Spenser's Monstrous Regiment

Spenser's Monstrous Regiment

Elizabethan Ireland and the Poetics of Difference

RICHARD A. McCABE

OXFORD

UNIVERSITY PRESS

OXFORD
UNIVERSITY PRESS

Great Clarendon Street, Oxford OX2 6DP

Oxford University Press is a department of the University of Oxford.
It furthers the University's objective of excellence in research, scholarship,
and education by publishing worldwide in

Oxford New York

Auckland Bangkok Buenos Aires Cape Town Chennai
Dar es Salaam Delhi Hong Kong Istanbul Karachi Kolkata
Kuala Lumpur Madrid Melbourne Mexico City Mumbai Nairobi
São Paulo Shanghai Taipei Tokyo Toronto

Oxford is a registered trade mark of Oxford University Press
in the UK and in certain other countries

Published in the United States
by Oxford University Press Inc., New York

British Library Cataloguing in Publication Data
Data available

Library of Congress Cataloging in Publication Data
Data available
ISBN 0–19–818734–3

1 3 5 7 9 10 8 6 4 2

Typeset in Garamond
by Hope Services (Abingdon) Ltd.
Printed in Great Britain
on acid-free paper by
Biddles Ltd.,
Guildford and King's Lynn

Cuirim leis Elizabeth phéisteach,
nár phós fear is nár stad ó éinneach.
Iomdha dream ar ar fheall an mhéirdreach.
Do rinne sí fásach do Chlár Éibhir.
A mná 's a bhfir do sgriosadh léithe.
Tug sí bás do Mháire Stéabhard.

(An Síogaí Rómhánach, c.1650)

With [Henry VIII] I class the pestilential Elizabeth,
Who wed no man, nor resisted any.
That harlot treacherously undid whole races,
And turned all of Munster into a desert,
Killing women as well as men without distinction.
She caused the death of Mary Stewart.

(The Roman Fay)

Acknowledgements

The writing of this book was made possible by the award of a British Academy Research Readership and it gives me great pleasure to record my gratitude for such generous support. Indeed, I have reason to be doubly grateful in that the invitation to deliver the British Academy Chatterton Lecture on Poetry in 1991 led me to write 'Edmund Spenser: Poet of Exile' in which I adumbrated some of the central concerns of the present study.[1] I should also like to express my gratitude to the Warden and Fellows of Merton College Oxford, and to the many scholars who lent their assistance at different stages of the writing process. In particular, I wish to acknowledge my debt to Cathal Ó Háinle, Professor of Irish at my alma mater, Trinity College Dublin, for his invaluable advice on matters Gaelic, and to the undergraduate and graduate students at Dublin and Oxford whose interest in the Irish facet of Spenser's canon helped to inspire my work. I am also grateful for advice on various literary, historical and bibliographical matters to Ciaran Brady, Nicholas Canny, Patrick Cheney, Sam Eidinow, Howard Erskine-Hill, Antony Griffiths, Steve Gunn, Ralph Hanna, Bernard O'Donoghue, Nicholas Richardson, Suzanne Romaine, Bart Van Es, Colin Wilcockson, and Andrew Zurcher.

---

[1] Richard A. McCabe, 'Edmund Spenser: Poet of Exile', *Proceedings of the British Academy*, 1991 Lectures and Memoirs, 80 (1993), 73–103.

Contents

Part V: *The Faerie Queene* (1596)

Part VI: Spenser's Ireland 1609–1650

List of Illustrations

The figures are reproduced by kind permission of the following: Edinburgh University Library for Figs. 1, 3–8; the British Library for Fig. 2 (MS Royal 18. A. xlviii); the Bodleian Library, Oxford for Figs. 9, 11, and 12 (Mal 504, Douce V. 170, and Mason BB 49, respectively); the Trustees of the British Museum for Fig. 10 (1957-4-13-35)

Abbreviations

All primary sources are cited in the notes by author (or editor) and date. Full bibliographical details are supplied on pp. 288–97. For example, Davies (1612) refers to Sir John Davies, *A Discoverie of the True Causes why Ireland was never entirely Subdued* (London, 1612). Other commonly cited works are abbreviated throughout as follows:

Cal. Car. MSS	*Calendar of Carew Manuscripts*
CSPI	*Calendar of State Papers Irish*
CSPD	*Calendar of State Papers Domestic*
CSPS	*Calendar of State Papers Spanish*
NHI	*A New History of Ireland*, ed. by T. W. Moody, F. X. Martin, and F. J. Byrne, 9 vols (Oxford: Clarendon Press, 1976–84).
Prose	*Spenser's Prose Works*, Variorum Edition, IX (1949)
PRO	Public Record Office, London
SP	State Papers, Public Record Office (MSS)
Variorum	*The Works of Edmund Spenser.* Variorum Edition

FURTHER ABBREVIATIONS

EA	*Études Anglaises*
EHR	*English Historical Review*
EIC	*Essays in Criticism*
ELH	*English Literary History*
ELN	*English Language Notes*
ELR	*English Literary Renaissance*
ES	*English Studies*
HLQ	*Huntington Library Quarterly*
IHS	*Irish Historical Studies*
JEGP	*Journal of English and Germanic Philology*
JHI	*Journal of the History of Ideas*
JMRS	*Journal of Medieval and Renaissance Studies*
MLN	*Modern Language Notes*
MLQ	*Modern Language Quarterly*
MLR	*Modern Language Review*
MP	*Modern Philology*

N&Q	*Notes and Queries*
OED	*Oxford English Dictionary*
PMLA	*Publications of the Modern Language Association of America*
PQ	*Philological Quarterly*
REL	*Review of English Literature*
RES	*Review of English Studies*
RQ	*Renaissance Quarterly*
SEL	*Studies in English Literature*
SP	*Studies in Philology*
SQ	*Shakespeare Quarterly*
SpE	*The Spenser Encyclopedia*
SpN	*Spenser Newsletter*
SR	*Studies in the Renaissance*
SSt	*Spenser Studies*
TLS	*Times Literary Supplement*
TSLL	*Texas Studies in Language and Literature*
UJA	*Ulster Journal of Archaeology*
UTQ	*University of Toronto Quarterly*
YES	*Yearbook of English Studies*

Introduction: Beyond the Pale

I OWE the idea for this book to a question posed by a disgruntled student at a Spenser seminar in Dublin: 'If King Arthur was Celtic how can he be the hero of an English national epic?' As I was preoccupied at the time with explaining the influence of Neoplatonism on the Gardens of Adonis, this salvo from the blue, or rather from the green, was most unwelcome. I mentioned 'poetic licence' and passed swiftly on, but the question lingered in my mind and I thought of it again when I visited Kilcolman for the first time. It reminded me that the Irish dimension of *The Faerie Queene* is as much a matter of text as context, as much a concern of poetic fabric as polemical allusion. It reaches to the heart of the poem's Briton and fairy mythologies, and to Spenser's conception of his role as 'poet historicall'. The poem abounds in Irish topographical references most of which are employed by way of analogy or comparison: the mob besieging Alma's castle is likened to a 'swarme of Gnats' arising from the Bog of Allan (2. 9. 16), and the conflict between Cambell and Triamond resembles the 'contrarie' tides in the Shannon estuary (4. 3. 27). Such instances demonstrate the degree to which the poem is, if not set, at least 'mindset' in Ireland, the degree to which Spenser's Irish experience had come to provide a frame of reference for so much else. It is less a question of territorial than of psychological 'chorography'. Although commonly remembered as the Elizabethan court poet par excellence, Spenser spent remarkably little time at the court of 'Gloriana'. The years of his poetic and political maturity were passed not at the centre but on the periphery of the Elizabethan state, and the effect on the poetry is evident from the moment that his decentred narrative begins to deviate from the court-centred template provided in the letter to his fellow planter, Sir Walter Ralegh. As the work stands, the fairy queen is to the world of *The Faerie Queene* what Elizabeth I was to Ireland, a remote authority figure acting through deputies and substitutes. Yet it was primarily in Ireland that Spenser witnessed the errantry, and errancy, of Gloriana's knights.

It is not, of course, as if 'Ireland' has been neglected of recent years with monographs by such critics as Willy Maley, Andrew Hadfield, Christopher Highley, and Andrew Murphy, numerous critical anthologies and scores of articles.[1] Planter Ireland has been densely replanted from the groves of academe, but few have ventured far beyond the Pale. Gaelic Ireland has been all but ignored. Although the rise of 'British' or 'Archipelagic' history has intensified interest in the Irish dimension of Spenser's canon, the resulting studies have remained rigidly anglophone despite their avowed hostility to anglocentrism. The language of the majority population is now a minority interest. Ireland is commonly regarded as a 'text', and we hear of the process of 'representing Ireland' or 'writing Ireland', but it would be more illuminating to speak in terms of a palimpsest, or a set of palimpsests, and to begin to consider the process of erasure that enabled the process of inscription. As it is, there is much talk of the 'other' and 'otherness' in abstract terms but little, if any, engagement with it. Irenius's 'bards' are mentioned but seldom quoted— and never in Gaelic. This is all the more remarkable in view of the innovative work conducted in the field of Renaissance Gaelic literature by Brendán Ó Buachalla, Marc Caball, and Joseph Leerssen.[2] The dialogical format of *A View of the Present Ireland* efficiently functions to exclude the Gaelic voice, and modern criticism, even when of a 'post-colonial' or 'new-historicist' cast, has unwittingly participated in this exclusion. This book represents an attempt to redress the balance by examining Spenser's response to Irish colonial experience with reference to contemporary Gaelic literature, and particularly bardic poetry. The enterprise is all the more significant to colonial studies in general in that Spenser heavily influenced the techniques of interpretation, and denigration, that remained prevalent in colonial discourse for over three centuries. They were remarkably effective. Even the names of the Gaelic writers from whom I quote will be unfamiliar to most readers: poets such as Tadhg Dall Ó hUiginn,

---

[1] Willy Maley, *Salvaging Spenser: Colonialism, Culture and Identity* (Basingstoke: Macmillan, 1997); Andrew Hadfield, *Spenser's Irish Experience: Wilde Fruit and Salvage Soyl* (Cambridge: Cambridge University Press, 1997); Christopher Highley, *Shakespeare, Spenser and the Crisis in Ireland* (Cambridge: Cambridge University Press, 1997); Andrew Murphy, *'But the Irish Sea Betwixt Us': Ireland, Colonialism, and Renaissance Literature* (Lexington: University Press of Kentucky, 1999). See my review of Maley, Hadfield, and Highley, 'Embarrassing Spenser', *Bullán*, 2 (1999/2000), 164–73. For my review of Brendan Bradshaw, Andrew Hadfield, and Willy Maley (eds.), *Representing Ireland: Literature and the Origins of Conflict, 1534–1600* (Cambridge: Cambridge University Press, 1993) see *IHS* 29 (1995), 394–8.

[2] Brendán Ó Buachalla, *Aisling Ghéar: Na Stíobhartaigh agus an t-Aos Léinn 1603–1788* (Dublin: An Clóchomhar, 1996); Marc Caball, *Poets and Politics: Reaction and Continuity in Irish Poetry, 1558–1625* (Cork: Cork University Press in association with Field Day, 1998); Joseph Th. Leerssen, *Mere Irish & Fíor-Ghael: Studies in the Idea of Irish Nationality, its Development and Literary Expression prior to the Nineteenth Century* (Amsterdam: John Benjamins Publishing Company, 1986).

Eochaidh Ó hEódhasa, or Eoghan Ruadh Mac an Bhaird; historians and polemicists such as Seathrún Céitinn, Lughaidh Ó Clérigh, Pilib Ó Súilleabháin Béarra, Mícheál Ó Clérigh and his collaborators on *Annála Ríoghachta Éireann* [*Annals of the Kingdom of Ireland*]. Although it is often necessary, for practical reasons, to use the now commonly accepted Anglicizations of Gaelic names, I have chosen to employ the original forms wherever possible (or at least to provide them at the point of first usage) in recognition of their cultural valence. It is essential to recognize that the alleged 'otherness' of the Irish was located *in their identity*. Irish family names, according to Fynes Moryson, rather resembled 'the names of Devowring Giants then Christian Subiects'.[3] But these giants had an equally low opinion of the oddly sounding Edmund Spensers and Valentine Brownes who settled among them—and said so.[4] It was their civility not their savagery, their similarity rather than their difference, that rendered them so dangerous. What I have termed Spenser's 'poetics of difference' were premised upon an uneasy sense of kinship. This was, perhaps, one of the darkest 'secrets' that Lord Grey's secretary could never quite keep.

Central to the present study is the argument that the experience of writing from Ireland intensified Spenser's sense of alienation from female sovereignty—evident even as early as *The Shepheardes Calender*—and progressively displaced 'Virgilian' with 'Ovidian' perspectives as the would-be laureate became, or adopted the pose of, the critic in exile.[5] It is not that the Virgilian canon is lacking in political discontent nor that the Ovidian is devoid of 'Caesar's praise', but rather that Ovid did something that Virgil never did. He wrote of Rome from a wilderness that he termed 'Scythia'. Spenser asserts that *The Faerie Queene* was 'bred in salvage soyl', and in *A View of the Present State of Ireland* Irenius attributes its savagery to the Scythian ancestry of the Gaelic Irish. Ovid feared to die in exile by 'Scythian arrows' and every New English planter harboured similar fears.[6] But fear can be a powerful literary stimulus. By *writing* from the wilderness Ovid created a new poetics. From his exile he fashioned a master-trope that could be used to express all forms of alienation and dissatisfaction. By drawing explicit comparisons between himself and Virgil

---

[3] Moryson (1903), 195.

[4] For Aogán Ó Rathaille's poem on Valentine Browne see Ó Tuama (1981), 160–3.

[5] For an excellent account of the classical career-roles available see Patrick Cheney, *Spenser's Famous Flight: A Renaissance Idea of a Literary Career* (Toronto: University of Toronto Press, 1993).

[6] *Epistulae ex Ponto*, II. 1. 65.

he even became the first to demonstrate the literary advantages of setting the 'Ovidian' against the 'Virgilian'. By calling Augustus' attention to the presence of erotic elements within what he termed 'your *Aeneid*' ['tuae Aeneidos'] he revealed the uncomfortable similarity between the laureate and the outlaw, Bonfont and Malfont.[7] The template he bequeathed to posterity was complex and Spenser uses it in a complex manner. It was never a question of 'choosing' between Virgil and Ovid so much as exploiting the literary advantages that arose from the ever-present possibility of making such a choice. Spenser was quick to realize the literary benefits of writing from a 'salvage soyl', of writing a sort of *Aeneid ex Ponto*, and Ovid's poetics of metamorphosis provided a perfect means of exploring the phenomenon of cultural 'degeneration' that posed the single greatest threat to the Irish colonial enterprise. I do not wish to imply, however, that nothing more was involved in all of this than an exercise in literary modelling. Spenser's political position was, if anything, more difficult than Ovid's. Left to its own devices, Ireland's New English community lacked the resources to maintain its position. It needed the 'court', as 'The Legend of Courtesie' demonstrates. Grand gestures of poetic isolation, of attempting to 'fashion' civil nations from the slopes of Mount Acidale, were beside the point when the 'barbarians' were in the foothills. By negotiating between the personae of Virgil and Ovid, Spenser was articulating real political needs and disappointments. His literary templates provided vehicles for apprehending and analysing lived experience.

It has become common of late to use *A View* as a sort of prose 'gloss' to the poetry, but their relationship is far more intricate. It is often forgotten that the prose is, in so many respects, just as 'fictive' as the verse. Indeed there are occasions when the verse seems to 'gloss' the prose by entertaining disquieting possibilities that neither Irenius nor Eudoxus may be allowed to broach. Stephen Greenblatt has argued that 'it is art whose status is questioned in Spenser, not ideology: indeed, art is questioned precisely to spare ideology that internal distantiation'.[8] I hold the opposite to be the case. It is the ideology rather than the art that suffers. Indeed the art draws power from ideological contradiction. Spenser's poetics interrogate his politics so profoundly as to discover the heart of darkness at the centre of the colonial enterprise. The implications of narrative are harder to

---

[7] *Tristia*, II. 533.

[8] Stephen Greenblatt, *Renaissance Self-fashioning: From More to Shakespeare* (Chicago: University of Chicago Press, 1980), 192.

contain than those of deliberative rhetoric, and truth is one of the most surprising consequences of fiction. The 'Letter to Ralegh' promises to deliver a 'pleasing Analysis' of all of the poem's narrative complications but, as Seamus Heaney has said, 'poetry of any power is always deeper than its declared meaning'.[9] He was speaking, as it happens, of Gaelic poetry but, as I shall argue, Spenser's kinship with the 'bards' was closer than either party realized, or cared to admit.

I do not subscribe to the view, recently advanced by Nicholas Canny, that Spenser 'set the [political] agenda' in Ireland.[10] Within his own lifetime his opinions were often unpalatable to the government and he fell foul of the censor in both England and Scotland. He was certainly popular with John Milton but the history of his reception in the 1640s is complicated. It makes very little sense to refer to him as a 'republican' or even as a 'proto-republican'.[11] Dissatisfaction with the policies of an individual monarch does not constitute a rejection of monarchy, and disillusionment with female regiment may even serve to strengthen the desire for a stronger male successor. *A View* affords considerable evidence of discontent with Elizabeth's Irish policy, but it also criticizes the Irish Parliament for damaging the royal prerogative. During the civil wars and interregnum Spenser was selectively read and cited by both Royalists and Parliamentarians in order to buttress opposing viewpoints. Generally speaking it was less a question of influence than opportunistic appropriation. Spenser, it was discovered, had much to say of the relationship between the 'three kingdoms', and with good reason. As the rise of 'British' history has served to remind us, the prevailing political circumstances of the 1580s and 1590s were such that no self-styled 'poet historicall' could isolate the 'history' of England from that of its neighbours.[12] The King of Scotland was a claimant to the English throne, and Scottish mercenaries sustained the Gaelic clans of Ulster. Hugh O'Donnell's Scottish wife

---

[9] Seamus Heaney, 'The God in the Tree', in *The Pleasures of Gaelic Poetry*, ed. Seán Mac Réamoinn (London: Allen Lane, 1982), 25–34 (p. 30).

[10] Nicholas Canny, *Making Ireland British, 1580–1650* (Oxford: Oxford University Press, 2001), 1–58.

[11] Andrew Hadfield, 'Was Spenser a Republican?', *English*, 47 (1998), 169–82.

[12] For the 'British' perspective on Spenser see David J. Baker, *Between Nations: Shakespeare, Spenser, Marvell, and the Question of Britain* (Stanford, Calif.: Stanford University Press, 1997), 1–10; 'Spenser and the Uses of British History', in Patrick Cheney and Lauren Silberman (eds.), *Worldmaking Spenser: Explorations in the Early Modern Age* (Lexington. Ky.: University Press of Kentucky, 2000), 193–203; John Morrill, 'The Fashioning of Britain' and Ciaran Brady, 'Comparable Histories?: Tudor Reform in Wales and Ireland', in Steven G. Ellis and Sarah Barber (eds.), *Conquest and Union: Fashioning a British State, 1485–1725* (London: Longman, 1995), 8–39, 64–86.

was, according to one of the clan's official historians, 'the head of advice and counsel of the Cenél Conaill [the O'Donnells], and though she was calm and very deliberate and much praised for her womanly qualities, she had the heart of a hero and the mind of a soldier'.[13] In other words she was a sort of Gaelic 'Eliza', but one far more involved in the country's affairs than the distant and frequently recalcitrant monarch upon whom Spenser was forced to rely. Yet it was evident to New English observers that the cause of 'St George' might be won or lost in Ireland, and that its success or failure might well determine whether England was to become an 'imperial' power in its own right or a mere province of Philip II's Catholic empire.

I have previously written, in *The Pillars of Eternity: Time and Providence in 'The Faerie Queene'* (1989), on the philosophical background to Spenser's work. The present study seeks to engage more closely with the relationship between the philosophical and the political, with the transformation wrought upon the humanist agenda when it is imposed upon a colony rather than inculcated in a people. Contemporary colonial treatises frequently struck a philosophical pose. Richard Beacon characterizes England as 'Athens' throughout *Solon His Follie* (1594) and Sir William Herbert upholds the ideals of 'Pallas Athenae' in *Croftus sive De Hibernia Liber* (1591). In the following pages I examine the various ways in which these self-styled 'Greeks' construed their opponents as 'barbarians'. In doing so I have made no attempt to read the poetry as a 'continued' *roman-à-clef*, nor to scan the text for every possible allusion to the minutiae of Irish politics. My interest lies in the 'legends' of idolatry, intemperance, promiscuity, enmity, injustice and incivility that provide the subtext to the moral allegory. I am concerned with Spenser's aesthetic response to the *idea* of Ireland, with the genesis of the savage knighthood (and savage poetics) of book five, and with the various ways in which Gaelic Ireland helped to influence these matters.

---

[13] Ó Clérigh (1948–57), i (1948), 39.

Part I: The Imperial Theme

1   *Arms and the Woman*

She was a beautiful woman, but proud and haughty, and could not bear that anyone else's beauty should excel her own. She possessed a magic mirror, and when she stood in front of it and looked at herself she would say:

> 'Mirror, mirror on the wall,
> Who is the fairest of us all?'

The mirror would answer:

> 'My lady queen is fairest of all.'

And this satisfied her, for she knew that the mirror spoke the truth.

(Jacob and Wilhelm Grimm, 'Snow White')[1]

The Faerie Queene presents itself as a sort of magic 'mirrhor' in which England's 'dread' sovereign is invited to 'behold thy face, | And thine owne realmes in the lond of Faery, | And in this antique Image thy great auncestry' (2 Proem 4). This 'mirrhor' repeatedly assures her that its lady queen is 'fairest of all', and even that she herself may be regarded as a 'mirrour of grace and Maiestie divine' (1 Proem 4). The 'poet historical' has, it seems, found timeless truth in the contemplation of a unique political icon, 'like as two mirrours by oppos'd reflexion, | Doe both express the faces first impression'.[2] Yet the tale of Snow White reminds us that it would be quite unwarranted to expect an enchanted mirror to ignore

---

[1] Grimm (1982), 74.
[2] *An Hymne in Honour of Beautie*, ll. 181–2. For Elizabeth as an ideal see David Lee Miller, *The Poem's Two Bodies: The Poetics of the 1590 'Faerie Queene'* (Princeton: Princeton University Press, 1988), 98–111.

changing circumstance. That is not how enchanted mirrors, or enchanted makers, behave. The proem to book six delivers a stern warning to those 'Which see not perfect things but in a glass: | Yet is that glasse so gay, that it can blynd | The wisest sight, to thinke gold that is bras' (6 Proem 5). Depending on how they were used, mirrors might promote self-knowledge or self-delusion. Elizabeth would understand the point. She had translated Marguerite of Navarre's *Le Miroir de l'âme pécheresse* as *The Glass of the Sinfull Soul*.[3] In any case, Spenser invites her to view herself 'in mirrours more then one' (3 Proem 5), and as she moves amongst them her image veers from the ideal to the grotesque. If experimentation with multiple mirrors in contemporary 'perspective cabinets' can be seen to have promoted a new awareness of the relativity of human perception, the multiple mode of 'reflection' chosen for *The Faerie Queene* seems equally calculated to call in question not just the validity of its 'official' iconography, but the psychology of icon-making.[4]

The notion of Virgil's covert hostility to the policies of Augustus was generally accepted by Spenser's day, and the creation of national epic did not automatically entail unqualified endorsement of the nation's leaders.[5] It was well understood that at moments of political crisis the business of 'opposd reflexion' became potentially oppositional. For an ageing woman the 'faces first impression' may be little more than a sad reminder of decay. 'Queen Elizabeth', Ben Jonson reported, 'never saw her self after she became old jn a true Glass, they painted her, and sometymes would vermilion her nose.'[6] The portraits of the 1590s tell much the same story. Officially the queen did not age.[7] Yet, as every courtier knew, Elizabeth Tudor did, and it was the courtly class who were most likely to see or possess her portraits.[8] 'Considering she beareth two persons', Spenser tells Sir Walter Ralegh, 'the one of a most royall Queene or Empresse, the other of

---

[3]   The full text is reproduced in Shell (1993).

[4]   See Herbert Grabes, *The Mutable Glass: Mirror-imagery in Titles and Texts of the Middle Ages and English Renaissance*, trans. Gordon Collier (Cambridge: Cambridge University Press, 1982), 113.

[5]   See Richard A. McCabe, 'Annotating Anonymity, or Putting a Gloss on *The Shepheardes Calender*', in Joe Bray, Miriam Hendley, and Anne Henry (eds.), *Ma(r)king the Text: The Presentation of Meaning on the Literary Page* (Aldershot: Ashgate, 2000), 35–54 (pp. 41–4).

[6]   Jonson (1925–52), i. 141–2.

[7]   See Sir Roy Strong, *Gloriana: The Portraits of Queen Elizabeth I* (London: Thames and Hudson, 1987), 19–21, 34–43. See also S. P. Cerasano and Marion Wynne-Davies (eds.), *Gloriana's Face: Women, Public and Private, in the English Renaissance* (New York: Harvester Wheatsheaf, 1992), 1–24 (p. 14).

[8]   See Dennis Kay, ' "She was a queen, and therefore beautiful": Sidney, his Mother, and Queen Elizabeth', *RES* 43 (1992), 18–39 (pp. 29–32).

a most vertuous and beautifull Lady, this latter part in some places I doe expresse in Belphœbe, fashioning her name to your owne excellent conceipt of Cynthia.'[9] The doctrine of the monarch's 'two bodies' was a commonplace of Elizabethan political theory but, as the comparison with *The Book of the Ocean to Cynthia* suggests, Spenser's use of it was anything but commonplace.[10] Ralegh's poem is in the nature of a personal and political complaint written from the depths of frustrated ambition, and Spenser's depiction of Belphœbe increasingly betrays its genesis. If he is liable to accusations of political 'idolatry' in creating Gloriana, his portrait of Belphœbe constitutes an act of conscious iconoclasm.[11] All too often the woman eclipses the monarch, a phenomenon identified by John Knox in his *First Blast of the Trumpet against the Monstrous Regiment of Women* (1558) as the central problem of female rule.[12] Knox's works were suppressed in England, but many of Elizabeth's subjects were equally disposed to blame the public failures of 'Gloriana' on the personal failings of 'Belphœbe'. Anti-feminism was the 'default' position of political discontent in Elizabeth's England. To the nation's cost, it was frequently insinuated, the monarch's other 'body' was female.

Contemporary medical literature placed so much emphasis on the relative inferiority of the female body—judged by Aristotle to be an 'imperfect' version of the male—that its effect on the doctrine of the body politic was well nigh inevitable.[13] The contrasting connotations of 'male' and 'female' in this context are disclosed in Spenser's account of the 'proportions' of the Castle of Alma: 'the one imperfect, mortall, fœminine; | Th'other immortall, perfect, masculine' (2. 9. 22). Like the Castle of Alma, the feminized body politic was generally perceived to be acutely vulnerable to threats of invasion (2. 11. 2–7). Knox went further still. For him, the 'naturall bodie of man' and the 'politik or civile body of [the]

---

[9] Spenser (1978), 16.

[10] See Ernst H. Kantorowicz, *The King's Two Bodies: A Study in Medieval Political Theology* (Princeton: Princeton University Press, 1957), 7–23, 314–450; Marie Axton, *The Queen's Two Bodies* (London: Royal Historical Society, 1977), 11–17.

[11] For a more positive view of the relationship see Susanne Woods, 'Spenser and the Problem of Women's Rule', *HLQ* 48 (1985), 141–58.

[12] Knox (1846–64), iv. 373–9.

[13] See Ian Maclean, *The Renaissance Notion of Woman: A Study in the Fortunes of Scholasticism and Medical Science in European Intellectual Life* (Cambridge: Cambridge University Press, 1980), 31–3; Peter Stallybrass, 'Patriarchal Territories: The Body Enclosed', in Margaret W. Ferguson, Maureen Quilligan, and Nancy J. Vickers (eds.), *Rewriting the Renaissance: The Discourses of Sexual Difference in Early Modern Europe* (Chicago: University of Chicago Press, 1986), 123–42; David George Hale, *The Body Politic: A Political Metaphor in Renaissance English Literature* (The Hague: Mouton, 1971), 69–107.

common welth' were divinely ordained as perfect 'mirrors and glasses' of one another. 'Monstruous is the bodie of that Common welth', he concluded, 'where a Woman beareth empire.'[14] By the 1590s the evident debility of the queen's ageing, childless body had come to symbolize the debility of the Elizabethan state. Herein lay what was, perhaps, the single greatest paradox of Spenser's endeavour: the attempt to idealize a situation that was never regarded as ideal. Female 'regiment' might possibly be justified by reference to 'the grace of God' but, as the Radigund episode reminds us, it was never to be preferred to 'mans well ruling hand' (5. 5. 25). In George Buchanan, one of the principal authorities cited in *A View of the Present State of Ireland*, Spenser would have encountered the sentiment that 'no people who ever had the freedom of choice, preferred women when they had a sufficient number of men'.[15] Even Bishop Aylmer, author of the official response to Knox, *An Harborowe for Faithfull and Trewe Subiectes, agaynst the late blowne Blaste, concerninge the Government of Wemen* (1559), admitted that male rulers were generally superior.[16] His immediate concern in defending Elizabeth was the maintenance of political stability. He was anxious to ensure that arguments originally honed against the monstrous regiment of Catholic women would not jeopardize the title of a Protestant monarch. While he refuted the assertion that female regiment was inherently 'unnatural', he also suggested that such misgivings 'might better have been moved when the Sceptre was *or shable* in the hand of the male' (my emphasis).[17] The champion of female regiment was already anticipating a male succession. The matter might then be decided one way or the other 'without manifest and violent wrong of them that be in place'.[18]

Nowhere was the queen's apparent deficiency more evident to contemporary observers than in Ireland. Elizabeth is specifically told that she will find not her 'owne realme' but her 'owne realmes' in the 'lond of Faery' (2 Proem 4), and amongst the 'mirrors more then one' in which Spenser invites her to look there lurks a carefully angled piece of Irish 'glass'. It is predominantly in its engagement with the Irish colonial enterprise that *The Faerie Queene* registers the failure of the fairy queen, a failure implicitly attributable to the monarch's lack of 'masculine' resolve. Spenser was not

---

[14] Knox (1846–64), iv. 390–1.   [15] Buchanan (1856), ii. 122.

[16] See James E. Phillips, Jr., 'The Background of Spenser's Attitude Toward Women Rulers', *HLQ* 5 (1941–2), 5–32 (p. 16). If the Morrell of *The Shepheardes Calender* is to be identified with Aylmer, Spenser pays scant compliment to the foremost defender of female regiment.

[17] Aylmer (1559), sig. B2r.   [18] Ibid.

alone in this perception. According to Fynes Moryson, for example, Lord Grey's failure to reduce Ireland to submission was occasioned by an excess of 'pittye in the Royall (may I with leave say womanly) breast of the late famous Queene'.[19] Much of Spenser's political outlook is articulated in Moryson's polite, yet damning, parenthesis. The needs of empire, it seemed, were even less well served by female regiment than those of monarchy. To sing of arms and the woman proved far more difficult than to sing of arms and the man. The queen's apparent frustration of the military aspirations of Grey, Leicester, and Ralegh—and also of the dynastic needs of the monarchy itself—led to the remarkable fusion of colonial and sexual anxieties manifest in Spenser's pervasive images of anti-heroic emasculation. It is no coincidence that the most remarkable of such images—that of the cross-dressed Artegall enslaved to the regiment of Radigund—occurs in 'The Legend of Justice'.

Elizabeth was intensely suspicious of her Irish deputies and they were invariably disappointed in her. 'Silly woman', cried Sir John Perrot in a characteristic fit of rage, 'now she shall not curb me, she shall not rule me now'. And yet again, 'this it is to serve a base bastard piss kitchen woman'.[20] The choice of language reflects the speaker's notoriously irascible temperament, but the burden of his complaint runs throughout the papers of numerous deputies. Such tensions were artfully exploited by both the Gaelic Irish and the Old English and the policies of the Dublin administration suffered accordingly.[21] The experience of Sir Henry Sidney, Lord Grey's immediate predecessor, provides a notable, and particularly instructive, case in point. 'Three tymes', he tells Walsingham in his *Memoir*, 'her Majestie hath sent me her Deputie into Ireland, and in everie of the three tymes I susteyned a great and a violent rebellion, everie one of which I subdued, and (with honorable peace) lefte the countrey in quiet.'[22] He proceeds to allege, however, that all three administrations were bedevilled by the queen's interference—and by the Earl of Ormond's baleful influence upon her.[23] While Sidney laboured in Ireland, Ormond spent his time at court levelling dangerous accusations of bias and

---

[19] Moryson (1903), 260.
[20] Hiram Morgan, 'The Fall of Sir John Perrot', in John Alexander Guy (ed.), *The Reign of Elizabeth I: Court and Culture in the Last Decade* (Cambridge: Cambridge University Press, 1995), 109–25 (p. 121).
[21] See e.g. Lombard (1930), 81. [22] Sir Henry Sidney (1855), 38.
[23] See Ciaran Brady, *The Chief Governors: The Rise and Fall of Reform Government in Tudor Ireland, 1536–88* (Cambridge: Cambridge University Press, 1994), 122–3.

corruption, and his victim was condemned to suffer a fate very similar to that of Lord Grey: 'The Earl of Ormond (my professed foe) sometyme with clamour, but oftner with whispering, did bitterly backbite me; saying that his brethren were dryven by my cruelty to rebell, and that he nor his could never have any justice of me, nor any constituted by me in auctority to mynister justice.'[24] Here, as in *The Faerie Queene*, detraction and envy undo the legend of justice.

'Almost wekely' Sidney received a flood of 'sharpe and bitter letters' from the queen, and was driven to seek his own recall.[25] 'I lothed . . . to tarry any longer in that land', he records, 'for that I saw the Queene make so little account of my service.'[26] Holinshed reports Elizabeth's unfailing support of Sidney during his dispute with the Irish Parliament concerning the imposition of 'cess' (or 'composition' in lieu of cess) but, as Sidney himself realized, what she actually supported was the royal prerogative.[27] Once that point had been conceded, Sidney's interests were largely ignored. 'These things', he writes, 'had well nere broken my heart.'[28] Although he eventually received some 'comfortable and thankful letters' from the queen 'signed with her own hand', his material rewards were minimal. After all his years of service, he complains, 'I am now fifty-four yeres of age, toothlesse and trembling, being five thousand pounds in debt, yea and £30,000 worse than I was at the death of my most deere king and master, King Edward the VIth.' His conclusion is stark: *dura est conditio servorum* ['hard is the condition of servants'—or is it 'slaves'?].[29] 'So hard it is to be a womans slave', remarks the narrator of the 'Legend of Justice' (5. 5. 23). Sidney's reference to Edward VI evokes a powerful leitmotif of his memoir. He has experienced the ideal alternative to female regiment, a 'king and master' who knew how to nurture his followers: 'while I was present with him he would allwayes be cheerfull and pleasant with me, and in my absence give me such wordes of praise as farre exceeded my desert, Sondry tymes he bountifully rewarded me . . . Lastly, not only to my own still felt grief, but also to the universall woe of England, he dyed in my armes.'[30] What is lamented here, the death of a king or that of male regiment? Had Edward lived, Elizabeth might never have succeeded to the throne. 'Yf women be not permitted by Civile policies to rule in inferior offices,' argued Christopher Goodman in the year of

---

[24] Sir Henry Sidney (1857), 308.   [25] Sir Henry Sidney (1856), 94.
[26] Sir Henry Sidney (1860), 189.   [27] See Holinshed (1808), vi. 389–95.
[28] Sir Henry Sidney (1860), 181–4 (p. 184).   [29] Ibid. 194.
[30] Ibid. 193.

Elizabeth's accession, 'I make your selves iudges, whither it be mete for them to governe whole Realmes and nations?'[31] Yet Sidney chose Goodman as his private chaplain in 1566 and recommended him—with a predictable lack of success—for appointment as Bishop of Dublin and Dean of St Patrick's Cathedral. 'If ever man on earth, since the apostles' days deserved to be held a saint', he told Cecil, 'he is one.'[32] The queen could be forgiven for demurring.

The imperial pretensions of *The Faerie Queene* (1590) are signalled at the very outset in its dedication 'To the Most Mightie and Magnificent Empresse Elizabeth, by the Grace of God Queene of England, France and Ireland Defender of the Faith, &c.' The designation of Elizabeth as 'Empresse' as well as 'Queene'—with the implication that an 'empresse' is 'queene' of numerous 'realmes'—immediately links the poem's colonial agenda to its celebration, or otherwise, of female regiment The association is remarkable in that the 'imperial' virtues were traditionally regarded as the province of the male, and within the poem itself 'might' and 'magnificence' are ascribed to Prince Arthur, England's once and future *king*. Fynes Moryson was by no means unique in regarding 'womanly' virtues as inimical to 'conquest' and the ascendancy of an 'empresse' as potentially fatal to the imperial enterprise. In 1597, just a year before his appointment as Lord Lieutenant of Ireland, the Earl of Essex told the French Ambassador that 'they laboured under two things at this Court, delay and inconstancy, which proceeded chiefly from the sex of the Queen'.[33] The remark reflects the most influential political theory of the day. Bodin had asserted that 'people . . . of a great and couragious spirit, will deeme a womans government but ignominious'. 'A Monarchy', he concluded, 'ought to descend unto the heires male, considering that the rule and government of women, is directly against the law of nature, which hath given unto men wisdom, strength, courage and power to commaund; and taken the same from women.'[34] In so far as virility was expected to identify itself, as Bourdieu claims, by a constant process of differentiation from the feminine, Lord Grey could be perceived as most 'heroicke' in his opposition to his sovereign's enervating 'mercye and

---

[31] Goodman (1558), 52. See Louis Adrian Montrose, '*A Midsummer Night's Dream* and the Shaping Fantasies of Elizabethan Culture: Gender, Power, Form', in Ferguson (ed.), *Rewriting the Renaissance*, 65–87 (p. 80).

[32] See James E. Phillips, Jr., 'The Woman Ruler in Spenser's *Faerie Queene*', in *HLQ* 5 (1941–2), 211–34 (pp. 214–15). See also James E. Phillips, 'George Buchanan and the Sidney Circle', *HLQ* 12 (1948), 23–55 (pp. 28–30).

[33] Hurault (1931), 115.   [34] Bodin (1606), 746.

Clemencye' (*Prose*, 159).[35] The 'proper' role of the female monarch was that assigned to Gloriana, to inspire great deeds and leave their fulfilment to 'heroicke' males. From this most ironic of perspectives, 'absence' was her national duty. In reality, however, Elizabeth was all too intrusive, and her frequent use of 'masculine' rhetoric only exacerbated the problem.[36] She was even more dangerous in her attempted usurpation of the male role—the claim to possess 'the heart and stomach of a king'—than in her frequent professions of womanly frailty—the disparagement of her 'weak and feeble' female 'body'.[37] The figure of the Amazon or Virago was, for Knox, the most suspect of all female stereotypes.[38] Its recurrence in the portraits of *both* Belphœbe (2. 5. 27–31) *and* Radigund (5. 5. 1–3) is indicative of the problem with which Spenser wrestled.[39] In the 'virtual reality' that is 'fairyland' even the most widely divergent political and sexual possibilities may be canvassed simultaneously and polar opposites display a disconcerting tendency to coalesce.

The frustration of *The Faerie Queene*'s imperial agenda is suggested by its 'feminine' form. What Bakhtin describes as the 'male' structure of classical epic (characterized by linear progression, achievement, and closure) is progressively distorted into the 'female' structure of medieval romance (pervaded by patterns of inconclusiveness and self-repetition). 'There is no place in the epic world', argues Bakhtin 'for any openendedness, indecision, indeterminacy'—no place, that is, for the determining traits of Spenserian narrative.[40] It is as though the genre itself has become emasculated, as though the body of the text has grown to resemble the effeminate

---

[35] See Pierre Bourdieu, 'La Domination Masculine', *Actes de la Recherche en Sciences Sociales*, 84 (1990), 2–31 (pp. 13–20). See also Ann Rosalind Jones and Peter Stallybrass, 'Dismantling Irena: The Sexualizing of Ireland in Early Modern England', in Andrew Parker, Mary Russo, Doris Sommer, and Patricia Yaeger (eds.), *Nationalisms and Sexualities* (London: Routledge, 1992), 157–71.

[36] See Leah S. Marcus, 'Shakespeare's Comic Heroines, Elizabeth I, and the Political Uses of Androgyny', in Mary Beth Rose (ed.), *Women in the Middle Ages and the Renaissance: Literary and Historical Perspectives* (Syracuse, NY: Syracuse University Press, 1986), 135–53 (pp. 137–42).

[37] See Frances Teague, 'Queen Elizabeth in her Speeches', in Cerasano and Wynne-Davies (eds.), *Gloriana's Face*, 63–78 (pp. 66–9). See also Susan Frye, *Elizabeth I: The Competition for Representation* (New York: Oxford University Press, 1993), 13. For the contrary argument that Spenser 'finds strength' in the paradoxes of female rule see Pamela Joseph Benson, *The Invention of the Renaissance Woman: The Challenge of Female Independence in the Literature and Thought of Italy and England* (University Park, Pa.: Pennsylvania State University Press, 1992), 251–306 (p. 253).

[38] Knox (1846–64), iv. 375.

[39] See Mary Villeponteaux, ' "Not as women wonted be": Spenser's Amazon Queen', in Julia M. Walker (ed.), *Dissing Elizabeth: Negative Representations of Gloriana* (Durham, NC: Duke University Press, 1998), 209–25.

[40] M. M. Bakhtin, *The Dialogic Imagination: Four Essays*, ed. Michael Holquist, trans. Caryl Emerson and Michael Holquist (Austin: University of Texas Press, 1981), 16. See also Patricia A. Parker, *Literary Fat Ladies: Rhetoric, Gender, Property* (London: Methuen, 1987), 8–17.

body politic.[41] Spenser's imaginative response to the twin pressures of colonial conquest and female regiment is largely responsible for transforming England's first national epic into its first colonial romance. Because of its engagement with the problems of racial difference *The Faerie Queene* was, in any case, always more likely to resemble the work of Camões than of Ariosto or Tasso. One salient distinction, however, is that *Os Lusíadas* can boast of 'a line of kings who kept ever advancing the boundaries of faith and empire' while the problems of Spenser's imperial poetics are located at their core.[42] It is Gloriana herself who, to adapt Coleridge's famous phrase, constitutes the 'true imaginative absence' at the heart of her poem.[43] As the work progresses, the fairy queen's remarkable absence comes to evoke the poet's frustrated yearning for the presence of a fairy king. Only when Arthur succeeds will the needs of the nation be satisfied. His quest for the fairy queen is the quest to displace her.

So far as the matter of female regiment is concerned, it is entirely appropriate that *The Faerie Queene* should describe itself as 'a continued allegory'. 'Allegory' implies 'a speaking of the other', and 'otherness' is located not just at the margins but at the very heart of fairyland, in the fairy monarch herself.[44] The cultural and racial differences experienced on the borders of the empire are exacerbated by the sexual difference located at its centre. As E.K.'s notes to *The Shepheardes Calender* remind us, the notion of 'fairy' is at best ambivalent. The fairy queen of English and Gaelic folklore was a profoundly enigmatic figure who, like Lady Fortuna or Morgan Le Fey, arbitrarily dispensed pain or pleasure with little concern for merit. If she reflects divine grace, it is the grace of a Calvinist god, electing and reprobating in accordance with the dictates of a mysterious will. For Spenser's purposes the figure of the fairy queen was brilliantly calculated to capture the ambiguous character of England's 'dread' sovereign, and Prince Arthur's dream vision—what Gaelic poets would later term an 'aisling'—encapsulates her fraught relationship with her subjects. It is

[41] See Katherine Eggert, ' "Changing all that Forme of common weale": Genre and the Repeal of Queenship in *The Faerie Queene*, Book 5', *ELR* 26 (1996), 259–90.
[42] Camões (1952), 39.
[43] Coleridge (1936), 36. For the problem of female rule see Andrew Hadfield, 'The Trials of Jove: Spenser's Irish Allegory and the Mastery of the Irish', *Bullán*, 4 (1996). 1–15.
[44] See Elizabeth J. Bellamy, 'The Vocative and the Vocational: the Unreadability of Elizabeth in *The Faerie Queene*', *ELH* 54 (1987), 1–30 (p. 6); Dorothy Stephens, ' "Newes of devils": Feminine Sprights in Masculine Minds in *The Faerie Queene*', *ELR* 2: (1993), 363–81. For the contrary, and to my mind unconvincing, view that Spenser successfully 'internalizes' the female see Stevie Davies, *The Feminine Reclaimed: The Idea of Woman in Spenser, Shakespeare and Milton* (Lexington, Ky.: University Press of Kentucky, 1986), 37–54.

virtually impossible to decide whether the 'vision' is substantial or delusive, whether the queen is Mercilla or La Belle Dame sans Merci.[45] The fact that Arthur's moment of epiphany is drawn from Chaucer's parodic *Tale of Sir Thopas* (778–96) merely compounds the problem (1. 9. 13–15).[46] Spenser's residence in Ireland may also have familiarized him with stories of the Gaelic banshee (the 'bean sídhe', or fairy woman) and, if so, his fairy queen may have acquired even darker associations.[47] What is unquestionable, however, is that his fairy myth takes us to the heart of his political reality, and if it compensates to some extent for that reality it also exposes it.

The fault was partly Spenser's own. In her first speech to Parliament, Elizabeth warned her subjects that they must not seek to 'frame my will to your fantasies'.[48] She might therefore be said to have given fair warning that she would not be 'framed and fashioned' to the demands of allegorical fiction, or even that she was determined to create and maintain regal fictions of her own. *The Faerie Queene* undertakes to 'reflect' both the monarch and the nation but increasingly attempts to appropriate both to an agenda to which neither was fully committed. The creators of political and social 'myths' are best placed to recognize their distance from reality, and unfounded eulogy inevitably promotes satire. Had Elizabeth sat for one of her later portraits the disparity between image and reality would have been intolerable. Yet this is precisely what happens in *The Faerie Queene* where the 'image' of Gloriana is repeatedly juxtaposed with suspiciously familiar, if officially malign, avatars.[49] Lucifera, 'a mayden Queene, that shone as *Titans* ray' (1. 4. 8), is a case in point:

> And in her hand she held a mirrhour bright,
> Wherein her face she often vewed fayne,
> And in her selfe-lov'd semblance tooke delight;
> For she was wondrous faire, as any living wight.
>
> (1. 4. 10)

[45] See Minor White Latham, *The Elizabethan Fairies: The Fairies of Folklore and the Fairies of Shakespeare* (New York: Columbia University Press, 1930), 33–64; Isabel E. Rathborne, *The Meaning of Spenser's Fairyland* (New York: Russell and Russell, 1965—first pub. 1957), 213–17.

[46] *The Tale of Sir Thopas* is cited in *A View* (*Prose*, 121). See Judith H. Anderson, 'Arthur, Argante, and the Ideal Vision: An Exercise in Speculation and Parody', in Christopher Baswell and William Sharpe (eds.), *The Passing of Arthur: New Essays in Arthurian Tradition* (New York: Garland, 1988), 193–206.

[47] For Celtic elements in Spenser's fairy lore see Edwin Greenlaw, 'Spenser's Fairy Mythology', *SP* 15 (1918), 105–22 (108–16).

[48] Elizabeth I (2000), 57.

[49] See Jeffrey P. Fruen, '"True Glorious Type": The Place of Gloriana in *The Faerie Queene*', *SSt* 7 (1986—but pub. 1987), 147–73.

Looking in the 'mirrhor' of Spenser's poem, the fairy queen sees a fairy queen (of sorts) obsessed by the desire to be 'fairest of all'. A traditional emblem of female vanity is made to portray not just the narcissism of power but, more particularly, the perilous self-absorption of female 'regiment'. In Gabriel Harvey's *Gratulationes Valdinenses* the courtly lady is advised to 'govern all the parts of her body by the advice of her mirror', but only one type of mirror will do.[50] Erasmus's *Conjugium* counsels the good wife to 'see' herself in the 'mirror' of her husband, 'for as a glasse (if it be a true stone) representeth ever the physnamy of hym that loketh in it, so lykewyse it becommeth a wedded woman alway to agre unto the appetite of her husbande'.[51] If Elizabeth is England's 'wife' she must fashion herself after the image of her 'husband's' imperial designs—she is wedded to her male subjects and is, to that extent, their subject. The 'mirror' that consolidates male identity reconstitutes female identity. From the male viewpoint, as Irigaray has argued, 'successful femininity cannot lay claim to being ideal or confer an ideal upon itself. It lacks a mirror appropriate for doing so. The narcissistic ideal for a woman will have been and theoretically is still the man she desired to become.'[52] Far from discouraging the queen's 'narcissism', *The Faerie Queene* seeks to exploit it. Gazing in the 'mirror' of Spenser's text she will 'love' the image he has created and 'govern all the parts of her body', and of her body politic, accordingly. She never did.

The second edition of *The Faerie Queene* saw the appearance of three further books and a suitably expanded dedication 'To the Most High, Mightie and Magnificent Empresse renowmed for Pietie, Vertue, and all Gratious Government Elizabeth by the Grace of God Queene of England Fraunce and Ireland and of Virginia, Defendour of the Faith, etc.' The addition of Virginia is very telling. It is as though the poetic and political 'realmes' have expanded simultaneously, or even symbiotically, as though the Virgilian aspirations of the poetry mirror the Augustan aspirations of the nation. The queen who once described herself as 'barren stock' has had prolific issue in 'fruitfullest *Virginia*' and, as contemporary readers would recognize, the 'father' was none other than Sir Walter Ralegh

---

[50] See George L. Barnett, 'Gabriel Harvey's *Castilio, sive Aulicus* and *De Aulica*: A Study of their Place in the Literature of Courtesy', *SP* 42 (1945), 146–63 (p. 152). E.K. praises the work in *The Shepheardes Calender* in his gloss to 'September', 176.

[51] Erasmus (1557), sig. A7.

[52] Luce Irigaray, *Speculum of the Other Woman*, trans. Gillian C. Gill (Ithaca, NY: Cornell University Press, 1985), 105.

(2 Proem 2). Ideally, at least, frustrated personal relationships are resolved in the public sphere as the energies of 'love' are channelled into those of conquest. The allegory of Timias and Belphœbe tells a very different story, however. Her displeasure transforms the civil English squire into a 'wild' Irishman 'with heary glib deform'd' (4. 8. 12).[53] The bizarre imagery touched a raw nerve. Sir Francis Allen reported in 1589 that 'my Lord of Essex hath chased Mr. Ralegh from the Court and hath confined him in Ireland'. Ralegh responded by claiming that his 'retrait from court' was occasioned by the need to take possession of his 'seignory' in Munster.[54] Depending on the attitude of the queen, departure for Ireland could be seen either as an opportunity for advancement or as a mark of banishment. The borders of empire were also the precincts of exile. Yet the queen's favour could prove to be just as detrimental as her anger since she was generally disposed to detain her favourites at court. Belphœbe's 'love' for Timias separates him from Arthur and all that the Arthurian enterprise involves. To remain with Belphœbe is, paradoxically, to forsake the quest for Gloriana. The 'Letter to Ralegh' identifies the goal of Arthur's quest as 'glory' and the 'virtue' that sustains him as 'magnificence'. Both concepts are susceptible of a purely 'moral' interpretation, but those acquainted with Skelton's *Magnyfycence*—not to mention the prolific literature of Spanish imperialism—would note their strong political associations.[55] Spenser is writing as a 'poet historicall' and moral virtues are habitually appropriated to political policies, yet this gives rise to one of the poem's greatest problems. Moral allegory has a strong tendency to internalize its demons whereas colonial allegory is inherently resistant to any suggestion that the 'other' is somehow latent in the self, if only for fear of compromising the sense of identity that the contrast functions to sustain. The tension between the moral and colonial aspects of Spenserian allegory is to this extent intractable.

Particularly significant in both versions of *The Faerie Queene*'s dedication is the close association, relentlessly pursued in the subsequent allegory, between sovereignty, good government, territorial expansion and the advancement of Christianity. This denotes an 'imperial' agenda, yet care must be had in the interpretation of terms. The queen is an 'Empresse', but the word may be variously understood. The term 'imperium'

[53] For the Irish 'glib' see *Prose*, 99.

[54] See Kathrine Koller, 'Spenser and Ralegh', *ELH* 1 (1934), 37–60 (pp. 40–1).

[55] See Anthony Pagden, *Lords of All the World: Ideologies of Empire in Spain, Britain and France c.1500–c.1800* (New Haven: Yale University Press, 1995), 64.

had a wide range of connotations extending from the absolute rule of a single individual to the collective hegemony of a 'civilization'.[56] The *Imperium Romanum,* which served as the paradigm for the various self-styled 'empires' of the sixteenth and seventeenth centuries, was perceived no less as a cultural than as a political entity. Under Constantine and his successors the term *imperium* acquired an almost theocratic aura: 'in hoc signo vinces'. Henceforward 'barbarians' were also 'pagans' and to 'civil-ize' was to Christianize. The act of suppression was regarded as an act of 'charity', an attitude which eventually gave rise to the claim that the Irish were 'beholding to God for being conquered'.[57] It is therefore highly ironic that the earliest assertion of England's 'imperial' status is to be found in the Henrician Act in Restraint of Appeals to Rome (1533). 'This Realm of England', it maintains, 'is an Empire.' As the context demon-strates, the term 'empire' is here employed in a restrictive rather than an expansionist sense.[58] England is an 'empire' because it enjoys independ-ent sovereignty, and is *not* subject to the jurisdiction of Rome, even though (or rather, especially because) its sovereign and his successors continued to use the papal title of 'Defender of the Faith'. In due course, however, the retention of that title would be used to promote another sort of English 'empire'. According to Richard Hakluyt's *A Discourse on West-ern Planting* (1584), for example, it entailed an obligation not only 'to maintain and patronize the faith of Christ, but also to enlarge and ad-vance the same'.[59] It was England's peculiar duty to bring the reformed faith to the New World, and the break with Rome was merely a prelude to the assumption of the imperial mantle. The tale of King Arthur's 'con-quest' of Rome, fabricated by Geoffrey of Monmouth and elaborated by Malory, was used to lend topical urgency to an ancient legend. A. Kent Hieatt has made a strong case for supposing that the original plan for a twenty-four-book *Faerie Queene* envisaged the presentation of the Roman campaign as the culmination of Arthur's career, as the supreme expression of the 'politicke vertues'. The 'Briton Moniments' recall how the country was 'tributarie made | T'ambitious *Rome,* and did their rule

---

[56] Ibid. 12–17.   [57] Cox (1689–90), sig. A3v.

[58] See Jenny Wormald, 'The Creation of Britain: Multiple Kingdoms or Core and Colonies?', *Transactions of the Royal Historical Society,* 6th ser., 2 (1992), 175–94 (p. 190); Walter Ullmann, ' "This Realm of England is an Empire" ', *Journal of Ecclesiastical History,* 30 (1979), 175–203; Brian P. Levack, *The Formation of the British State: England, Scotland, and the Union 1603–1707* (Oxford: Clarendon Press, 1987), 2; Willy Maley, ' "This Sceptred Isle": Shakespeare and the British Problem', in John Joughin (ed.), *Shakespeare and National Culture* (Manchester: Manchester University Press, 1997), 83–108.

[59] Hakluyt (1935), i. 215.

obay, | Till *Arthur* all that reckoning did defray' (2. 10. 49). In contemporary terms Arthur's defeat of Rome would signify the defeat of Roman Catholicism by the Defenders of the Faith. 'To have formulated in an epic such a master-stroke of *translatio imperii* westward to Britain', Hieatt concludes, 'would have seemed a potent, ultimate gesture among the contending nationalistic mythologies of Renaissance Europe'.[60] Literary interest in the once and future king reflected political interest in the once and future 'empire'.[61]

But all of this was little more than wish-fulfilment. As Jeffrey Knapp has observed, the Elizabethan reality was quite different. England lost its last foothold in France the very year that the queen ascended to the throne, and by the 1590s the Virginia enterprise was seen to have failed.[62] 'The loss of Calais', observes Josephine Bennett, 'the last bit of British empire on the Continent, made the vaunting tales of Arthur's conquests an empty mockery.'[63] Of the many titles ascribed to Elizabeth in Spenser's dedication only one might conceivably be 'imperial' in the Roman sense, but even this was questionable. Elizabeth was indeed 'Queene of Ireland' but she was not, technically speaking, its 'empresse' for the simple reason that, under both English and Irish law, Ireland was not a subservient 'colony' but a separate 'kingdom', a status that prospective planters found highly inconvenient.[64] In 1541 the Irish Parliament for the first time acknowledged an English monarch as 'king', rather than 'lord', of Ireland, an event celebrated by hereditary Palesmen but deplored by New English observers such as Spenser.[65] According to *A View*, for example, 'nothinge

[60] A. Kent Hieatt, 'The Passing of Arthur in Malory, Spenser, and Shakespeare: The Avoidance of Closure', in Baswell and Sharpe (eds.), *The Passing of Arthur*, 173–92 (p. 184). For Arthur's role in the extant poem see Richard A. McCabe, 'Prince Arthur's "Vertuous and Gentle Discipline"', in Eileán Ní Cuilleanáin and J. D. Pheifer (eds.), *Noble and Joyous Histories: English Romances, 1375–1650* (Dublin: Irish Academic Press, 1993), 221–43.

[61] See Charles Bowie Millican, *Spenser and the Table Round* (Cambridge, Mass.: Harvard University Press, 1932), 7–36.

[62] Jeffrey Knapp, *An Empire Nowhere: England, America, and Literature from 'Utopia' to 'The Tempest'* (Berkeley: University of California Press, 1992), 62–3.

[63] Josephine Waters Bennett, *The Evolution of 'The Faerie Queene'* (Chicago: University of Chicago Press, 1942), 69.

[64] See Karl S. Bottigheimer, 'Kingdom and Colony: Ireland in the Westward Enterprise 1536–1660', in K. R. Andrews, N. P. Canny, and P. E. H. Hair (eds.), *The Westward Enterprise: English Activities in Ireland, the Atlantic, and America 1480–1650* (Liverpool: Liverpool University Press, 1978), 45–64 (p. 46).

[65] Colm Lennon, *Sixteenth-Century Ireland: The Incomplete Conquest* (Dublin: Gill and Macmillan, 1994), 154–5; Steven G. Ellis, 'Tudor State Formation and the Shaping of the British Isles', in Steven G. Ellis and Sarah Barber (eds.), *Conquest and Union: Fashioning a British State, 1485–1725* (London: Longman, 1995), 40–63 (pp. 56–7).

was given to Kinge Henrye [in 1541] which he had not before from his Auncestors, but onelye the bare name of a Kinge. for all other absolute power of Principalitye he had in himselfe before derived from manye former Kinges his famous progenitours and worthie Conquerours of that lande' (*Prose*, 52). This argument is crucial to an understanding of Spenser's attitude towards Ireland. The Act for the Kingly Title was particularly important in paving the way for the policy of 'surrender and regrant' whereby native Gaelic chieftains were invited to cede their territories to the crown and receive them back under English titles.[66] This process was central to the political philosophy which sought to achieve the Anglicization of Ireland through 'reform' rather than military intervention. Spenser was well aware of this but, as a leading proponent of the opposite policy, he had no option but to resist such developments. Hence the insistent argument that military conquest must precede civil or religious 'reform'.

At the heart of the issue lay the vexed problem of land tenure. The act of 'surrender' implied a prior right of possession and contradicted the claim to total 'conquest'. Worse still, because of the Gaelic practice of 'tanistry' (from tánaiste, the Gaelic for heir or deputy), a form of succession by election rather than primogeniture, the chieftain did not own most of the lands he was prevailed upon to 'surrender' and his successor was not regarded in brehon law as bound by his submission (*Prose*, 48–53).[67] Many of the accusations of treachery and duplicity levelled by both sides in the ensuing conflicts had their roots in this cultural impasse. The concept of sovereignty upon which *The Faerie Queene* is premised, that of the monarchy as a body corporate, was largely alien to the people upon whom Spenser wished to impose it.[68] The Gaelic high kingship had never operated on such a basis, but on a delicate negotiation between contract and constraint.[69] As Seathrún Céitinn explained in *Foras Feasa ar Éirinn*, the high king obtained sovereignty 'by the choice of the people, by the excellence of his exploits, and by the strength of his hand'.[70] Such sovereignty was personal not dynastic. 'It was not the custom in Ireland', Céitinn tells us, 'that the son should succeed the father . . . but the sovereignty of Ireland was given

---

[66] For surrender and regrant see Lennon, *Sixteenth-Century Ireland*, 155–9.

[67] See Kenneth Nicholls, *Gaelic and Gaelicised Ireland in the Middle Ages* (Dublin: Gill and Macmillan, 1972), 21–43.

[68] For developments in the Jacobean period see below pp. 51–3.

[69] See T. M. Charles-Edward, 'A Contract Between King and People in Early Medieval Ireland? *Críth Gablach* on Kingship', *Peritia*, 8 (1994), 107–19.

[70] Céitinn (1902–13), iii. 182–3.

to him who was most powerful in action and exploit.'[71] In order to command Gaelic support an English monarch needed to demonstrate a commensurate power to compel it—mere 'title', in the English sense, would not do. As Spenser recognized, local chieftains participated in the scheme of surrender and regrant more for pragmatic than ideological reasons. Adopting the pose of the honest Englishman bemused by foreign duplicity, Eudoxus asks 'dothe not the Acte of the parent in anye lawfull graunte or Conveyaunce binde his heires for ever theareunto?' 'They saie noe', Irenius replies, 'for theire Auncestors had not estate in anye theire Landes, Segniories, or hereditamentes longer then duringe theire owne lives' (*Prose*, 49). Similarly, those who had subscribed to the Act for the Kingly Title had done so 'reservinge yet (as some saye) unto themselves all theire owne former priviledges and seigniories inviolate' (*Prose*, 48). It might therefore appear that Elizabeth's sovereignty over Ireland depended upon the consent of the governed rather than upon the claim of conquest 'derived from manye former Kinges':

> Thearefore me semes in steade of so great and meritorious a service as they boste they performed to the Kinge In bringinge all the Irishe to acknowledge him for theire Leige, they did great hurte to his title and have lefte a perpetuall gall in the minde of that people, who before beinge absolutelye bounde to his obedience are now tyed but with tenures. (*Prose*, 52)

It was vital to remember that 'the Earle Strangbowe, havinge Conquered that Lande, delivered up the same unto the handes of Henrye the Second' (*Prose*, 96). The consequence for present policy was plain: 'all is the Conquerours' (*Prose*, 52). This myth of 'conquest' was one of the most potent weapons in the arsenal of New English polemic, and contemporary historiographers could be relied upon to provide apparent corroboration.[72] As the first Elizabethan Englishman to write a history of Ireland, Edmund Campion speaks of the country's 'conquest' by Henry II as though it were every bit as comprehensive as England's conquest by William I.[73] He then proceeds to chronicle the events of 'Irish' history under the reigns of the relevant English kings thereby ensuring that the work's structure dictates its political outlook. Although the manifest anachronism of this account of affairs was admitted by Sir John Davies in

---

[71] Céitinn (1902–13), iii. 256–7.

[72] For the Irish viewpoint see Bernadette Cunningham, *The World of Geoffrey Keating: History, Myth and Religion in Seventeenth-Century Ireland* (Dublin: Four Courts Press, 2000), 149–52.

[73] Campion (1963), 63.

1612, Elizabethan commentators clung to the contrary assertion that 'the kings of this our Britain had an elder right to the realme of Ireland, [even] than by the conquest of Henrie the second'.[74] Irenius characteristically asserts that 'kinge Arthur and before him Gurgunt had all that Ilande in his Allegiance and Subieccion' (*Prose*, 95).

Few were prepared to defend the claims of the shadowy 'Gurgunt', but the role of Arthur was treated quite seriously. Hakluyt opens *The Principal Navigations Voyages Traffiques and Discoveries of the English Nation* (1589) with Geoffrey of Monmouth's account of how the 'Brittish' Arthur subdued Ireland as the first stage in a series of conquests which eventually embraced 'Ireland, Island, Gotland, Orkney, Norway, and Denmarke'.[75] Spenser directly alludes to this proto-empire when he has Merlin speak of 'the six Islands, comprovinciall | In auncient times unto great Britainee' (3. 3. 32). According to Hakluyt, the people Arthur encountered 'were wild and savage, and had not in them the love of God nor of their neighbors . . . But king Arthur was an exceeding good Christian, and caused them to be baptized'.[76] As Arthur's descendant and Defender of the Faith, Elizabeth could be said to have inherited his imperial mission—and nowhere more so than in Ireland, the first Arthurian 'colony'. Spenser's claim to have chosen Arthur as a figure 'furthest from the daunger of envy, and suspition of present time' is thus doubly disingenuous in its application to Ireland, as Gaelic historians noted.[77] To Céitinn, for example, it was evident from the Gaelic chronicles that 'neither Arthur, nor any other foreign potentate, ever had supremacy over Ireland from the beginning till the "Norman" invasion [gabháltas Gall]'.[78] In matters such as these Spenser preferred to dismiss the Gaelic chronicles, yet the argument from conquest raised as many problems as it solved since the process is variously represented as both total and incomplete, accomplished and ongoing. Despite this evident illogicality, however, the concept of conquest proved too potent to resist, integral as it was to the martial heroism of national epic. It was all the more infuriating on that account that Elizabeth deplored the use of the term 'conquest' in an Irish context and actively discouraged the more

---

[74] Davies (1612), 286; Holinshed (1808), vi. 77.   [75] Hakluyt (1903–5), i. 3, 4.
[76] Ibid. 6.
[77] Spenser (1978), 15. For the imperial uses of Arthur see David A. Summers, *Spenser's Arthur: The British Arthurian Tradition and the Faerie Queene* (Lanham, Md.: Oxford University Press of America, 1997), 177–202.
[78] Céitinn (1902–13), i. 16–17.

grandiose ambitions of would-be conquistadors [79] Such attitudes necessitated the adoption of complex strategies of self-justification on the part of the New English.

Writing at the point of first contact, Giraldus Cambrensis had asserted that Pope Alexander III had granted to Henry II the right 'to rule over the Irish people [Hibernico populo] and, as it was very ignorant of the rudiments of the faith, to instruct it in the laws and disciplines of the church according to the usage of the church in England [iuxta Anglicane ecclesie mores]'. By such means, 'this barbarous nation, Christian only in name [barbara nacio, que Christiano censetur nomine]' would eventually 'earn the name of Christian which they now profess'. The English Pope Adrian IV enthusiastically concurred.[80] The immediate application of such attitudes to contemporary affairs was evident to John Hooker whose translation of Cambrensis was incorporated into the 1587 edition of Holinshed's *Chronicles* as 'The Conquest of Ireland'.[81] Into his accompanying *Supplie of the Irish Chronicles* Hooker weaves a subtle pattern of allusions to the *Expugnatio Hibernica* designed to cast the New English as the spiritual descendants of the original 'conquerors'—as latter-day crusaders labouring to reclaim a famous victory shamefully betrayed by the degeneracy of the victors' unworthy offspring. To those involved in what was increasingly regarded as the 'reconquest' of Ireland, the *Expugnatio* acquired an almost typological relevance.[82] Once again it was morally necessary for the 'barbarous people of Ireland' to be 'reformed and recovered from their filthie life and abhominable conversation; that as in name so in maners and conversation they may be Christians'.[83] The translator's choice of vocabulary is subtly polemical. The issue of 'reforme' had acquired a precise sectarian resonance, and the association of spiritual 'reformation' with the cultivation of civil 'maners and conversation' established a link that all New English commentators were anxious to forge. In the context of the

[79] See David Beers Quinn, *The Elizabethans and the Irish* (Ithaca, NY: Cornell University Press, 1966), 137; Mary Dewar, *Sir Thomas Smith: A Tudor Intellectual in Office* (London: Athlone Press, 1964), 159; Lisa Jardine, 'Mastering the Uncouth: Gabriel Harvey, Edmund Spenser and the English Experience in Ireland', in John Henry and Sarah Hutton (eds.), *New Perspectives on Renaissance Thought: Essays in the History of Science, Education and Philosophy in Memory of C. B. Schmitt* (London: Duckworth, 1990), 68–82 (pp. 72–4).

[80] Giraldus Cambrensis (1978), 143, 147.

[81] For colonial translation generally see Michael Cronin, *Translating Ireland: Translation, Languages, Cultures* (Cork: Cork University Press, 1996), 47–90.

[82] See Richard A. McCabe, 'Making History: Holinshed's Irish Chronicles, 1577 and 1587', in Willy Maley and David Baker (eds.), *British Identities and English Renaissance Literature* (Cambridge: Cambridge University Press, 2002), 51–67.

[83] Holinshed (1808), vi. 187.

Reformation to 'civilize' is to Protestantize and Catholics are the new 'pagans'. For both poetic and political reasons, therefore, Spenser eagerly espoused the 'reformed' version of Roman imperialism ingeniously applied to the Irish enterprise by Sir Thomas Smith.[84] Had not Camden lamented the Romans' failure to reach Ireland 'to the plague and spolie of Britaine'?[85]

Yet, as every Renaissance reader knew, Rome was a highly problematic model. Jan Van der Noot's *Theatre for Voluptuous Worldlings* (1569), in which Spenser published his earliest verse, is much preoccupied with the progressive degradation of imperial Rome, and in *The Faerie Queene* 'the antique ruines of the *Romaines* fall' are duly located in the dungeon of the House of Pride, that precarious structure governed by a 'mayden Queene' (1. 5. 49). Noot's principal target was the papacy but, by adopting Rome as the paradigm of empire, the work comes close to representing moral corruption as the spiritual consequence of imperial power. The 'Bishop of Rome' is, in this sense, a fit successor to the emperors, a matter recalled in Duessa's claim to be 'the sole daughter' of a Roman 'Emperour' (1. 2. 22).[86] It might well follow that the goals of empire and Christianity were fundamentally incompatible—a suspicion that haunts the Spenserian canon. Noot's illustrations enforce the point. The arrogance of ancient Rome is evident in its imperial architecture. The first woodcut illustrating the 'Sonets' displays the ruins of a classical temple bearing the inscription SPQR, and the third shows the collapse of a triumphall arch erected in honour of Augustus.[87] By concluding with the fall of the Whore of Babylon and the glimpse of a kingdom not of this world, the sequence suggests that those who imitate Rome are destined to share its fate, in this world and the next. Such, for example, is the unidentified 'king' who 'studieth . . . to increase his dominions daily, that at length he might attaine to the Monarchie of all *Europe*, and then to become Lorde of the whole worlde'.[88] The primary target is Philip II, but the criticism is deliberately couched in general terms. Yet in the fulsome—and, to readers of Spenser, almost proleptic—dedication to 'the moste high, puissant,

---

[84] For Smith see Dewar, *Sir Thomas Smith*, 156–70; Nicholas Canny, 'The Permissive Frontier: The Problem of Social Control in English Settlements in Ireland and Virginia 1550–1650', in Andrews et al. (eds.), *The Westward Enterprise*, 17–44 (pp. 18–19); Walter J. Ong, 'Spenser's *View* and the Tradition of the "Wild" Irish', *MLQ* 3 (1942), 561–71 (pp. 564–5); Hiram Morgan, 'The Colonial Venture of Sir Thomas Smith in Ulster, 1571–1575', *The Historical Journal*, 28 (1985), 261–78.

[85] Camden (1610), 'Ireland', 66. See also Davies (1612), 124–6.

[86] Noot (1569), sigs. 17r–v.   [87] Ibid., sigs. C1r, C3r.   [88] Ibid., sig. 1v.

noble, vertuous, and righte Christian Princesse *Elizabeth, by the grace of God* Quene of Englande, Fraunce, and Ireland etc', the queen is compared to the 'Virgin Astrea' and complimented on her management of the 'croune imperiall'.[89] The dichotomous context of Spenser's earliest verse may, therefore, be seen to inform the ambivalent agenda of his maturity. The problem was one of moral differentiation. How could one advance the imperialism of 'St George' while denigrating that of 'St Peter'? The publication of Las Casas's condemnation of Spanish brutality—if not of Spanish imperialism per se—and its translation into English as *The Spanish Colonie, or Briefe Chronicle of the Actes and Gestes of the Spaniardes* (1583), engaged all patrons of the English venture in a constant exercise of disclaimer. Otherwise the 'Legend of Justice' might prove to be no more than a further chapter of the 'Black Legend'.[90] It was presented in just that way by Catholic commentators such as Peter Lombard whose *De Hibernia Insula Commentarius* (1600), records such gruesomely familiar topoi as 'the cruel spectacle of mothers hanging on crosses, the little ones still lying or crying on their breasts strangeled in their hair and hanging from this new fashioned halter'.[91] Was it sufficient to reply, either in the New World or the Old, that the victims were 'salvages'?

Because of its engagement with current affairs, *The Faerie Queene* functions not as a passive reflection of political events but as an active expression of history in the making, a manifesto of the imperial ideal 'fashioned' by one of its most articulate exponents. Yet the practice of defining civil ideals by their 'savage' antitheses is notoriously hazardous, particularly in the context of continuing military conflict. In such circumstances intended contrasts collapse all too easily into unintentional comparisons, betraying the common heritage of the 'civil' and the 'savage', the embarrassing kinship of self and other. It may then prove, 'that what were conceived as distinguishing characteristics of the marginal are in fact the defining qualities of the central object of consideration'.[92] *The Faerie Queene* presents 'virtue' militant rather than achieved, embattled rather than secure, with the result that negative, repressive energies frequently usurp their positive counterparts. The fashioning of 'civil' selves necessitates the suppression of savage others, but the act of suppression licenses

---

[89] Noot (1569), sigs. A3v, A6r.

[90] See William S. Maltby, *The Black Legend in England: The Development of Anti-Spanish Sentiment, 1558–1660* (Durham, NC: Duke University Press, 1971), 12–28.

[91] Lombard (1930), 17.

[92] Jonathan Culler, 'Jacques Derrida', in John Sturrock (ed.), *Structuralism and Since* (Oxford: Oxford University Press, 1979), 154–81 (p. 168).

the savage self. As a result, the pervasive imagery of monstrosity, viewed in the self-styled 'mirror' of the text, becomes increasingly self-reflective until the hybrid figure of the 'salvage knight' emerges as the 'hero' of Spenser's own poetry and prose. In allegorical narrative, Coleridge remarked, 'difference is everywhere presented to the eye or imagination while . . . likeness is suggested to the mind'.[93] Spenser's colonial allegory bears particularly ironic testimony to the truth of this statement.

[93] Coleridge (1936), 30.

2   Spenser and the Rival Poets

LAMENTING the forlorn state of poetry in Ireland in his sonnet to
Thomas Butler (1531–1614), tenth Earl of Ormond and Ossory, Spenser
asserts that the country affords 'not one Parnassus, nor one Helicone' except for that maintained by Ormond himself:

> There in deede dwel faire Graces many one.
> And gentle Nymphes, delights of learned wits,
> And in thy person without Paragone
> All goodly bountie and true honour sits,
> Such therefore, as that wasted soyl doth yield,
> Receive dear Lord in worth, the fruit of barren field.

Of the seventeen dedicatory sonnets that preface the first edition of *The
Faerie Queene*, this is the only one addressed to an 'Irish' aristocrat. I use
the term 'Irish' with considerable circumspection, however. Ormond was
not Gaelic Irish but Old English, what the Irish termed 'Sean-Ghall' or
'Old Foreigner'. The Butlers had been established in Ireland since the
twelfth century and were commonly reputed by New English commentators to be amongst the least 'Gaelicized' of the surviving Old English
families.[1] Black Thomas (or Tomás Dubh), as he was known to his contemporaries, was the first of the Butlers of Ormond to be professedly
Protestant and, as the queen's kinsman, exercised considerable influence
at court.[2] That influence was highly detrimental to the interests of New
English settlers, yet Spenser praises Ormond for providing a haven for
civility within an otherwise 'barren field'.[3] His 'brave mansion' at
Kilkenny affords a blessed space where 'dwel faire Graces many one. | And
gentle Nymphes, delights of learned wits'.[4] Ideally he has created an

---

[1] The Butlers were at their most Gaelicized in the early 16th cent. following the accession of Sir
Piers Butler, ninth Earl of Ormond, whose mother was of the MacMurrough Kavanagh family.

[2] See Ciaran Brady, 'Thomas Butler, Earl of Ormond (1531–1614) and Reform in Tudor
Ireland', in Ciaran Brady (ed.), *Worsted in the Game: Losers in Irish History* (Dublin: The Lilliput
Press, 1989), 49–59.

[3] For Ormond and the New English see Nicholas Canny, *Making Ireland British, 1580–1650*
(Oxford: Oxford University Press, 2001), 125–9.

[4] Ormond had recently built another 'brave mansion' at Carrick-on-Suir, but Spenser is
probably referring to his principal seat at Kilkenny.

English oasis in an otherwise 'brutish' desert, an Acidalian paradise in 'salvage soyl'. It is highly indicative of Spenser's attitude that the only poem
in the canon expressly addressed to an 'Irish' aristocrat should praise him
for being 'English'. This was how Ormond portrayed himself at court and
the sonnet dutifully endorses the official image. Yet Spenser was well
aware that the reality was far more complex. Lord Grey engineered
Ormond's dismissal from command of the army in Munster on the
grounds that only 'an Englishe goovernor' could be trusted to oppose the
Desmonds. To Grey's way of thinking, Ormond was not quite 'English'
enough to guarantee loyalty to the crown.[5] His connections with the
'Irishrie' were far too close. His widowed mother, Joan Fitzgerald, had
married the Earl of Desmond and his brothers had joined the Desmonds
in open rebellion in the late 1560s, infuriated by the land-grabbing
schemes of Sir Peter Carew and his New English associates.[6] Though subsequently pardoned, they were never restored in blood, a circumstance
that eventually threatened the dissolution of the earldom.

In *A View of the Present State of Ireland* Irenius identifies Ormond's personal fiefdom, the 'Countie Pallatine' of Tipperary not as a centre of
civility but as a lawless 'border' area perilously situated 'in the verye lapp of
all the lande' (*Prose*, 74). Compensatory praise of the 'righte noble man
that is the Lorde of the libertye' does little to blunt the force of such criticism.[7] Culturally, socially, and politically, Ormond's 'Countie Pallatine' is
characterized as what the French would term 'terrain vague'. It is somewhat remarkable, therefore, that Spenser should raise the issue of literary
patronage in the Butler sonnet at all. One suspects that Ormond is being
cajoled into demonstrating some of the 'bountie' for which he is praised—
or, perhaps, that he was simply too powerful, and too dangerous, to ignore. There is no evidence that he ever afforded patronage to Spenser, but
he certainly patronized the 'bards' whom Irenius takes such pains to denigrate. If there was a patronly 'Parnassus' at Kilkenny it was primarily a
Gaelic one. Like many other members of his family, Ormond was a fluent
Irish speaker. His father had acted as interpreter for the House of Lords
during the passage of the Act for the Kingly Title in 1541.[8] The Ormonds'

---

[5] SP 63/81/36. For Ormond's alleged links with the 'Irishrie' see SP 63/82/50.

[6] See Richard A. McCabe, 'Making History: Holinshed's Irish *Chronicles*, 1577 and 1587', in
Willy Maley and David Baker (eds.), *British Identities and English Renaissance Literature* (Cambridge: Cambridge University Press, 2002), 51–67.

[7] See David J. Baker, *Between Nations: Shakespeare, Spenser, Marvell, and the Question of
Britain* (Stanford, Calif.: Stanford University Press, 1997), 80–5.

[8] Brian Ó Cuív, 'The Irish Language in the Early Modern Period', *NHI* iii. 509–45 (p. 510).

bilingualism equipped them to work in both worlds and, in the internecine climate of clan rivalries, Black Thomas's activities were sufficiently 'Irish' to lend themselves to bardic encomium of the sort accorded to such 'rebels' as the notorious Feagh mac Hugh O'Byrne [Fiachaidh mac Aodha Ó Broin]. Indeed, when read from a New English perspective, the surviving poems tend to corroborate Irenius's account of the palatinate. In Flann mac Eoghain Mac Craith's elegy 'Eólach mé ar mheirge an iarla' ['I know the Earl's standard'] (1614), for example, Ormond is praised for raiding and spoiling neighbouring fiefdoms in the traditional Gaelic manner. Mac Craith takes full account of his services to the crown but incorporates them into the traditional 'caithréim' or battle role. Where Spenser would have put down markers of change and difference, Mac Craith see continuity and similarity.[9] Nor was he alone in this. Another of the Butler poets, the anonymous author of 'Taghaim Tomás', expressly refers to Ormond as an Irishman ['Éirionnach'].[10] Bardic poetry praises Ormond for being precisely what Spenser's sonnet pretends that he is not. Spenser would have him display the 'civil' English virtues of *The Faerie Queene*; Mac Craith would assimilate him to the ancient traditions of Gaelic panegyric—and it was Mac Craith, not Spenser, who benefited from Ormond's 'bountie'.

Few members of the Gaelic and Old English community attracted quite so much condemnation as the professional caste known to New English observers as the 'bards'. The example of the Butlers explains the need to speak in terms of the 'Gaelic *and Old English* community'. By the mid-sixteenth century the phenomenon of acculturation deplored by Spenser, and celebrated by the 'bards', had established a socially cohesive—if politically discordant—community from which the New English found themselves excluded. The bards formed a crucial link between Ireland's two most powerful 'nations' and, more dangerously still, frequently urged Gaeil and 'Sean-Ghaill' to regard themselves as one 'nation'. In 'Fearann cloidhimh críoch Bhanbha' ['Banbha's land is swordland'], for example, Tadhg Dall Ó hUiginn acknowledges the Burkes' territorial claims by right of conquest while at the same time celebrating their assimilation to the culture of the conquered.[11] The association worked to the

<hr />

[9] Carney (1945), 67–73.

[10] Ibid. 74. The poem is not in *dán díreach*. See below p. 51.

[11] See Ó hUiginn (1922–6), i. 120–31; ii. 80–90. For Old English patronage of Gaelic verse see Katharine Simms, 'Bards and Barons: The Anglo-Irish Aristocracy and the Native Culture', in Robert Bartlett and Angus MacKay (eds.), *Medieval Frontier Societies* (Oxford: Clarendon Press, 1989), 177–97.

advantage of both parties: in return for patronage the Burkes gained legit-imacy. Language lay at the heart of the matter. As Irenius complains, some Old English families had ceased to speak or even to understand English, while many, and possibly most, of the others, were bilingual—and this situation obtained not just outside the Pale but also within it.[12] The use of Gaelic was so prevalent that even such a stalwart New Englishman as Richard Boyle, first Earl of Cork, was careful to have his sons taught Gaelic.[13]

In late 1580 Lord Grey arrested Christopher Nugent, the fourteenth Baron Delvin, for alleged complicity in the rebellion of Viscount Baltin-glass. In a letter to the queen, a copy of which survives in Spenser's hand, he professed himself horrified to discover such treachery at the very heart of the English Pale.[14] The sense of sheer incomprehension evident in Grey's attitude is quite understandable in someone of his outlook. Delvin was, on the face of it, a most unlikely 'traitor'. He had been brought up as the ward of the Earl of Sussex and educated at Clare Hall in Cambridge. He spoke English perfectly, but did not regard it as his 'mother tongue'.[15] In 1564 he was granted an audience with the queen during the course of which she expressed an interest in learning Gaelic. In response he pro-duced an elegant 'Primer' designed to instruct her in the rudiments of Irish grammar. In the preface he suggests that she will never truly com-prehend her Irish subjects until she learns their language: 'For as speache is the spetiall mean whereby all subjectes learne obedience, and their Prynces, or Governors, understande their greves and harmes; so the same beinge delyvered by an interpretor, cann never carye that grace, or proper intellygence, which the tonge itselfe beinge understode expressith.'[16] The Irish cannot be 'understood' in English, only misunderstood. Their lan-guage articulates their nature.

It is now impossible to assess Elizabeth's personal attitude to the Gaelic language, but the political import of her curiosity is clear. In the early years of her reign there was considerable interest in using Gaelic to pro-mote policies of religious and political reform. Shortly after her interview

---

[12] Ó Cuív, 'The Irish Language', 509–12.

[13] Nicholas Canny, *The Upstart Earl: A Study of the Social and Mental World of Richard Boyle, First Earl of Cork, 1566–1643* (Cambridge: Cambridge University Press, 1982), 126–8.

[14] SP 63/79/24.

[15] See Vincent Carey, ' "Neither good English nor good Irish": Bi-lingualism and Identity Formation in Sixteenth-century Ireland', in Hiram Morgan (ed.), *Political Ideology in Ireland, 1541–1641* (Dublin: Four Courts Press, 1999), 45–61 (pp. 52–6).

[16] See Gilbert (1882), p. xxxv.

with Delvin in 1564, the queen provided a substantial sum of money 'for the making of Carecter to print the New Testament in Irish' in the hope of furthering the country's reformation by providing a vernacular Bible. By 1567, frustrated by the evident lack of progress, she was threatening to demand her money back.[17] In the event, the New Testament [*Tiomna Nuadh*] was delayed until 1603 but two preliminary publications did appear in the meantime, both in 1571.[18] One of these was a broadside containing 'Tuar ferge foighide dhe' ['God's patience portends anger'], a poem on the last judgement by the fifteenth-century poet Pilib Bocht Ó hUiginn. It may seem somewhat ironic that the first 'bardic' poem to appear in print in Ireland should be sponsored by the administration that sought to proscribe the 'bards', but the poem in question is exceptionally well chosen, being as overtly apolitical and non-sectarian as might be had.[19] Even so, a degree of subtle editing is certainly in evidence. The insertion of two pointing 'hands' draws attention to the opening lines of stanza eleven: 'Breath dé mona dheacha leam | ní shaorfaidh índ ó ifreand: | Sí do ghuidhe an duilimh dhamh, | ar gluínibh muire mhathar' ['If God's judgement is not in my favour, it will not save me from hell that Mother Mary beseech the Creator for me on her knees']. A pre-Reformation poem is hereby (mis)placed in the context of Reformation polemic. Reflecting popular habits of devotion rather than orthodox Catholic theology, bardic poetry frequently exaggerated Mary's powers to the point at which Protestant observers might well detect 'blasphemy'.[20] The editorial intervention is designed to suggest that Ó hUiginn shared the reformers' misgivings. In fact he did not, and the general tenor of bardic poetry was far less easy to appropriate than the chosen example.

Lord Delvin was not the 'traitor' that Grey imagined and the charges against him were subsequently dismissed, but neither was he a simple servant of the crown.[21] His loyalties were divided and the best expression of the complexity of that division is to be found in the accomplished Gaelic verse written by his brother William Nugent while studying at Hart Hall in Oxford. Ireland is William's 'native land' ['mo dhomhan dúthchais']

---

[17] See Bruce Dickins, 'The Irish Broadside of 1571 and Queen Elizabeth's Types', *Transactions of the Cambridge Bibliographical Society*, 1 (1949), 48–60 (p. 49).

[18] For the second Gaelic publication of 1571 see below p. 178.

[19] For the text and translation see Ó Cuív (1994), 191–208.

[20] Ibid. 203. See Peter O'Dwyer, *Mary: A History of Devotion in Ireland* (Dublin: Four Courts Press, 1988), 175–99.

[21] Delvin was arrested for suspected treason during the Nine Years' War and died in Dublin Castle while awaiting trial.

and he takes no comfort amongst 'the families of England's nobles' ['clan-naibh séaghainn Saxon']. His sense of kindred binds his heart instead to 'the musicians who were my companions, and the poets of that land where Gall and Gael dwell' ['a haos ciúil (mo chompánuigh), | filidh cláir Ghall a's Ghaoidheal'].[22] So far as the authorities were concerned, how-ever, 'the poets of that land' were the very 'bablers' and 'rymours' respons-ible for the 'degeneracy' evident in Nugent's own verse. They were legislated against as early as the Statutes of Kilkenny (1366) and were banned from all Anglicized territories in 1435—and again in 1534—as ma-licious fomenters of treason and bloodshed.[23] Holinshed, for example, attributes the rebellion of Silken Thomas, one of the Geraldines of Kil-dare, to the incitement of 'an Irish rithmour . . . a rotten sheepe able to in-fect an whole flocke'.[24] Lord Grey's principal opponents were the Geraldines of Desmond, and it was regarded as no coincidence that some seventy Gaelic poets were active in Munster during that period.[25] The Geraldines were lineally descended from the heroes of Giraldus Cam-brensis's *Expugnatio Hibernica* and numbered Giraldus himself amongst their ancestors.[26] Through generations of intermarriage, however, they had gradually assimilated to Gaelic culture while at the same time main-taining official links with the crown. So far as was possible they exploited their dual kinship to secure their pre-eminence. Gearóid Iarla, the third Earl of Desmond (1338–98), was both a minister of the crown and an ac-complished Gaelic poet. He favoured a policy of cultural and political in-tegration and, when compelled to enact segregationist policies, expressed his dilemma in Gaelic verse:

> Fuilngim tír na nÉireannach
> nach rachainn i gceann Ghaoidheal
> mina tíosadh éigeantas
> ó ríogh Shaxan dom laoidheadh.

---

[22] Murphy (1948), 8–15 (pp. 12, 15). See also Ó Tuathail (1940).

[23] For the ordinance of 1579 against 'rhymers, bards, harpers or such idle persons' see Pauline Henley, *Spenser in Ireland* (Cork: Cork University Press, 1928), 106. Thomas Smyth alleged that the bards would compare 'anye younge man discended of the septs of *Ose* or *Max*' to 'Aniball, or Scipio, or Hercules' by commending 'his father and his aunchetours, nowmbrying howe many heades they have cut of, howe many townes they have burned'. He links their power to witch-craft. Hore (1858), 166.

[24] Holinshed (1808), vi. 292.

[25] Michael MacCarthy-Morrogh, *The Munster Plantation: English Migration to Southern Ireland 1583–1641* (Oxford: Clarendon Press, 1986), 14.

[26] See Holinshed (1808), vi. 46–8.

[I swear by the land of the Irish
That I would not oppose the Gaels
Were it not that I am forced to do so,
By orders of the Saxon King.][27]

Although it would be quite anachronistic to interpret such passages as supplying evidence for any form of emergent 'nationalism', the terminology nevertheless anticipates by three centuries Seathrún Céitinn's designation of the Gaelic Irish ('Gaedhil') and Catholic Old English ('Sean-Ghaill') as 'Éireannaigh' or 'Irishmen', a common term indicative of a joint political agenda as well as a shared culture.[28] Even allowing for an element of shrewd special pleading on the author's part, Gearóid's poetry displays a considerable conflict between political obedience and cultural affinity, particularly as it proceeds to refer to the Irish as 'brothers' ('bráithreachaibh'). Even by the mid-fourteenth century many of the Gaelic Irish and Old English had far more in common with each other than either had with the 'Saxons' king'. The process of assimilation was so complete in some families as to allow the professional poets to function with equanimity as spokesman for both parties. As Gofraidh Fionn Ó Dálaigh, one of the poets patronized by Gearóid Iarla, disarmingly asserted:

In poetry for the English [i ndán na nGall] we promise that the Gaels shall be banished from Ireland, while in poetry for the Gaels [i ndán na nGaoidheal] we promise that the English shall be hunted across the sea.[29]

Though often dismissed as an exercise in political cynicism, this is rather to be seen as a testament to the degree of cultural integration achieved by the Old English families. The result of centuries of intermarriage was that most of the Old English shared a common genealogy with the Irish and could therefore be eulogized in the traditional manner through praise of an heroic ancestry stretching back to Míl Espáinne, the mythical progenitor of the Gaelic race. 'Although their surnames are not like those of the Gaeil', argued Tadhg Mac Bruaideadha, 'they are descended from our women folk'. And, he continued, 'on the female side from our race comes Thomas Earl of Ormond'.[30] These remarks activate

---

[27] Mac Niocaill (1963), 18.
[28] For the term 'Éireannach' see See Brendán Ó Buachalla, '*Annála Ríoghachta Éireann* is *Foras Feasa ar Éirinn*: an Comhthéacs Comhaimseartha', *Studia Hibernica*, 22–3 (1985), 59–105 (pp. 79–81).
[29] Ó hUiginn (1922–6), i, p. xlvii.   [30] See McKenna (1918–19), ii. 246–7.

every nuance of anxiety detectable in Spenser's lengthy discussion of mis-cegenation. By the end of the sixteenth century many New English ob-servers had come to regard inculturation as the single greatest threat to their position, and the bards were seen to promote it.[31] They, like their English equivalents, acted not merely as the custodians but as the adapters and inventors of genealogy. Although they drew their material from the distant past, they invariably employed it with an eye to present circumstance. Their genealogies, for example, could be used to validate, or extend, contemporary territorial claims.[32] In the absence of political unity they functioned to promote a cultural empathy that might eventu-ally issue in political unity.

The willingness of Gaelic poets to write on behalf of Old English patrons has led to the assertion that 'bardic' poetry was largely 'apolitical' in the sense that the poets' overriding concern was the maintenance of their professional status.[33] Such wider interests as they had, it has been alleged, were purely 'cultural'.[34] But this is to conceive of 'culture' and 'politics' as exclusive categories although they are self-evidently related in practice, and nowhere more so than in a colonial situation.[35] The New English made a point of politicizing cultural difference. Accusations of cultural 'degeneracy' were potent weapons in their struggle to supplant their Old English rivals. Long before Céitinn spoke of the Gaelic Irish and Old English as 'Éireannaigh', Sir Henry Sidney and Lord Grey habit-ually collapsed the traditional distinction by speaking of both as 'Irish'— a practice popularized by the New English partisan John Hooker in his contributions to Holinshed.[36] In effect, the attitudes of the New English

---

[31] See Marc Caball, *Poets and Politics: Reaction and Continuity in Irish Poetry, 1558–1625* (Cork: Cork University Press in association with Field Day, 1998), 128; Marc Caball, 'Innova-tion and Tradition: Irish Gaelic Responses to Early Modern Conquest and Colonization', in Morgan (ed.), *Political Ideology in Ireland*, 62–82 (pp. 70–7).

[32] See e.g. McKenna (1980), 258–75.

[33] T. J. Dunne, 'The Gaelic Response to Conquest and Colonisation: The Evidence of the Poetry', *Studia Hibernica*, 20 (1980), 7–30 (p. 29). For an extreme statement of this viewpoint see Michelle O Riordan, *The Gaelic Mind and the Collapse of the Gaelic World* (Cork: Cork Univer-sity Press, 1990). For a trenchant response see Brendán Ó Buachalla, 'Poetry and Politics in Early Modern Ireland', *Eighteenth-Century Ireland: Iris an dá Chultúr*, 7 (1992), 149–75.

[34] Joseph Th. Leerssen, *Mere Irish & Fíor-Ghael: Studies in the Idea of Irish Nationality, its Development and Literary Expression prior to the Nineteenth Century* (Amsterdam: John Benjamins Publishing Company, 1986), 177, 206–18, 220, 224. But Leerssen's argument is contradictory and he is occasionally led to recognize the emergence of 'a national-Gaelic stance' (p. 205).

[35] See Marc Caball, 'Faith, Culture and Sovereignty: Irish Nationality and its Development, 1558–1625', in Brendan Bradshaw and Peter Roberts (eds.), *British Consciousness and Identity: the Making of Britain, 1533–1707* (Cambridge: Cambridge University Press, 1998), 112–39.

[36] See McCabe, 'Making History', 63.

helped to promote the development of the embryonic 'nationalism' they opposed by providing the Irish and Old English with a common enemy.[37] Although religious difference played its part, the outbreak of the Desmond wars in the late 1570s was largely the result of New English attempts to break the power of the local magnates by subordinating them to provincial presidencies and abolishing the much maligned practices of 'coyne and livery' through which they derived much of their revenue.[38] Existing tensions were greatly exacerbated by the adoption of increasingly aggressive tactics by crown agents such as Sir John Perrot, Sir Nicholas Malby, and Sir Humphrey Gilbert.[39] To their way of thinking, the association between culture and politics was absolute. The practice of 'tanistry' is a case in point since it functioned both as an expression of ancestral Gaelic culture and as a principle of current Gaelic politics. The policy of 'surrender and regrant', which was designed to suppress it, aimed at the very heart of Gaelic identity, as at least one bardic poet recognized as early as the 1540s.[40] 'Fúbún fúibh, a shluagh Gaoidheal' ['Shame on you, O men of the Gael'] is addressed, contrary to usual bardic practice, to the Gaelic Irish as a whole and not to a particular clan or sept. It is forthright in its identification of the Gaels' common enemy and displays an acute awareness of the politics of 'culture':

Ó Néill of Oileach and Eamhain Macha [Con Bacach Ó Néill], the king of Tara and Tailte, has exchanged in foolish submission his kingship [ríoghacht] for the Ulster earldom [iarlacht Uladh].[41]

The titles attributed to Ó Néill deserve particular attention in view of their connection with the ancient high kingship.[42] As applied to local chieftains, the term 'rí' [king] had become little more than a poetic

---

[37] See G. H. Hayes-McCoy, 'The Completion of the Tudor Conquest and the Advance of the Counter-reformation, 1571–1603', *NHI* iii. 94–141 (p. 111).

[38] See Ciaran Brady, 'Faction and the Origins of the Desmond Rebellion of 1579', *IHS* 22 (1981), 289–312. 'Coyne and livery' is a characteristically hybrid formulation since 'coyne' derives from the Gaelic 'coinmheadh' signifying billeting or quartering.

[39] See Ciaran Brady, 'The Road to the View: on the Decline of Reform Thought in Tudor Ireland', in Patricia Coughlan (ed.), *Spenser and Ireland: An Interdisciplinary Perspective* (Cork: Cork University Press, 1989), 25–45.

[40] For the threat posed by 'surrender and regrant' see Steven G. Ellis, *Ireland in the Age of the Tudors 1447–1603: English Expansion and the End of Gaelic Rule* (London: Longman, 1998), 254–7; Leerssen, *Mere Irish & Fíor-Ghael*, 203–6.

[41] Ó Cuív (1973–4), 273.

[42] Tara was the seat of the ancient high kings, and the great fair at Tailte (or Tailtiu) was the principal assembly of the Uí Néill at which the high king generally presided. Emain Macha was the ancient capital of Ulster.

archaism by the sixteenth century, yet the poets frequently urge their patrons to assume the ancient high kingship—in abeyance since the Old English incursions of the twelfth century—and 'unite' the country under their personal leadership.[43] In accordance with the ancient trope whereby a chieftain was said to 'marry' his lands, the patron is presented as the only fit 'mate' for 'Ireland', usually figured as a beautiful woman in need of a strong, protective husband. A bard may make similar claims for a number of different, and even mutually hostile, patrons and, in the vast majority of cases, those claims are entirely unrealistic. Thus, for example, the beleaguered Cú Chonnacht Mág Uidhir, is urged by Ferghal Óg Mac an Bhaird to assume the high kingship and lead his countrymen against the foreigner. The Maguires, he is informed, *are* Ireland ('Leath re Fódla fuil Uidhir').[44] The very 'conventionality' of such material has been used to dismiss the notion that the bards ever managed to articulate a potentially 'nationalist' stance despite their frequent calls for united action, but this is to misunderstand the nature of poetic 'convention' and ignore the importance of context.[45] Just a few years prior to the writing of 'Fúbún fúibh, a shluagh Gaoidheal' the Dublin administration was deeply disturbed by reports that Con Bacach Ó Néill was indeed planning to occupy Tara (the seat of the ancient high kingship) and proclaim himself 'Kinge of Irelande' in that deeply symbolic location.[46] In times of political emergency the standard topoi of bardic encomia were perceived to be more than mere 'rhetoric'. 'If we had a king like other nations', argued James Fitzmaurice, at the outbreak of the Desmond wars, 'none would venture to attack us.' Bardic poetry implicitly endorsed such ideology by keeping the notion of the ancient high kingship alive.[47] Although individual bards frequently addressed their poems to patrons who were most unlikely to command the united support of the various clans, collectively they preserved the *idea* of the high kingship, the idea that someone not only might, but certainly should, lead a pan-Gaelic alliance:

What is this plight of Ireland? Throughout old Europe from sea to sea there is no island without a high-king [airdrígh] except the rightful wife of Cobhthach

---

[43] Katherine Simms, *From Kings to Warlords: The Changing Political Structure of Gaelic Ireland in the Later Middle Ages* (Woodbridge: Boydell, 1987), 38–40, 147.

[44] Greene (1972), pp. 3, 5.

[45] See Marc Caball, 'Bardic Poetry and the Analysis of Gaelic Mentalities', *History Ireland*, 2/2 (1994), 46–50.

[46] Ó Cuív (1973–4), 264.

[47] See Hayes-McCoy, 'The Completion of the Tudor Conquest', 105.

[Ireland] . . . she will accept a single mate again—[and renew] the glory of the Irish which was quenched.[48]

Such ambitions were beyond Cú Chonnacht Maguire but during the Nine Years' War his son helped Hugh O'Neill [Aodh Ó Néill] to all but realize them.[49] In 1597, at the height of the conflict, Nicholas Dawtrey reported that O'Neill 'holds himselfe king of Ulster, and his rymer Bards . . . and other parrasites, do call him so in many of their flattering rymes, or orations, which did ever lift up the olde Oneales'.[50] Irenius goes even further than Dawtry in alleging that Tyrone has 'set . . . before his eyes the hope of a kingedome'—not just Ulster but Ireland (*Prose*, 166).[51] In so far as the New English read bardic poetry at all they read it politically, and no one knew better than the author of *The Faerie Queene* that reliance on medieval poetic conventions posed no barrier to topical allusion. The bards' penchant for citing supposedly ancient prophecies in support of current policies would be entirely familiar to him.[52] Far from impeding political engagement, 'convention' might even promote it.

In assessing Spenser's attitude towards the bards it is essential to recognize that during the 1590s serious, and relatively successful, efforts were being made to construct a pan-Gaelic alliance under Ó Néill and Ó Dónaill and to draw towards it as many of the Catholic Old English as possible. In 1595 the leaders of the emergent confederacy offered the Irish 'crown' to Philip II—the most terrifying of all possibilities for New English observers.[53] The 'conventions' of bardic rhetoric had at last found an echo in political reality and there is abundant evidence that many of the poets realized this.[54] To mention but one instance, Eoghan Ruadh Mac an Bhaird speaks of a confederacy of clans embracing 'the Old English of the Land of the Fair, with whom we, the warriors of Ireland, have united' ['ar Sheanghallaibh fóid na bhFionn, | lér cheanglamair óig Éirionn']. The work, he tells the young Hugh O'Donnell [Aodh Ó Dónaill], is written in the common 'mother tongue' ['teanguidh ar máthar'] of the Irish and Sean-Ghaill and he wishes it to journey through-

---

[48] Greene (1972), 17, 35.

[49] For Hugh Maguire see Hiram Morgan, *Tyrone's Rebellion: The Outbreak of the Nine Years War in Tudor Ireland* (Woodbridge: Boydell Press, 1999—first pub. 1993), 119, 142–59.

[50] Dawtrey (1995), 88.   [51] For similar allegations see Hogan and O'Farrell (1959), 174.

[52] See Eugene O'Curry, *Lectures on the Manuscript Materials of Ancient Irish History* (Dublin: James Duffy, 1861), 382–96.

[53] Morgan, *Tyrone's Rebellion*, 139–92, 194–5.

[54] See Aodh De Blácam, *Gaelic Literature Surveyed* (Dublin: Talbot Press, 1973—first pub. 1929), 136–48.

out the land and share its contents with every Irishman ['ris gach n-aon d'Éirionnchaibh'].[55] In terms of 'national' consciousness, and the importance of the 'mother tongue' to the development of such consciousness, these sentiments are strongly reminiscent of those expressed in the prefatory material to *The Shepheardes Calender*, not to mention Irenius's concerns with the linguistic, and hence political, influence of Gaelic mothers and wet-nurses.[56]

In the cultural attitudes of the bards Spenser might detect a dangerous inversion of his own political agenda. They promoted the unity of the Irish and Old English and actively opposed the policy of Anglicization which lay at the heart of New English ideology.[57] Worse still, as Seathrún Céitinn pointed out, the very existence of the bardic order, and the extraordinary honour accorded to it, challenged the classification of Gaelic society as 'barbarous'.[58] Poetry, and particularly written poetry, was widely regarded as the hallmark of civility, and poets as agents of civilization.[59] The writers pejoratively called 'bards' or 'rhymers' never referred to themselves in such a manner.[60] The 'bard' was usually an 'ollamh', or at least a 'file', a learned man who might well combine the roles of poet, chronicler, genealogist, and counsellor.[61] They regarded themselves as the supreme guardians of the Gaelic language and considered English to be a 'barbarous' tongue.[62] It took seven years to qualify as an 'ollamh' in one of the many schools run by the hereditary 'bardic' families and the successful candidates were highly conscious of their status. They were regarded as an elite caste and treated accordingly even during times of conflict.[63] Functioning exclusively as court poets at the service of the Gaelic nobility they articulated a predominantly aristocratic outlook on social and political issues.[64] Their work lent endorsement to their patrons'

[55] Bergin (1970), 25–7, 219–20. [56] See Spenser (1999), p. xii.
[57] See my discussion of Laoisioch Mac an Bhaird's attitudes in 'Ireland: Policy, Poetics and Parody', in Andrew Hadfield (ed.), *The Cambridge Companion to Spenser* (Cambridge: Cambridge University Press, 2001), 60–78 (pp. 72–3).
[58] Céitinn (1902–13), i. 5, 73. [59] See Smith (1904), ii. 6–10.
[60] For the use of the term 'bard' see Bergin (1970), 4.
[61] See Proinsias Mac Cana, 'The Rise of the Later Schools of Filidheacht', *Ériu*, 25 (1974), 126–46; Ó Cuív, 'The Irish Language', 523.
[62] Attitudes would change in the 17th cent., however. See Nicholas Canny, 'The Formation of the Irish Mind: Religion, Politics and Gaelic Irish Literature 1580–1750', *Past and Present*, 95 (1982), 91–116 (p. 105).
[63] For a notable example see Ó Clérigh (1948–57), i. 209–11.
[64] See Eleanor Knott, *Irish Classical Poetry: Filíocht na Sgol* (Dublin: Cultural Relations Committee of Ireland, 1957), 49–54; Pádraig A. Breatnach, 'The Chief's Poet', *Proceedings of the Royal Irish Academy*, 83, sect. C, no. 3 (1983), 37–79.

claims to authority and they sometimes arbitrated in political disputes.[65] The relationship between poet and patron was so close as to bear comparison with that of husband and wife.[66] It was this intimate access to the highest echelons of Gaelic society that rendered the 'bards' so menacing. Their poetry was perceived to achieve that crucial effect of 'praxis', that 'moving' of the emotions, and influencing of actions, that Sir Philip Sidney identified as the peculiar effect of legitimate poetic discourse.[67] They afforded proof, or at least seemed to do so, that poets could exercise real political power and the call for their suppression is, in this respect, a bizarre form of aesthetic appreciation. They confronted Spenser with the enticing image of his own dearest ambitions: his 'Gloriana', like Ralegh's 'Cynthia', is the creation of a would-be laureate writing from the 'wilderness', but the ollamh *was* a courtly laureate. It is therefore quite misleading to claim that Spenser attempted to 'appropriate' a 'bardic persona' in poems such as *Colin Clouts Come Home Againe*.[68] The term 'bard' is never applied to Colin and its absence is significant. Spenser laments Colin's lack of bardic status, portraying him as an isolated figure disillusioned at court, imperilled in the wilderness, and truly at 'home' in neither.

The bards, by contrast, knew their place and frequently mocked the low social status of the New English and, after the fall of the old Gaelic order, that of the *nouveaux riches* in general.[69] They regarded patronage as their right and often responded with vicious satire when it was refused.[70] Since the lack of equivalent patronage in England forms one of the central themes of Spenserian 'complaint', it is difficult to resist the suspicion that at least some of the hostility directed towards the 'bards' is the product of professional envy. In the case of the Earl of Ormond, for example, Spenser was literally in competition with the 'bards' for a share in the patron's 'bountie'. Just how close the rivalry might become is illustrated by a remarkable Gaelic eulogy of Elizabeth I written for Ormond sometime after 1588. It bears ready comparison with Spenser's *Aprill* eclogue in language, tone and imagery:

[65] See Marc Caball, 'Innovation and Tradition', 66–8.

[66] James Carney, *The Irish Bardic Poet: A Study in the Relationship of Poet and Patron* (Dublin: Dolmen Press, 1967), 12–13, 37–8.

[67] See Smith (1904), i. 171.

[68] For the opposite view see Sue Pettitt Starke, 'Briton Knight or Irish Bard? Spenser's Pastoral Persona and the Epic Project in *A View of the Present State of Ireland* and *Colin Clouts Come Home Againe*', in *SSt* 12 (1991—but pub. 1998), 133–50 (p. 137); Christopher Highley, *Shakespeare, Spenser, and the Crisis in Ireland* (Cambridge: Cambridge University Press, 1997), 36.

[69] See Leerssen, *Mere Irish & Fíor-Ghael*, 224–6.

[70] E. C. Quiggin, *Prolegomena to the Study of the Later Irish Bards 1200–1500* (London: Oxford University Press for the British Academy, 1911), 29–30.

Doghéan aiste do phrionnsa Shacsan
  cúmtha cneasta cóirighthe
bhias dá haithris ag lucht aitis
  ar feadh faithche feorghloine
is bhias 'na sólás in gach comhdháil
  le gléas comhlán ceolchruite.[71]

[I shall make for the sovereign of England a poem
  Well fashioned, courteous, and orderly,
That will surely be often recited on many
  A green-swarded fair green by merry folk,
And will be as a solace in every assembly,
  By melodious harps fully accompanied.]

The poem proceeds to recall the uniting of the Houses of York and Lan-
caster in the Tudor dynasty, to offer a blazon of the queen's personal beauty,
to compare her to King Arthur, to celebrate her conquests in the New
World, and to praise her for holding Ireland in England's 'protection' ['féach
Éire aice i gcléith Sacsan'].[72] Even though it falls short of hailing Elizabeth
as 'Queen of Ireland', this is somewhat too close for Spenserian comfort,
and none of it corresponds to the Renaissance notion of the 'salvage'.

The same might be said of the poets' patrons, some of whom were immensely learned in their own right.[73] Literary patronage is habitually represented in Spenserian verse as the hallmark of the culturally magnificent.
'Salvage' chieftains such as the notorious Feagh mac Hugh O'Byrne who
defeated Lord Grey at Glenmalure should not, in theory, patronize
poetry. It is not consistent with the stereotype. Sir Henry Sidney described the O'Byrnes as 'vermin' and encouraged Lord Grey to 'extirp'
them.[74] Yet Feagh mac Hugh and his forebears patronized the writers
who contributed to the *Leabhar Branach*, one of the most sophisticated of
the 'duanaireadha', or poem books, assembled during the sixteenth century. Their devotion to poetry was such that in 1579 Sir Henry Harring-
ton was instructed to 'make proclamation that no idle person, vagabond
or masterless man, bard, rymor, or other notorious malefactor' be allowed
to remain in their territory.[75] In this he was remarkably unsuccessful.

---

[71] Ó Bruadair (1910–17), iii. 64, 65. The poem is not in *dán díreach* and the traditional attribution to Flann Mac Craith has been disputed. See Carney (1945), 136–7.

[72] Ó Bruadair (1910–17), iii. 68, 69.

[73] See Brendan Bradshaw, 'Manus "the Magnificent": O'Donnell as a Renaissance Prince',
in Art Cosgrove and Donal MacCartney (eds.), *Studies in Irish History presented to R. Dudley
Edwards* (Dublin: University College Dublin, 1979), 15–36.

[74] See Grey (1847), 70.   [75] See Leerssen, *Mere Irish & Fíor-Ghael*, 292.

Irenius bristles with impotent indignation at 'the insolent outrages and spoiles of Pheagh Mac Hugh' (*Prose*, 64), but the *Leabhar Branach* represents his raids on the Pale in an heroic register that would have been disconcertingly familiar to readers of *The Faerie Queene*. His father, Hugh mac Shane O'Byrne [Aodh mac Sheaáin Ó Broin], is equipped by Tadhg Dall Ó hUiginn with an invincible fairy lance, much like that wielded by Britomart, and with armour impervious to enemy blades, much like that worn by Arthur and George. He is a sort of 'fairy' knight locked in conflict with the barbarous forces of the New English. In fact, the use of 'fairy' was a staple feature of bardic panegyric. There, as in *The Faerie Queene*, to approach the state of 'fairy', particularly in artistic matters, was to approach perfection.[76] Weighed against such familiar sensitivities, the crude rhetoric of cultural inferiority may be seen to supply even more vital succour to the unconscious psychology of colonialism—to its desperate need for justification through differentiation—than to its conscious politics.

Condemnation seems to struggle with appreciation throughout *A View* even though the dialogue is elaborately constructed to exclude such discordant undersongs. Feagh mac Hugh O'Byrne constituted an imminent threat to the well-being of the Pale and all that it represented, yet in a remarkable passage, indicative of a radical, if unconscious, disquiet in Spenser's attitudes, he is grudgingly praised for raising himself 'to that heighte that he nowe dare front Princes And make termes with greate Potentates, the which as it is to him honorable so is to them moste disgracefull to be bearded of suche a base varlet' (*Prose*, 172). The shifts in register in this passage are quite remarkable. Spenser's instinctive respect for heroic self-fashioning, the very stuff of his own aesthetic, appears to have extorted a complimentary aside before the mentality of the public official reasserted itself in the more orthodox condemnation of a 'varlet'. Yet the real insult is not to O'Byrne but to 'the great Potentate' whose failure to oppose him is 'moste disgracefull'—an adjective antithetical to the mythology of Gloriana. Spenser's ambivalence towards O'Byrne reveals a deeper ambivalence towards his queen and, taken as a whole, the dialogue displays as much discontent with the present state of England as that of Ireland.

Many of the poets patronized by the O'Byrnes expressly associate such patronage with military opposition to the Dublin administration. Hugh

---

[76] Mac Airt (1944), 54–5. See also Greene (1972), 144–7. The usage sometimes involves wordplay on the homophone 'sídh' [peace].

mac Shane O'Byrne is the sort of man who 'never bowed to Foreigners' customs' ['fear nach umhal do nós Gall'] and is therefore a generous patron. The O'Tooles, by contrast, are said to have made terms with the English ['go gcuirid suas do shídh Gall'] and to have forsaken the poets.[77] Some of the poems proceed further still in urging Feagh mac Hugh O'Byrne to abandon factionalism and unite all of the local clans against their common enemy. For this reason the *Leabhar Branach* has been interpreted as signalling 'the first stages of development of a national political consciousness, and of the creation of an image of the Gaelic dynast as a national rebel leader'.[78] This is to overstate the case somewhat, but poems such as 'Dia libh, a laochruidh Gaoidhiol' ['God be with you, Gaelic warriors'] certainly inculcate a highly polarized vision of the current situation.[79] Such attitudes were fostered by the O'Byrnes' geographical location. They owed their success to the strategic advantage of possessing virtually impregnable terrain on the very borders of the Pale, at the flashpoint between the two civilizations (*Prose*, 170). Feagh mac Hugh was never likely to lead a national crusade or proclaim himself high king, but the autonomy he symbolized was more potent than the man. His proximity to the Pale emphasized his contempt for it. He embodied an idea, and it was that idea that Lord Grey had vainly attempted to destroy when he sent his forces into Glenmalure. Irenius recognizes this when he asserts that it is 'the greateste indignitye to the Quene that maie be to suffer suche a Caitiffe playe suche Rex, and by his ensample not onelie to give harte and Couragement to all suche bolde Rebells but allso to yealde them succour and refuge againste her maiestie' (*Prose*, 170). Therein lay the problem: in the absence of strong military intervention from England's queen, the 'bards' might encourage any Gaelic lord to 'playe' the 'king'. The point about affording 'succour and refuge' was highly topical. Although he could not lead a national crusade, O'Byrne could assist others to do so. In 1592 he had sheltered Red Hugh O'Donnell [Aodh Rua Ó Dónaill] on his escape from Dublin Castle and arranged for his safe return to Ulster. This enabled the formation of an unprecedented alliance between the O'Neills and O'Donnells and facilitated the countrywide

---

[77] For a discussion of this poem see Paul Walsh, *Gleanings from Irish Manuscripts*, 2nd edn. (Dublin: Three Candles, 1933), 182–93.

[78] Brendan Bradshaw, 'Native Reaction to the Westward Enterprise: A Case-Study in Gaelic Ideology', in K. R. Andrews, N. P. Canny, and P. E. Hair (eds.), *The Westward Enterprise: English Activities in Ireland, the Atlantic, and America 1480–1650* (Liverpool: Liverpool University Press, 1978), 65–80 (p. 74).

[79] Mac Airt (1944), 142–4.

campaigns of the Nine Years' War. During that period even the most apparently unrealistic expectations of the *Leabhar Branach* were almost fulfilled, as was Tadhg Dall Ó hUiginn's prediction that, under the right leader, 'Ireland will join in one united war' ['raghaidh Éire ar aon-chogadh'].[80] Day by day, as Spenser watched, bardic rhetoric was being translated into political reality.

For the purposes of New English polemic it was the elevated status of the Gaelic poets that necessitated their denigration. The object of the exercise was to transform the courtly 'ollamh' into the wild 'bard'. The third woodcut in John Derricke's *Image of Irelande* (1581) shows a Gaelic lord and his followers dining in the open air on cattle stolen from 'civil' settlers in a raid depicted in the previous woodcut (Fig. 1). A friar blesses the stolen banquet while a bard and harpist celebrate it. The whole of Gaelic society is here: its political, social, religious, and cultural orders joined in a conspiracy against 'civility' in the occulted seclusion of a wild landscape. Comparison with the well-known image of George Gascoigne presenting his works to Elizabeth in an elaborately courtly interior aptly illustrates the competing iconographies of 'bonfont' and 'malfont' (Fig. 2).[81] Yet, as Katherine Simms has recently demonstrated, a substantial number of bardic poems from this period focus upon the elaborate castles and banqueting halls of the Gaelic and Old English chieftains.[82] The poets did not, in fact, perform their own verse as the woodcut suggests, but employed a professional reciter ['reacaire'] and a harpist.[83] But the image of a courtly 'ollamh' sitting by his patron's side in an elaborate banqueting hall while his subordinates perform his work is not the 'image of irelande' that Derricke wished to project. Rather, it is essential that the bard be 'seen' to instigate barbarity in a wild environment:

> This Barde he doeth report,
>   the noble conquestes done,
> And eke in Rimes shewes forth at large,
>   their glorie thereby wonne.

---

[80] Ó hUiginn (1922–6), i. 110.

[81] Gascoigne fell foul of the censor nonetheless. See Cyndia Susan Clegg, *Press Censorship in Elizabethan England* (Cambridge: Cambridge University Press, 1997), 103–22.

[82] Katherine Simms, 'Native Sources for Gaelic Settlement: The House Poems', in Patrick J. Duffy, David Edwards, and Elizabeth Fitzpatrick (eds.), *Gaelic Ireland: Land, Lordship and Settlement c.1250–c.1650* (Dublin: Four Courts Press, 2001), 246–67 (pp. 254–6).

[83] See the anonymous poem beginning 'Go, my reciter [reacaire], recite my words', Bergin (1970), 200–1, 306–7. Only in the declined circumstances following the Flight of the Earls did this system break down. See Caball, *Poets and Politics*, 140–1.

1. John Derricke,
*The Image of
Ireland* (1581). A
Gaelic victory
banquet.

2. George Gascoigne presenting his works to Elizabeth I. BL, MS Royal 18. A. xlviii.

Thus he at randome ronneth
he pricks the Rebells on:
And shewes by suche externall deeds,
their honour lyes upon.[84]

As here portrayed, the aesthetic values of Gaelic society are merely the expression of a 'barbarous', not to say criminal, mentality: the bard is an instigator of theft and a receiver of stolen goods, a promoter and beneficiary of violence.

Spenser's procedure, by contrast, is far less self-assured than Derricke's. From the outset, Irenius presents the Gaelic 'bard' as the antithesis of the civil English 'poet', but an undertone of uncertainty struggles through the vocabulary of condemnation. The bards may be evil men but they are allowed to employ 'goodlye wordes' (*Prose*, 125). The manoeuvring here is both complex and subtle. Given Spenser's hostility to the Irish language it would be quite inconsistent for the New English Irenius to admit to reading or speaking Gaelic. He therefore has recourse to the tactic of translation as a means of simultaneously appropriating and distancing bardic literature. He explains his familiarity with Gaelic poetry with considerable circumspection when he asserts that, 'I have Cawsed diverse of them to be translated unto me that I mighte understande them' (*Prose*, 127). But Baron Delvin had asserted that the Irish could not be understood in translation, and Spenser proceeds to illustrate the point.[85] Distinctive Gaelic virtues are 'translated' into familiar English vices through the common ethnographic technique of negative analogy.[86] As François Hartog contends in *The Mirror of Herodotus*, 'a rhetoric of otherness is basically an operation of translation' and the 'translator' can always rely upon 'the handy figure of inversion, whereby otherness is transcribed as anti-sameness'.[87] Just as

---

[84] Derricke (1985), 55–6. For a comparison with Spenser see Maryclaire Moroney, 'Apocalypse, Ethnography, and Empire in John Derricke's *Image of Ireland* (1581) and Spenser's *View of the Present State of Ireland* (1596)', ELR 29 (1999), 355–74.

[85] For the 'ethnocentric violence of translation' see Lawrence Venuti, *The Translator's Invisibility: A History of Translation* (London: Routledge, 1995), 310.

[86] For the political uses of translation see Eric Cheyfitz, *The Poetics of Imperialism: Translation and Colonization from 'The Tempest' to 'Tarzan'* (New York: Oxford University Press, 1991), 59–103; Michael Cronin, *Translating Ireland: Translation, Languages, Cultures* (Cork: Cork University Press, 1996), 47–90; Lawrence Venuti, *The Scandals of Translation. Towards an Ethics of Difference* (London: Routledge, 1998), 67–87.

[87] François Hartog, *The Mirror of Herodotus: The Representation of the Other in the Writing of History*, trans. Janet Lloyd (Berkeley: University of California Press, 1988), 213, 237. Interestingly, the sole use of the term 'translated' in *The Faerie Queene* recounts how warrior women have 'translated' their 'dainty parts' to uses other than 'nature' intended (5. 7. 29). Female regiment, by implication, may be a 'mistranslation' of 'proper' political roles

Herodotus 'translated' the Scythians, Irenius 'translates' their supposed descendants, citing the example of 'a moste notorious Thiefe and wicked outlawe' of whom an unidentified bard is alleged to have said,

> that he was none of those Idle milkesopps that was broughte up by the fire side but that moste of his daies he spente in armes and valiante enterprises . . . that he laye not slugginge all nighte in a Cabbyn under his mantle But used Comonlye to kepe others wakinge to defende theire lives . . . that his musicke was not the harpe nor layes of love but the Cryes of people and Clashinge of Armour, and that finallye he died not bewaylled of manye but made manye waile when he died that dearely boughte his deathe.

'Doe youe not thinke', Irenius concludes, 'that manye of these praises mighte be applied to men of beste deserte?' (*Prose*, 126). The question might well be in the reader's mind since the attempt to illustrate difference has actually betrayed similarity. Despite the impression created by Irenius's vocabulary of moral denunciation, the issue is clearly less moral than political and the major charge levelled against the bards is that their work '[tends] for the moste parte to the hurte of the Englishe or mayntenaunce of theire owne lewd libertie' (*Prose*, 125). Several bardic poems display an acute awareness of this point.[88] The invariably pejorative use of the term 'libertie', as a synonym for lawlessness, perfectly encapsulates Spenser's rhetorical strategy. As in *The Faerie Queene* the political appropriates the moral. By contrast, or rather by comparison, the bards may be seen to appropriate to the Gaelic cause all of the moral propriety, and all of the language of heroic endeavour, that Spenser appropriates to the English. When Tadhg Dall Ó hUiginn urged Brian na Múrtha Ó Ruairc to adopt a scorched earth policy and drown the Pale in blood, he justified the advice in terms that recall Spenser's defence of Grey's strategy in Munster.[89] Captured in the 'mirror' of Celtic verse the demonic alter-ego of the bard reflects a peculiarly disturbing parody of the self. As Bakhtin has argued, 'in parodic discourse two styles, two "languages" . . . come together and to a certain extent are crossed with each other: the language being parodied . . . and the language that parodies'. This is particularly true of parodic translation where the exercise enables the parodist, in a very literal sense, 'to look at language from the outside . . . from the point

---

[88] See Caball, *Poets and Politics*, 33–7, 56–8.

[89] For the assertion that it is the poets' duty to advise Gaelic chieftains to 'declare war on the foreigner' see Ó hUiginn (1922–6), i. 108–19; ii. 72–9.

of view of a potentially different language and style'.[90] Parody necessitates
a fusion of distinct voices, yet at the point of 'dialogical contact' their very
distinctiveness threatens to break down, an effect noted by Northrop Frye
when he speaks of 'the constant tendency to self-parody in satiric
rhetoric'.[91] When Eudoxus first hears Irenius's description of bardic
poetry he declares himself at a loss to understand 'what kinde of speaches
they can finde or what face they Cane put on to praise suche lewde per-
sones . . . or howe Cane they thinke that anie good minde will applaude
or approve the same' (*Prose*, 125). Yet Spenser faced much the same problem in his depiction of Lord Grey, and generations of readers have responded with something like Eudoxus's scepticism.[92] As the episode
of Detraction and Envie clearly indicates, Spenser was well aware that
his national hero was not, in fact, a national hero (5. 12. 28–43). Artegall
encounters his critics not in Irena's 'salvage island' but upon his return
'there . . . whence forth he set' (28). To many contemporary readers it
must have seemed as if Spenser, no less than the 'bards', had attempted to
'fashion' heroism from savagery, and the strain of this endeavour largely
accounts both for the uneasy quality of book five and for the disconcerting manner in which Irenius's parody of Gaelic poetry threatens to resolve
into Spenserian self-parody.

Whereas many extant bardic poems conform to the general pattern of
Irenius's description, none proffers an irresponsible encouragement to indiscriminate violence. Rather, working within a standard matrix of
received literary conventions, the Gaelic poets evoke and inculcate
traditions of martial endeavour, and social beneficence, stretching back to
the heroes of ancient Celtic saga. Their theme is chivalry and their patrons are accordingly praised for intellectual as well as physical prowess, for
beauty as well as strength, for establishing peace as well as prosecuting
war.[93] Cormac O'Hara [Cormac Ó hEadhra] is credited by Tadhg Dall Ó
hUiginn with transforming the troubled land of Leyney ('críoch
Luighne') into 'a restful fairy plain . . . without enmity, wrath, plunder-
lust, or conflict' ['n-a haonchlár shuaimhneach shídhe . . . gan fholuidh,
gan fhích | gan toil d'fhoghoil ná dh'eissíoth'].[94] Another eulogy in the

---

[90] M. M. Bakhtin, *The Dialogic Imagination: Four Essays*, ed. Michael Holquist, trans. Caryl
Emerson and Michael Holquist (Austin: University of Texas Press, 1981), 60, 75.

[91] Northrop Frye, *Anatomy of Criticism: Four Essays* (Princeton: Princeton University Press,
1973—first pub. 1957), 234.

[92] For Spenser's account of the massacre at Smerwick see *Prose*, 524–30.

[93] For the elements of Gaelic panegyric see Quiggin, *Prolegomena*, 25–8.

[94] McKenna (1980), 46, 47.

O'Hara *duanaire* argues that Cormac engaged in combat solely in the interests of justice and civility. He is 'no lover of evil' ['nar char cionta']:

> Triath Luighne na dtoirbheart dtrom,
> mór fhuair Ó hEadhra dh'fhorlonn
> fa chlár mín na magh sreaphghlas
> gur ghabh tír is tighearnas . . .

[Ó hEadhra, Lord of Luighne, bestower of weighty gifts—great was the hardship he bore for the smooth land with its verdant stream-fed plains until in the end he won his land and his chieftainship.][95]

Particular praise was always reserved for a chieftain's largess in patronizing poetry—hence the phrase 'bestower of weighty gifts'. In return, like Spenser, Gaelic poets promised fame.[96] Each poem is therefore addressed to a specific individual or family since the bards were expected to celebrate their patrons' illustrious genealogy just as assiduously as English poets were expected to celebrate that of Elizabeth Tudor. By omitting the dedicatee's proper name and replacing it with the terms 'thiefe' and 'outlawe', Spenser 'translates' an exercise in heroic particularity into a general *exemplum* of cultural inferiority. In his version of the poem an anonymous demagogue incites a nameless outlaw. This parodic effect was relatively easy to accomplish, given the immensely sophisticated nature of bardic verse, since the boundaries between the highly stylized and the parodic are inherently unstable. The reader is given no more access to the bard's real sentiments than to his actual language. Hence the deletion of all of the dense mythological and historical detail that form the staple of bardic poetry but would, quite literally, 'mean nothing' to readers unfamiliar with its cultural frame of reference. The elements that constitute the heart of Gaelic verse are accordingly excised from its 'translation'. Furthermore, because it is virtually impossible to capture the complexity of bardic vocabulary (which, like Spenser's, was self-consciously archaic), or the intricacy of bardic metres, in any language other than Gaelic, the act of translation strips away the artistry of the poems so thoroughly that one of the most highly-wrought and consciously rhetorical forms of European poetry is made to appear like the artless expression of an unsophisticated and 'salvage' culture. Ironically, contemporary English poetry was often deemed 'barbarous' by classical purists on account of its reliance on rhyme rather than quantitative metres, and Spenser's own youthful

---

[95] McKenna (1980) 122, 123.   [96] See ibid. 58–75.

experiments in classical metrics display his insecurity in this area.[97] The strict syllabic metres of the bardic *dán díreach* afford a far closer approximation to classical precedent than his own verse, but none of this survives the process of 'translation'. Through various effects of rhythm and alliteration the paraphrase preserves something of the vigour and energy of the original but only at the level of burlesque. It is as though we are allowed to hear the voice of the bard through that of a highly gifted, satiric impressionist who replicates and caricatures simultaneously. George Puttenham allowed for a type of 'naturall poesie' amongst 'wilde and savage people' and Irenius accordingly finds that the poems translated for him 'savored of swete witt and good invencion but skilled not of the goodlie ornamentes of Poetrye, yet weare they sprinkled with some prettie flowers of theire owne naturall devise which gave good grace and Comlinesse unto them' (*Prose*, 127).[98] Bardic poetry is hereby 'translated' out of 'art' into 'nature', and nature requires 'cultivation'.[99] The bards can achieve their aesthetic potential only when they cease to be 'bards' and become English-speaking, and English-thinking, 'poets'. In Ben Jonson's *Irish Masque at Court*, for example, a reformed Gaelic 'bard', introduced by 'a civill gentleman of the nation', sings—in English, of course—a paean of praise to James I, the monarch destined to redeem Ireland from 'barbarisme'.[100]

Jonson's vision was very much the product of its times. Coinciding closely with the end of the Nine Years' War, the accession of the Stuarts occasioned a major transformation in the Gaelic outlook. As the poets were quick to point out, the Scottish king possessed an impeccable Gaelic pedigree and a rapprochement with the crown was therefore seen to be in

---

[97] See Smith (1904), ii. 10. See also S. Weiner, 'Spenser's Study of English Syllables and its Completion by Thomas Campion', *SSt* 3 (1982), 3–56; Richard Helgerson, *Forms of Nationhood: The Elizabethan Writing of England* (Chicago: University of Chicago Press, 1992), 25–40.

[98] Smith (1904), ii. 10.

[99] Cheyfitz observes that native eloquence is always conceptualized as natural', while European eloquence is nature 'aided and amended by art', an interesting counter-example being Montaigne's appreciative reception of Native American poetry. *The Poetics of Imperialism*, 121, 145–57.

[100] Jonson (1925–52), vii. 403–5. See Andrew Murphy, *'But the Irish Sea Betwixt Us': Ireland, Colonialism, and Renaissance Literature* (Lexington, Ky.: The University Press of Kentucky, 1999), 124–50; Kathleen Rabl, 'Taming the "Wild Irish" in English Renaissance Drama', in Wolfgang Zach and Heinz Kosok (eds.), *Literary Interrelations: Ireland, England and the World* (Tübingen: Narr, 1987), 47–60; Elizabeth Fowler, 'The Rhetoric of Fit in Political Forms: Social Persons and the Criterion of Fit in Colonial Law, *Macbeth*, and *The Irish Masque at Court*', in Amy Boesky and Mary Thomas Crane (eds.), *Form and Reform in Renaissance England: Essays in Honor of Barbara Kiefer Lewalski* (Newark, Del.: University of Delaware Press, 2000), 70–103.

order.[101] James VI and I could claim ancestral title to the Irish crown, he and his heirs could be represented as successors to the ancient high kings.[102] During the great *Contention of the Bards* [*Iomarbhágh na bh-Fileadh*], poets from the north and south competed for the honour of claiming him as their kinsman, but both sides agreed that 'to James today belong England, Scotland, and Ireland' ['le Séamus aniú ma le | Sacsa, Alba agus Éire'].[103] Mary Queen of Scots was highly respected in Ireland and it was hoped, wrongly as it proved, that her Protestant son would show tolerance towards his mother's fellow Catholics. He was represented not as a wilful heretic but as a good Christian, misguided in his minority by heretical Protestant ministers.[104] Spenser, by contrast, had far less reason to welcome the prospect of a Stuart accession. As is well known, his gratuitously insulting depiction of Mary Queen of Scots in the second instalment of *The Faerie Queene* gave great offence in Scotland where the work was immediately banned on the king's personal order.[105] By 1596 those who wished to see a Stuart succession had long since revised their attitude to Mary.[106] *The Faerie Queene* was risking rejection by the next fairy king, but Gaelic poets made no such miscalculation.[107] The Stuarts were amongst their preferred candidates for the English throne and James's accession was accordingly greeted by Fearghal Óg Mac an Bhaird with a remarkably clear statement of support:

The three crowns in James's charter [Trí coróna i gcairt Shéamais]—have you not seen the three of them with pleasure? . . .
The Saxon's land [críoch Sagsan] has long been—'tis well known—prophesied for thee; so too is Éire due to thee; thou art her spouse by all signs.
No high-king's blood [fuil airdríogh], however noble—except for that of the Virgin's son—surpasses yours.[108]

---

[101] See Brendán Ó Buachalla, *Aisling Ghéar: Na Stíobhartaigh agus an t-Aos Léinn 1603–1788* (Dublin: An Clóchomhar, 1996), 3–66.

[102] See Céitinn (1902–13), i. 208–9.

[103] See McKenna (1918–19), i. 138. See Joseph Th. Leerssen, *The Contention of the Bards (Iomarbhágh na bhFileadh) and its Place in Irish Political and Literary History* (London: Irish Texts Society, 1994).

[104] See Mac Aingil (1952), 166–7.

[105] See F. I. Carpenter, *A Reference Guide to Edmund Spenser* (Chicago: University of Chicago Press, 1923), 41–2.

[106] See Richard A. McCabe, 'The Masks of Duessa: Spenser, Mary Queen of Scots, and James VI', *ELR* 17 (1987), 224–42; Jonathan Goldberg, *James I and the Politics of Literature: Jonson, Shakespeare, Donne, and their Contemporaries* (Stanford, Calif.: Stanford University Press, 1989), 1–17.

[107] See Caball, *Poets and Politics*, 85–93.

[108] McKenna (1939–40), i. 177–80. I have made minor alterations to McKenna's translation (ii. 104–6).

In terms of traditional bardic encomium no greater compliment could be paid to James than the assertion than that he was Ireland's legitimate 'spouse'. This was one of the principal topoi of Gaelic panegyric.[109] The treatment of Mary Queen of Scots is equally significant. Mac an Bhaird is prepared to rewrite history in a manner quite distinct from Spenser: 'this noble high king's mother ruled Alba from coast to coast [Badh lé Alba ó mhuir go muir | máthair an airdríogh uasail], she put the crown upon her head, an honour that will never end'. All taint of treachery, and even tragedy, is excised. As Mary's son and Elizabeth's successor, James is a 'high king' with legitimate claims over Gael and Gall ['rígh slóigh Gall is Gaoidheal'].[110] Eochaidh Ó hEódhasa, ollamh to Hugh Maguire, described the transformation wrought by the Stuart accession as a sort of Ovidian metamorphosis and, like Spenser, he evoked the goddess Nature to guarantee the ultimate benefits of change: 'Let it be understood that there is no refuting Nature, what she says is to be believed . . . From evil or from envious eye or from reversal of Fortune may no second change come for us soon again: we have experienced every transformation [gach athrughadh uaramar]'.[111] His efforts were obviously appreciated since he received lands in the Plantation of Ulster.[112]

Yet, despite all of this Jacobean celebration, a deep sense of loss persisted. The Stuart king lived outside Ireland and made no attempt to meet his new subjects. The poet who celebrated his 'three crowns'—and ended his own life in exile—also composed the great elegy or 'marbhna' for Red Hugh O'Donnell who died in 1602 while seeking help from Philip III. 'Ireland', he asserted 'has perished in Spain . . . The champion of Ireland was not spared to obtain the sovereignty of Ireland' ['Teasda Éire san Easbáinn . . . Níor hanadh tuir Tholcha Fáil | re flaitheas Éirionn d'fhagháil'].[113] Resignation to what had occurred struggled for many years with the sense of what might have been. After the Flight of the Earls (1607) and the subsequent death of Ruairí Ó Dónaill, Eoghan Ruadh Mac an Bhaird asserted that now, 'despite the men of Ulster, without war, without conflict, the Saxon king [rí Sagsan] can say that the Plain of Dathí is in his title . . . A new plant [planda nuaidhe] is planted today in place of the old.'[114] In the context of Gaelic dispossession, James reverts to being an 'English' king. If something new was being born, something

[109] Carney, *Irish Bardic Poet*, II, 19–20.
[110] McKenna (1939–40), i. 177, 178.
[111] Breatnach (1977), 177, 178.
[112] Caball, *Poets and Politics*, 112–13.
[113] Breatnach (1973), 31–50 (pp. 34, 42).
[114] Mac an Bhaird (1930), 198, 200, 368, 369.

very ancient was perceived to be dying. It is indicative of the new era that many of its poems of complaint are addressed to no one individual or family but to the Gaelic world in general. They are elegies for a nation and mark the slow emergence of a 'communal' voice in Gaelic poetry.[115] The Flight of the Earls sounded the death-knell for the traditional bardic schools. After the fall of the House of Desmond in 1583 many southern poets sought patronage in the north.[116] After 1607, however, few options remained.[117] One observer described the poets engaged in the *Contention of the Bards* as hounds wrangling over an empty dish.[118] From this point on, 'bardic' poetry grows even more similar to Spenser's in its obsession with lack of patronage. 'Who will buy a poem?' ['cia do cheinneóchadh dán?'], asked Mathghamhain Ó hIfearnáin in the 1620s, recognizing as he did so that the question had already become rhetorical.[119] But 'yet the end was not', as Spenser might have said. Freed from the metrical conventions, and the consciously archaic diction, of the bardic schools, Gaelic poetry entered one of its most stylistically innovative periods.[120] The remnants of the bardic order deplored the shift into what they regarded as facile metres and demotic idioms, but the fall was surprisingly fortunate.[121] Flexible new forms, such as the 'aisling' [dream vision], emerged, and the engagement with political issues intensified.[122] In the writings of Pádraigín Haicéad, Piaras Feiritéar, Dáibhí Ó Bruadair, and Aogán Ó Rathaille, the 'mother tongue' found vigorous new exponents.[123] Like the Gaelic language itself, Irish poetry was never more articulate than in its 'decline'.[124]

---

[115] See Ó Buachalla, 'Poetry and Politics', 173.   [116] See Greene (1972), 170–9.

[117] A few poets took refuge in Scotland. See Caball, *Poets and Politics*, 138.

[118] Ó Cuív, 'The Irish Language', 539.   [119] Bergin (1970), 145, 279.

[120] See Brendán Ó Buachalla, 'James our True King: the Ideology of Irish Royalism in the Seventeenth Century', in D. G. Boyce, Robert Eccleshall, and Vincent Geoghegan (eds.), *Political Thought in Ireland since the Seventeenth Century* (London: Routledge, 1993), 7–35 (p. 8). For the divergence between classical and colloquial Gaelic see Allan Macinnes, 'Gaelic Culture in the Seventeenth Century: Polarization and Assimilation', in Steven G. Ellis and Sarah Barber (eds.), *Conquest and Union: Fashioning a British State, 1485–1725* (London: Longman, 1995), 162–94 (pp. 163–9).

[121] See Leerssen, *Mere Irish & Fíor-Ghael*, 229–50.

[122] See Mícheál Mac Craith, 'Gaelic Ireland and the Renaissance', in Glanmor Williams and Robert Owen Jones (eds.), *The Celts and the Renaissance: Tradition and Innovation* (Cardiff: University of Wales Press, 1990), 57–89.

[123] See Seán Ó Tuama, 'Gaelic Culture in Crisis: The Literary Response 1600–1850', in Thomas Bartlett, Chris Curtin, Riana O'Dwyer, and Gearóid Ó Tuathaigh (eds.), *Irish Studies: A General Introduction* (Dublin: Gill and Macmillan, 1988), 28–43.

[124] See Victor Edward Durkacz, *The Decline of the Celtic Languages: A Study of Linguistic and Cultural Conflict in Scotland, Wales, and Ireland from the Reformation to the Twentieth Century* (Edinburgh: John Donald, 1983), 1–23.

From this later period comes the celebrated poem 'Cill Chais' which stands as something of an epitaph both to the bards' integrationist role in Irish society in general and to their close associations with the Butlers in particular. Spenser's Black Thomas professed Protestantism (at least in the reign of Elizabeth), but his chosen heir was his Roman Catholic nephew Walter Butler of Kilcash, known in New English circles as 'Walter of the Beads and Rosaries'.[125] Walter was eventually recognized as the eleventh Earl of Ormond but during his absence in England (contesting protracted litigation conducted by Black Thomas's son-in-law, Sir Richard Preston) Kilcash served as home to his recusant brother and sister-in-law, Sir Richard and Lady Francis, whose chapel was famed for the frequent celebration of the mass by seminary priests.[126] During the same period the Roman Catholic Butlers of Dunboyne afforded patronage to Pádraigín Haicéad, a stalwart supporter during the 1640s of the papal nuncio, Rinuccini.[127] The nuncio's principal opponent, James Butler, twelfth Earl and first Duke of Ormond, admitted to being the only Protestant member of his family of any social significance.[128] He was, in fact, the grandson of Walter of the Beads and Rosaries and born of Roman Catholic parents.[129] Following the collapse of the Confederation of Kilkenny—presided over by Richard Butler, third Viscount Mountgarret—and the subsequent Cromwellian confiscations, Kilcash fell into decay and the 'wild' woodlands that surrounded it were finally felled. An anonymous poet of the late seventeenth century contrasted the ethos of the place in its heyday with its current dereliction:

> Cad a dhéanfaimid feasta gan adhmad?
>   Tá deireadh na gcoillte ar lár;
> Níl trácht ar Chill Chais ná ar a teaghlach
>   is ní bainfear a cling go bráth.
> An áit úd a gcónaíodh an deighbhean
>   fuair gradam is meidhir thar mhnáibh,
> bhíodh iarlaí ag tarraingt tar toinn ann
>   is an t-aifreann binn á rá.

---

[125] See Cyril Falls, 'Black Tom of Ormonde', *The Irish Sword*, 5 (1961–2). 10–22 (pp. 20–1).

[126] See Paul of St Ubald (1654), sigs. A2r–v.

[127] For Haicéad and Dunboyne see Haicéad (1993), poems 15, 16, 17 and 29.

[128] See Raymond Gillespie, 'The Religion of the first Duke of Ormond', in Toby Barnard and Jane Fenlon (eds.), *The Dukes of Ormonde, 1610–1745* (Cambridge: Boydell Press, 2000), 101–13 (pp. 101–2).

[129] See David Edwards, 'The Poisoned Chalice: The Ormond Inheritance, Sectarian Division and the Emergence of James Butler, 1614–1642', in Fenlon (ed.), *The Dukes of Ormonde*, 55–82.

[Now what will we do for timber,
With the last of the woods laid low?
There's no talk of Cill Chais or its household
and its bell will be struck no more.
That dwelling where lived the good lady,
most honoured and joyous of women,
Earls made their way over wave there
and the sweet Mass used to be said.][130]

What the poet nostalgically envisages here is the total integration of Gaeil and Sean-Ghaill: the Gaelic-speaking, Catholic Butlers hearing mass in the heart of the ancestral Irish woodlands. He prays that this situation may one day be restored but for the time being can only lament its loss.

It is often claimed that history is written by winners but the accounts they produce necessarily resemble palimpsests, overwritten upon the erased texts of the losers. *The Faerie Queene* provides us with a perfect example of this—and in direct relation to poetry. On their way into the Court of Mercilla Prince Arthur and Artegall see a poet with his tongue nailed to a post. A sign above his head gives his name as 'Malfont', but looking more closely at the 'cyphers strange, that few could rightly read' the knights notice that '*bon* that once had written bin | Was raced out, and *Mal* was now put in. | So now *Malfont* was plainely to be red' (5. 9. 26). The overwritten text is what first strikes the eye, but lurking beneath lies a challenging subtext. What I have attempted to do in the present chapter is to read Irenius's account of Gaelic poetry as a political palimpsest, disclosing the erased 'ollamh' beneath the overwritten 'bard', the 'bon' beneath the 'mal'. This is not to suggest the superiority of Gaelic ollamhs over English poets but rather to reveal their underlying similarity, because it is precisely in a situation of similarity that it becomes so important to construct a 'difference'. Yet even in Spenser's own allegory 'Malfont' and 'Bonfont' are the same person. The distinction, in so far as it exists, is purely a matter of political inscription, of providing suitable captions for the signposts that are so carefully positioned to lead us from the 'wilderness' into Mercilla's court.

[130] See Ó Tuama (1981), 328–9.

Part II: 'Salvagesse sans finesse'

3   'Salvage Nacion'

LONG before the composition of *The Faerie Queene*, Ireland was constructed as an 'allegorical' space, a precinct of monstrosity and 'otherness' precariously perched on the edge of the known world. As Marina Warner reminds us, however, 'monsters' are made not born, and Spenser was fully aware of the mind's capacity to create illusory terrors: 'why make ye such Monster of your mind?' (3. 2. 40), Glauce asks the adolescent Britomart whose subsequent experience in the House of Busirane is related to the 'phastasies' of 'wavering wemens wit' (3. 12. 26).[1] The 'monsters' of colonial poetics are equally indebted to hidden demons. If *The Faerie Queene* was 'bred' by 'salvage soyl' its landscape reflects its genesis: 'the danger hid, the place unknowne and wilde, | Breedes dreadfull doubts' (1. 1. 12). Self-doubts for the most part. To relax one's guard is to release the inner 'other' and become 'wild Irish'. Throughout the poem the landscape functions not just as a scenic backdrop but as a formidable agent which may, at any moment, assimilate person to place through some bizarre stroke of Ovidian metamorphosis—as in the case of Fraudubio and Fraelissa (1. 2. 30–44)—thereby realizing the colonists' deepest fears.[2]

Spenser was writing in an established tradition.[3] The image of Ireland inherited by Elizabethan colonists was largely the creation of Giraldus

---

[1] Marina Warner, *Managing Monsters: Six Myths of Our Time* (London: Vintage, 1994), 31. See also pp. 65–79.

[2] See Shirley Clay Scott, 'From Polydorus to Fradubio: The History of a *Topos*', *SSt* 7 (1986—but pub. 1987), 27–57.

[3] See Walter J. Ong, 'Spenser's *View* and the Tradition of the "Wild" Irish', *MLQ* 3 (1942), 561–71.

Cambrensis.[4] Regarding the 'remote' and the 'savage' as interchangeable
categories, earlier accounts of the country had emphasized its strangeness
and 'barbarity', but his was the first to be conceived and written in the interests of 'conquest', the first to exploit the atavistic power of the traditional topoi for immediate political effect.[5] Yet even Giraldus was
fascinated by the imaginative possibilities of Ireland's marginality. 'What
new things,' he wondered, 'what secret things not in accordance with her
usual course has nature hidden away in those farthest western lands?'[6]
Writing some four centuries later from within the 'civil' confines of the
Pale, Richard Stanyhurst felt no compunction in populating the outlands
of the 'Irishrie' with Giraldus's marvels and monsters, much as contemporary cartographers filled the blank spaces of otherwise up-to-date maps
with Medieval prodigies.[7] His account of the great urban centres of the
Pale bears comparison with Stow's *Survey of London*, but that of the bor-
derlands reverts to the ethos of *Mandeville's Travels*.[8] 'Stanihurst has not
understood', replied Seathrún Céitinn, 'that Ireland [developed] as a
kingdom apart by herself, like a little world [ríoghacht ar leith léi féin,
amhail domhan mbeag]', that its marginality guaranteed its cultural integrity.[9] But this was to miss his opponent's point. As I have argued in the
previous chapter, the Elizabethan revival of interest in Giraldus was far
from accidental. The *Historia et Topographia Hiberniae* was now seen to
serve as an explanatory preface to the *Expugnatio Hibernica*. The country's 'savagery' had justified its original conquest and would do so again.
From the moment that the rhetoric of 'conquest' began to supplant that
of 'reform', monsters were back in vogue.[10] It is no coincidence that
Artegall's career is modelled upon that of Hercules, the archetypal

---

[4] Extensive trading contacts with Britain and the continent had existed previously. See
Norman Davies, *The Isles: A History* (London: Macmillan, 1999), 229–302.

[5] See W. R. Jones, '*Giraldus Redivivus*—English Historians, Irish Apologists, and the
Works of Gerald of Wales', *Éire-Ireland*, 9 (1974), 3–20. See also Hiram Morgan, 'Giraldus
Cambrensis and the Tudor Conquest of Ireland', in Hiram Morgan (ed.), *Political Ideology in
Ireland, 1541–1641* (Dublin: Four Courts Press, 1999), 22–44.

[6] Giraldus Cambrensis (1982), 31. For the uses of 'wonder' see Steven Mullaney, 'Strange
Things, Gross Terms, Curious Customs: The Rehearsal of Cultures in the Late Renaissance', in
Stephen Greenblatt (ed.), *Representing the English Renaissance* (Berkeley: University of California
Press, 1988), 65–92 (p. 68).

[7] See Holinshed (1808), vi. 36–42.

[8] For *Mandeville's Travels* see Stephen Greenblatt, *Marvelous Possessions: The Wonder of the
New World* (Oxford: Clarendon Press, 1991), 26–51. See also John Block Friedman, *The Monstrous Races in Medieval Art and Thought* (Syracuse, NY: Syracuse University Press, 2000), 5–36.

[9] Céitinn (1902–13). i. 38–41.

[10] For the uses of monstrosity see Margaret T. Hodgen, *Early Anthropology in the Sixteenth
and Seventeenth Centuries* (Philadelphia: University of Pennsylvania Press, 1964), 127–8.

monster-slayer (5. 5. 24), nor that *The Faerie Queene* is set in England's
heroic age.[11] Spenser's 'archaism' is a facet of his modernity.

The translation of the *Expugnatio* that John Hooker contributed to the
1587 edition of Holinshed was intended to complement the material from
the *Historia et Topographia* that Stanyhurst had contributed to the edition of
1577. Camden incorporated much of Giraldus's material into his *Britannia*
(1586) and published the Latin texts of both the *Historia* and the *Expugnatio*
in 1602.[12] It was the immense influence of these publications that inspired
the concerted Gaelic attack upon Giraldus in the seventeenth century. It
represents a response not to a four-hundred-year-old text but to a powerful
contemporary influence. 'The calumnies of which Giraldus is the author',
complained John Lynch in his *Cambrensis Eversus*, 'are published in the language and writings of every nation, no new geography, no history of the
world . . . appearing, in which his calumnious charges against the Irish are
not chronicled as undoubted facts.'[13] Stephen White claimed that Camden
had published Cambrensis in order to justify the colonial venture by
'promoting among other nations a contempt for the native Irish of past and
present ages'.[14] Such denigration served the cause of self-aggrandisement.
Virgil's attitude towards Britain was not greatly dissimilar to Giraldus's
attitude towards Ireland. Once upon a time it too was a savage, isolated place
'wholly sundered from the world'.[15] By adopting a suitably 'Virgilian' attitude towards Ireland, therefore, contemporary 'Britons' could enforce their
new status. Dismissed by the great Latin poet as marginal to civilization,
their homeland had advanced so far as to produce in Spenser an epic poet
equally dismissive of all that was savage, isolated and peripheral.

Towards the close of his discussion of Gaelic customs Irenius informs
Eudoxus that he has seen an Irish foster mother drink the blood of her
executed stepson 'sayinge that the earthe was not worthie to drinke it and
thearewith allso steped her face, and breste and torne heare Cryinge and
shrikinge out moste terrible' (*Prose*, 112). To drink blood is to engage in a
species of cannibalism, and cannibalism has traditionally been regarded
as the ultimate index of racial inferiority.[16] Sir Henry Sidney accordingly

---

[11] See Jane Aptekar, *Icons of Justice: Iconography and Thematic Imagery in Book V of 'The
Faerie Queene'* (New York: Columbia University Press, 1969), 153–200.
[12] See Rudolf B. Gottfried, 'The Early Development of the Section on Ireland in Camden's
Britannia', *ELH* 10 (1943), 117–30; the Latin texts appeared in Camden (1602), 692–813.
[13] Lynch (1848), i. 107. [14] White (1849), p. v. [15] See Virgil, *Eclogues*, I. 66.
[16] See Francis Barker, Peter Hulme, and Margaret Ivessen (eds.), *Cannibalism and the
Colonial World* (Cambridge: Cambridge University Press, 1998), 1–38; Peter Hulme, *Colonial
Encounters: Europe and the Native Caribbean, 1492–1797* (London: Methuen, 1986), 78–87.

warned Lord Grey to beware of the 'caniballs' of Glenmalure.[17] To drink blood in a ritualistic manner is to compound the abomination by enacting a sort of savage Eucharist, a demonic antitype of the Christian sacrament. It is to be 'other' both racially and spiritually. So powerful is the impact of Irenius's image that although the execution of Murrogh O'Brien occurred in 1577, three years prior to Spenser's officially documented arrival in Ireland, commentators have long sought to adapt the author's biography to his polemic.[18] Spenser, so the argument runs, must surely have 'seen' what Irenius claims to have seen. Not a particularly convincing argument in itself, but therein lies the insidious power of the colonial 'image'. If we conclude that Spenser 'saw' the execution of Murrogh O'Brien must we also conclude that he 'saw' his foster mother drink blood? And if the account of the blood-drinking is fictitious why should we assume that Spenser was present at all? From the time of Herodotus onwards professedly 'eyewitness' testimony has been employed to lend credence to sensational descriptions of alien cultures.[19] What is involved, as Michel de Certeau argues, is no less than the 'fabrication and accreditation of the *text as a witness of the other*'.[20]

In Ireland's case the practice of appealing to 'eyewitness' testimony was established, like so much else, by Giraldus, the single most influential authority to allege that the Irish drank blood, and the creator of the first 'heroic' narrative to represent 'English' civility as the antithesis of Gaelic 'barbarity'.[21] In order to underscore the importance of the topos Giraldus invoked John 3: 11: 'we speak that we do know, and testify that we have seen'.[22] This would imply that he writes 'gospel truth', but later statements complicate matters considerably: 'I protest solemnly that I have put down nothing in this book the truth of which I have not found out either by the testimony of my own eyes, or that of reliable men found

---

[17] Grey (1847), 70. For the term 'cannibal' see Eric Cheyfitz, *The Poetics of Imperialism: Translation and Colonization from 'The Tempest' to 'Tarzan'* (New York: Oxford University Press, 1991), 41–3.

[18] The inference was first drawn in the anonymous article 'Edmund Spenser—the State Papers', *Dublin University Magazine*, 58 (1861), 131–44 (pp. 132–3). See also Paul E. McLane, 'Was Spenser in Ireland in Early November 1579?', *N&Q* 204 (1959), 99–101; Willy Maley, *Salvaging Spenser: Colonialism, Culture and Identity* (Basingstoke: Macmillan, 1997), 11–33.

[19] See Greenblatt, *Marvelous Possessions*, 123–9. See also Mercedes Maroto Camino, ' "Methinks I see an evil lurk unspied": Visualizing Conquest in Spenser's *A View of the Present State of Ireland*', *SSt* 12 (1991—but pub. 1998), 169–94.

[20] Michel de Certeau, *Heterologies: Discourse on the Other*, trans. Brian Massumi (Manchester: Manchester University Press, 1986), 68.

[21] Giraldus Cambrensis (1982), 57, 108.   [22] Giraldus Cambrensis (1978), 238.

worthy of credence.'[23] 'Eyewitness' is thus equated with hearsay and those 'worthy of credence' are those who report what the hearer is disposed to believe. So far as the colonial enterprise is concerned believing is seeing. It is therefore entirely consistent with Irenius's characterization that he should appeal to personal experience ('so have I sene . . . I sawe') in order to validate what his creator has 'read': 'the *Gaules* used to drinke theire enemyes blodd and to painte themselues therewith So allsoe they write that the owlde Irishe weare wonte And so have I sene some of the Irishe doe' (*Prose*, 112). Central to Irenius's argument is the assertion that the Irish are primarily descended from the 'Scythians', the blood-drinking barbarians represented by Herodotus as the antithesis of Greek civilization: 'the *Scythyans* used when they would binde anie solempe vowe or Combinacion to drinke a bowle of blodd togeather vowinge theareby to spende theire laste blodd in that quarrell' (*Prose*, 108).[24] As this is precisely what Giraldus reports of the Irish, it is taken to confirm the genealogical link. But Giraldus also alleges that vows taken in blood issue in blood: 'woe to brothers amongst a barbarous peopie.'[25] The implication is plain: for the Irish, as for their 'savage' ancestors, even the 'social' virtues of friendship and alliance are tinged with peculiarly murderous intent.

By the close of the sixteenth century extensive new frontiers had opened up three thousand miles to Ireland's west. It might have been expected that the country's 'image' would benefit substantially but exactly the opposite occurred. From mid-century onwards comparisons between the Gaelic Irish and American 'Indians' become increasingly frequent and Ireland is more commonly assimilated to the New World than to the Old.[26] Adventurers such as Sir Walter Ralegh and Sir Humphrey Gilbert began their careers in the Irish service before crossing the Atlantic, and Ireland became, in the words of Jane Ohlmeyer, 'a laboratory for empire'.[27] Self-evident distinctions between Gaelic and 'Indian' societies were confounded in the common category of the 'savage'. This was only to be expected in view of what Homi Bhabha terms the 'Manichaean'

[23] Giraldus Cambrensis (1982), 57.
[24] For the alleged blood-drinking see Herodotus, *History*, IV. 62.
[25] Giraldus Cambrensis (1982), 108.
[26] See David Beers Quinn, *The Elizabethans and the Irish* (Ithaca, NY: Cornell University Press, 1966), 21–7, 106–22. Nicholas Canny, *Kingdom and Colony: Ireland in the Atlantic World 1560–1800* (Baltimore: Johns Hopkins University Press, 1988), 1–29.
[27] Jane Ohlmeyer, 'Seventeenth-Century Ireland and the New British and Atlantic Histories', *American Historical Review*, 104 (1999), 446–62 (p. 460).

nature of an outlook preconditioned to identify stereotypes and obscure 'the preconstruction or working up of difference'.[28] Colonial rhetoric provides not just a means of representation but of apprehension. Exceptions merely prove the rule. Campion informs his readers that any relative improvement detectable in the condition of contemporary Irishmen is wholly attributable to the civilizing influence of conquest.[29] 'Eyewitness' experience of Gaelic civility is hereby degraded into evidence of primeval barbarism. The suspicion therefore arises that the obsessive insistence upon 'savagery' which characterizes Elizabethan colonial literature represents an attempt to achieve by sheer repetition what could not be achieved by demonstration.

What is not 'seen' is apprehended more powerfully than what is in plain view. In the impenetrable fastnesses of the woods, hidden from 'eye and observation', the Irish 'encreased and multiplied unto infinite numbers, by promiscuous generation among themselves; there they made their Assemblies and Conspiracies without discovery'.[30] This conflation of 'promiscuous' sex and treasonable conspiracy is highly revealing: 'eyewitness' testimony draws its voyeuristic power from claiming to penetrate the most private recesses of habit and habitat, from 'discovering' what no 'Englishman' is supposed to see, from prying, like Guyon, into the corrupting bower of bliss. For the New English observer Ireland was a land of 'hidden things': 'they hide under the grounde all the riches they have', says Nicholas Dawtrey, 'whether it be silver, gold, or other necessaryes of house, or household, and that with such secrecy as if it were possible, god himselfe should not knowe where.'[31] One recalls the Cave of Mammon or the 'hollow caves, that no man mote discover' to which the brigands of book six convey their booty:

> But darkenesse dred and daily night did hover
> Through all the inner parts, wherein they dwelt,
> Ne lightned was with window, nor with lover,
> But with continuall candlelight, which delt
> A doubtfull sense of things, not so well seene, as felt.

(6. 10. 42)

It is this occulted 'state' that must be brought into 'view': 'we' must witness what transpires when 'they' are 'togeather . . . amongst themselves', particularly when civil ladies like Pastorella are brought below. 'A doubt-

---

[28] Homi K. Bhabha, *The Location of Culture* (London: Routledge, 1994), 61, 79.
[29] Campion (1963), 20–1.   [30] Davies (1612), 160–1.   [31] Dawtrey (1995), 96–7.

full sense of things, not so well seene, as felt' perfectly encapsulates the prurient innuendo that characterizes most New English accounts of Ireland.

Who was to blame for the 'state' of Ireland? Could 'barbarity' be regarded in any sense as a moral condition? Giraldus had no doubts on the matter. For him, topography was a branch of what would now be termed ethnography, and ethnography was a branch of ethics. The 'wildness' of the Irish countryside was directly attributable to the indolence of the inhabitants. The country's moral health might best be gauged by the geographical expansion or contraction of the Pale:

> While man usually progresses from the woods to the fields and from the fields to settlements and communities of citizens, this people despises work on the land, has little use for the money-making of towns, contemns the rights and privileges of citizenship, and desires neither to abandon, or lose respect for, the life which it has been accustomed to lead in the woods and countryside.

Properly speaking, Giraldus concluded, 'the Irish cannot be said to have any culture'.[32] Similar attitudes inform Spenser's obsession with the Irish woodlands. At a time when Germanic writers were rehabilitating the reputation of the ancient forests as the cradle of a virile 'Teutonic' race, Irenius calls for 'the Cuttinge downe and openinge of all places thoroughe the wodes' (*Prose*, 224).[33] 'The Legend of Holinesse' begins with St George's ill-advised foray into the Wood of Error thereby recalling Spenser's first experience of the Irish campaign, Lord Grey's disastrous defeat in the woods of Glenmalure at the hands of the O'Byrnes and O'Tooles whose names, Irenius asserts, signified 'woddye' and 'hillye': 'wiche names it semethe they toke of the Countrye which they inhabited' (*Prose*, 170–1).[34] This presents us with a perfect example of the colonial cast of Spenser's 'reading', if not a paradigm for colonial reading in general. The 'allegory' of Ireland is deciphered by a 'civil' reader to disclose the symbiotic relationship between outlaws and outlands. Under 'etymological' analysis the very names of the O'Byrnes and O'Tooles are made to reveal their true nature and justify their suppression. Yet, as Céitinn was later to point out, Irenius's etymologies are wrong and so, too, is his

---

[32] Giraldus Cambrensis (1982), 101–2.

[33] See Simon Schama, *Landscape and Memory* (London: Harper Collins, 1995), 81–100; Eileen McCracken, *The Irish Woods since Tudor Times: Distribution and Exploitation* (Newton Abbot: David and Charles, 1971), 26–9, 45.

[34] For a contemporary account of Glenmalure see Holinshed (1808), vi. 435–6. For references to the locality in *A View* see *Prose*, 57, 171–2, 191.

history.[35] The ancestral homelands of the O'Byrnes and O'Tooles lay on the plains of Kildare but they had been progressively dispossessed by previous waves of settlers. Had Spenser read the relevant Gaelic chronicles he would have discovered that Wicklow was not their place of origin but their place of refuge.[36]

From the satyrs of book one to the savages of book six, the landscape of *The Faerie Queene* is populated by wild, ill-natured sub-races generally impervious to nurture: 'lawlesse people . . . That never used to live by plough nor spade, | But fed on spoile and booty' (6. 10. 39). But moving amongst them are even more problematic figures such as Sir Satyrane, the hybrid offspring of gross miscegenation, born in the 'forrest wyld' of a civil 'lady' and 'salvage sire' (1. 6. 21–3). Like the 'degenerate' Old English he hovers between the wilderness and the court, and his existence challenges the traditional polarity of 'civil' and 'savage'. But Giraldus had anticipated even this phenomenon. Over the course of centuries, he warned, 'barbarous habits' come to constitute 'another nature'—effectively an 'other' nature in that it supplants 'proper' instincts—with the result that 'newcomers may be contaminated' by 'the inborn vice of the country, a vice that is most contagious': 'he who touches pitch will be defiled by it [Ecclesiasticus 13: 1]'.[37] Here was a ready-made, and biblically attested, solution to the problem of those who had 'degenerated and growen allmoste meare Irishe' (*Prose*, 96). Ethnic 'degeneration' (playing on the Latin sense of 'gens') is moral degeneration and the practice of miscegenation implies a lack of cultural and sexual 'continence' of the sort displayed by Sir Guyon. Contemporary Gaelic writers reversed the perspective, berating the New English for their reluctance to intermarry: 'I conceive not whence it is', remarked the Old English Céitinn, 'that they do not contract alliance with the nobles of Ireland, unless it be from disesteem for their own obscurity, so that they did not deem themselves worthy to have such noble Gaels in their kinship.'[38] There is nothing 'salvage' here except the satire, but Céitinn's efforts were unavailing. One New English tract warned that the true offspring of miscegenation was sedition: 'shee that at night suckes from yore bosome, what soever the store house of yore harte containeth, laboreth in the morninge (as if she were

---

[35] See below pp. 277–9.

[36] See Rolf Loeber, 'An Architectural History of Gaelic Castes and Settlements, 1370–1600', in Patrick J. Duffy, David Edwards, and Elizabeth Fitzpatrick (eds.), *Gaelic Ireland: Land, Lordship and Settlement c.1250–c.1650* (Dublin: Four Courts Press, 2001), 271–314 (p. 279).

[37] Giraldus Cambrensis (1982), 103, 109.   [38] Céitinn (1902–13), i. 35.

with childe) untill she have delivered it either to her brother, her sonne in lawe, or some of her kinsmen.'[39] In order to ensure that 'the coine of a yoong England was like to shoot in Ireland' the indigenous culture had to be suppressed—if only because there was no other way of preventing 'civilized' Palesman from adopting it.[40] Pilib Ó Súilleabháin Béarra [Philip O'Sullivan Beare] was quick to spot the ironic implications of this attitude. It was historically evident, he argued, that inferior cultures were assimilated to superior ones and the same was true of Ireland. What Stanyhurst termed 'degeneration' was actually regenerative acculturation.[41] Similarly, argued John Lynch, by the application of Stanyhurst's three criteria for conquest (language, law, and dress), 'it will follow that the English were conquered by the Irish, not the Irish by the English'.[42]

The phenomenon of hybridity, one of the cardinal features of 'monstrosity', informed every aspect of Giraldus's work and is inherent in the polemical template he bequeathed to posterity.[43] He was himself of mixed antecedents, equally related to the Marcher lords and the Welsh nobility. As Robert Bartlett explains, 'his *morum institutio* and *conversatio* (his upbringing and active life) were among the English, his *natio* and *cognatio* (descent and family connections) in Wales'. The result, as he frequently complained, was that both peoples regarded him as a 'stranger'.[44] In the *Expugnatio* he has an 'Old Englishman' remark that 'just as we are English ['Angli'] as far as the Irish are concerned, likewise to the English we are Irish ['Hibernici']'.[45] As Bartlett shrewdly observes, 'the subsequent course of Anglo-Irish history is prefigured in that insight'.[46] Writing some four hundred years later, Edmund Campion speaks of the conflicting political interests of 'the Englishe of birthe and thenglishe of bloude'.[47] The problem with this neat dichotomy was that remarkably few of the 'englishe of bloude' could claim to be wholly English of blood, not even within the House of Ormond. Confronted by this impasse, Stanyhurst coined the term 'Anglo-Hiberni' in an attempt to assert a cultural identity distinct from both the Gaelic Irish ('antiqui Hibernici') and the native English.[48] Yet whatever the intention behind it, the composite

[39] Maley (1995), 30.
[40] Holinshed (1808), vi. 4.
[41] O'Sullivan Beare (1960), 68–9.
[42] Lynch (1848), i. 231.
[43] See the list of hybrid monsters at *Mother Hubberds Tale*, ll. 1122–4.
[44] Robert Bartlett, *Gerald of Wales, 1146–1223* (Oxford: Clarendon Press, 1982), 17–18.
[45] Giraldus Cambrensis (1978), 81.
[46] Bartlett, *Gerald of Wales*, 18.
[47] Campion (1963), 98.
[48] Colm Lennon, *Richard Stanihurst, The Dubliner 1547–1618* (Dublin: Irish Academic Press, 1981), 82, 126.

term 'Anglo-Hiberni' is more redolent of the culturally hybrid than the culturally autonomous. In the long run religion proved to be the decisive factor for the anglophone Stanyhurst. When eventually driven into exile, he sought some measure of rapprochement with his Gaelic-speaking fellow Catholics.[49]

What, then, really lay beyond the Pale? John Derricke's *Image of Irelande* (1581) is primarily designed to answer that question and duly sets the tone by praising Sir Henry Sidney for his unique prowess in 'conflictyng' Irish 'monsters'.[50] The twelve remarkable woodcuts that illustrate the text seek to create a legion of 'eyewitnesses' to the country's 'barbarity'. As the explanatory verses indicate, the plates are arranged in an organized sequence designed to convey a clear political message, and in all cases the topography of the scene is as operative as the figures within it. The Gaelic lord pictured in the first woodcut is found in a mountainous, woody terrain with no buildings or cultivated fields in sight. He appears to have emerged from a nearby forest. An attendant woodkern 'gripes' an axe 'fast with his murd'ring hand' while offering his master a long dart or spear (Fig. 3). The second plate illustrates their subsequent attack on a 'civil' settlement and the accompanying verse instructs us to read the image counter-clockwise thereby conveying the graphic impression of an outrage in progress (Fig. 4). To the left of the picture a band of heavily armed kerns bursts from the fastness of the forest led by a bagpiper, a detail perhaps recalled in the sixth book of *The Faerie Queene* when 'salvages' prepare to slaughter Serena:

> Then gan the bagpypes and the hornes to shrill,
> And shrieke aloud, that with the peoples voyce
> Confused, did the ayre with terror fill,
> And made the wood to tremble at the noyce.
>
> (6. 8. 46)[51]

To the right, in the foreground, the kerns are seen burning the settlers' cottage while the hapless owners throw up their hands in horror. In the centre, at the back, the spoil is driven into the forest and the cycle of destruction is complete.

[49] See Brendan Bradshaw, 'The Beginnings of Modern Ireland', in Brian Farrell, *The Irish Parliamentary Tradition* (Dublin: Gill and Macmillan, 1973), 68–87 (p. 83), and *The Irish Constitutional Revolution of the Sixteenth Century* (Cambridge: Cambridge University Press, 1979), 282–8. See also Lennon, *Richard Stanihurst*, 125–8.

[50] Derricke (1985), 9.

[51] For 'bagpipes' and 'shrieking Hububs' see 3. 10. 43. For the 'hubbub' see *Prose*, 103, 105.

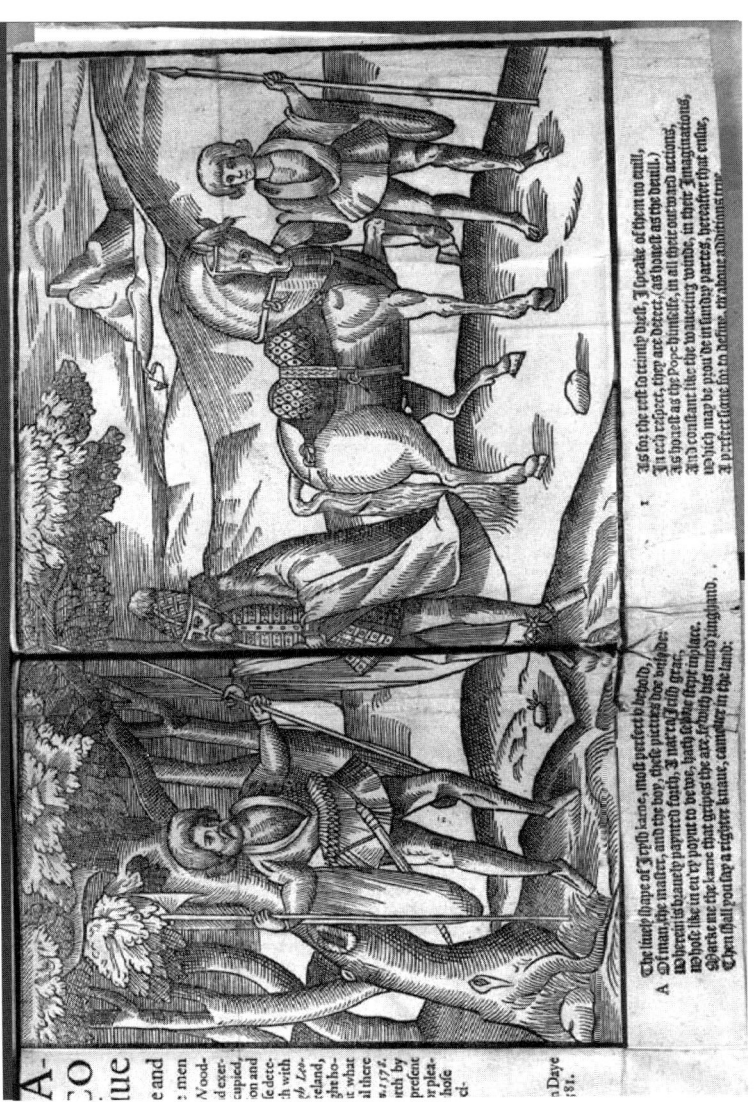

3. John Derricke,
*The Image of
Ireland* (1581).
An Irish lord
and his kerns.

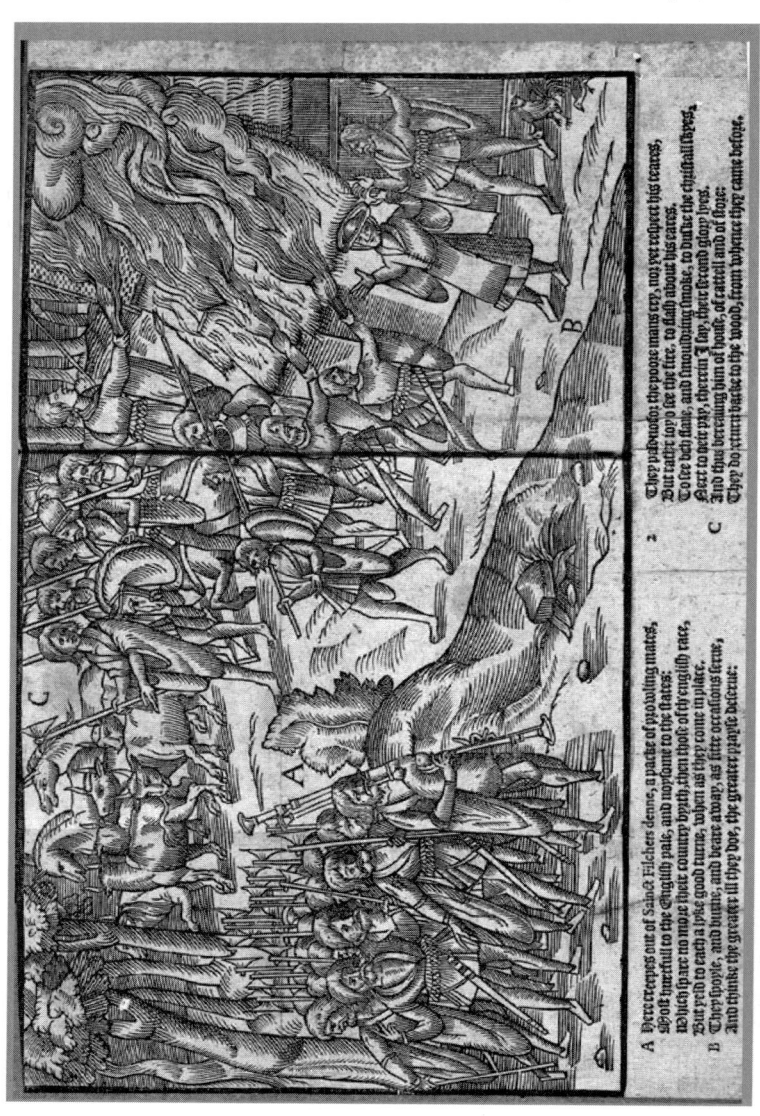

4. John Derricke, *The Image of Ireland* (1581). An attack by kerns.

Plate six, by well-contrived contrast, removes us to the massive, urban solidity of Dublin, the heart of the English Pale (Fig. 5). This is the landscape of 'civility' and serves to remind us that behind the preference for 'georgic' over 'pastoral' lifestyles lies an even deeper prejudice for town over country.[52] Giraldus had remarked that the Irish 'had little use for the money-making of towns', but in the intervening centuries urban development, always significant, had become the supreme emblem of civility—and of empire. Spenser was a Londoner and his imagination invariably focuses upon images of the city whether his concerns be panegyrical (Cleopolis), political (Troynovant), or spiritual (the New Jerusalem).[53] In charting the course of the Thames from the 'meadow' to the city—'at length they all to mery *London* came, | To mery London my most kyndly Nurse' (127–8)—*Prothalamion* plots the vector of the poet's imagination, and it ends, characteristically, with the counter-Ovidian transformation of 'birds' into 'brides', the natural into the social. The establishment of 'corporate townes' throughout Ireland is one of the main recommendations of *A View* (*Prose*, 188). Well-garrisoned towns guarantee the safety of plantations, plantations encourage trade, and trade produces 'comoditye' or 'proffitte' (*Prose*, 183). The alternative is a lifestyle of 'wilfull want' in 'a little cottage, built of stickes and reeces | In homely wize, and wald with sods around', a caricature of Gaelic practice all the more potent for its association with witchcraft, malice, and isolation (3. 7. 6). The Irish are 'barbarous' not merely because they cultivate a 'pastoral' lifestyle (and by the 1590s it was well known that many did not), but because they do not aspire to become 'urban'. For an observer such as Sir John Davies this was sufficient in itself to negate all other signs of civility: 'though the Irishry be a nation of great Antiquity . . . and though they had received the Christian Faith, above 1200 yeares since; and were Lovers of Musicke, Poetry, and all kinde of learning; and possessed a Land abounding with all thinges necessary for the Civill life of man; yet (which is strange to bee related) they did never builde any houses of Bricke or stone (some few poor Religious Houses excepted) before the raigne of King *Henrie* the second.'[54] The problem with the Irish is that, unlike Colin Clout (as portrayed, for example, in the woodcut to the 'Januarye'

---

[52] See James Clifford, 'On Ethnographic Allegory', in James Clifford (ed.), *Writing Culture: The Poetics and Politics of Ethnography* (Berkeley: University of California Press, 1988), 98–121 (p. 113).

[53] See L. Manley, 'Spenser and the City: the Minor Poems', *MLQ* 43 (1982), 203–27.

[54] Davies (1612), 169.

eclogue of *The Shepheardes Calender*) they do not gaze longingly towards a distant town. In retrospect it might well seem that Colin was always a poetic 'shepheard' in search of a city—an imperial city, if we are to judge by the classical architecture of the 'October' woodcut.[55] Derricke supplies such a city, and a Lord Deputy who sets forth 'to iustifie his Princes cause' much as Artegall might have ridden from Cleopolis. Sidney issues from Dublin Castle in state, and marches towards Christ Church Cathedral, a minister of the crown devoted to the Protestant religion. He wears civilian clothes but also, significantly, a breastplate. Over the gate from which he emerges are displayed the severed heads of three 'rebeles', an incongruously 'barbarous' detail to the modern reader but, for Derricke, an emblem for the defeat of 'rebellion':

> These trunckles heddes do playnly showe each rebelles fatall ende,
> And what a haynous crime it is, the Queene for to offend.

Spenser agreed, and 'The Legend of Justice' duly recalls such gruesomely familiar scenes in its description of the fate suffered by Pollente by the banks of the River Lee, a very specific topographical detail that locates the episode in time as well as place:

> His corps was carried downe along the Lee,
> Whose waters with his filthy bloud it stayned:
> But his blasphemous head, that all might see,
> He pitcht upon a pole on high ordayned;
> Where many years it afterwards remayned,
> To be a mirrour to all mighty men.

(5. 2. 19)

During Lord Grey's campaign of 1581, Sir John of Desmond's decapitated corpse was hung over the River Lee on the North Gate of Cork while his 'blasphemous head' was impaled on a spike outside Dublin Castle. Poetic licence struggles to accommodate political fact.[56] Contemporary Gaelic poets looked in such 'mirrours' and saw a very different reflection from the one Spenser intended. Following the executions of Brian and Domhnall Ó hEadhra in 1580 their severed heads were displayed outside the walls of Galway and Sligo. Moved by this spectacle, Tadhg Dall Ó hUiginn wrote an extraordinary elegy apostrophizing their remains:

---

[55] See Spenser (1999), 35, 128.
[56] Pauline Henley, *Spenser in Ireland* (Cork: Cork University Press, 1928), 139.

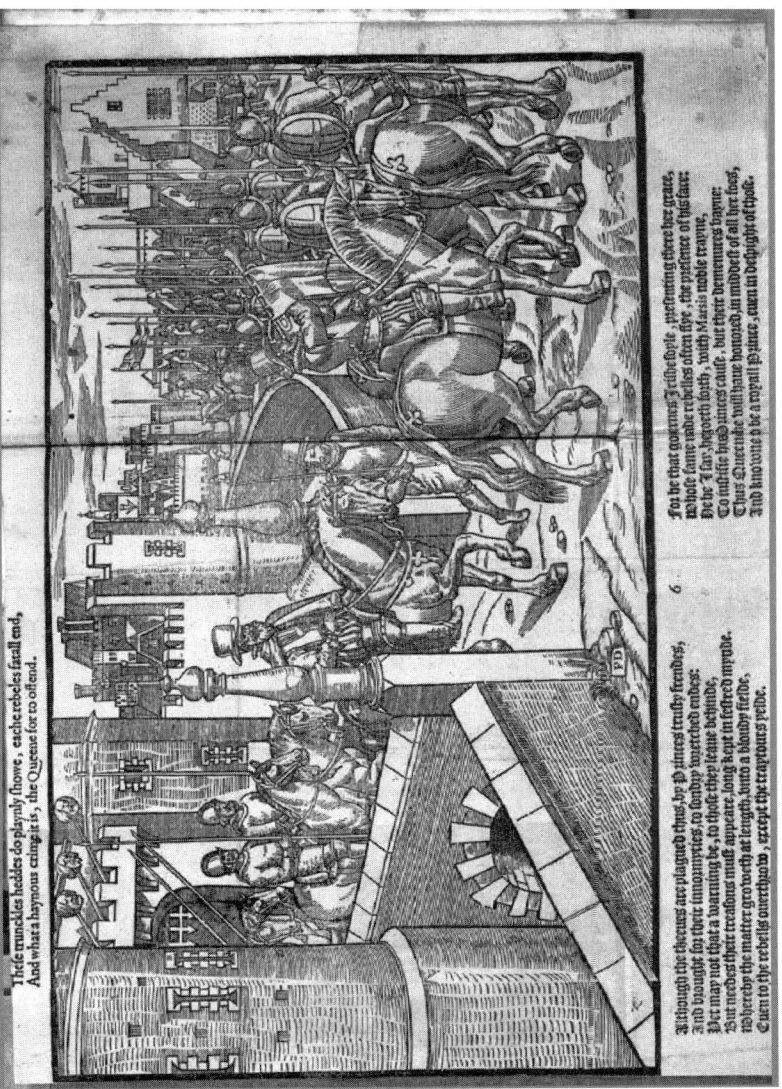

5. John Derricke, *The Image of Ireland* (1581). Sir Henry Sidney sets out from Dublin Castle.

How often in days gone by did those heads rest in fair maidens' arms, the heads I
now see on poles, the heads whose downfall has meant the ruin of Flann's Plain.
O head of Brian [a chinn Bhriain], to be raised aloft never caused thee shame till
today—how sad! It was never imagined that thou shouldst be as thou now art.
O head of Domhnall [a chinn Domhnoill], 'twas a dread disaster that thou in presence of thy men should be cut off by the foe; this will be the ruin of Éire forever.[57]

The studied grotesqueness of the trope functions to expose the monstrosity of the practice, while at the same time rehumanizing the dehumanized
by exposing public examples of 'justice' as personal instances of tragedy.

Derricke's message is reinforced in plate eight which displays the mas-
sive force at Sidney's command (Fig. 6).[58] Taken collectively, the dense,
serried ranks of heavily armed harquebusiers, halberdiers, pike-men, and
cavalry constitute 'Talus', the military arm of the deputy's government.
But this, ideally, is an image of disciplined power, not uncontrolled violence. It suggests order, formality, and 'degree'. The meticulous detail of
the uniforms is in marked contrast to the clothing of the loosely garbed,
bare-legged kern. Sidney himself wears chain-armour but with a soft hat
instead of a helmet. The warrior and the gentleman are one. The following plates display Sidney's glorious success in battle and triumphal return
to Dublin preceded by the 'sword of state' which Irenius takes to symbolize 'the Royall power of the Prince' (*Prose*, 148). The Lord Deputy is duly
received 'with Ioy on every parte'.

The two final woodcuts illustrate the consequences of conquest with
two diametrically conflicting images: the despair of the recalcitrant 'rebel'
Rory Oge O'More [Ruairí Óg Ó Mórdha] and the submission of Turlough Luineach O'Neill [Toirdhealbhach Luinneach Ó Néill]. The clear
implication is that the Irish must choose one destiny or the other. O'More
had long been a thorn in the side of the administration, persistently en-
gaging in the sort of raids illustrated in the second plate. In a letter of 3
March 1576 Sir Henry Sidney records how '*Rorie Oge Omore*, and *Cormocke Mac Cormocke Oconnor* . . . bourned betwene vij or viij C. thatched
Howsies, in a Markett Towne, called the *Naas* . . . they ranne thorough the
Towne, beinge open, like Haggs and Furies of Hell, with Flakes of Fier
fastened on Pooles Ends, and so fiered the lowe thatched Howsies'.[59] In

---

[57] McKenna (1980), 294–5.
[58] Aristotle regarded the practice of decapitation as characteristic of savagery. See Anthony
Pagden, *The Fall of Natural Man: The American Indian and the Origins of Comparative Ethnology* (Cambridge: Cambridge University Press, 1982), 17.
[59] Collins (1746), i. 166–7.

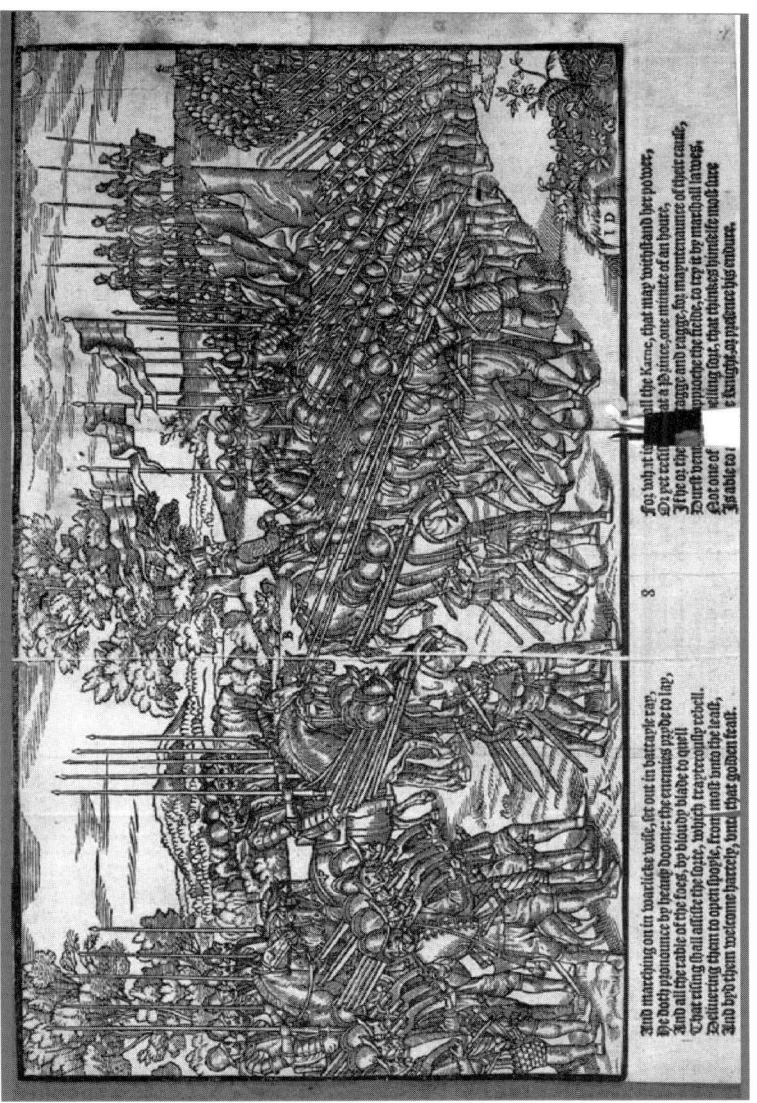

6. John Derricke, *The Image of Ireland* (1581). Sir Henry Sidney's army in the field.

the eyes of Ó Súilleabháin Béarra, however, O'More was a hero who had desperately endeavoured 'to recover his patrimony by arms in a fierce struggle of six years' duration'.[60] During the Nine Years' War his son lead the assault on Munster which routed Spenser and his fellow planters. In plate eleven, however, O'More is portrayed as 'a grose and corpulent man, lapped in a mantle, overwhelmed with miserie, beyng in a Wood (an ill-favoured Churle) standyng on a Hillocke enclosed with a shaking Bogge (his onely refuge in the tyme of trouble), utteryng moste lamentably, with brynishe salte wolvishe teares, his life as enseweth' (Fig. 7).[61] Into his mouth is placed a confession of treachery which resolves cultural differ-ence into moral apostasy: O'More is a 'rebell' because he is evil and evil because he is a rebel. He has refused both the Queen's 'grace' and God's. 'The howre is at hande', he foretells, 'in which the cept of my rebellyng race, | Shall be extirp't, and bolishte cleane the lande'.[62] This is particu-larly important in that it illustrates the tendency for the 'woodkerne' to be employed as a metonym for Gaelic society generally, a polemical strategy noted, and deplored, in the *Leabhar Branach*.[63] The woodcut takes us to the heart of the colonial issue. Here in the midst of wild woods and bogs, surrounded by prowling wolves and 'wolvishe' by nature, Gaelic society repents of being Gaelic. It recognizes its autonomy as barbarous isolation, its Anglicization as redemption. And this is, perhaps, the ultimate colo-nial fantasy: the voluntary recognition on the part of the 'other' that it has received nothing but 'Justice'—it is as though O'More were to write the fifth book of *The Faerie Queene* on Spenser's behalf, reducing himself to an allegorical abstraction by way of public confession. Subsequent to the news of O'More's death in a skirmish, Derricke added a second mono-logue spoken by the traitor's severed head hoist upon 'the highest toppe of the Castell of Dublin': 'Thus God of Justice, doeth traitours confounde: | When from their sinnes thaile not be removed.'[64]

The final woodcut illustrates the sole alternative by presenting the 'submission' of Turlough Luineach O'Neill to Sir Henry Sidney (Fig. 8). In the foreground, the Lord Deputy sits in state, effectively as Vice Regent, with the sword of justice lying by him on a cushion. Turlough, sporting English dress, kneels before him, 'civil' hat in hand. His retinue, all dressed in Irish mantles, kneel in his wake in acceptance of his submis-sion. This is certainly not how Gaelic poets pictured Turlough, but the

[60] O'Sullivan Beare (1903), 6–7.   [61] Derricke (1985), 70.   [62] Ibid. 79.
[63] Mac Airt (1944), 143.   [64] Derricke (1985), 92, 97.

7. John Derricke, *The Image of Ireland* (1581). Rory Oge O'More in defeat.

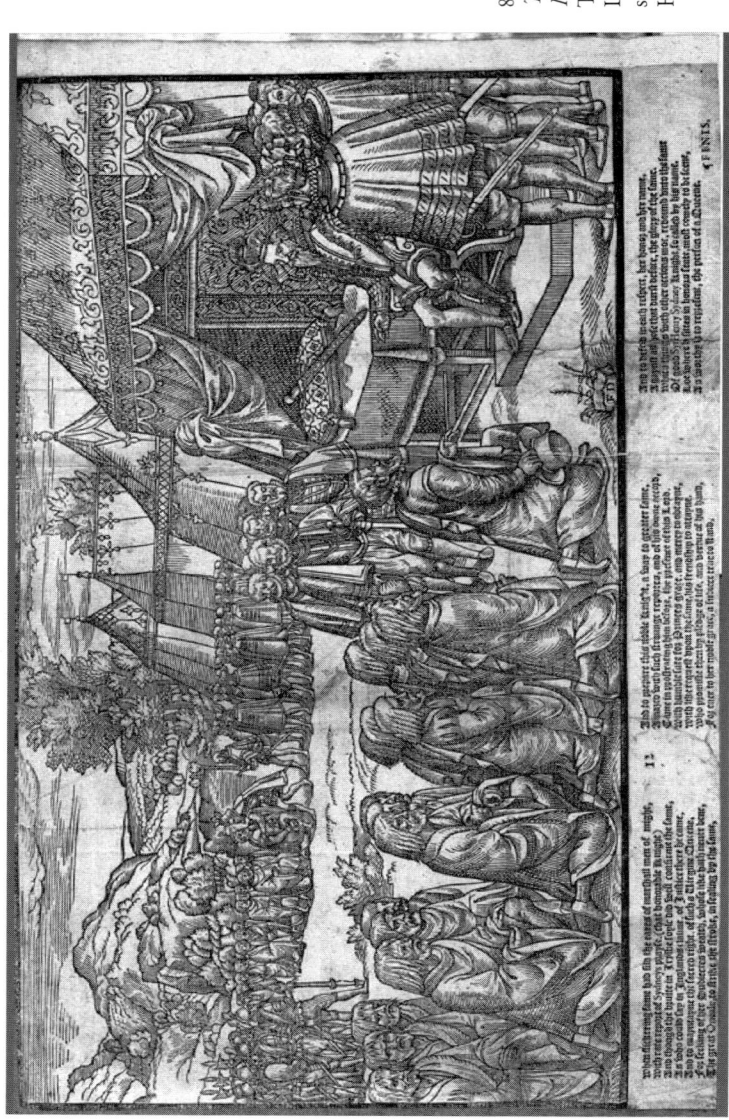

8. John Derricke, *The Image of Ireland* (1581). Turlough Luineach O'Neill submits to Sir Henry Sidney.

clothing supplies the key to Derricke's allegory.[65] Sidney recorded how
the Earl of Clanrickard's sons had signified their rejection of his authority
by 'shaking off and cutting in pieces their English garments upon the
ryver of Shenan' thereby abandoning their 'civil' identities before crossing
over into the Gaelic strongholds of Connaught.[66] By contrast, Derricke's
O'Neill has abandoned his mantle and led all of his mantled allies out of
the undergrowth where their activities may be supervised. In the background the Lord Deputy courteously bends to embrace him. *The Image
of Irelande* ends with Gaelic chieftains kneeling to English officials, a
scene which perfectly encapsulates the agenda underlying the construction of all such 'images'. The reality, however, was less encouraging. Even
as Derricke's woodcuts appeared in print, Spenser's secretarial letters reported the continuing dangers posed by Turlough Luineach O'Neill, who
was described by Lodowick Bryskett as 'the very roote, or seedeman of all
the rebellion of Ireland'.[67] The imagery anticipates Spenser's Garden of
Ate, 'full of wicked weedes, | Which she her selfe hath sowen all about':

> The seedes of evill wordes, and factious deedes;
> Which when to ripenesse due they growen arre,
> Bring foorth an infinite increase, that breedes
> Tumultuous trouble and contentious iarre,
> The which most often end in bloudshed and in warre.

> (4. 1. 25)

Such was the garden state in which Spenser operated. The very term
'plantation' suggests the cultivation of previously 'wild' soil, and the
figurative meaning invariably draws moral support from the literal. Hus-
bandry is at once the 'moste naturall' of all human occupations and the
essential prelude to urbanization, but in order to husband the soil one
must 'plant' colonies of cultivators, and in order to 'plant' colonists one
must 'plant' garrisons to protect them: 'as the Poet saiethe *Bella execrata
Colonis*, for husbandrie beinge the nurse of thrifte and daughter of indus-
trie and labour, detestethe all that maie worke her scathe and destroye the
travell of her handes' (*Prose*, 216). The source of the quotation remains
unidentified but it is surely significant that 'colonus' signifies both husbandman *and* colonist.[68] The coincidence of meanings serves to remind

---

[65] For the bardic view see Dáibhí I. Ó Cróinín, 'A Poem to Toirdhealbhach Luinneach Ó
Néill', *Éigse*, 16 (1975), 50–66.

[66] Sir Henry Sidney (1857), 313.   [67] See e.g. SP 63/84/ 13; 63/84/14; Bryskett (1927), 23.

[68] Spenser may be misquoting 'bellaque matribus | detestata' (Horace, *Carmina*, I. 1. 24–5).
If so, the substitution of 'colonis' for 'matribus' is particularly noteworthy.

us that, for Spenser and his fellow 'undertakers', the enterprise of Ireland was as much personal as public. Ireland's 'barbarity' was the planter's opportunity, and to dismiss the indigenous population as 'savages' was *ipso facto* to legitimize their conquest while at the same time insulating the conqueror from the more disturbing implications of perceived cultural difference.[69] By repeatedly personifying the land while dehumanizing its inhabitants, Spenser transformed poetic allegory into a powerful tool of colonial polemic, facilitating the presentation of violent conquest as civil reclamation. Through the carefully deployed imagery of pruning and physic, the destructive energies of conquest are sublimated into charitable duties. We are given to understand—or rather one might say that Spenser gives himself to understand, since Irenius and Eudoxus are twin *personae* of the one author—that the New English have undertaken no more than the cultivation of an estate gone to seed, the 'cure' of a sick body politic (*Prose*, 146), and 'wheare no other remedye maie be devized nor no hope of recoverie had theare muste neds this violent meanes be used' (*Prose*, 148). Thus an agricultural image gradually develops military connotations with the result that dubious policies appear to acquire the validity of natural law: Talus, in an action uncannily reminiscent of Ate, 'scatters' the Irish landscape with the corpses of recalcitrant rebels, 'as thicke as . . . seede after the sowers hand' (5. 12. 7). By contrast, in one of the most celebrated of all Gaelic exile poems, 'Óm sceol ar ardmhagh Fáil' ('At the news from Fál's high plain'), Céitinn inverts Spenser's imagery by comparing the proliferation of colonists to that of cockle in a wheatfield. The sole remaining hope is that a carefully winnowed harvest may be shipped overseas.[70]

[69] See A. Bartlett Giamatti, 'Primitivism and the Process of Civility in Spenser's *Faerie Queene*', in Fredi Chiapelli (ed.), *First Images of America: The Impact of the New World on the Old*, 2 vols. (Berkeley: University of California Press,1976), i. 71–82; Quinn, *The Elizabethans and the Irish*, 106–22.

[70] For similar uses of the imagery of planting see Eamon Grennan, 'Language and Politics: A Note on Some Metaphors in Spenser's *A View of the Present State of Ireland*', *SSt* 3 (1982), 99–110 (pp. 100–2). For Céitinn see Ó Tuama (1981), 84–7.

4 'Salvage Knight'

> A good and virtuous nature may recoil
> In an imperial charge.
>
> (*Macbeth*, 4. 3. 20–1)

THERE is no documentary evidence for Spenser's presence in Ireland prior to his arrival with Lord Grey in August 1580, but there is much to indicate an association with the Sidney circle. *The Shepheardes Calender* is dedicated to Sir Philip Sidney and the *Familiar Letters* suggest that both Spenser and Harvey were anxious to cultivate his acquaintance, and to be seen to do so.[1] Sir Henry Sidney had greater experience of Irish politics than any of his contemporaries and Spenser's relationship with his son may well have impelled him into the Irish service. In response to Grey's request for advice, Sir Henry penned a long and detailed letter supplying an overview of the conditions in Ireland and of the difficulties incident to the office of Lord Deputy—an office in which, he claims, his son has 'ernestlie and often' expressed an interest.[2] This is by no means unlikely. Philip Sidney had recently drafted an aggressive defence of his father's third administration in which he suggested that the queen should exercise greater discretion in her response to malicious Irish slanders designed 'to discreddit, not so muche the governour as the governement'. Like Grey, he opposes her policy of 'lenity' on the grounds that the Irish are inherently untrustworthy and prone to lend support 'to any invadinge force'. The policy to be preferred is one of 'directe conquest' and is 'in her Majesties handes' to implement 'when it shall please her'.[3] The implication that it does not please her insinuates a criticism that the document is careful never to articulate.

---

[1] S. K. Heninger, Jr., 'Spenser and Sidney at Leicester House', *SSt* 8 (1987, but pub. 1990), 239–49.
[2] Grey (1847), 71. Sir Henry Sidney was contemplating a fourth term of office in 1582 in the hope that his son would succeed him. See Bart Westerweel, 'Astrophel and Ulster: Sidney's Ireland', in C. C. Barfoot and Theo D'haen (eds.), *The Clash of Ireland: Literary Contrasts and Connections* (Amsterdam: Rodopi Press, 1989), 5–22 (pp. 14–15).
[3] Sir Philip Sidney (1912–26), iii. 46–50.

Sidney was in bad odour with the queen for other reasons. In 1579 the contentious matter of her proposed marriage to the Catholic Duc d'Alençon eclipsed even the Desmond wars, and Sidney's contribution to that debate had earned him temporary exile from the court.[4] The two issues were, however, intimately related. Catholicism was widely perceived as the greatest stumbling block to the 'reform' of Ireland and the proposed marriage threatened to confound the 'religious' basis of the whole enterprise. It is richly expressive of the moment that Sidney should begin his assault on Alençon with an analogy drawn from his Irish experience. 'Irishmen', he informs the queen, 'are wont to tell them that dye, they are ritche, they are feare [healthy], what nede they to dye? So truely to you indued with felicities beyond all others . . . a man may well aske, what maketh you in such a calme to chaunge course, to so helthfull a body to applye such a weary medecine?' For the queen to wed Alençon was to encompass 'the manifest death' of her 'estate' for 'as in bodies naturall any soudain change is not without perill, so in this body politick wherof you are the onely head, it is so much the more as there are more humours to receave a hurtfull impression'.[5] But Elizabeth was no less 'head' of the Irish 'body politic' than the English, and out of such complex crosscurrents was born Spenser's first major, but significantly anonymous, engagement with his sovereign's public image.[6]

Published less than a year before Spenser's arrival in Ireland, *The Shepheardes Calender* provides what has long been regarded as the ultimate image of the virgin queen in its portrayal of 'fayre *Elisa*, Queene of shepheardes all' (*Aprill*, 34). Yet Elizabeth is praised for her virginity at the very moment when, to the dismay of her Protestant subjects, she was planning to abandon it, and 'Colin' is too 'alienate and with drawen' to 'sing' a eulogy composed in happier times.[7] He is sufficiently engaged, however, to

    [4] See Blair Worden, *The Sound of Vertue: Philip Sidney's 'Arcadia' and Elizabethan Politics* (New Haven: Yale University Press, 1996), 89–124. See also Maureen Quilligan, 'Sidney and his Queen', in Heather Dubrow and Richard Strier (eds.), *The Historical Renaissance: New Essays on Tudor and Stuart Literature and Culture* (Chicago: University of Chicago Press, 1988), 171–96. For the courtship generally see Susan Doran, *Monarchy and Matrimony: The Courtships of Elizabeth I* (London: Routledge, 1996), 154–94.
    [5] Sir Philip Sidney (1912–26), iii. 51, 52, 59.
    [6] See Brendan Bradshaw, 'The Beginnings of Modern Ireland', in Brian Farrell (ed.), *The Irish Parliamentary Tradition* (Dublin: Gill and Macmillan, 1973), 68–87 (p. 85).
    [7] For the historical background see Wallace T. MacCaffrey, *Queen Elizabeth and the Making of Policy, 1572–88* (Princeton: Princeton University Press, 1981), 243–66. See also Louis Adrian Montrose, 'Of Gentlemen and Shepherds: The Politics of Elizabethan Pastoral Form', *ELH* 50 (1983), 415–59. For Colin as an 'oppositional voice' see Andrew Hadfield, *Literature, Politics and National Identity: Reformation to Renaissance* (Cambridge: Cambridge University Press, 1994), 170–201.

'sing' November's elegy for the mysterious 'Dido' whose name inevitably evokes memories of the Virgilian queen who perished for love of an untrustworthy foreign prince.[8] The overt cause of Colin's distress is the pain of unrequited love but, as Arthur Marotti has valuably reminded us, 'love is not love' in the context of political allegory.[9] One of the principal literary consequences of female regiment was the representation of political ambition as amorous desire and political disappointment as unrequited love. In Colin's discontent with 'Rosalind' readers might recognize the country's discontent with 'fayre *Elisa*'. At a time when the future fairy queen was contemplating marriage to a Catholic, E.K. caustically associates the fairies with Catholic superstition.[10] Feelings were running high. The proposed marriage revived memories of Mary Tudor's alliance with Philip II and threatened to reopen the whole issue of female regiment. John Stubbs's *Discoverie of a Gaping Gulf Whereinto England is Like to be Swallowed* (1579), may even be regarded as a *Second Blast of the Trumpet against the Monstrous Regiment of Women* since Knox had intended the sequel to deal with the problems arising from the marriage of female rulers to 'straingiers' or aliens.[11] Although Stubbs is overtly supportive of Elizabeth, his imagery is implicitly anti-feminist. As a mere woman, Elizabeth would be the 'weaker vessel' in any marriage, and her husband would of necessity be her 'governor'.[12] Sir Philip Sidney perfectly articulated such fears when he observed that Alençon was 'of the Romishe religion, and if he be a man, must nedes have that manlike propertye to desire that all men be of his mind'.[13] In matters of such moment as a royal marriage, a female monarch should not be allowed to choose for herself but should accept the advice of a male Parliament as a 'daughter' accepts the counsel of a 'parent'.[14] In this manner patriarchy is slyly reimposed within gynarchy. The issue of the queen's marriage was, moreover, perceived to be

[8] Paul E. McLane, *Spenser's Shepheardes Calender: A Study in Elizabethan Allegory* (Notre Dame, Ind.: University of Notre Dame Press, 1961), 47–60. For the association of Elizabeth with Dido see also John Watkins, *The Specter of Dido: Spenser and Virgilian Epic* (New Haven: Yale University Press, 1995), 75–82.

[9] Arthur F. Marotti, '"Love is Not Love": Elizabethan Sonnet Sequences and the Social Order', *ELH* 49 (1982), 396–428. See also Stephen Greenblatt, *Renaissance Self-Fashioning: from More to Shakespeare* (Chicago: University of Chicago Press, 1980), 165–9.

[10] See E.K.'s gloss to 'June', 25. Elizabeth had been associated with the fairy queen four years previously at Woodstock. See *The Queenes Majesties Entertainment at Woodstocke*, ed. J. W. Cunliffe, *PMLA* 26 (1911), 92–141 (pp. 98–9); Charles Read Baskervill, 'The Genesis of Spenser's Queen of Faerie', *MP* 18 (1920), 49–54.

[11] Knox (1846–64), iv. 397, 404, 410–11. [12] Stubbs (1968), 11, 69.
[13] Sir Philip Sidney (1912–26), iii. 56. [14] Stubbs (1968), 68–70.

closely related to that of Ireland. 'Unless we ourselves close our own eyes', Stubbs asserted,

we may see that it is a very French Popish wooing to send hither smooth-tongued Simiers to gloss and glaver and hold talk of marriage, and yet, in the meanwhile, Jacques Fitzmaurice, who had been in France . . . even now came immediately thence into Ireland to invade our Queen's dominion there and assemble the traitorous Papists *in nomine domini, domini papae* [in the name of the Lord, of the Lord Pope].[15]

'Jacques Fitzmaurice' is, of course, James Fitzmaurice Fitzgerald who initiated the Desmond wars by landing at Smerwick in July 1579 and urging his fellow countrymen to rise up against 'the pretensed queen of England'. The mercenaries who accompanied him were Spanish and Italian rather than French, but Stubbs was disposed to ignore such distinctions in view of the general threat from continental Catholicism.[16] His right hand was struck off for his pains, and his printer, Hugh Singleton, very nearly suffered the same fate.[17] There was therefore every reason for *The Shepheardes Calender* to appear anonymously. By praising Elizabeth for her spotless virginity, by dedicating the work to Sir Philip Sidney and by using the same printer as Stubbs, Spenser could be interpreted as indicating his opposition to both the foreign and domestic policies of the queen he claimed to be celebrating.[18] His subsequent experience as Grey's secretary did little to reassure him.

Spenser's secretarial letters afford a unique insight into the genesis of epic heroism not because they expose the 'fact' behind the fiction but because they compromise the distinction between 'fact' and 'fiction', between 'politics' and 'poetics'.[19] The record is 'fictionalized' at every level,

[15] Stubbs (1968), 80.
[16] Steven G. Ellis, *Ireland in the Age of the Tudors 1447–1603: English Expansion and the End of Gaelic Rule* (London: Longman, 1998), 312–13.
[17] For Singleton see H. J. Byrom, 'Edmund Spenser's First Printer, Hugh Singleton', *Library*, 4th ser., 14 (1933), 121–56.
[18] See Richard A. McCabe, ' "Little booke: thy selfe present": The Politics of Presentation in *The Shepheardes Calender*', in Howard Erskine-Hill and Richard A. McCabe (eds.), *Presenting Poetry: Composition, Publication, Reception. Essays in Honour of Ian Jack* (Cambridge: Cambridge University Press, 1995), 15–40; Doris Adler, 'Imaginary Toads in Real Gardens', *ELR* 11 (1981), 235–60.
[19] Spenser's secretarial letters are catalogued by Roland M. Smith in 'Spenser's Scholarly Script and "Right Writing" ', in Don Cameron Allen (ed.), *Studies in Honour of T. W. Baldwin* (Urbana: University of Illinois Press, 1958), 67–111 (pp. 69–75), and by Anthony G. Petti in *The Spenser Encyclopedia* (Toronto: University of Toronto Press, 1990), 345–6. Petti rejects a small group of letters in italic script attributed to Spenser by Smith and a number of earlier commentators: SP 63/78/29; 82/54; 85/5; 86/50; 88/39; 92/11 (I). On balance I am inclined to accept Smith's attributions.

but the fictions are inconsistent, not to say mutually contradictory. The complex process whereby Arthur Grey 'became' Artegall illustrates the psychology of colonial experience even more vividly than the often self-contradictory defence mounted in *A View*. The cult of heroism answered the need for moral validation, and the fiction of glorious endeavour functioned not only as a cloak for failure but more insidiously as a cloak for success. The role of the 'secretary' and that of 'poet historicall' were remarkably comparable. As 'secretary' to the nation the 'poet historicall' sought to represent the historical process as a spiritual quest, turning mere 'records' into 'legends'. In so doing he kept both his nation's and his patron's political 'secrets'.[20]

Lord Grey was mooted for Ireland as early as 1571 but was recognized as a risky choice because of the uncompromising nature of his religious views. Writing to Burghley in 1572 he deplored 'the late horryble and tirannicall dealings' of the St Bartholomew's Day Massacre and expressed the hope that 'hyr Majestie may have the wysedoome too follow and magnitude to execute the thynges that maye divert the same from hence'.[21] He moves on immediately to the prospect of his appointment as Lord Deputy. The implication is clear: promoting ministers such as himself is one of 'the thynges' that Elizabeth can do in order to secure the Protestant state. Grey's family, which boasted a distinguished tradition of public service stretching back to the reign of Henry III, was one of the earliest to embrace the tenets of the Reformation. His father, William Grey, had rallied to Northumberland's assistance in the attempt to dispossess Mary Tudor and usurp the throne for Lady Jane Grey. David Lloyd captured the essence of William Grey's character when he described him as 'that great Souldier and good Christian, in whom Religion was not a *softness*, (as *Machiavil* discoursed,) but a *resolution*'.[22] His religion, in other words, was of a distinctly 'masculine' and martial character and he bequeathed its spirit to an heir equally hostile to all things 'Catholic'—even within Anglicanism. 'But a back-friend to Bishops', Arthur Grey was commonly

[20] For the role of the secretary see Richard Rambuss, *Spenser's Secret Career* (Cambridge: Cambridge University Press, 1993), 5–24. For Spenser's appointment see Jean R. Brink, ' "All his minde on honour fixed": The Preferment of Edmund Spenser', in Judith H. Anderson, Donald Cheney, and David A. Richardson (eds.), *Spenser's Life and the Subject of Biography* (Amherst: University of Massachusetts Press, 1996), 45–64. For the type of work involved see Raymond Jenkins, '*Newes out of Munster*, A Document in Spenser's Hand', *SP* 32 (1935), 125–30.

[21] Grey (1847), 66.

[22] Lloyd (1670), 571. See Richard A. McCabe, 'The Fate of Irena: Spenser and Political Violence', in *Spenser and Ireland: An Interdisciplinary Perspective* (Cork: Cork University Press, 1989), 109–25.

suspected of promoting Puritanism. 'In all divisions of Votes in Parliament or Council-Table', observes Lloyd, '[he] sided with the Anti-prelatial party'.[23] Mindful of the dangers of sending such a person to Ireland, the queen cautioned him to exercise religious tolerance, but in one of his earliest letters as Lord Deputy—dated 22 December 1580 and copied by Spenser—he signalled his disagreement with official policy: 'Your Highness at my leave taking gave me a warning for being strict in dealing with religion, I have observed yt, how obediently soever, yett most unwillingly I confesse, and I doubt as harmefully to your and gods service, a Canker never receiving Cure without corrosive medicines.'[24] Catholicism was Ireland's 'canker' and military action was its 'cure'. The letter's uneasy blend of implicit criticism and piously paternalistic advice set the tone for the unhappy correspondence that was to follow.

Grey's initial expectations of extraordinary royal favour were informed by his father's relationship with Henry VIII, or rather by the myth of that relationship which he created for Holinshed's use. By comparing Grey's holograph with the version eventually presented to the general public, one can see how an apparently 'objective' chronicle was fashioned from a highly subjective memoir. Grey writes in the first person, Holinshed in the third, and the emphasis varies accordingly. Holinshed regarded William Grey as a worthy instrument of national policy, but his son presents him as a moral hero. The two versions of the narrative tell essentially the same story but to quite different effect. Both begin with an account of William Grey's attack on the fortifications of Chatillon but, in a sentence omitted by Holinshed, Grey alleges that the incident illustrates 'the *expression* of the kynges noble *mynde* and courage, with the greate secret trust that hee reposed in my lord'.[25] His father was the keeper of the king's political 'secrets', his 'secretary' in the fullest sense of the term—the sense in which Spenser was doubtless employed. It is perhaps indicative of the trust that eventually grew between Spenser and Grey that the Lord Deputy's first report from Ireland is an untidy holograph 'whytche, for secresie sake, I chose rather myselfe yllfavooredly to sett downe, then too impart to oothers fayrer drawght'.[26] The destruction of the fortifications at Chatillon was essential to the national interest but contrary to the terms of a recently negotiated truce. As such, it constituted a flagrant breach of international law. Henry VIII therefore sent two contradictory

[23] Lloyd (1670), 589.   [24] SP 63/79/24 (I) (in Spenser's hand).
[25] Grey (1847), 3.   [26] Ibid. 78.

messages to William Grey. An official letter instructing him to observe the terms of the truce and an oral message urging him to ignore them:

Byd him call too mynde how that hys breetherne and hymself, not awhyle, but eeven from chyldisshe yeeares, nor far of, but styll neere too owre persone, wee have browght up; the which tell hym, not unjustly, yf that bee in hym that wee conceave doothe breede in us an greater trust of hys fervencie too serve us then of a common servant or subject. By that toaken, wyll hym, whatsoever I have wrytten too the contrarie, that presently hee empeatcche the fortification of Chastilion, and rase it yf it bee possible; and this my message shall bee hys cleering therin, and the servyce gratefully accepted.[27]

The courier was 'estonyed' at the 'contrarietie of the letter and message' but the recipient acted without hesitation in eager conspiracy with his sovereign. The tone of the holograph makes it clear that this is precisely the sort of relationship that Grey had hoped to enjoy with Elizabeth, a relationship based on the mutual recognition of the prior claims of national interest over the letter of international law.[28]

Initially such hopes seemed justified.[29] Though widely condemned as a gross violation of the law of arms and nations, Grey's ruthless extermination of (by his own account) some 600 disarmed mercenaries at Smerwick prompted an official letter of thanks from Elizabeth.[30] She even appended a note in her own hand asserting that 'the mightie hand of the Almightiest power hathe showed manifest the force of his strengthe in the weakenes of feeblest sexe and mynds this yere to make men asshamed ever hereafter to disdaine us, in which Action I joye that you have bin chose the Instrument of his glory which I meane to give you no cause to forthincke'. Here was the perfect union of female sovereign and male servant, the masculine fortitude of the one supporting the 'feeble' strength of the other. Yet, even amid such glowing praise, there was much in Elizabeth's letter to make her Deputy 'forthincke'. While expressing no overt objection to the slaughter of the mercenaries, the queen signalled her discontent at the decision to spare the leaders for ransom. 'We could have wished', she wrote, 'that the principal persons of the said invaders to

---

[27] Ibid. 5–6.
[28] For a different perspective see Christopher Highley, *Shakespeare, Spenser, and the Crisis in Ireland* (Cambridge: Cambridge University Press, 1997), 110–33.
[29] For exhaustive accounts of Grey's campaign see Richard Bagwell, *Ireland Under the Tudors*, 3 vols. (London: Longman, 1885–90), iii. 59–115; Cyril Falls, *Elizabeth's Irish Wars* (London: Constable, 1996—first pub. 1950), 123–52.
[30] For Smerwick see *Prose*, 524–30.

whome youe have promised grace . . . had been reserved for us, to have extended towards them eyther Justice or mercy . . . ffor that it seemeth to us most agreable to reason that a principall should receave punishment before an accessary.'[31] Grey had executed the wrong people and, quite possibly, for the wrong reasons. From this point onwards, the tone of his letters is invariably at odds with those of his sovereign. He writes as an idealist, she as a pragmatist. She was more interested in fiscal than religious reform, but he was intent on ridding Ireland of Catholicism in order to secure the safety of the Protestant state.[32] Grey's personal account of the massacre at Smerwick accordingly emphasizes its European context. According to him, one of the mercenaries' leaders claimed that 'they were all sent by the Pope for the defence of the Catholica fede'. 'My answer was', he asserts,

that I would not greatly have marvelled if men being commanded by natural and absolute princes did sometimes take in hand wrong actions, but that men . . . should be carried into unjust, desperate and wicked actions by one that neither from God nor man could claim any princely power or empire, but indeed a detestable shaveling, the right Antichrist and general ambitious tyrant over all right principalities, and patron of the diabolica fede, I could not but greatly rest in wonder.[33]

Finding their 'fault' to be 'aggravated by the vileness of their commander,' Grey demanded unconditional surrender, offering them no option but to 'yield their selves to my will for life or death'. Contemporary Gaelic commentators strongly contested this claim. Ó Súilleabháin Béarra, for example, alleges that Sebastiano di san Giuseppe, the Italian leader of the garrison, surrendered 'on the one condition, which was secured to the besieged by the oath of the viceroy, that he might march out safe with soldiers, arms, bag and baggage'. In the event, however, 'heretical faithlessness held itself bound neither by honour nor the sanctity of an oath, nor by the laws held inviolate amongst all people civilized and barbarous . . . Hence "Grey's faith" became a proverb for monstrous and inhuman perfidy.'[34] From the Irish perspective savagery and monstrosity were located squarely in the supposed instrument of English civility. This, in itself, is

---

[31] SP 63/79/13.
[32] For the queen's fiscal concerns see Hogan and O'Farrell (1959), 38–62.
[33] SP 63/78/29 (attributed to Spenser by Smith).
[34] O'Sullivan Beare (1903), 24–5. In letter of 9 January 1581 the Jesuit Nicholas Sander alleges that Sebastiano di San Giuseppe was falsely given the impression that his followers' lives were to be spared. See O'Rahilly (1938), 7–8.

hardly surprising, but even English commentators were uneasy. By way of attempted mitigation Camden fabricated the story that Grey 'shed Tears' at Smerwick and that 'the Queen wished it had not been done, detesting from her Heart such Cruelty, though necessary, against persons who had yielded themselves; and hardly did she allow of the Reasons for the Slaughter committed'.[35] As the parenthetical 'though necessary' indicates, the queen, like her father before her, was playing a double game—if scarcely the one that Grey had anticipated. Even as early as November 1580 the adoption of a 'merciful' pose presented itself as a ready strategy for distancing the crown from an increasingly isolated and unpopular minister. It was essential that Mercilla be seen to deplore Artegall's 'zeal'.

From this point onwards Grey's hopes of royal favour evaporated. The government complained of escalating expenditure while the Lord Deputy complained of inadequate provisions 'considering the present great Extremitie of Need, wherewith the Garrison is pinched, whom how to relieve by any Means I see not, unless it be thought that Men may feed of Air'.[36] The letter in question is written in Spenser's secretary hand, as was an even more desperate appeal to Walsingham to which the poet added the apparently personal plea 'Hast hast post hast for lyfe'.[37] The problem was that Grey had now committed himself to a 'thorough' policy of 'reformation' and, unlike the government, was quite unwilling to compromise. In a remarkable letter of 26 April 1581, penned in what appears to be Spenser's italic hand, he tells the queen that while 'your highness charge indeed is very great . . . your Majesty in this case is not to looke onely upon the chardge, but upon the cause as well'. Since God also keeps 'accounts' she needs to act 'in your own honours behalf and especially in gods respect, who having betaken unto you the interest and government of this land with nolesse duety of care and charge, then of the same wherein you abyde, will doubtles challenge no lesse accoumpt at your handes for the one then for the other'. Matters might well be 'patched up', he concedes, and 'a face of peace and quietnes made to appeare' at lesser expense, but the result would be morally unsatisfactory and politically unpalatable: 'I know the great feare, due reverence and sound knowledge your Highness hath of god, besides the naturall regard

[35] Camden (1675), 243.
[36] Hatfield House, Cecil Papers, 12. 19 (no. 1081). The letter is dated 10 December 1581.
[37] SP 63/84/14 (in Spenser's hand). See Raymond Jenkins, 'Spenser with Lord Grey in Ireland', *PMLA* 52 (1937), 338–53 (p. 340).

to your honour and place cannot suffer you to like or rather not to detest such kynde of government.' Unlike Ralegh, Grey opposed the queen's intention to issue a general pardon to the rebels on the grounds that 'mercifull dealinges have ever lifted them up to greater insolencies' while 'feare' alone bred obedience.[38]

The pardon was proclaimed nonetheless.[39] Elizabeth was preoccupied by very different concerns. She was incensed by reports that escheated lands had been granted to Grey's favourites on terms that seemed highly disadvantageous to the crown. This was undoubtedly true but hardly unusual. It was a recognized fact of Irish political life that the Lord Deputy needed to dispense lavish patronage in order to secure his position: Artegall allows Talus to cut off the golden hands and silver feet of 'Lady Munera' but he pities her fate (5. 2. 25–6).[40] Grey had done no more than his predecessors and was devastated to find his integrity challenged. The accusation of profiteering was one to which he was peculiarly vulnerable. The cost of ransoming his father from French captivity had seriously damaged the family's fortunes and even Wilton Castle had been sold to meet its mounting debts. Finding his pious rhetoric undermined by insinuations of graft, he reacted with ill-disguised anger denying that any concern for 'private commoditie' had motivated his demands for increased funding.[41] Turning the tables on Elizabeth's courtiers he represented himself, as his secretary would later represent him, as a victim of 'privie malice' and begged not to be judged by those 'whose setting up hath come by commodity of offices, and therefore the readier by them selves to measure and coniecture of me'.[42] 'Commoditie' was now a pejorative term.[43] Grey claims that his failure to provide detailed

[38] SP 63/82/54 (attributed to Spenser by Smith).

[39] SP 63/91/4. For Grey's reply to the pardon see SP 63/92/78. For Ralegh's support of the use of pardons see SP 63/96/30–1. For Grey's poor opinion of Ralegh see SP 63/92/10 (in Spenser's hand): 'for myne owne part I must bee playne I nether lyke his carriage nor Company, and therefore other then by direccion and commaundment and what his right can require, he is not to expect at my handes.'

[40] The episode of Munera and Pollente seems intended to represent the sort of extortion that Gaelic and Old English chieftains were accused of practising (5. 2. 4–28). It is particularly ironic, however, that it was Spenser himself who suggested 'tythinge' the country 'by the polle' (*Prose*, 204)

[41] SP 63/86/50 (attributed to Spenser by Smith). Questionable rewards (in the form of 'custodiams') were made to Grey's subordinates, including Spenser. See Michael MacCarthy-Morrogh, *The Munster Plantation: English Migration to Southern Ireland 1583–1641* (Oxford: Clarendon Press, 1986), 54; Frederic Ives Carpenter, 'Spenser in Ireland', *MP* 19 (1921–2), 405–19 (pp. 415–16).

[42] SP 63/88/39 (attributed to Spenser by Smith).

[43] For the issue of 'commodity' see below pp. 125–6.

accounts was occasioned solely by 'the infinitenes of the other service, which the general trouble of this land required'. Sailing very close to the wind, he contrasts the government's concern with 'proffit' with his own higher aspirations, and maintains that he might well have 'reformed the state' if the queen had remained 'resolute',

But when before one halfe yeare fully expired your Majesty grieved with the warre by reason of the charge, beganne to thinck the tyme long, and to esteeme of no service, bycause all was not doen at once . . . and settled in that conceipt fell to temporizing and pardoning them, whome your warre had now brought to that exigent, as by thende of this winter of necessitie they must have farnished, fought, or yielded to your mercye; here, with humblenes and all submission I speake it, was the overthrow of the service, and making vayne of all former cost and travayle.[44]

It is impossible to overestimate the effect that this must have had on Spenser. Here was the man who would be 'Artegall' blaming the queen who would be 'Gloriana' for a mercenary lack of moral resolve. To 'temporize' in matters religious is characteristic of the wily Burbon who thought Paris well worth a mass, and Artegall condemns all such practices as 'forgerie' (5. 11. 56). *The Faerie Queene* all but quotes Grey's words when it recalls how Artegall's efforts to 'reforme that ragged common-weale' were frustrated:

> But ere he could reforme it thoroughly,
> He through occasion called was away,
> To Faerie Court, that of necessity
> His course of Iustice he was forst to stay,
> And *Talus* to revoke from the right way,
> In which he was that Realme for to redresse.
>
> (5. 12. 27)

In point of fact, Grey had persistently petitioned for his own recall on the grounds that the queen had made his position untenable. 'The bruit of this your Highness dislyke', he informed her, 'hath brought me into such discredit with all, and so amated and distracted me in my selfe, as nether powre nor sence is lefte me to hold on the service.'[45] Summarizing his discontent he asserted that:

---

[44] SP 63/86/50 (attributed to Spenser by Smith).
[45] SP 63/88/39 (attributed to Spenser by Smith).

I see that the sore of this countrey without force will not bee cured, I see that force is chargeable to your Highness. I see that charge is grievous and dislyking, I see that it pleaseth not God to give the short successe and end to things, that your Majesty expecteth, I see that my service thus becomes altogether condemned and dissavored . . . am I then to be blamed, if I seeke to bee rid of that causeth me my greatest grief, which is your dissavour.[46]

In a letter of May 1582 the queen sought to reassure Grey of her continuing favour, 'though in very deede we have conceaved some mislike of the continuance of our great chardgs in that realme and for that things weare not so carefully looked unto and husbanded for our most proffit, as yt seemid unto us they might have ben'.[47] One can appreciate why the issue of 'chardge' features so prominently in Irenius's calculations (*Prose*, 149). Despite her renewed expressions of confidence, however, Elizabeth issued Grey's recall just two months later on the pretext of needing his advice on weighty matters—a circumstance echoed in Spenser's careful phrasing 'he through occasion called was away, | To Faerie Court' (5. 12. 27).[48]

Even as Grey prepared to return home reports of the famine devastating Munster began to flood into court. What he had described merely as 'this winter of necessitie' was delineated for the queen in graphic terms by Sir Warham St Leger. Writing in March 1582 he claimed that upwards of thirty thousand people had died within the last six months. The fault, as he saw it, lay squarely with Grey. 'In this government', he observed, 'it is thought good policy to make waste the five counties within this province . . . holding it the only means to subdue and famish the traitors. A government no doubt meant to good purpose, but (under correction) far wide from the due course of government that ought to be, and so have I sundry times told the Governor since my coming hither.' There was an imminent danger, he claimed, to the 'corporate towns' because 'victuals' had grown so scarce that 'the poorer sort of people are driven for preserving them from famine to live (saving your Highness reverence) upon starven cows and horses, being glad to give for each carcase, so dead, 4s sterling'.[49] Not everyone shared St Leger's viewpoint. Responding to Burghley's demands for an explanation, Chief Justices Loftus and Wallop conceded that under normal circumstances, 'it is indeed a lamentable thing . . . that the people under a Christian Prince should be driven to eat the carcasses of dead horses' but, they continued, 'it is less lamentable or

[46] SP 63/85/5 (attributed to Spenser by Smith). [47] SP 63/92/123.
[48] SP 63/94/17. [49] SP 63/91/41 (I).

strange here, considering the beastly disposition of many among this
people, who undoubtedly, not only in time of war, but even in time of
peace, and not only upon the borders, where waste may drive them to it,
but even in the pale . . . will always eat the carcasses of any cattle or of their
garans that die, be they never so loathsome to civil people'.[50] Ireland, according to this account, is to be judged by different standards than the
Christian world at large, and no great harm has been done. Such attitudes
help to place Spenser's own well-known account of the famine in its
proper context. 'Out of everie Corner of the woods and glinnes', Irenius
reports,

they Came Crepinge forthe upon theire handes for theire Legs Coulde not
beare them, they loked like Anotomies of deathe, they spake like ghostes Crynge
out of theire graves, they did eate of the dead Carrions, happie wheare they
Coulde finde them, Yea and one another sone after, in so muche as the verye
carkasses they spared not to scrape out of theire graves . . . in shorte space theare
weare non allmoste lefte and a moste populous and plentifull Countrye sodenlye
lefte voide of man or beaste, yeat sure in all that warr theare perished not manie
by the sworde but all by the extreamitye of famine which they themselves had
wroughte (*Prose*, 158).

The image, as Irenius notes, is such that 'anie stonie harte would have
rewed', yet pity would be inappropriate. The famine is one which the victims themselves 'had wrought'—presumably by opposing the authority
of the Lord Deputy—and 'of suche desperate persons as will willfullie followe the Course of theire owne follie theare is no Compassion to be had'
(*Prose*, 157). It has often been claimed that the vision of the Munster
famine filled Spenser with horror and haunted him for the rest of his life,
but one must distinguish between the graphic description of something
horrible in itself and a horrified account of something from which the
author recoils. Describing the miserable condition of the 'Indians', Las
Casas remarks that the spectacle 'is enough to melt the hardest of hearts',
a sentiment superficially similar to that of Irenius.[51] The difference, however, is that Las Casas calls for an end to the policies responsible whereas
Irenius calls for their repetition. As the opinions of Loftus and Wallop indicate, one of the principal advantages of the argument from cultural or
racial 'degeneracy' is that it deflects attention from—and even serves to
'justify'—the questionable morality of the methods of 'conquest'. What
is at issue in *A View* is not the tragedy of human suffering but the efficacy

---

[50] SP 63/98/23.   [51] Las Casas (1992), 55–6.

of famine as a military tactic. The thrust of Spenser's argument informs his choice of language. The image of human horror is also the image of military success. Famine works:

> The profe wheareof I sawe sufficientlye ensampled in Those late warrs of mounster, for notwithstandinge that the same was a moste ritche and plentifull Countrye full of Corne and Cattell . . . ere one yeare and a haulfe they weare broughte to soe wonderfull wretchednes as that anie stonie harte would have rewed the same. (*Prose*, 158)

He is not saying that he pitied their condition but that they were reduced to a *pitiable* condition. A nice distinction in words but a huge dichotomy in sentiment. Far from recoiling from the experience of the 1580s Spenser demands that it be repeated in the 1590s and, to the extent that Ulster is less fertile than Munster, the results of a Northern famine will be proportionately worse: 'they would quicklye Consume themselves and devour one another' (*Prose*, 158). The plan is not just to repeat, but to outdo, the horrors of recent history by suppressing the impediment of 'compassion':

> Therefore by all meanes it muste be forsene and assured that after once entringe into this Course of reformacion, theare be afterwardes no remorse or drawinge backe, for the sighte of anie suche rufull obiectes as muste theareuppon followe, nor for Compassion of theire Callamityes, seinge that by no other meanes it is possible to recure them, and that these are not of will but of verye urgente necessitye. (*Prose*, 163)

The 'objectes' that any 'stonie harte' would rew, the imperial heart must ignore. Grey's policy was eventually readopted by Lord Mountjoy and the grim results were approvingly described by *his* secretary, Fynes Moryson.[52] In times of political necessity 'compassion' can be seen as a vice. In the fifth book of *The Faerie Queene* (where political necessity is invariably allegorized as moral necessity) 'foolish pity' is identified as one of the obstacles that justice must learn to overcome (5. 5. 13). According to Irenius's account of the matter, it was Elizabeth's false sense of clemency that denied victory to Grey—'yf it bee clemency', Grey had wryly commented, 'to spare iustice'.[53] No sooner had the country been 'made readie for reformacion' when 'Complainte was made . . . that he was a blodye man and regarded not the lief of her subiectes no more then dogges . . . Eare was sone lente thearunto, all sodenlye turned topsydeturvey, He noble Lord eftsones was blamed the wretched people pittied and new

---

Councells plotted in which it was Concluded that a generall pardone shoulde be sente over to all that woulde accepte of it' (*Prose*, 159–60). Grey argued in October 1581 that the queen had undermined the tactical efficacy of the Munster famine by granting a reprieve to rebels 'who otherwise must have starved, if the Pardon had not been published, whereby the Soldiers was letted from the Destruction of their corn'.[54] Elizabeth, he implied, had reacted like a 'feeble' woman rather than a resolute monarch, apparently choosing 'to bee contented with the English pale, or somuch thereof as the Irish borderers will suffer you to enioy, and herewith the name of Queene'.[55] Eudoxus fears that the same may occur again: 'her sacred maiestye beinge by nature full of mercye and Clemencye . . . will not endure to heare suche tragedies made of her people and poore subiectes as some aboute her maie insinuate, then shee perhaps for verye Compassion of suche Calamities will not onelye stopp the streame of suche violence and retorne to her wonted mildenes, but also con them litle thankes which have bene the Aucthors and Counsellours of suche blodye platformes' (*Prose*, 159). In passages such as this the apparently neutral personal and possessive pronouns imply a form of discontent far too dangerous for overt expression. It is the queen's feminine 'nature', expressed in a 'wonted mildenes' of temperament, that makes her 'moste inclynable' to 'pittifull Complaintes' and thereby confounds the work of her male ministers.

Justice, according to Marsilio Ficino, is properly to be figured neither as male nor female but 'bisexual': 'courage in men because of their strength and bravery is called Masculine. Temperance is called Feminine because of a certain relaxed and cooler nature of Woman's passion and her gentle disposition. Justice is called Bi-Sexual; feminine inasmuch as because of its inherent innocence it does no one any wrong, but masculine inasmuch as it allows no harm to be brought to others, and with more severe censure frowns upon unjust men.'[56] It is to be feared, therefore, that a female monarch will upset the balance, effectively emasculating her ministers by blunting the phallic edge of Justice's 'sword'. An allegorical portrait of Francis I, now in the Bibliothèque Nationale, represents him as an androgynous figure displaying a unique complementarity of human virtues. His right arm, in full armour, brandishes aloft the 'sword' that Spenser attributes to Artegall, 'so firme and hard, | But it would pierce or

---

[54] Murdin (1759), 363.   [55] SP 63/86/50 (attributed to Spenser by Smith).

[56] Ficino (1944), 160.

cleave, where so it came' (5. 1. 10). His bare left arm demurely bears the ca-
duceus, the 'rod of peace' assigned to Cambina (4. 3. 42).[57] Here, as
often in *The Faerie Queene*, the figure of the hermaphrodite signifies the
totality of human experience. The 'Legend of Justice', by contrast, presents us with a bitter reprise of the myth of Hercules and Omphale. Artegall is overcome by Radigund, dressed in women's clothes 'that is to
manhood shame', and forced to hold a distaff in place of his broken sword
(5. 5. 20–1).[58] The 'bi-sexuality' of Ficinian justice is hereby travestied in
an image of unnatural effeminacy. 'Such', comments the narrator,

> is the crueltie of womenkynd,
> When they have shaken off the shamefast band,
> With which wise Nature did them strongly bynd,
> T'obay the heasts of mans well ruling hand.
>
> (5. 5. 25)

The argument may have been suggested by a passage in George
Buchanan's *History of Scotland* which approvingly quotes the opinion that
'nature . . . has attributed to each sex their respective duties . . . How little
less indecorous would it be in a woman to sit in judgement, to muster a
levy, to lead an army, or to give the signal for battle, than for a man to
handle the distaff, manage the loom, or perform the other services of the
weaker sex?'[59] But this was dangerous matter and Spenser is careful to in-
sert an escape clause:

> But vertuous women wisely understand,
> That they were borne to base humilitie,
> Unlesse the heavens them lift to lawfull soveraintie.
>
> (5. 5. 25)

There is no question of Elizabeth's right to rule. Rather, that very right
exacerbates the problem. The female sovereign must rule herself, control-
ling those elements of her feminine 'nature' that impede the business of
government. Radigund, who forces men to don women's clothing, is defeated by Britomart, a woman posing as a male knight. Female rulers

---

[57] See Edgar Wind, *Pagan Mysteries in the Renaissance* (London: Faber and Faber, 1958), 214.
[58] Artegall's defeat by Radigund has also been related to the 'degendering' of Old English
men by Gaelic women. See Clare Carroll, 'The Construction of Gender and the Cultural and
Political Other in *The Faerie Queene* 5 and *A View of the Present State of Ireland*: The Critics, the
Context, and the Case of Radigund', *Criticism*, 32 (1990), 163–92.
[59] Buchanan (1856), ii. 117. See I. D. McFarlane, *Buchanan* (London: Duckworth, 1981),
431–7.

must be 'manly' enough to overcome their own feminine nature. The cross-dressed Artegall reminds Britomart of the male Maid Marians of the May games, and the sight fills her with such 'secrete shame' that 'she turnd her head aside, as nothing glad, | To have beheld a spectacle so bad' (5. 7. 38–40).[60] This is the 'proper' female response to effeminacy: the recognition that it is no less a 'shame' to women than to men. Forced to rescue her transvestite damsell in distress, Britomart acts to ensure that the situation can never recur:

> And changing all that forme of common weale,
> The liberty of women did repeale,
> Which they had long usurpt; and them restoring
> To mens subiection, did true Iustice deale.
>
> (5. 7. 42)

It is the paradoxical duty of the female sovereign to protect the patriarchal order and encourage martial prowess. She should be 'Amazonian' only in the cause of male suffrage. Britomart's true quest is to marry Artegall and bear him children—an essentially marital destiny despite its deceptively martial ethos—but the fate of 'Irena' rests with him. He might well have accomplished his quest, becoming 'equal to Arthur' in deed as well as name, had he not been recalled by 'Gloriana'—or is it by 'Radigund'? Does Artegall ever really escape the tyranny of female regiment? By the time book five was published Lord Grey was three years dead, but in the intervening period Elizabeth had frequently opposed the imposition of martial law in Ireland, insisting instead that her ministers govern in accordance with common law. Such a policy was anathema to Spenser and many other New English commentators.[61] His 'historical' allegory may be retrospective, but its 'political' import was as current as ever. In delineating the fate of Artegall, the 'poet historicall' is doing precisely what he promised to do in the 'Letter to Ralegh': 'recoursing to the thinges forepaste, and divining of thinges to come'.[62] It was imperative that Grey's failure should not be repeated in the even more dangerous political climate of the 1590s and Spenser's policy was designed accordingly.

---

[60] For sexual inversion during public festivities see Natalie Zemon Davis, *Society and Culture in Early Modern France: Eight Essays* (London: Duckworth, 1975), 131–51.

[61] David Edwards, 'Ideology and Experience: Spenser's *View* and Martial Law in Ireland', in Hiram Morgan (ed.), *Political Ideology in Ireland 1541–1641* (Dublin: Four Courts Press, 1999), 127–57 (pp. 137–42).

[62] Spenser (1978), 17.

Central to his plans for Ireland was the establishment of a central, male authority at liberty to act with relative autonomy from the queen:

> this shoulde be one principall in the Appointement of the Lord deputies aucthoritye that it shoulde be more ample and absolute then it is and that he shoulde have uncomptrolled power to doe anie thinge that he with the Advizement of the Councell shoulde thinke mete to be done for it is not possible for the Councell heare [in England] to directe a governour theare whoe shalbe forced oftentimes to followe the necessitye of present occasions and to take the sodaine advantage of time which beinge once loste will not be recovered. (*Prose*, 229)

The effect is greatly reinforced by the call for the appointment of a strong 'Lord Liuetennante'—conceived as a sort of Vice Regent—to underwrite the Lord Deputy's power by working to 'defende the good Course of that governement againste all maligners' (*Prose*, 228).

Close analysis of Spenser's defence of Grey illustrates the process whereby the historical figure was transformed into the fictional hero. The decision to make him 'equal to Arthur' may have been suggested by his association with the English version of Leland's *Assertio Inclytissimi Arturii* (1582), a work dedicated to him by the translator. As presented in *A View*, he appears as a man of 'heroicke spirite' endowed with all of the qualities that confer epic stature (*Prose*, 162). Though 'blotted with the name of a bloddye man' he was 'gentle affable Lovinge and temperate' and 'so farr from delightinge in blodd that oftentimes he suffered not iuste vengeance to fall wheare it was deserved' (*Prose*, 160). By this account he displayed the ideal Ficinian blend of masculine courage and feminine temperance and was therefore the ideal 'patron of justice'. This is hardly the impression created by Grey's activities but it accurately reflects his self-image. 'I fear', he told the queen, 'I shall do your Highness little service amongst them [the Irish], for certainly a hard and forcible hand I too well find must bring them to duty, which I confess falls not with my nature.'[63] In the same letter, however, he proceeds to recount the details of the massacre at Smerwick. Reviewing the campaign after his recall, he estimated the number of dead at 1,485 but this was 'not accounting those of the meaner sort nor yet executions by lawe and killing of churles, the accompt of which is beesides number'.[64] In retrospect it seems evident that the very strength of Grey's religious convictions rendered him uniquely unsuited to his position. He was very much a Cromwell before his time.

---

[63] SP 63/78/29 (attributed to Spenser by Smith).   [64] SP 63/106/62.

Spenser has much to say of the dangers of clemency, yet even he sensed that something untoward had happened to Grey in Ireland. Writing from similar colonial experience, Las Casas had warned of the moral degeneration incident to the business of conquest. 'The longer men have operated in the New World', he observed, 'and the more they have become accustomed to the carnage and butchery around them, the more brutal and the more wicked have been the crimes they commit against God and their fellow-men.'[65] There is much to suggest that Spenser recognized the validity of this argument. Indeed he was one of the first Englishmen to recognize it, and book five may consequently be ranked amongst the earliest precursors of Conrad's *Heart of Darkness*. The very location of the Irena episode within the 'Legend of Justice' risks, if not promotes, exposure of the moral vulnerability that Irenius's rhetoric is designed to occlude. But the policy's loss was the poetry's gain. In attempting to justify the ways of Grey to man Spenser embarked on a profoundly disturbing exploration of colonial policy.[66] He was uncomfortably aware of how the experience of the Irish campaign had altered the nature of his epic hero, almost to the point of parodic inversion. When discussing the 'sinister suggestions of Crueltye' attaching to Grey's reputation (*Prose*, 162), Irenius describes how 'the necessitye of that presente state of thinges forced him to that violence and allmoste Changed his verye naturall disposicion' (*Prose*, 160). The final clause of this chilling sentence cannot but prompt speculation upon the nature of a 'salvage knight' whose success depends upon the suppression of 'pittie'—a quality elsewhere identified as a hallmark of humanity (6. 4. 3). It was, after all, allegedly characteristic of the Gaelic Irish to show themselves 'mercyles where they overcome, which is declaration that ther vallour is but barbarous'.[67]

On his first entrance into *The Faerie Queene*—significantly as an enemy to the Knights of Maydenhead—Artegall appears to be undergoing a sort of Ovidian metamorphosis into the 'salvage' landscape surrounding him:

> For all his armour was like salvage weed,
> With woody mosse bedight, and all his steed

[65] Las Casas (1992), 103.
[66] For Spenser's relationship to Grey see H. S. V. Jones, 'Spenser's Defence of Lord Grey', *University of Illinois Studies in Language and Literature*, 5 (1919), 7–75; Vincent P. Carey and Clare Carroll, 'Factions and Fictions: Spenser's Reflections of and on Elizabethan Politics', in Anderson (ed.), *Spenser's Life and the Subject of Biography*, 31–44.
[67] Dawtrey (1995), 103.

With oaken leaves attrapt, that seemed fit
For salvage wight, and thereto well agreed
His word, which on his ragged shield was writ,
Salvagesse sans finesse, shewing secret wit.

(4. 4. 39)

The nature of the motto's 'secret wit' (and who better to devise it than
Grey's secretary?) doubtless relates to the extent to which Artegall's outward appearance reveals or obscures his inner nature. Were the normal
expectations of chivalric pageantry to be fulfilled, the 'quyent disguise' of
salvagesse sans finesse would prove to be an instance of 'finesse'. Gheer-
aedts's extraordinary portrait of Captain Thomas Lee—an English
gentleman standing in an Irish wilderness as bare-legged as any kern—
suggests that such paradoxical depictions were currently in vogue.[68] But
there is more to Spenser's 'darke conceit' than mere fashion, and it is hard
to resist the suspicion that his depiction of Artegall responds to the 'violence' that 'allmoste Changed' Lord Grey's 'verye naturall disposicion'.
The figure of the 'salvage knight' explores the consequences of Irenius's
words, implicitly recognizing the possibility that 'Artegall' may have become as 'salvage' as his opponents, that his 'ragged shield' took its character from Ireland's 'ragged common-weale' (5. 12. 26). But the figure of
'Talus' seems equally designed to deflect that recognition. Overtly at least,
violence cannot be allowed to corrupt an epic hero's 'naturall disposicion'.
Another character must bear the burden of blood-guilt and who better
than an 'iron' man incapable of self-recrimination? Artegall is commonly
portrayed as attempting to restrain Talus, especially during the Irena
episode where he informs Grantorto that it was 'not for such slaughters
sake | He thether came, but for to trie the right | Of fayre *Irenaes* cause
with him in single fight' (5. 12. 8). Fiction here takes leave of reality and we
are invited to view the episode in strictly conceptual terms as a conflict
between 'justice' and 'tort', a conflict in which the only casualties are
'monsters'. Grey himself cultivated a similar abstraction, justifying the
execution of one chieftain's hostages by asserting that 'I committed to
Justice his first Pledges'.[69] In the real world, however, such decisions
are made by judges not 'justice' and, if Spenser's allegory is to retain any
objective correlative, Talus must correspond to some human agency.

[68] See Hiram Morgan, 'Tom Lee: the Posing Peacemaker', in Brendan Bradshaw, Andrew
Hadfield, and Willy Maley (eds.), *Representing Ireland: Literature and the Origins of Conflict,
1534–1660* (Cambridge: Cambridge University Press, 1993), 132–65.
[69] Murdin (1759), 362.

Comparison with Camões is instructive at this point for a similar unease is detectable in *Os Lusíadas*. There is abundant evidence that Camões privately deplored much that he publicly idealized. He was profoundly disturbed by the massacre at Chembé in 1553 and expressed his disgust at the corruption of the colonial administration in his 'Disparates da India' ['Follies in India'] and the uncompromising sonnet 'Cá nesta Babilónia' ['Here in this Babylon']. The mysterious 'old man of venerable aspect' who, at the close of the epic's fourth canto, condemns Da Gama's enterprise as motivated by greed and promoted by cruelty, may therefore be seen to articulate many of the poet's own misgivings. The various 'hermit' figures who interrupt the action and interrogate the ethos of *The Faerie Queene* may well serve a similar function for Spenser.[70] They acknowledge the knights', and possibly also the text's, 'sins' even as they bestow an empowering absolution.

In retrospect Grey came to 'accurse' his appointment to Ireland and to fall back upon the argument that 'successe' was the 'uniustest measure' of loyal service.[71] Spenser admits that his patron failed in his attempt to 're-form' Ireland, but blames that failure in both verse and prose on the malice of powerful enemies at court. By portraying them as Envie and Detraction he seeks to discredit their allegations in the very utterance.[72] They continued to have wide currency even after Grey's death, however, and he was commonly believed to have stained 'that bright sword, the sword of Justice . . . In guiltlesse blood of many an innocent' (5. 12. 40). In Spenser's immediate circle, by contrast, there was little doubt that the real cause of Grey's downfall was the queen. According to Lodowick Bryskett, she had denied him the resources to reward his followers and recalled him without due consideration to the state of the country. Given the proper support, he was a minister 'whose wisdome might . . . governe a whole Empyre'.[73] The fairy queen had undone the imperial cause. Five years later, in the aftermath of Mary Queen of Scots' execution, Grey vigorously defended the secretary who had allegedly dispatched the death warrant without Elizabeth's knowledge. He would not condemn a man who had acted against the queen's orders but in her own best interests and

---

[70] Camões (1952), 119–21. See Henry H. Hart, *Luis de Camoëns and The Epic of the Lusiads* (Norman: University of Oklahoma Press, 1962), 98–101, 124–6. See below p. 215.

[71] SP 63/87/29 (not in Spenser's hand).

[72] 'Moste untrewlye and malitiouslye do these evill tonges backebite and slaunder the sacred ashes of that most iuste and honorable personage' (*Prose*, 162).

[73] Bryskett (1927), 39. Grey made the same points, SP 63/88/39 (attributed to Spenser by Smith).

those of Protestantism.[74] The case resembled his own: 'though I have not
followed that your Highness direction', he told Elizabeth, 'the glory of
God, your Highness honour, and well willing to a true reformation of this
most forwandered state, are the causes of yt.'[75] Spenser accurately
portrays his attitude in *The Faerie Queene* by representing Artegall as im-
placably 'bent' upon Duessa's death in 'zeale of Iustice' (5. 9. 49)—professions of 'zeal' being frequent in the letters he had penned on Grey's behalf.
Only within the fiction of *The Faerie Queene* could his royal lady be seen
to fulfil the heroic expectations of her more 'zealous' subjects—and increasingly not even there.

[74] See Richard A. McCabe, 'The Masks of Duessa: Spenser, Mary Queen of Scots, and James
VI', *ELR* 17 (1987), 224–42 (pp. 238–9).
[75] SP 63/86/50 (attributed to Spenser by Smith).

Part III: *The Faerie Queene* (1590)

5   *St George for Ireland*

ABOUT a month after Lord Grey's arrival in Ireland, Sir William Pelham,
then President of Munster, issued a proclamation requiring 'every hors-
mane' in the service of the crown 'both Englishe and Irishe' to display 'two
rede crosses, either of Silke or Cloth, the one to be fastened on the breste,
the other on the backe'.[1] On his first visit to the province in which he
would finally take up residence, Spenser could have seen bands of 'Redcross knights' pricking across the plains of Desmond in pursuit of what
the Lord Deputy regarded as the papal dragon. By happy coincidence a
winged dragon was indeed the emblem of Pope Gregory XIII, the pontiff
who, according to Grey's personal account of the matter, dispatched the
mercenaries he had put to death at Smerwick.[2] Pelham's proclamation
serves to remind us that 'The Legend of Holinesse' is not, as has often
been claimed, exclusively related to the history of England. Nor could it
be. 'St George' had wandered further afield. 'That the State might not
seeme utterly to neglect the defence of the Pale,' records Sir John Davies,
'there was a fraternity of men at armes, called the *Brother-hood of S.
George*, erected by Parlament, the 14. of *Edward* the fourth, consisting of
thirteene the most Noble and woorthy persons within the foure shires
. . . These and their successors, were to meet yearely upon *S. Georges* day;
and to choose one of themselves to be Captaine of that Brother-hood, for

<hr>

[1] For Pelham's proclamation see Roland M. Smith, 'Origines Arthurianae: The Two Crosses
of Spenser's Red Cross Knight', *JEGP* 54 (1955), 670–83 (pp. 673–4).
[2] Robert J. Clements, 'Iconography on the Nature and Inspiration of Poetry in Renaissance
Emblem Literature', *PMLA* 70 (1955), 781–804 (p. 792).

the next yeare to come.'³ The set-up is familiar to any reader of *The Faerie Queene* and was doubtless influential upon its author. Here we have thirteen questing knights, the celebration of an annual feast day that is both national and religious, and the choice of one predominant knight for each new year—or should we say for each new year's adventures?

The original members of this 'Brother-hood of S. George' were drawn from the ranks of the Old English, including the Geraldines, and therein lay the government's problem. The majority of their descendants had rejected the Reformation. Despite the best efforts of Prince Arthur's Tudor successors, the Irish 'St George', who was 'English' by blood but not by birth, continued to believe that 'Duessa' was 'Fidessa'. Their loyalty to 'Una' was correspondingly doubtful and the excommunication of the queen in 1570 only served to make matters worse. The papal bull 'Regnans in Excelsis' formally pronounced Elizabeth's deposition and absolved her subjects from all duties of obedience. Thereafter Catholicism could be regarded as potentially treasonable per se. It is particularly noteworthy in this regard that the letters dispatched by Duessa in an attempt to frustrate Una's union with St George claim that he has plighted his troth not only 'unto another love' but, more significantly, 'to another land' (1. 12. 26).⁴ During the Nine Years' War every effort was made to draw the Catholic Old English into an alliance with their Gaelic co-religionists in defence of 'faith and fatherland' ['creideamh agus athardha'].⁵ According to Fynes Moryson, the 'grand cause' of their 'alienation' from the New English was their 'firme consent' with the Gaelic Irish 'in the Roman Religion'.⁶ This was to overstate the case but not the fear. The notion of Ireland as a pan-Catholic 'fatherland' was terrifying to the New English but took many decades to mature.⁷ Since 'athardha' could mean both 'fatherland', in the sense of Ireland, and 'fathers' lands', in the sense of familial domain, the very word intended to arouse an embryonic form of 'nationalism' also connoted the local loyal-

---

³ Davies (1612), 61–2.

⁴ In the months prior to Spenser's arrival in Ireland Walsingham claimed that 'infinite' copies of defamatory papal letters were circulating in the country. See Hogan and O'Farrell (1959), 167, 178. One of Spenser's secretarial letters notes Hugh O'Donnell's receipt of a letter from the Holy See (SP 63/91/26).

⁵ See Mícheál Mac Craith, 'The Gaelic Reaction to the Reformation', in Steven G. Ellis and Sarah Barber (eds.), *Conquest and Union: Fashioning a British State, 1485–1725* (London: Longman, 1995), 139–61 (pp. 147–8, 156).

⁶ Moryson (1903), 211.

⁷ See Brendan Bradshaw, *The Irish Constitutional Revolution of the Sixteenth Century* (Cambridge: Cambridge University Press, 1979), 276–88.

ties than impeded it.[8] Even during the Nine Years' War rival claimants to Gaelic and Old English chieftaincies were all too willing to prosecute their claims with English support.

By the time Spenser arrived in Ireland, the official celebration of St George's Day had been appropriated to a New English, and staunchly Protestant, cause. Sir Henry Sidney took particular pains to observe the occasion in such a manner as to reflect an implicit association between loyalty and Protestantism, a tradition eagerly continued by Lord Grey.[9] Both were disposed to assess the worth of their Irish subjects by their 'willingness to become English'.[10] But, as the 'Legend of Holinesse' reminds us, becoming 'English'—or at least becoming aware of one's Englishness—necessitates the rejection of 'Duessa' and all that she represents. On the Mount of Contemplation the Redcross Knight experiences a moment of apocalyptic epiphany in which he discovers his personal, national, and spiritual identity simultaneously, and the simultaneity is allegorically functional in that all three are regarded as inherently interdependent:

> For thou emongst those Saints, whom thou doest see,
> Shalt be a Saint, and thine owne nations frend
> And Patrone: thou Saint *George* shalt called bee,
> Saint *George* of mery England, the signe of victoree.

> (1. 10. 61)

'In hoc signo vinces', one might say, except that the Garter 'George' has now replaced Constantine's mystical cross. In order to undermine these grandiose pretensions Gaelic historians such as Ó Súilleabháin Béarra ridiculed the traditional account of the origin of the Garter as a tale of bawdry.[11] Nor did the festivities themselves go unchallenged. The celebrations of 1600, for example, suffered an embarrassing subversion of official symbolism. One of the Butler poets notes that in 1588 the Earl of Ormond 'received the Knighthood of the Garter as a mark of his distinction, an unusual honour for an Irishman' ['Fuair sé d'airdchéim Ridireacht Gáirtéir, | ainm nár ghnáth é ar Éirionnach'].[12] Thereafter, Peter

---

[8] After the Battle of Kinsale, it was considered best that 'each prince and each lord of a district should return to defend his own patrimony ['a athardha']' rather than pursue a united campaign. Ó Clérigh (1948–57), i. 338, 339.

[9] See Sir Roy Strong, *The Cult of Elizabeth: Elizabethan Portraiture and Pageantry* (London: Thames and Hudson, 1977), 175. For Lord Grey's observance of St George's Day see Bryskett (1927), 22.

[10] Sir Henry Sidney (1857), 311.   [11] O'Sullivan Beare (196c), p. xxx.

[12] Carney (1945), 74. Ormond was reputed to wear his George even in bed. See Cyril Falls, 'Black Tom of Ormonde', *The Irish Sword*, 5 (1961–2), 10–22 (p. 20).

Lombard records, he was accustomed 'to celebrate the feast [of St George] with great pomp and circumstance, in a splendid and magnificent palace that he had at Kilkenny'. In order to prevent this, he was captured en route 'and the golden garter which is the insignia of that English military order was seized, and he was detained in Leix until the feast of St George, which in his presence and view was there celebrated in Catholic fashion [Catholico ritu]'. In this manner, Lombard notes, the festival of St George was restored to 'its ancient, and still, Catholic rites'.[13] The point is shrewdly made. The practice of promoting a Protestant cause through the celebration of a Roman Catholic 'saint' was one, as we shortly shall see, that offended many of Spenser's fellow countrymen.

The tradition of the 'Irish' St George reached its apogee a few months after Spenser's death in the extravagant celebrations hosted by the Earl of Essex. A contemporary ballad accurately captures their political import:

> Of ioyfull triumphes I must speake,
> Which our *english* friends did make,
> For that renowned mayden's sake,
>   that weares the crowne of *England.*
> In *Ireland* S[ain]ct *George's* Day
> Was honored bravelye every waye,
> By lords and knights in rich array,
>   as though they had been in *England.*
> *Therefore let all trew English men,*
> *With every faythfull subiect then,*
> *Unto my prayers say Amen!*
>   *Now God and s[ain]ct George for England!*[14]

The juxtaposing of 'England' and 'Ireland' throughout this ballad, and the insistence that all ceremonies be observed 'as though they had been in *England*', serves to remind us that Ireland was commonly viewed as a 'proving ground' for English identity, as the place where a 'clownishe younge man', like the untested Redcrosse Knight, was most likely to 'prove his puissance in battell brave' and win his spurs (1. 1. 3).[15] This, as E.K. might have said, was 'no poetical fiction'.[16] Knighthoods were bestowed with uncommon frequency in the Irish service, often to the queen's displeasure.[17] If it was 'even the other daye since Englande grewe Civill', it was scarcely a few hours since it grew Protestant (*Prose*, 118). By

---

[13] Lombard (1930), 87–8.   [14] Clark (1907), 321–6 (p. 322).
[15] See Spenser (1978), 17.   [16] See E.K.'s gloss to *The Shepheardes Calender*, 'June', 18.
[17] For the conferring of knighthoods see Holinshed (1808), i. 267.

converting others it could 'prove' the security of its own profession and establish its imperial credentials. Assuming the role of Prince Arthur, the Protestant New English would redeem the Catholic Old English, the old 'St George', from 'thraldome' to Rome. Success or failure in Ireland reflected upon the great 'national' project, the creation of a Protestant 'empire' under the crown. The Essex ballad ends with the hope that 'the Traytor, base Terone' and all of his accomplices will soon suffer defeat. Like his father before him, however, Essex experienced nothing but failure in Ireland. The land of opportunity was also the land of disenchantment, a place in which reputations were more commonly lost than won. Holinshed records how the first Earl of Essex came close to 'the gulfe of despaire'—like Spenser's St George—and a remarkably similar fate overtook his son.[18] His ignominious failure disproved the current prophecy that in 1599 'the Irish shall tire all and some | St Patrick to St George a horseboye shalbe sene'.[19] When Tyrone was eventually defeated by Lord Mountjoy, however, a revisionist ballad duly represented the event as a victory for England, God and 'St George'.[20]

The battle against Roman Catholicism was worldwide but Ireland was the theatre of conflict in which Spenser was directly engaged and, in so far as the pursuit of 'holinesse' entails a rejection of 'Duessa', book one inevitably concerns itself with the site of that rejection. Grey's actions at Smerwick were reportedly prompted by the sight of 'the Pope's banner' flying over the inner fort, and matters were not helped by the Earl of Desmond's alleged declaration that he and his allies 'were all entered into the defense of the catholike faith, with great authoritie both from the popes holinesse and king Philip'.[21] Spenser obliquely applies the allegory of 'holinesse' to Ireland when he has Irenius explain the history of the Irish Church to Eudoxus. According to this account, St Patrick, 'beinge by nacion a Britton', brought Christianity to Ireland at a time when 'religion was generallie Corrupted with . . . Popishe trumperie, Therefore what other Coulde they learne then suche trashe as was taughte them, And drinke of that Cupp of fornicacion with which the purple Harlott had then made all nacions drunken' (*Prose*, 137). One remembers Duessa's 'golden cup' of 'secret poyson' (1. 8. 14). Like the dissolute St George who drinks from a spiritually debilitating spring (1. 7. 4–6), the Old English have 'tasted' corruption from the Gaelic well: 'they drunke not from the

---

[18] Holinshed (1808), vi. 374.
[19] For the prophecy see 'A Brief Note of Ireland' (*Prose*, 245).
[20] Clark (1907), 123–8 (p. 125).   [21] Holinshed (1808), vi. 428.

pure springe of life but onelye tasted of suche trobled waters as weare broughte unto them, the druggs theareof have bred greate Contagion in theire Soules the which . . . Cannot but onelye with verye stronge purgacions be Clensed and Carryed awaie' (*Prose*, 137–8). According to St George's spiritual guide, only 'chosen people purg'd from sinfull guilt' can enter, or even glimpse, the Protestant New Jerusalem (1. 10. 57). In his own troops Grey detected clear signs of election.[22] By stark contrast, the descendants of the Irish 'St George' remained locked in the Dungeon of Ignorance, but could not be exonerated on that account: 'for the sinne or ignoraunce of the Priestes shall not excuse the people nor the auctoritye of the greate Pastor Peters successours shall not excuse the priestes but they shall all dye in theire sinnes for they have all erred and gone out of the waye togeather' (*Prose*, 138). The knight errant had become the knight aberrant but, through the kindly offices of Prince Arthur (a hero of St Patrick's own 'nation'), all might yet be well.

The relevant paradigm was established in 1553 with the publication of *The Vocacyon of Johan Bale to the Bishoprick of Ossorie in Ireland*. The woodcut on the title page displays two contrasting figures, 'The English Christian' and 'The Irishe Papist' (Fig. 9). The one is meek and civil, like the sheep that shelters by his legs, the other violent and savage, like the wolf that accompanies him. If God is an Englishman, the Devil is an Irishman. Bale's 'vocacyon' is to bring the Christian civility of 'our nacion' to the 'wilde nacyon' amongst whom he has fallen, 'to preache the . . . Gospel to the Irishe heathens which never hearde of it afore'. He regards 'Papists' as idolatrous 'paganes'.[23] *The Faerie Queene* similarly envisages a world divided between civil Christians and barbarous Infidels, a pattern established in Ariosto and Tasso but ingeniously adapted to a crusade far closer to home. To attempt 'to fashion a gentleman or noble person in vertuous and gentle discipline' in an Irish context was to confront a people who were 'all Papistes by theire profession but in the same so blindelye and brutishly enformed . . . that ye woulde rather thinke them *Atheists* or infidles' (*Prose*, 136). Civil 'fashions' rapidly degrade into colonial 'disciplines' when transplanted to such an alien environment. Here it is savage Gaels and degenerate 'Englishe Irishe' who must, in the words of Irenius, be 'framed and fashoned' in order to draw them 'from theire delighte of licentious barbarisme unto the love of goodnes and Civilitye' (*Prose*, 54, 240). The point was well taken on the opposing side. Ó Súilleabháin Béarra's *Historiae Catholicae Iberniae Compendium* (1621) presents the

---

[22] See SP 63/78/29.   [23] Bale (1990), 33, 43, 58, 84.

The vocacyon
of Joh̄a Bale to the
bischopzick of Ossozie in Jre
lāde his perfecuciōs in ẏ fame/ẓ
finall delyueraunce.

The English Chziftiā / The Jrifhe Papift.

¶ God hath deliuered me from the fnare of the
hunter/ẓ frō ẏ noyfome peftilēce. Pfal. xcj.
¶ Jf J muft nedes reiopce/ J wil reiopce
of myne infirmytees. ij. Coz. xj.

9. John Bale, *The Vocacyon of Johan Bale* (1553). Title page.

Irish conflict as an episode in the struggle for worldwide Counter-
Reformation.[24] The parties are 'Catholics' and 'Heretics' and Philip IV,
to whom the treatise is dedicated, is urged to resume his grandfather's
interventionist policies on the grounds that it would be preferable for
Ireland to become part of a universal Catholic empire than remain under
Protestant sway. The author was one of the first Irishmen to be knighted
by a Spanish monarch.[25]

The Irish context of *The Faerie Queene* is signalled at the outset by the
inclusion of dedicatory sonnets to Grey, Ormond, and Sir John Norris.
The latter was Lord President of Munster but was relieved of duty in order
to serve in the Netherlands. During his absence, Spenser acted as secretary to the Council of Munster under his brother Sir Thomas Norris, a
fellow 'undertaker' in the plantation. Collectively these sonnets attest to a
desperate sense of cultural isolation in a 'savadge soyle, far from Parnasso
mount' where the 'civilizing' effects of poetry are locked in unremitting
conflict with the 'degenerative' effects of cultural assimilation. But
sharply counterpointed against these three 'Ovidian' sonnets written, as it
were, 'ex Ponto', are a set of 'Virgilian' counterparts addressed to the
leading courtiers of the day. The sequence begins with a sonnet to Sir
Christopher Hatton designed to emphasize the relationship between imperialism, poetry, and patronage. The 'prudent heads' who 'taught ambi-
tious *Rome* to tyrannise | And in the neck of all the world to rayne' drew
pleasure and inspiration from epic verse: 'So *Ennius* the elder Africane, |
So *Maro* oft did *Cæsars* cares allay'. Ennius gave Rome its first national
epic and was patronized by Scipio Africanus; Virgil celebrated the birth of
empire and won the favour of Augustus. The detail is carefully chosen.
Hatton was yet another of Spenser's fellow 'undertakers' with a 'seignory'
of some twelve thousand acres.[26] As a senior member of the Privy Council, he was perfectly placed to espouse the cause of a 'national' poet writing from the permeable borders of an emergent 'empire'. The same might
be said of Sir Francis Walsingham, one of the principal architects of the

[24] See Ruth Dudley Edwards, 'Ireland, Elizabeth I, and the Counter-Reformation', in
S. T. Bindoff, J. Hurstfield, and C. H. Williams (eds.), *Elizabethan Government and Society.
Essays Presented to Sir John Neale* (London: Athlone Press, 1961), 315–39; John Bossy, 'The
Counter-Reformation and the People of Catholic Ireland, 1596–1641', *Historical Studies; Papers
Read before the Irish Conference of Historians*, 8 (1971), 155–69.

[25] See Clare Carroll, 'Irish and Spanish Cultural and Political Relations in the Work of
O'Sullivan Beare', in Hiram Morgan (ed.), *Political Ideology in Ireland, 1541–1641* (Dublin: Four
Courts Press, 1999), 229–53 (p. 248).

[26] Michael MacCarthy-Morrogh, *The Munster Plantation: English Migration to Southern
Ireland 1583–1641* (Oxford: Clarendon Press, 1986), 40–1.

plantation, who is reminded of how Maecenas 'aduaunst' Virgil 'to great *Augustus* grace' thereby fostering a talent which might otherwise 'have lien in silence bace, | Ne bene so much admir'd of later age'. The New English Virgil 'flies for like aide unto your Patronage; | That are the great *Mecenas* of this age'. Together with Lord Burghley, Walsingham had personally overseen the administration of Irish affairs for some dozen years and was intimately acquainted with every aspect of the government's policy. He had also been an 'undertaker' for a brief period before financial pressures forced him to withdraw.[27] There is, therefore, a precise correlation in the dedicatory sonnets between the imagery of imperial patronage and the matter of Ireland. It is in no sense coincidental that Spenser addresses the prefatory letter 'expounding his whole intention' to Sir Walter Ralegh, Grey's henchman at Smerwick, and now in possession of some 42,000 acres of Munster soil, the single largest 'seignory' in the plantation. The estate eventually passed to Richard Boyle, first Earl of Cork, and a close kinsman of Spenser's second wife. Ralegh was widely acknowledged as the foremost exponent of Elizabethan expansionism but, as *Colin Clouts Come Home Againe* suggests, he was important to Spenser primarily for combining an interest in Ireland with privileged access to the queen, for his ability, when in favour, to join the margins of the empire to its centre. Paradoxically, the 'Irish' context of *The Faerie Queene* functions very much as an intrinsic expression of its 'Englishness'.

C. S. Lewis famously suggested that '*The Faerie Queene* should perhaps be regarded as the work of one who is turning into an Irishman' but it would be more accurate to regard it as the work of one who feared that his descendants might turn into Irishmen.[28] The New English were far from immune to the wiles of 'Duessa'. In 1595 Sir John Dowdall complained of how 'young men both of the Irish *and English* nation' travelled to the continent 'in the company of Jesuits' only to return to Ireland 'to seduce the people to disobedience and rebellion'.[29] Living 'downe in a dale, hard by a forests side', Archimago, who fashions both the false St George and the phantasmal Una, looks suspiciously like a caricature of a seminary priest—'he told of Saintes and Popes, and evermore | He strowd an *Ave-Mary* after and before' (I. I. 34–5).[30] Typical of the kind—and a possible

[27] Michael MacCarthy-Morrogh, *The Munster Plantation: English Migration to Southern Ireland 1583–1641* (Oxford: Clarendon Press, 1986), 39–40.

[28] C. S. Lewis, *Studies in Medieval and Renaissance Literature* (Cambridge: Cambridge University Press, 1966), 126. See below pp. 284–6.

[29] Maxwell (1923), 147.

[30] See *Prose*, 136.

model for Archimago—was the Jesuit James Archer who even attempted to convert, or reconvert, the Earl of Ormond to Catholicism. 'He was held not merely in awe by the heretics', writes Ó Súilleabháin Béarra, 'but even in a kind of admiration or superstitious terror and they believed him able to walk dry-footed over the sea; to fly through the air; and to possess other superhuman power, arguing thence that he ought to be called Archdevil rather than Archer.'[31] In view of the ever-present Spanish threat, it was well understood that Ireland's religious character might eventually determine England's political destiny.[32] Irish ports offered a perfect 'ingate to the Spanniarde' (*Prose*, 194). 'The Legend of Holinesse' prefaces St George's slaying of the Dragon with the prospect of a final battle 'twixt that great faery Queene and Paynim king'—undoubtedly Elizabeth I and Philip II (1. 11. 7). But recusants constituted a dangerous fifth column within the fairy queen's domains, and it was widely known that large numbers of them had taken refuge in Ireland. Fynes Moryson attributed the failure of the Munster plantation to the number of 'papists' amongst the undertakers.[33] His account is undoubtedly exaggerated, but it illustrates the common perception of Ireland as a receptacle for politically disaffected Catholics. Those who fled there did so with good reason for, as John Lynch notes, although Catholicism was notionally proscribed at the beginning of Elizabeth's reign, 'no statute was passed, in any subsequent Parliament, abolishing the profession of the Catholic faith'.[34] Catholics were 'borne with for their conscience sake' in Ireland and yet, observed Robert Payne, 'from such consciences spring all the Traiterous practises agaynst her Maiestie'.[35]

The contrasting figures of Una and Duessa, about whom so much of the 'Legend of Holinesse' is structured, owe a considerable debt to Bale's *Image of Both Churches* (1548) which takes the form of a commentary on Revelation. Bale is concerned to distinguish the Whore of Babylon (the 'Romish Religion') from the Woman Clothed with the Sun ('the true Christian church') but, as Claire McEachern has argued, the contrast is everywhere beset by misgivings concerning the contemporary state of the Anglican Church.[36] *The Vocacyon of Johan Bale* concludes by switching its attention from the Church of Ireland to the Church of England, the

---

[31] O'Sullivan Beare (1903), 123. See Thomas Morrissey, *James Archer of Kilkenny* (Dublin: Studies Special Publications, 1979), 4–5, 22–6.

[32] MacCarthy-Morrogh, *The Munster Plantation*, 193–4.   [33] Moryson (1903), 209.

[34] Lynch (1848), i. 33.   [35] Payne (1589), 8.

[36] Bale (1849), 404–5, 495–7; Claire McEachern, *The Poetics of English Nationhood, 1590–1612* (Cambridge: Cambridge University Press, 1996), 29–30.

supposedly 'elect vyneyarde' that has 'brought fourth ydolatrie'. It objects, in particular, to the continuing cult of the saints and inveighs against 'subtylle devysers of sanctes legendes' and 'subtile allegories'.[37] Read in such a context, Spenser's allegorical 'legend' of St George may be seen to encapsulate the dilemma of a Church caught in an ill-defined 'via media' between the iconology of Rome and the iconoclasm of Geneva. The Protestantism that the New English sought to impose upon Ireland was deeply fissured and wracked by internal dissension and schism, and the figure that Spenser selected to 'patronize' reform—a figure from the *Golden Legend* whose image was venerated in Catholic churches throughout the continent—threatens to compromise the very values he represents. On this level the poem seems to be imaginatively rooted in the ethos it deplores.

The figure of the queen posed similar problems. Radical Protestants objected to the Order of the Garter (and the associated observance of St George's Day) because of its potentially 'idolatrous' associations with the discredited cult of the saints, and the 'cult' of Elizabeth spawned discontent in similar circles precisely because it was thought to be developing into a 'cult'.[38] In Ireland the matter was even more divisive. At the outset of the Desmond wars, James Fitzmaurice, echoing the terms of 'Regnans in Excelsis', invited the insurgents to disclaim allegiance to 'that she-tyrant' who 'by refusing to hear Christ in the person of His vicar, and even by daring to subject the Church of Christ to the ruling of a woman in matters of faith, on which she has no right to pronounce, has deservedly forfeited her royal authority'.[39] At about the same time Viscount Baltinglass told the Earl of Ormond that 'a woman, uncapax of all holy orders' could never be acknowledged as head of the Church.[40] The Elizabethan settlement had anticipated such objections, and the title of 'supreme governor' rather than 'supreme head' of the Church served, amongst other things, as a concession to male sensibilities, but the distinction did little to reassure the sceptical.[41] The Jesuit Nicholas Sander, bitterly described

[37] Bale (1990), 45, 46, 86.

[38] Strong, *Cult of Elizabeth*, 166, 178. For Elizabeth's association with the Order of the Garter see Robin Headlam Wells, *Spenser's 'Faerie Queene' and the Cult of Elizabeth* (London: Croom Helm, 1983), 98–9.

[39] See Myles V. Ronan, *The Reformation in Ireland under Elizabeth 1558–1580* (London: Longmans, Green, 1930), 620. See Wallace MacCaffrey, *Elizabeth I* (London: Edward Arnold, 1993), 328.

[40] *Cal. Car. MSS* (1575–88), 289.

[41] Parker (1853), 66. See also Philippa Berry, *Of Chastity and Power: Elizabethan Literature and the Unmarried Queen* (London: Routledge, 1989), 68–73.

by Lord Grey as the Desmonds' 'honest apostle', vigorously defended Elizabeth's excommunication in *De Visibili Monarchia Ecclesiae* (1573) and proceeded in *De Origine et Progressu Schismati Anglicani* (1585) to represent the spiritual ascendancy of a female monarch as a divine judgement upon the English nation.[42] Edward Rishton endorsed the notion on the grounds that Elizabeth 'on account of her sex, never could be a minister of the Word, without which the government of the Church becomes impossible'.[43] It was an opinion with which many radical Protestants had considerable sympathy, although they were forced to concede exceptional status to those who acted as 'nursing mothers' to the Protestant faith.[44] Sander found a ready answer to such devices in the allegation that Anne Boleyn was the natural daughter of Henry VIII and, consequently, that the Church of England's 'nursing mother' was the contaminated offspring of incest. Outside the Pale 'Archimagos' such as Archer and Sander reified the worst fears of Spenserian allegory by demeaning Una's public image (both sexually and politically) in order to suggest that 'St George' had made the wrong 'choice of queens' (1. 1. 47–55).

Spenser's St George sets out on the annual feast of the Fairy Queen, an event which recalls the annual festivities of Elizabeth's Accession Day, but in 1582 one Robert Wright, Lord Rich's chaplain, was arrested on the grounds that 'he had spoke some Time ago against keeping the Queen's Day. Which, he said, was, *To make her an Idol*.'[45] Catholic observers shared his misgivings. Rishton complained that Elizabeth's festivities were 'kept with more solemnity throughout the kingdom than the festivals of Christ and of the saints . . . And to show the greater contempt for our Blessed Lady, they keep the birthday of queen Elizabeth in the most solemn way on the 7th day of September, which is the eve of the feast of the Mother of God.'[46] In so far as the 'cult of Elizabeth' consciously or unconsciously appropriated facets of the officially discredited worship of the Blessed Virgin, it could be represented to the queen's Catholic subjects as little more than a blasphemous parody.[47] 'Blessed is he', wrote the Gaelic

---

[42] See Sander (1877), 168. For Grey's assessment of Sander see Grey (1847), 77.

[43] Sander (1877), 237–8.   [44] Knox (1846–64), iv. 357.

[45] For the association with Elizabeth's accession day see Roy C. Strong, 'The Popular Celebration of the Accession Day of Queen Elizabeth I', *Journal of the Warburg and Courtauld Institute*, 21 (1958), 86–103 (pp. 86–7). For Wright's remarks see Strype (1735–7), iii. 123 and (1821), 54–6.

[46] See Sander (1877), 284.

[47] For the association of the virgin queen and the Virgin Mary see Elkin Calhoun Wilson, *England's Eliza* (New York: Octagon Books, 1966—first pub. 1939), 200–29; Frances Yates, *Astraea: The Imperial Theme in the Sixteenth Century* (Harmondsworth: Penguin Books, 1977—

poet Fear Flatha Ó Gnímh, 'who secures the love of the queen . . . for whom I fashion this artful poem . . . I will bind a pact with the sweet virgin-queen to wed whom no man may aspire.'[48] The sentiment is familiar to all readers of Spenser, but Ó Gnímh's 'queen' ['banríon'] is not Elizabeth but the 'Queen of Heaven'. The Counter-Reformation strongly reinforced the traditionally Marian temper of Irish Catholicism and during the Nine Years' War Irish troops were urged to fight for the Blessed Virgin rather than the virgin queen.[49] What many of the New English regarded as 'graven images' of the Virgin Mary were to be seen throughout Ireland, and Gaelic devotional poetry was replete with Marian theology.[50] The battle for the image of Ireland's 'Gloriana' was therefore fought on the issue of idolatry. A case in point was the trial for treason of Sir Brian O'Rourke in 1591. O'Rourke had been knighted by Sir Henry Sidney in 1567 in a characteristic attempt at 'Anglicization' but remained known to his clan as Brian na Múrtha Ó Ruairc, or Brian of the Ramparts, and in that capacity was urged by Tadhg Dall Ó hUiginn to march on Dublin and drown the Pale in blood.[51] During the proceedings he was accused of having 'scornfully dragged the queens picture at a horse-taile, and disgracefully cut the same in pieces'. The Gaelic Irish were thus in the peculiar position of being accused of the idolatrous worship of religious icons on the one hand and of the failure to revere secular icons on the other. When challenged to defend his attitudes, O'Rourke replied that 'there was a great difference between your queen and images of the saints'.[52] Most Roman Catholics would have agreed. Yet perhaps the most disconcerting aspect of the incident for English observers was the alleged complicity in O'Rourke's 'treason of the image' of none other than Elizabeth's own Lord Deputy, Sir John Perrot.[53] That the accusation was undoubtedly false merely serves to emphasize the radical insecurity of the

first pub. 1975), 34–6, 78–9; Helen Hackett, *Virgin Mother, Maiden Queen. Elizabeth I and the Cult of the Virgin Mary* (London: Macmillan, 1995), 1–12 and *passim*.

[48] McKenna (1939–40), i. 274–5; ii. 167–8.

[49] See Colm Lennon, 'The Counter-Reformation in Ireland, 1542–1641', in Ciaran Brady and Raymond Gillespie (eds.), *Natives and Newcomers: Essays on the Making of Irish Colonial Society 1534–1641* (Dublin: Irish Academic Press, 1986), 75–92; O' Sullivan Beare (1903), 127–8.

[50] Peter O'Dwyer, *Mary: A History of Devotion in Ireland* (Dublin: Four Courts Press, 1988), 175–99.

[51] See Ó hUiginn (1922–6), i. 117–19; ii. 77–8.

[52] See Daniel Gallogly, 'Brian of the Ramparts O'Rourke (1566–1591)', *Breifne*, 2 (1962), 50–79; Hiram Morgan, 'Extradition and Treason-Trial of a Gaelic Lord: The Case of Brian O'Rourke', *The Irish Jurist*, 22 (1987), 285–301; Christopher Highley, *Shakespeare, Spenser and the Crisis in Ireland* (Cambridge: Cambridge University Press, 1997), 110–11.

[53] For 'treason of the image' see *CSPI* (1588–92), 405.

colonial regime. In Ireland even a Lord Deputy might become politically 'degenerate'; in Ireland anyone might be transformed into his polar opposite.[54]

Richard Hakluyt reported the near-idolatrous adoration of the queen's portrait amongst the 'salvages' of the Americas, but O'Rourke's riposte to his accusers relocates such 'idolatry' amongst the 'civilized' denizens of the court.[55] The matter was of vital concern in view of Knox's allegation that 'the Empire of a Woman is an Idol'.[56] *The Faerie Queene* is full of 'idols' and the business of discrimination between the 'good' and the 'bad'
T is highly problematic.[57] After her separation from St George, Una, like Revelation's Woman Clothed with the Sun, flies to the wilderness. Unlike her avatar, however, she encounters a 'salvage nation', a 'rude, mishapen, monstrous rablement' of 'woodborne people' remarkably reminiscent of John Derricke's Irish 'woodkerne' (1. 6. 8–16). The term 'salvage nacion', one remembers, is the phrase used to describe the Irish in the opening sentence of *A View*. Una attempts to teach these people 'truth' but instead, like Hakluyt's New World 'savages', they 'worshipt her', turning the would-be agent of reform into 'th'Image of Idolatryes' (1. 6. 19). The allegory at this point is polyvalent and complex but also uncomfortably self-reflexive. In Catholic theology the Woman Clothed with the Sun was often identified with the Virgin Mary, and the 'salvage nacion' amongst whom Spenser lived was commonly accused of the 'horrible blasphemie' of 'the worshippinge of our ladyes ymage'.[58] Considered exclusively from this viewpoint, the episode reads like an assault on the excesses of Marian devotion. The idolatry of the 'woodborne people' who are represented as half-bestial 'satyrs' proceeds from their lack of civility. They are capable only of 'barbarous truth', dim intimations of Christian verity (1. 6. 12). Irish Catholicism may therefore be regarded as the spiritual expression of the 'Ignorance of the people', satisfying a primitive need for painted idols and talismans (*Prose*, 138–9). Protestantism, by implication, is the spiritual expression of civil enlightenment. Una is eventually rescued by Sir

---

[54] Pauline Henley, 'The Treason of Sir John Perrot', *Studies: An Irish Quarterly Review*, 21 (1932): 404–22; Hiram Morgan, 'The Fall of Sir John Perrot', in John Guy (ed.), *The Reign of Elizabeth I: Court and Culture in the Last Decade* (Cambridge: Cambridge University Press, 1995), 109–25 (pp. 119–20). Perrot was also accused of failing to suppress the seditious slanders of Gaelic 'rhymers' (p. 118).

[55] Hakluyt (1903–5), x. 354.   [56] Knox (1846–64), iv. 391. See also pp. 413–14.

[57] See Kenneth Gross, *Spenserian Poetics: Idolatry, Iconoclasm and Magic* (Ithaca, NY: Cornell University Press, 1985), 27–77; Ernest B. Gilman, *Iconoclasm and Poetry in the English Reformation: Down Went Dagon* (Chicago: Chicago University Press, 1986), 61–83.

[58] Bale (1990), 84.

Satyrane, the 'civil' component of whose nature inspires him to learn Una's 'discipline of faith and veritie' (1. 6. 31). Like the hybrid Old English he may eventually be reclaimed, but the fate of the 'satyr' nation remains uncertain.

So much is clear and, perhaps, even predictable, but there remains a problem. Whatever else she may represent, Una is also a surrogate for the ever-absent Gloriana whose image the Irish steadfastly refused to 'worship' on the grounds that there was 'a great difference' between the virgin queen and the Virgin Mary. It is precisely that difference, however, that *The Faerie Queene* tends to blur by associating an image of the queen with the Woman Clothed with the Sun. In his account of 'The Queen's Majesty's Passage through the City of London to Westminster the Day before Her Coronation' (a work to which the iconography of *The Faerie Queene* is heavily indebted), Richard Mulcaster described how Elizabeth received 'the Bible in English' from the hands of 'Truth', the daughter of Time ('Temporis filia')—or rather through the hands of her intermediary Sir John Perrot, the future Lord Deputy who allegedly desecrated the image he helped to create. 'She', Mulcaster tells us, 'as soon as she had received the book, kissed it, and with both her hands held up the same and so laid it upon her breast with great thanks to the city therefore.'[59] The association was continued in 1568 when Elizabeth's portrait appeared on the title page of the Bishops' Bible, and it recurs in 'The Legend of Holinesse' when Una presents Arthur with a copy of the New Testament (or possibly the whole Bible) 'writ with golden letters rich and brave' (1. 9. 19). The symbolism of Mulcaster's pageant was remarkable not only for the compliment to Elizabeth's spirituality but for the calculated rebuff to Knox's *First Blast of the Trumpet against the Monstruous Regiment of Women*, the title page of which bears the proverb 'Veritas temporis filia' ['Truth is the daughter of Time']. 'And Time hath brought me hither', remarked Elizabeth in sublimely ironic response.[60] The eventual unveiling of Spenser's Una prior to her mystical union with St George gestures to a similar, and even more Apocalyptically charged, reclamation of the contested proverb from the anti-feminists (1. 12. 22–3).

The image of 'Una-Eliza' in her role of Woman Clothed with the Sun was not one that Ireland's 'salvage nacion' could justly be accused of idolizing. It was not they but 'Colin Clout' ('under which name this Poete secretly shadoweth himself') who declared 'shee is my goddesse plaine, |

---

[59] Kinney (1999), 28–9.   [60] Ibid. 27.

And I her shepherds swayne' (*Aprill,* 97–8)—although he does display considerable unease about such rhetoric: 'such follie great sorow to *Niobe* did breede' (87). But Hobbinol has no such compunction. 'O dea certe' is his response (165). All men, asserts Sir Guyon, 'do her adore with sacred reverence, | As th'Idole of her makers great magnificence' (2. 2. 41). Such imagery played into the hands of Spenser's opponents. If 'worship' of the Virgin Mary might be interpreted as 'idolatry', how much more might 'worship' of Elizabeth? The battle to reclaim female regiment from the aspersions of Knox had the odd effect of making the royal image potentially obnoxious, and even 'monstruous', to her Catholic subjects. To such hostile observers 'Una' was very much as 'Archimago' presents her since the attractions of an idol were agreed by all parties to resemble 'the flatteries of a wanton harlot'.[61] But there are subtle indications that Spenser too was uneasy. When we look more closely at his description of Una's reception amongst the satyrs we find that they first 'worship her, as Queene' while 'singing all a shepheards ryme' (1. 6. 13), just like Colin Clout. Like Colin, too, they then proceed to 'worship her as Goddesse of the wood' (1. 6. 16). Unlike Elizabeth, however, she attempts to stop them: 'their bootlesse zeale she did restraine | From her own worship' (1. 6. 19). What are we to make of this? Here amongst the 'salvage nation' is a conspicuous replica of the self. It is almost as if Spenser were endorsing O'Rourke's outlook, and detectable also is the ever-present fear of assimilation. The leader of the idolatrous 'salvage nation' is called Sylvanus, the name that Spenser chose for his eldest son. In this manner the Irish context of *The Faerie Queene* functions as a sort of dark 'mirror' in which an anti-Spenserian 'allegory' emerges from the text by ironic 'reflection'. Ireland revealed, in the felicitous words of Kenneth Gross, how 'the revelatory and the idolatrous poles may infect one another'.[62]

It is particularly ironic that the attempted 'reformation' of Ireland should have been impeded by the very 'Englishness' it sought to promote.[63] In 1536 the Irish Parliament formally recognized the Church of Ireland as 'annexed and united to the imperial Crown of England', but even Irenius concedes that 'moste of the Irishe' shun Protestantism less

---

[61] See Gilman, *Iconoclasm and Poetry,* 71. See also Linda Gregerson, 'Protestant Erotics: Idolatry and Interpretation in Spenser's *Faerie Queene', ELH* 58 (1991), 1–34.

[62] Gross, *Spenserian Poetics,* 69. See also Joan Fitzpatrick, 'Spenser's Nationalistic Images of Beauty: The Ideal and the Other in Relation to Protestant England and Catholic Ireland in *Faerie Queene* Book I', *Cahiers Elisabéthains* 53 (1998), 13–26.

[63] Alan Ford, 'The Protestant Reformation in Ireland', in Brady and Gillespie (eds.), *Natives and Newcomers,* 50–74 (pp. 51, 53).

from religious conviction than 'for the verye hatred which they have of the Englishe and theire governement' (*Prose*, 221).[64] There is much wish-fulfilment in evidence here, but the sentiment reveals the degree to which the New English faction hoped to utilize the Church of Ireland as a vehicle for 'Anglicization' in every sense of the term. While hereditary Palesmen jealously guarded the independence of both the Church of Ireland and the Irish Parliament, the New English sought to reduce both to subservience, 'for Religion . . . beinge but one, so as theare is but one waie thearein. for that which is trewe onelye is and the rest are not at all' (*Prose*, 221).[65] Or, to put it in terms of Spenserian allegory, St George's spouse must always be 'Una' whether the 'plaine' across which he rides be in England or Ireland. Had not the Irish Parliament passed the Act of Uniformity [or 'Una-formity'?] in 1560? If the Irish 'nacion' was ever to become 'one people' with the English, it was necessary to supply English ministers to a Church in which even 'the Bishoppe himself' might be 'an Irishe man' and consequently corrupt (*Prose*, 141). Yet Spenser acknowledged the possibility that cultural difference might frustrate this scheme for 'what good shall anye Englishe mynister doe amongest them by preachinge or teachinge which either Cannot understande him or will not heare him?' (*Prose*, 141). Part of the problem lay in the divergence of attitudes towards the Virgin Mary. 'These clergymen who have come from the other side', complained the poet Eoghan Ó Dubhthaigh, 'respect a dog more than Mary' ['ní mó leo Muire ná *dog*]. the macaronic use of the word 'dog' being intended to capture the semantic flavour of a peculiarly Anglican heresy.[66] One can understand why Irenius suggests that 'some discrete ministers of theire owne Cuntrymen be firste sente amongeste them which . . . maie drawe them firste to understande and afterwardes to imbrace the doctrine of theire salvacion' (*Prose*, 221). It was hoped that the 'new Collegde' at Dublin—which was also in receipt of escheated Munster lands—would eventually provide such 'discrete' Irish ministers (*Prose*, 142), but for the moment 'reformacion muste nowe be with the strengthe of a greate power' (*Prose*, 147).[67] In Ireland, as previously in England, the state would redeem the Church.

---

[64] Maxwell (1923), 122.

[65] For the truculent independence of the Irish Parliament see Brendan Bradshaw, 'The Beginnings of Modern Ireland', in Brian Farrell (ed.), *The Irish Parliamentary Tradition* (Dublin: Gill and Macmillan, 1973), 68–87.

[66] Mhág Craith (1980), i. 133; ii. 61.

[67] See MacCarthy-Morrogh, *The Munster Plantation*, 23–4, 169–70.

Readers of *The Shepheardes Calender* might well feel sceptical about such a claim, particularly in view of Irenius's admission that all of the 'disorders' of the Church of Ireland are also evident in the Anglican Church (*Prose*, 139). The ultimate responsibility in both cases lay with the 'supreme governor'. The episode of Corcaeca and Kirkrapine in the third canto of 'The Legend of Holinesse' is usually taken to reflect upon the condition of the Church of England following the dissolution of the monasteries but its location 'in exile, | In wildernesse and wastful deserts' rather recalls the vast ecclesiastical dilapidation that Spenser witnessed in Ireland (1. 3. 3).[68] Only in Ireland might he have encountered convents of 'blindhearted' nuns saying 'nine hundred *Pater nosters* every day, | And thrise nine hundred *Aves*' under the rule of an Abbess (1. 3. 13–18). Some three years before the publication of *The Shepheardes Calender*, Sir Henry Sidney sent the queen a personal memorandum concerning the 'lamentable Estate' of the Church in Ireland. Only by her 'gratious and relygious Order', he informs her, can its manifold abuses be 'cured, or at least amended'. Amongst the foremost of these are non-residence, pluralism, lay-impropriation (often by lease from the crown), illiteracy, and popish superstition ('Masses, Dirges, Shryvings and soch lyke Tromperye')—the very charges levelled in Spenser's 'moral' eclogues against the Church of England, and phrased in very similar terms.[69] The coincidence was profoundly disturbing. That the 'present' state of Ireland should reflect England's past was only to be expected; that it should reflect England's contemporary situation was a different matter. A further irony lurks in the suggested remedy. Sidney complains of widespread dilapidation, 'the very Walles of the Churches doune, verye fewe chauncells covered, Wyndowes and Dores ruyned, or spoyled'.[70] Irenius deplores the same phenomenon but concludes that mere repair is insufficient. Rather, 'all the Ruined Churches' should be 'builte in some better forme . . . for the outwarde shewe asure your selfe dothe greatlye drawe the rude people to the reverensinge and frequentinge thereof what ever some of our late too

---

[68] See Maryclaire Moroney, 'Spenser's Dissolution: Monasticism and Ruins in *The Faerie Queene* and *The Vewe of the Present State of Ireland*', *SSt* 12 (1991—but pub. 1998), 105–132. Moroney's contention that Spenser promoted in Ireland the sort of dissolution he deplored in England fails to account for Irenius's plan to re-edify dilapidated Irish churches. For the Irish dimension of book one see also Andrew Hadfield, ' "The Sacred Hunger of Ambitious Minds": Spenser's Savage Religion', in Donna B. Hamilton and Richard Strier (eds.), *Religion, Literature, and Politics in Post-Reformation England, 1540–1688* (Cambridge: Cambridge University Press, 1995), 27–45; John Breen, '*The Faerie Queene* Book I and the Theme of Protestant Exile', in *Irish University Review*, special issue, 'Spenser in Ireland 1596–1996', 26/2 (1996), 226–36.

[69] Collins (1746), i. 112–14 (p. 112).   [70] Ibid. 112.

nice foles saie that theare is nothinge in the semelye forme and Comelye order of the Churche' (*Prose*, 223). The 'moral' eclogues have often been interpreted as providing evidence for Spenser's sympathy with the 'Puritan' wing of the Anglican clergy—even though, or perhaps because, 'E.K.' is careful to disclaim such implications.[71] By contrast Irenius's defence of 'outwarde shewe' coupled with his dismissal of 'some of our late too nice foles' (such as Piers?) has been used as contrary evidence. Neither extrapolation is wholly justified by the relevant texts, but the passage from *A View* certainly suggests that the promotion of St George's cause in Ireland has at least occasioned a shift of emphasis. When operating in a largely Catholic environment, on the front lines of the religious conflict, the Protestant Church needs to resemble its opponent far more closely than radical Reformers might wish. In Ireland it is not merely unfortunate that Gloriana resembles Lucifera, it is also essential.

The avowed goal of Spenserian reform is 'civility' and, as the etymology of his name suggests, his patron of English 'holinesse' is also the patron of agrarian cultivation (1. 10. 66). He is a husbandman, a tiller of the soil brought up 'in ploughmans state', and by virtue of that fact an embodiment of the 'georgic' imperative. He represents not just the moral values of Piers Plowman, but the civic virtues of Virgilian culture.[72] 'The husbandman', explains Sir John Davies, 'must first breake the Land, before it bee made capeable of good seede . . . So a barbarous Country must be first broken by a warre, before it will be capeable of good Government.'[73] The project was no less literal than metaphorical. 'Since now we purpose to drawe the Irishe from desire of warrs and tumultes to the love of peace and Civillitye', Irenius explains, 'it is expediente to abridge theire greate Custome of heardinge and Augment theire more trade of Tillage and husbandrye' (*Prose*, 217–18). Remembering the pastoral 'otium' of *The Shepheardes Calender*, Yeats caustically remarked that 'though [Spenser] dreamed of Virgil's shepherds he wrote a book to advise . . . the harrying of all that followed flocks upon the hills, and of all "the wandering companies that keep the woods" '.[74] The choice of quotation is particularly apt since its poetic cadence resists its polemic intent (*Prose*, 149).

[71] For Spenser's religious sympathies see John N. King, *Spenser's Poetry and the Reformation Tradition* (Princeton: Princeton University Press, 1990), 14–46; Anthea Hume, *Edmund Spenser: Protestant Poet* (Cambridge: Cambridge University Press, 1984), 13–40.

[72] For Spenserian 'georgic' see Jane Tylus, 'Spenser, Virgil, and the Politics of Poetic Labour', *ELH* 55 (1988), 53–77.

[73] Davies (1612), 4–5.

[74] W. B. Yeats (ed.), *Poems of Spenser* (London: Caxton, 1906), p. xxxiv.

Acting as colonial 'planter', Spenser determined to destroy what he had
previously celebrated and branded as vagabonds figures he might previously have idealized.[75] In fact, most New English commentators were
well aware that the Gaelic economy was by no means exclusively 'pastoral'
but the notion of Ireland's 'savagery' was so deeply ingrained, and so politically useful, that counter-examples were readily dismissed.[76] Officially
Ireland remained 'uncultivated'. St George's quest in 'The Legend of
Holinesse' is the redemption of a fallen but potential 'Eden', a metaphor
frequently employed in colonial literature. The quest of the New English
'St George' is the redemption of a once 'holy island' but that was something that Spenser's fiction could merely adumbrate (7. 6. 37). Not the
least reason for Redcross's anticlimactic resumption of arms in the twelfth
canto was the ongoing struggle for a 'Georgic' Ireland.

[75] See *Prose*, 97–8, 128. Such attitudes are discussed in David Beers Quinn, *The Elizabethans and the Irish* (Ithaca, NY: Cornell University Press, 1966), 54–5, 77, 123, 148–9.

[76] See R. A. Butlin, 'Land and People, *c.*1600', *NHI* iii. 142–67 (pp. 148–50, 153); G. H. Hayes-McCoy, 'The Completion of the Tudor Conquest and the Advance of the Counter-Reformation, 1571–1603', *NHI* iii. 94–141 (p. 131).

6   Sins of Difference

Dark indeed is she I love . . .
But of barbarous lineage—no!

(Camões, 'Aquela cativa')

IT has recently been argued that 'The Legend of Temperaunce' is not
greatly concerned with Ireland, that its principal focus, as the proem suggests, is on the New World.[1] But this is to insist upon a distinction that
Elizabethan commentators laboured to obscure. To conquer Ireland, according to Sir William Herbert, was to facilitate 'our vast enterprises in
the Atlantic and West Indies'.[2] Fynes Moryson expressed the matter even
more succinctly when he described Ireland as 'this famous Iland in the
Virginian Sea'.[3] When it came to the business of settling colonists there
'no lesse Cautions were to be observed for uniting them and keeping them
from mixing with the other, then if these newe Colonyes were to be ledd
to inhabitt among the barbarous Indians'.[4] At the root of Moryson's fears
lay the 'legend' of Irish intemperance. Characteristically associating race
with topography, Camden asserts that the Irish are 'most intemperate, by
reason of the distemperature of the aire, and the moisture both of the
ground, and of their meats; in regard also that all law is exiled'.[5] As in the
Bowre of Blisse, the very landscape is morally enervating.[6] Given the nature of the problem, Irenius concludes that 'moderacion oughte to be had
in Temperinge and menaginge of this stubborne nacion of the Irishe to
bring them from theire delighte of licentious barbarisme unto the love of
goodnes and Civilitye' (*Prose*, 54). To conquer is merely to 'temper'. The
'despairefull outcries and ymoderate waylinges' encountered at Irish
'burialls' are indicative of the nation's 'Scythyan' origins, 'for it is the manner of all pagans and *Infidells* to be intemperate in theire waylinges of

---

[1] See David Read, *Temperate Conquests: Spenser and the Spanish New World* (Detroit: Wayne
State University Press, 2000), 83–92. For similar views see Andrew Murphy, 'Reviewing the
Paradigm: A New Look at Early Modern Ireland', *Éire*, 31 (1996), 13–40.

[2] Herbert (1992), 29.   [3] Moryson (1907–8), iv. 185.   [4] Moryson (1903), 249.

[5] Camden (1610), 143.

[6] By contrast, for the purposes of encouraging plantation, Ireland's climate is invariably said
to be 'temperate' (*Prose*, 62).

theare dead' (*Prose*, 105). At the very outset of his quest, Guyon encounters a remarkable instance of such immoderate bereavement in the person of Amavia. As early as 1758 the detail of Ruddymane's blood-stained hands was recognized by John Upton as an oblique allusion to the heraldic badge of the O'Neills, described by Edmund Campion as 'a tyrrible cognisaunce'.[7] 'The rebellion of the Oneals', Upton concluded, 'is imaged in this Episode, who drank so deep of the charm and venom of Acrasia'.[8] This is by no means the sole, or even the principal, significance of the incident, yet the association is highly likely in view of Irenius's observation that O'Neill's followers 'crye *Landargabo*, that is the bloddie hande which is *Oneles* badge' (*Prose*, 103). The 'general intention' of Spenser's allegory accommodates a wealth of 'particular' applications. '*Landargabo*' is a corruption of the Gaelic 'lámh dhearg abú' or 'the Red Hand Forever', and a bardic poem entitled 'Lámh Dhearg Éireann' or 'The Red Hand of Ireland' was still current in Spenser's time.[9] Guyon's failure to cleanse the child's hands recalls Campion's allegation that the Irish left 'the right armes of theire infantes males unchristoned (as they termed yt) to the intent yt might geave a more ungratious and deadely bloe'.[10] It is all the more disturbing, therefore, that Ruddymane's hand will serve as a 'sacred Symbole . . . to minde revengement'—and is presumably destined to deal an equally 'deadely bloe' in due course (2. 2. 10). The episode gestures yet again to the 'necessary' cycle of retributory violence, and the inevitable loss of 'innocence', that the Irish campaign entails.

The mingling of topographical references to Ireland and the New World throughout book two serves to remind us that the action is 'set' exclusively in neither but in a conflation of both, in the common 'land' of colonial opportunity. The enemies of the 'virgin Queene' Alma may resemble a 'swarme of Gnats at eventide' arising 'out of the fennes of Allan' (2. 9. 16), but they shoot such arrows 'as the *Indians* in their quivers hide' (2. 11. 21). By way of reply to those who enquire as to the whereabouts of 'that happy land of Faery' the proem invokes the prolific literature of discovery, recalling how 'dayly . . . through hardy enterprize, | Many great Regions are discovered, | Which to late age were never mentioned' (Proem 5). Fairyland is an expansionist space, a visionary realm in which

---

[7] Campion (1963), 138.   [8] See Spenser (1758), ii. 438.
[9] See Roland Smith, 'The Irish background of Spenser's *View*', *JEGP* 42 (1943), 499–515 (p. 504). For 'The Red Hand of Ireland' see Ó hUiginn (1922–6), i, pp. xvii–xviii.
[10] Campion (1963), 21. The detail is repeated in Holinshed (1808), vi. 69.

the poet explores the imaginative possibilities of founding an English empire on both shores of the 'Virginian' sea, and speculators such as Sir Walter Ralegh were equally active in both spheres.[11] Like the New World, Ireland was potentially another Eden,

> a moste bewtifull and swete Countrie as anye is under heaven, seamed thoroughe out with manye goodlye rivers . . . sprinckled with manye swete Ilandes and good-lye lakes like little Inlande seas, that will carye even shipps uppon theire waters, adorned with goodly woodes fitt for buildinge of howsses and shipps so comodi-ously as that if some princes in the worlde had them they woulde sone hope to be Lordes of all the seas and ere longe of all the worlde. (*Prose*, 62)

This is an extraordinary passage by any standards. Aesthetic appreciation of natural beauty gradually modulates, through plans for its commercial exploitation, into fantasies of world domination as beauty, money, and power coalesce and the diction of the civil colonist threatens to shade into that of Ben Jonson's Epicure Mammon—and Mammon is one of Guyon's most dangerous enemies. We are given to understand that Ireland's 'commodious' landscape is wasted upon its 'idle' inhabitants who choose to leave it unenclosed and, therefore, 'wyld' and 'desart'. 'This Chieflye redoundethe to the good of the whole Comon wealthe', Irenius remarks, apparently oblivious to the irony implicit in 'comon', 'to have the lande . . . enclosed and well fenced' (*Prose*, 135). Phædria navigates a 'wide Inland sea' of the sort he commends but hers is named 'the *Idle lake*' (2. 6. 10). To render it 'profitable' could be regarded as a moral duty.

According to such commentators as Thomas Bastard, however, the experience of the New World suggested otherwise. The commercial gain was scarcely worth the moral loss:

> *Indie* newe found the Christian faith doth holde,
> Reioycing in our heavenly merchandize.
> Which we have chang'd for pretious stones and gold
> And pearle and feathers, and for Popingyes.
> Now are they loving, meeke and vertuous,
> Contented, sweetly with poore godlinesse.
> Nowe are we salvage, fierce and barbarous,
> Rich with the fuell of all wickednesse.
>   So did *Elishaes* servant *Gehazye*,
>   With *Naamans* goold, buy *Naamans* leprosye.[12]

---

[11] Michael MacCarthy-Morrogh, *The Munster Plantation: English Migration to Southern Ireland 1583–1641* (Oxford: Clarendon Press, 1986), 124.

[12] Bastard (1598), 85–6.

Here is a nice reversal of the stereotypical image of the native selling his birthright for trifles.[13] The bargain has gone the other way, and there were many who suspected that the same thing had happened, and was happening again, in Ireland, and that this was the real reason for the colony's chronic 'degeneracy'. According to Edmund Tremayne, 'the sweetness and gain of the Irish government hath been such that it hath rather drawn our own nation to become Irish than any way wrought the reformation of the Irish to reduce them to English law.'[14] It was an argument with which Spenser was very familiar. In *A Theatre for Voluptuous Worldlings* Jan van der Noot associates the pursuit of empire with 'the service of wicked *Mammon*'.[15] Spenser's Cave of Mammon duly recalls the notorious—and much envied—gold mines of Spanish America, tracing with evident fascination the various stages of the refining process from the extraction of the raw ore to the minting of imperial coin:

> And round about him lay on every side
> Great heapes of gold, that never could be spent:
> Of which some were rude owre, not purifide
> Of *Mulcibers* devouring element;
> Some others were new driven, and distent
> Into great Ingoes, and to wedges square;
> Some in round plates withouten moniment;
> But most were stampt, and in their metall bare
> The antique shapes of kings and kesars straunge & rare.

(2. 7. 5)

While the Spaniards were condemned for making gold their 'god', the Irish were blamed for ignoring the country's mineral wealth.[16] According to Richard Stanyhurst, for example,

There are in this Iland such notable quaries of greie marble and touch, such store of pearle and other rich stones, such abundance of cole, such plentie of lead, iron, latin and tin, so manie rich mines furnished with all kind of metals, as nature seemed to have framed this countrie for the storehouse or iewelhouse of hir chiefest thesaure. Howbeit she hath not shewed hir selfe so bountifull a mother in powring foorth such riches, as she prooveth hir selfe an envious stepdame; in

---

[13] For objections to the practice of cheating the natives with 'trifles and gingles' see Bacon (1857–74), vi. 459.

[14] BL, Add. MSS, 48015, fo. 274. Quoted in Ciaran Brady, *The Chief Governors: The Rise and Fall of Reform Government in Ireland 1536–1588* (Cambridge: Cambridge University Press, 1994), 140.

[15] Noot (1569), fos. 2r.   [16] See Las Casas (1992), 27–8.

that she instilleth in the inhabitants a drousie lithernesse to withdraw them from the insearching of hir hourded and hidden iewels.[17]

Stanyhurst's juxtaposing of topics indicates the way in which Gaelic territories were commonly 'viewed'. His account of the island's 'strange and woonderfull places' immediately precedes that of its equally wonderous 'commoditie'.[18] In his writings we find the same bizarre combination of the exotic and the mercenary that pervades such descriptions of the New World as Ralegh's *Discovery of the Large, Rich and Beautiful Empire of Guiana* (1595).[19] As 'Lord Wardein of the Stannaryes'—a title employed in the dedications to both *The Faerie Queene* and *Colin Clouts Come Home Againe*—Ralegh had a particular interest in mining, and plans were already afoot to open up new mines and quarries in Munster.[20] It is readily understandable, therefore, that Stanyhurst should represent the native population as labouring, like the victims of Acrasia, under 'some secret enchantment' that prevents them from realizing the 'fruit and commoditie that the earth yeeldeth'.[21] The argument is overtly moral but the underlying concern is commercial.[22] The same emphasis is to be found in Robert Payne's *Briefe Description of Ireland* (1589), written to promote the plantation of Munster. 'The commodities of the countrie are many moe', Payne asserts, 'then eyther the people can well use or I recite.'[23] Irenius is merely following the official line when he argues that Ireland is 'full of verye good portes and havens openinge uppon Englande and Skotlande as invitinge us to Come unto them to see what excellente Comodities that Countrye Cane afforde' (*Prose*, 62). As in the New World, the land itself 'invites' the colonist with the prospect of 'commodity' despite the opposition of the indigenous population. In commercial terms Ireland, like America, is *terra nullius*.

  Edward Said has argued that imperialism invariably culminates in 'the domination, classification and universal commodification of all space, under the aegis of the metropolitan centre'.[24] The observation is pertinent

---

[17] Holinshed (1808), vi. 41.   [18] Ibid. 36–41.
  [19] For Ralegh's attitudes see Anthony Pagden, *Lords of All the World: Ideologies of Empire in Spain, Britain and France c.1500–c.1800* (New Haven: Yale University Press, 1995), 67–8.
  [20] See MacCarthy-Morrogh, *The Munster Plantation*, 224–5.
  [21] Holinshed (1808), vi. 41.
  [22] See Raymond Jenkins, 'Spenser: The Uncertain Years 1584–1589', *PMLA* 53 (1938), 350–62 (p. 356).
  [23] Payne (1589), 8. For the term 'commodity' see John Gillies, *Shakespeare and the Geography of Difference* (Cambridge: Cambridge University Press, 1994), 133.
  [24] Terry Eagleton, Fredric James, Edward W. Said, *Nationalism, Colonialism and Literature* (Minneapolis: University of Minnesota Press, 1988), 78.

because Spenser was a Londoner and, according to one contemporary observer, 'the citie of London standeth chiefly upon the traffique and intercourse of merchants and the use of buying and selling of their sundrie commodities'.[25] Yet this is exactly the sort of matter that chivalric romance traditionally eschews—if only because its own market value depends upon the creation of a very different ethos.[26] When it finally occurs in the sixth book of *The Faerie Queene* the word 'commodity' comes as something of a semantic shock, but the effect is carefully qualified by the context. Brigands demand that their prisoners be sold as 'bondslaves' and that the proceeds be 'shared equally' amongst them for 'their most commodity' (6. 11. 10). Here, as in the slave trade generally, human beings are turned into chattels, but the moral allegory strongly disapproves and dispatches Sir Calidore to the rescue. By employing chivalric metaphors for the colonial enterprise Spenser not only lends it the lustre of heroic tradition but effectively elides its mercenary nature—although it is perhaps unfortunate that the poem's most forthright dismissal of 'money' is delivered by Braggadocchio whose use of the term 'war-monger' is the earliest recorded in the *OED* (3. 10. 29–31). The narrative's vocabulary of denial impacts at every level upon its vocabulary of assertion.

Mammon is the 'Money God' (2. 7. 39), and seeks to recreate the Golden Age as an Age of Gold. Guyon refuses his 'offred grace' for the noblest of reasons: 'another blis before mine eyes I place, | Another happinesse, another end' (2. 7. 33). Yet the court of Philotime, where 'every one did strive his fellow downe to throw' (2. 7. 47), anticipates Colin Clout's description of Cynthia's court where 'each one seeks with malice and with strife, | To thrust downe other into foule disgrace'.[27] Polarities tend to collapse: Mammon and the Spaniards are condemned for doing what the Gaelic Irish are too 'idle' to do—and the New English have a moral duty to do for them. As David Read argues, 'Guyon's distinction from the model offered by the conquistador rests at the same time upon a basic consonance with that model . . . Guyon does most of the things that conquistadors do, but he does them with an "English" difference.'[28] The interesting point, however, is that Guyon is not 'English' but 'elfin' (2. 7. 19), and fairyland seems to be designed to allow 'difference' to be sustained despite convergence. In the real world condemnation of Spanish

---

[25] Anon., *Breefe Discourse* (1584), 21.

[26] Gabriel Harvey, commenting on the October eclogue, notes the financial concerns of '*Cuddie, alias* you know who' (*Prose*, 470–1).

[27] *Colin Clouts Come Home Againe*, ll. 690–1.   [28] Read, *Temperate Conquests*, 65.

methods went hand in hand with a desire to emulate Spanish gains.[29] In the very act of disclaiming 'greed', Guyon insists upon the imperial imperative:

> Regard of worldly mucke doth fowly blend,
> And low abase the high heroicke spright,
> That ioyes for crownes and kingdomes to contend.

(2. 7. 10)

Yet this is precisely what Mammon offers: 'Riches, renowme, and principality, | Honour, estate, and all this worldes good' (2. 7 8). Maureen Quilligan has related this episode to the rising commercialism of the era, but empire was its supreme expression.[30] If Guyon surveys Mammon's wealth with 'greedy vew', he is just as anxious to be 'seen' to reject it as to 'see' it (2. 7. 9). Throughout the episode, however, disapproval struggles with fascination. As he follows in Mammon's footsteps, Guyon 'with wonder all the way | Did feed his eyes, and fild his inner thought' (2. 7. 24), and it is quite unclear whether 'fild' is to be read as 'filled' or 'filed' in the common Elizabethan sense of 'defiled'.[31] Either way, the suggestion is that Guyon wants what he sees, as he wants the bathing ladies of the Bowre of Blisse who reveal their charms as 'spoiles to greedy eyes' (2. 12. 64). In the cave of Mammon Spenser explores the voyeurism of greed and as Guyon 'feed[s] his eyes' on forbidden gold his hunger increases—a hunger exacerbated by his refusal to 'eat' the golden apples of the Garden of Proserpina (2. 7. 54–6). It is little wonder, then, that the hero collapses at the close of canto seven since greed is as much an imperial virtue as an imperial vice.

In his *Short Account of the Destruction of the Indies* Las Casas rewrote the history of Spanish imperialism as that of grand larceny. Summarizing his argument in the final paragraph he concluded that 'everyone, young and old alike, who journeys to the New World is either openly or in secret a fortune-hunter'.[32] Similar accusations were levelled in Ireland as early as the twelfth century. In his eagerness to represent his relatives in an heroic light, Giraldus Cambrensis strongly denied that FitzStephen and Strongbow could 'in any sense be classed as mere robbers', at least so far as Leinster was concerned. He admits, however, that parts of Waterford, Desmond,

---

[29] William S. Maltby, *The Black Legend in England: The Development of Anti-Spanish Sentiment, 1558–1660* (Durham, NC; Duke University Press, 1971), 20–1, 23–4.

[30] Maureen Quilligan, *Milton's Spenser: The Politics of Reading* (Ithaca, NY: Cornell University Press, 1983), 55.

[31] For 'wonder' see above pp. 58–9.   [32] Las Casas (1992), 130.

Thomond, and Meath were 'seized unlawfully' and that many of the new colonists could justly be described as 'fugitives from Fortune, unarmed and destitute'. Nevertheless, since Strongbow transferred all of his legitimate rights to Henry II, to whom all of the Gaelic princes 'made a voluntary submission', 'it must be clear . . . that in entering Ireland the English ['Anglorum gentem'] were not guilty of injustice'.[33] Confronted by the entrenched power of their descendants, however, the New English expressed scepticism. Revisionism was the order of the day. For Sir John Davies, Strongbow and his associates were nothing more than mere 'adventurers' who 'came to seeke their fortunes in Ireland' whereas the New English were loyal servitors of the crown acting in the public interest.[34] Despite such attempts at moral differentiation, however, the Privy Council actively promoted the use of private 'adventurers' in the Irish service and Gaelic commentators were quick to brand the New English as mere 'praedones' or brigands.[35] The prevalent use of the term 'adventurer' in such contexts puts a somewhat unromantic gloss upon the 'adventures' of Gloriana's knights. Spenser criticized Gaelic society for its failure to observe the code of primogeniture but many of his fellow planters were its victims.[36] For second sons, impoverished soldiers, and indigent poets, Ireland afforded the otherwise impossible prospect of ascent to the ranks of the landed gentry.[37] 'The drifte of my purpose', remarks Irenius, is 'to settle an eternall peace in that Countrie and allsoe to make it verie profitable to her maiestie' (*Prose*, 197). The benefits of 'peace' are 'profit' and the moral values of the poetry are meticulously costed in the prose, sometimes to the last pound (*Prose*, 181–2). It was impossible to render such calculations 'poetic' and Spenser knew better than to try. For heroic purposes the 'quest' had to be altruistic, a selfless defence of the civil and vulnerable against the barbarous and inhumane.

Following his sojourn in the cave of Mammon, Guyon's next port of call is the Castle of Alma. Its association with the 'fennes of Allan' identifies it as an outpost of civility of the sort with which Spenser was personally familiar. His property at New Abbey in Kildare was 'adjacent to the north-

---

[33] Giraldus Cambrensis (1978), 31, 33, 229, 231.   [34] Davies (1612), p. 155.

[35] See Hogan and O'Farrell (1959), 157; O'Sullivan Beare (1960), 78–9.

[36] See David Beers Quinn, *The Elizabethans and the Irish* (Ithaca, NY: Cornell University Press, 1966), 39.

[37] For Spenser's personal interest in escheated lands see Raymond Jenkins, 'Spenser and the Clerkship in Munster', *PMLA* 47 (1932), 109–21 (pp. 116–17); Ray Heffner, 'Spenser's Acquisition of Kilcolman', *MLN* 46 (1931), 493–8; Simon Shepherd, *Spenser* (London: Harvester, 1989), 9, 51–5.

eastern border of the great Bog of Allen' and it is probably no coincidence that the poem's first mention of Artegall occurs immediately prior to our first encounter with the castle's enemies (2. 9. 6).[38] Irenius suggests that 'in all stretes and narrowe passages, as betwene Two Boggs . . . theare shoulde be some litle fortilage or woden Castle set' in order to prevent the incursion of 'rebelles' (*Prose*, 224). Stone castles were preferred but often proved too costly to construct. Like all such outposts, Alma's castle is represented as perpetually besieged by hoards of marauding enemies apparently spawned by the landscape itself. Like the kerns of *A View* they first raise an 'outragious cry' then 'swarm' out of 'rockes and caves', 'some with unweldy clubs, some with long speares, | Some rusty knives, some staves in fire warmd' (2. 9. 13). This, as Irenius might have said, is 'the verye Image of the Irish Hubub' (*Prose*, 103), and in his description of the castle's fabric the narrator recalls some of the more lucrative 'commodities' located in the 'wild', but invitingly rich, terrain inhabited by such savages: the 'porch' is constructed of 'stone more of valew, and more smooth and fine, | Then Iet or Marble far from Ireland brought' (2. 9. 24). Castles were first introduced to the Irish countryside by the Old English but by Spenser's day their taking, building, destroying, and re-edifying was an obsessive concern of New English reports and 'plots'.[39] The 'castle' of Alma, and all that it represents, can be saved from destruction only by the defeat of Maleger, a monster who loses strength, like the classical Antaeus, when lifted from the ground.[40] Sir William Herbert applied the myth directly to the Irish situation:

For just as when Hercules was fighting with Antaeus, the more often he threw his opponent to the ground so did the fight rage all the more fiercely and violently because the earth redoubled the giant's strength, until Hercules carried him from the ground and strangled him in the air; in the same way it cannot come about that justice and civilisation will prevail when they fight against evil and barbarism, however often they throw them down, unless they are dragged away from the evil laws and customs, which increase and double their strength, and are annihilated and vanish in the healthy and clear air of a legal and political administration.

---

[38] See Anon., 'Spenser in Ireland', *Edinburgh Review*, 201 (1905), 164–88 (p. 174).

[39] See Rolf Loeber, 'An Architectural History of Gaelic Castles and Settlements, 1370–1600', in *Gaelic Ireland: Land, Lordship and Settlement c.1250–c.1650* (Dublin: Four Courts Press, 2001), 271–314.

[40] See M. M. Gray, 'The Influence of Spenser's Irish Experiences on *The Faerie Queene*', *RES* 6 (1930), 413–28 (pp. 415–16).

In order to foster such a process he calls for 'the transplantation of inhabitants from one province to another' in an attempt to smash the relationship between ancestral homelands and ancestral identities.[41]

Ancestral identity is the Castle of Alma's major concern. Its status as a 'body politic' is confirmed by the discovery within its 'head' of the Briton and Fairy 'moniments'. As here presented, identity is very much a matter of 'record', or rather of respect for records. In the chamber of Eumnestes—itself 'ruinous and old'—the knights encounter an aged man 'of infinite remembrance' engaged in the 'endlesse exercise' of consulting 'old records from auncient times deriv'd, | Some made in books, some in long parchment scrolles, | That were all worme-eaten, and full of canker holes' (2. 9. 55–9). Collective 'remembrance' is locked in an unceasing conflict with oblivion and to lose the past is to lose the present. Henry VIII's 'Act in Restraint of Appeals to Rome' had recourse to 'old authentic histories and chronicles' to prove that 'this realm of England is an empire' and the 'Briton moniments' repeatedly confirm its status.[42] They are equally careful to record an 'English' claim to Ireland which precedes even that of the indigenous population (2. 10. 41). As J. G. A. Pocock has observed 'the court of record is the kernel of English government', and nowhere more so, one suspects, than in the handling of its colonies.[43] The entire New English enterprise rested on 'record'. In prosecuting the territorial claims of Sir Peter Carew, for example, John Hooker scoured the archives for corroborative evidence. One of the crucial documents, he tells us, 'had been trodden under the foot, and by that means the letters were almost worn out'.[44] It was held sufficient in law, however, to dispossess a number of Gaelic and Old English families. 'The Queen and her councillors and magistrates', remarked Ó Súilleabháin Béarra caustically, 'directed all their zeal and plots to despoil the Irish of their goods . . . This might easily be done, as most of the Irish had no patents and did not require them since they were the owners of their countries before the time of the English rule.'[45] Hooker was merely following a precedent set by Sir Henry Sidney. On consulting the archives at Dublin Castle, Sidney found that 'the records' were 'verie evill kept, not fensed or defended from raine and foule weather, but laie all in a chaos

---

[41] Herbert (1992), 113.   [42] See Bray (1994), 78.
[43] Pocock, 'British History: A Plea for a New Subject', *Journal of Modern History*, 47 (1974), 601–28 (p. 611).
[44] Hooker (1857), 72.   [45] O'Sullivan Beare (1903), 48, 49.

and a confused heap, without anie regard'. In order to rectify the situation he 'caused [them] to be viewed and sorted, and then prepared meete roomes, presses, and places for the keeping of them in safetie, and did appoint a speciall officer with a yearelie fee for the keeping of them'. Similarly, 'whereas there were manie good lawes & statutes established in the realme, which hitherto were laid up and shrouded in filth and cobwebs . . . he caused a through view, and a review to be made, and then a choise of all such statutes as were most necessarie to be put in use and execution: which being doone, he caused to be put in print, to the great benefit of that whole nation.'[46] Eumnestes' chamber was the seat of Irish government and Sidney was determined to supply it with an Anamnestes.

The Castle of Alma serves much the same function for Guyon as does the House of Holinesse for St George. Renewed by a sense of national and spiritual identity, he is at last prepared to confront Acrasia, and the very format of the subsequent cantos, that of an odyssey by sea to a strange, perilous land, encapsulates their colonial ethos.[47] It was generally agreed that Virgil had reinscribed Homer's *Odyssey* within the context of 'social' epic. Odysseus comes home alone, but Aeneas leads his nation to a land destined to be the centre of an empire. Yet Guyon is, in many respects, remarkably unlike Virgil's hero. Aeneas seeks to wed the daughter of King Latinus and secure his position by intermarriage, as the Old English did in *Ireland*. But Guyon is a knight of '*Maydenhead*' and struggles to preserve the 'self' from sexual contamination, as New English planters were enjoined to do (2. 2. 42). Comparison with Camões is illuminating at this point. It is probably in the final cantos of book two that *The Faerie Queene* and *Os Lusíadas* display their closest cultural and generic correspondences, yet even here the difference is more striking than the resemblance. In the ninth canto of Camões's poem, as Vasco da Gama and his companions approach their final destination, Venus prepares to receive them on an enchanted island in a sort of bower of bliss:

From the island, all joy and charm and loveliness, there rose three comely hills, their noble grace adorned with luxuriant vegetation. Limpid streams flowed from their summits, murmuring as they rippled over white pebbly beds . . . Jocund vine was interwoven with spreading elm, the grapes hanging in dark clusters of purple

[46] Holinshed (1808), vi. 402.
[47] See Stephen Greenblatt, *Renaissance Self-Fashioning: From More to Shakespeare* (Chicago: University of Chicago Press, 1980), 173–89.

and green . . . the flowery sward that carpeted the rustic scene . . . robbed Persia's tapestries of their sheen.[48]

As in Spenser, nature and art seem inextricable, but without the sinister implications. Venus provides Camões's sailors with willing 'nymphs' some of whom 'trusting to the unadorned beauty of a lovely form, had laid aside the enhancement of attire and were bathing naked'.[49] But there is no 'black Palmer' to warn the mariners off. Rather, Thetys is reserved for Da Gama himself and couples with him in a palace of crystal and gold.[50] The narrator intervenes to explain that all of the pleasures of the isle 'are but symbols of the honours . . . that can make life sublime'.[51] The fulfilment of sexual desire serves as a metaphor for the fulfilment of heroic potential. This difference in poetic technique reflects a fundamental divergence in colonial policy. The Portuguese governors of Goa encouraged intermarriage with the native population, and Camões responded by writing the celebrated love poem to an Indian slave girl which provides the epigraph to the present chapter. While stationed at Macao he lived for three years with 'Dinamene', a Chinese lady.[52] For him, miscegenation was not an issue. For Spenser it was, and sexuality functions very differently in the Bowre of Blisse. There, to succumb to the pleasures of the flesh is to compromise one's virtue and, paradoxically, to lose one's virility in the very act of exercising it. Guyon's most consistent attitude throughout book two is an attitude of refusal. 'Certes', he tells Mammon, 'I n'ill thine offred grace, | Ne to be made so happy do intend' (2. 7. 33). The remark is relevant here because the Cave of Mammon and the Bowre of Blisse are closely related by a carefully contrived coincidence of imagery. It is in the Cave of Mammon that Guyon first encounters Arachne who 'high did lift | Her cunning web, and spread her subtile net' above his head (2. 7. 28). He meets her again in the person of Acrasia:

> All in a vele of silke and silver thin,
> That hid no whit her alabaster skin,
> But rather shewd more white, if more might bee:
> More subtile web *Arachne* can not spin . . .
>
> (2. 12. 77)

---

[48] Camões (1952), 209–10. For the work's context see Ronald W. Sousa, *The Rediscoverers: Major Writers in the Portuguese Literature of National Regeneration* (University Park, Pa.: Pennsylvania State University Press, 1981), 11–45.

[49] Camões (1952), 211.   [50] Ibid., 215–16.   [51] Ibid., 216.

[52] See Henry H. Hart, *Luis de Camoëns and The Epic of the Lusiads* (Norman: University of Oklahoma Press, 1962), 95, 138, 268–9.

Greed and lust, two closely related forms of 'cupidity', offer only entrapment and loss of 'self'. Ralegh conflated the two when he remarked that Guiana 'is a Country that hath yet her Maidenhead, never sacked, turned, nor wrought'.[53] Even amongst Spenser's fellow 'undertakers', the principal agents of the plantation, profit increasingly motivated intermarriage with Gaelic families and many seemed destined for the same cultural fate as the Old English. The 'chronicles of Irelande' supplied a grim, and very personal, warning in this instance: it was the Old English of Munster 'which is the sweteste Soile of Irelande' that grew to be amongst the most 'degenerate': 'and some of them have quite shaken of theire Englishe names and put on Irishe that they mighte be alltogeather Irishe' (*Prose*, 115). 'Is it possible', Eudoxus asks in horror, 'that an Englisheman broughte up naturallye in suche swete Civilytie as Englande affordes . . . shoulde forgett his owne nature and forgoe his owne nacion? howe maie this be? . . . That is a moste daungerous *Lethargie*' (*Prose*, 96, 115). A powerful reply is proffered at the conclusion of book two, where Verdant is discovered in precisely such a 'daungerous *Lethargie*' as he reclines in the arms of the Circe-like Acrasia who undoes the 'framing' and 'fashioning' of noble gentlemen by transforming civil knights into savage beasts. Nearby lies the young man's 'brave shield' with the heraldic 'signes' of his ancestry 'fowly ra'st' (2. 12. 80). In the background sounds the song of the 'Virgin Rose', borrowed from Tasso, but recalling the popular belief that the Irish delighted 'above measure' in music as in all other sensual indulgences.[54] In New English polemic sexual licence served as a convenient metaphor for political apostasy, and the bards were regarded as 'sirens' for their ability to excite 'the unstable minds of fierce men to rebellion and crime'.[55]

The majority of the settlers brought to Munster by the 'undertakers' were single men of low social status whose likely intermarriage with Gaelic families posed the most serious threat to the colony's survival.[56] This was only to be expected since, as Irenius concedes, schemes for plantation are apt to attract 'the worste and moste decaied men' (*Prose*, 184). In a very real sense, therefore, sex, greed, and politics were intimately related.

[53] Ralegh (1986), 120.
[54] Camden (1610), 144. See Tasso, *Gerusalemme Liberata*, XVI. 14–15.
[55] Herbert (1992), 107, 109.
[56] See Nicholas Canny, 'The Permissive Frontier: the Problem of Social Control in English Settlements in Ireland and Virginia 1550–1650', in K. R. Andrews, N. P. Canny, and P. E. H. Hair (eds.), *The Westward Enterprise: English Activities in Ireland, the Atlantic and America 1480–1650* (Liverpool: Liverpool University Press, 1978), 17–44 (pp. 19–24).

In *The Image of Irelande* John Derricke weaves a pornographic reverie about the Gaelic 'nimphes' who 'scudd alongest | the woode and riverse side' until 'Cupid toul'th his sacryng bell, | to enter other Rites'. 'To see those naked sprites', he remarks pruriently, would 'revive a manne halfe dedde'. Yet herein lies the danger: 'wee knowe by good experience, | it is a daungerous thyng: | For one into his naked bedde, | a poysning Tode to bryng'.[57] As the 'allegory' vicariously indulges the very appetites it condemns, the shift to heavy moralization proves to be as unwittingly revealing as it is poetically jarring. The colonists must not be 'witched' with the 'externall sight' of Irish women,

> For why should men of Th'englishe pale,
>   in suche a Crewe delight
> Or eke repose suche confidence,
>   In that unhappie race:
> Since mischeef lurketh oftentimes
>   even in the smothest face?[58]

Approaching the matter from the opposite viewpoint Ó Súilleabháin Béarra paid tribute to the role of Gaelic 'mothers and nurses' in perpetuating the Catholic faith.[59] Irenius duly warns against 'licentious Conversinge with the Irishe or marryinge and fosteringe with them' (*Prose*, 117). 'How cane suche matchinge but bringe forthe an evill race', he asks, 'seinge that Comonlye the Childe takethe moste of his nature of the mother besides speache, manners, inclynacion . . . for by them they are firste framed and fashioned soe as what they receave once from them they will hardelye ever after forgoe' (*Prose*, 120). By usurping the very task of 'framing' and 'fashioning' that Spenser claims for himself in the 'Letter to Ralegh', and Irenius assigns to the New English in *A View*, Irish Acrasias defeat English Guyons.

Entrance to Acrasia's bower is by way of the porters Genius and Excesse. Despite his name, however, the former is 'quite contrary' to the guardian spirit 'that is our Selfe, whom though we do not see, | Yet each doth in him selfe it well perceive to bee'. He is, in fact, the demonic alter ego 'that secretly doth us procure to fall', the 'other' latent in the self (47–8). Yet it is he who possesses the 'governall' of the garden, a term which perfectly encapsulates the well-established relationship between the 'government' of the bodies private and politic. The false Genius is described as an androgynous figure of 'semblaunce pleasing, more than

---

[57] Derricke (1985), 28–9, 30.   [58] Ibid. 31.   [59] O'Sullivan Beare (1903), 43.

naturall' and clad 'in wanton wize, | Not fit for speedy pace, or manly ex-
ercize' (46). It is worth pausing on this detail. *A View* is much concerned
with the semiotics of clothing because 'theare is not a litle in the garment
to the fashioninge of the minde'. 'Therefore', Eudoxus informs us,

> it is written by *Aristotle* that when *Cirus* had overcome the Lidians that weare a
> warlike nacion and devised to bringe them to a more peaceable liffe he Chaunged
> theire Apparrell and musicke And in steade of theire shorte warlike Coate
> cloathed them in longe garmentes like weomen and in steade of theire warlike
> musicke appointed to them certaine Lascivious layes and loose gigs by which in
> shorte space theire mindes weare so mollified and abated that they forgate theire
> former firesnes and became moste tender and effeminate. (*Prose*, 121)

This passage well illustrates the a priori assumptions of 'natural' hegemony informing Elizabethan perceptions of gender. Masculinity implies
governance, femininity (or effeminacy) implies subservience. The trouble, however, was that the Irish saw matters in very similar terms and frequently perceived the New English as effeminate. Gaelic clansmen did
not dress like the false Agdistes or the effete Lydians. Their apparel, as
Irenius complains, was all too 'warlike' and fit for 'manly exercize'. What
is deplored in one context is therefore commended in another. Colonists
must not be emasculated by Gaelic women, but conquered nations must
be rendered 'tender and effeminate' and dressed accordingly for 'the persone that is gowned is by his gowne putt in minde of gravetye and allsoe
Restrained from lightenes by the verye unaptnes of his wede' (*Prose*, 121).
Richard Beacon approvingly pointed to the example of the Lacedemoni-
ans who rendered the Thebans 'soft and effeminate' by forbidding them
to be trained as soldiers.[60] The English 'Acrasia' is to be commended for
stripping the Irish 'Verdant' of his arms. Yet Irenius proceeds to admit
that all of the uncivil clothes to which he objects 'be not Irishe garmentes
but Englishe' (*Prose*, 121). Masculinity, desired in the self must be
repressed in the 'other'—which, as it turns out, is actually the other self.
Paradoxically, the false Agdistes is berated for being as the Irish should be,
and the Irish are condemned for not being as he is.

Richard Stanyhurst's 'Description of Ireland', incorporated into the
1577 edition of Holinshed, closely anticipates, and may well have influenced, the central imagery of Spenser's Bowre of Blisse when it comments

---

[60] See Beacon (1996), 131. For the notions of hegemony encoded in gender see Clare Carroll,
'Representations of Women in Some Early Modern Tracts on the Colonization of Ireland',
Albion, 25 (1993), 379–93.

upon the manner in which 'the verie Englishe of birth, conversant with the savage sort of that people [the Gaelic Irish] become degenerat, and as though they had tasted of Circes poisoned cup, are quite altered'.[61] Similarly, writing in 1612, and possibly influenced by Spenser, Sir John Davies complains of how English colonists 'became degenerate and metamorphosed . . . like those who had drunke of *Circes* Cuppe, and were turned into very Beasts: and yet tooke such pleasure in their beastly manner of life, as they would not returne to their shape of men againe'.[62] Spenser's fable concludes with the swinish Gryll who 'chooseth, with vile difference, | To be a beast' (2. 12. 87), as did so many of the families castigated for being 'muche degenerate from theire firste natures' (*Prose*, 114). Prominent amongst them were the MacSweeneys [Mac Suibhne] whose name Spenser degrades into 'Macswines' thereby contriving an astonishingly convenient accommodation of classical myth to contemporary circumstance (*Prose*, 115–16).[63] Cultural difference is 'vile difference' and a matter of moral choice. It must be resisted like sin. The false Genius ushers the traveller towards Excesse who proffers a cup of sensual delights (2. 12. 56) that is highly reminiscent of Duessa's cup of spiritual abominations (1. 8. 14). Sexual, political, and religious corruption are hereby inferred to be interwoven. Lord Grey therefore urged the queen to undertake the 'reformation' of 'this yet most miserable nation, utterly devoyde of [God's] knowledge, and nowhitt regarding you his annoynted nor guided by any other rule then sensuall libertie'.[64] In this manner the concept of political 'liberty' is repeatedly confounded in that of moral libertinism.[65] From Ó Súilleabháin Béarra's viewpoint, however, it was English 'civility' ('urbanitas') that constituted the real 'Circaean cup' ('Circaeum poculum') by compromising the purity of Gaelic culture and threatening the religion that served as its spiritual expression.[66]

Allegorical depictions of the discovery of America afford many similar images to that of the Bowre of Blisse. Jan van der Street, for example, shows Amerigo Vespucci (Fig. 10) encountering a buxom, naked 'America' in a lush, exotic landscape filled with strange creatures such as tapirs and sloths while in the background a group of naked cannibals cook human flesh.

[61] Holinshed (1808), vi. 69.   [62] Davies (1612), 182.

[63] For the 'hoggishe fashion' of the 'Macke Swines' see Derricke (1985), 11.

[64] SP 63/82/54 (commonly attributed to Spenser). See also Raymond Jenkins, 'Spenser with Lord Grey in Ireland', *PMLA* 52 (1937), 338–53 (p. 345).

[65] See William Palmer, 'That "Insolent Liberty": Honor, Rites of Power, and Persuasion in Sixteenth-Century Ireland', *RQ* 46 (1993), 308–27.

[66] O'Sullivan Beare (1960), 67.

10. Amerigo
Vespucci in
the New
World.
Theodor Galle
after
Stradanus.
BM, 1957-4-
13-35.

This is a savage Eden in which the newcomer may well fall, but Vespucci is on his guard. Like Calidore, he wears armour 'privily' beneath his tunic, and holds a banner with the Southern Cross in one hand and an astrolabe in the other (6. 11. 36). He knows where he is both morally and culturally. It is particularly noteworthy in this respect that the fifteenth canto of Tasso's *Gerusalemme Liberata*, upon which the Bowre of Blisse is closely modelled, incorporates a hymn of praise to Columbus.[67] Even in Spenser's immediate sources the pursuit of empire and the perils of exotic temptation are juxtaposed. Like the New World, Ireland was commonly envisioned as 'virgin' territory ripe for the possession of questing knights. According to Luke Gernon, for example, 'this Nymph of Ireland, is at all poynts like a yong wenche that hath the greene sicknes for want of occupying. She is verye fayre of visage, and hath a smooth skinn of tender grasse . . . Her flesh is of a softe and delicat mould of earthe, and her blew vaynes trayling through every part of her like ryvoletts.'[68] In the Bowre of Blisse, however, the louche eroticism of conquest is reversed. The female 'occupies' the male, and the effect is one of cultural 'depasturing' (2 . 12. 73).[69] Acrasia's association with the mantle-wearing 'monashul', or Gaelic wandering women, may be inferred from the fact that her bower is 'mantled with greene' (2. 12. 50). Irenius is much preoccupied with the sexual possibilities of this 'mantle'. The same garment that serves as 'a fitt howsse for an outlawe a mete bedd for a Rebell and an Apte cloake for a thefe' also provides a covering for 'these wanderinge weomen Called of them *monashul*': 'for in sommer ye shall finde her arayed Comonlye but in her smocke and mantle to be more readye for her lighte services. In winter and in her travell it is her Cloake and safegarde and allsoe a Coverlett for her Lewed exercises. And when she hathe filled her vessell under it she maye hide bothe her burden and her blame' (*Prose*, 100–1).[70] But it was not just a matter of sexual licence. According to Thomas Smyth such 'goyng women' travelled 'from contry to contry, soynge sedicione amongst the people'.[71] Defence of the 'Romish religion', remarked Camden, was the 'mantle for all rebellion' in Ireland.[72] The 'monashul' were whores of

---

[67] *Gerusalemme Liberata*, xv. 31–2.   [68] Hadfield and McVeagh (1994), 66.

[69] See Louis A. Montrose, '*A Midsummer Night's Dream* and the Shaping Fantasies of Elizabethan Culture: Gender, Power, Form', in Margaret W. Ferguson, Maureen Quilligan, and Nancy J. Vickers (eds.), *Rewriting the Renaissance: The Discourses of Sexual Difference in Early Modern Europe* (Chicago: University of Chicago Press, 1986), 65–87 (pp. 79, 86).

[70] 'Monashul' is a corruption of the Gaelic 'mná siúbhail' or vagrant women.

[71] Hore, 'Irish Bardism in 1561', *UJA* 6 (1858), 165–7 (p. 167).

[72] Camden (1610), 123 (mispaginated as p. 111).

Babylon. Yet in order to destroy the Bowre of Blisse Spenser first had to create it, and the act of creation reveals the object of fear as an object of desire. Fynes Moryson bears unwitting testimony to the truth of this when, in the course of condemning the 'licentiousnes' of Irish women, he takes exception to their unaccountable preference for extending the 'ill fruites of love' to any 'Irish horsboy, [rather] then to any English of better condition'.[73] They sin with the wrong people and that, at least, is unpardonable.

Colonial anxieties are writ large in the Acrasia episode, but so too are even more fundamental concerns concerning the government of the home country. According to John Knox both England and Scotland 'hath dronken . . . the enchantment and venom of *Circes* [*sic*] . . . to their owne shame and confusion' in their acceptance of female rule.[74] Modern commentators have accordingly related Acrasia to Mary Queen of Scots, but the imagery affords a more general picture of male heroism overcome by female luxury, of Mars slumbering in the arms of Venus as his weapons lie derelict in the background: 'his warlike armes, the idle instruments | Of sleeping praise, were hong upon a tree' (2. 12. 80).[75] The scenario is familiar in Renaissance paintings and was sometimes susceptible of a comfortingly moral interpretation (as conflict overcome by love, for example). The supplanting of Venus by Circe alters the matter, however. Acrasia's activity anticipates that of Radigund.[76] The wholesale destruction of the Bowre of Blisse populated by effeminate and 'unmanly' men (2. 12. 86), is indicative of the poem's resistance to the supposed source of its inspiration—as indeed are such incidents as the scatologically described stripping of Duessa. Though professedly active in the service of the fairy queen, the knight of 'maidenhead' is overtly suspicious of the power of female sexuality, and implicitly of female power. By appropriating his monarch's 'maidenhead' he insulates himself against her sexuality. Acrasia cannot die but she must be removed from power. It is not only her gardens but her 'Pallace brave' that must be torn down with 'rigour pittilesse' (2. 12. 83). To a greater extent than has hitherto been recognized the Bower of Blisse allegorizes the political 'landscape' of female regiment in all of its aspects, political as well as sexual. It is all the less surprising, therefore, that the anxieties generated by female ascendancy should find their

[73] Moryson (1903), 235.   [74] Knox (1846–64), iv. 392
[75] Kerby Neill, 'Spenser's Acrasia and Mary Queen of Scots', *PMLA* 60 (1945), 682–8.
[76] See Patricia Parker, 'Suspended Instruments: Lyric and Power in the Bower of Bliss', in Marjorie Garber (ed.), *Cannibals, Witches, and Divorce: Estranging the Renaissance* (Baltimore: Johns Hopkins University Press, 1987), 21–39 (pp. 26–8).

counterpart in Spenser's fear of Gaelic women, figures who embodied all varieties of 'otherness'—sexual, racial, political, and religious—and threatened to undo the colonial enterprise by seducing 'civil' planters and bearing hybrid children. The vices that Sir Henry Sidney and Sir Richard Bingham deplored in the redoubtable Gráinne Mhaol [Grace O'Malley]—a 'most famous femynyne sea-captain' and 'nurse of all the rebellions in Connacht'—were precisely those that might have won praise for her husband Richard Burke, or Richard in Irons, had she allowed him to exercise them. Instead, according to Henry Sidney, 'she was as well by sea as by land more than master's mate with him'. Sir William Drury considered her to have 'overstepped the part of womanhood'.[77]

Homi Bhabha has argued that 'the objective of colonial discourse is to construe the colonized as a population of degenerate types on the basis of racial origin, in order to justify conquest and to establish systems of administration and instruction'.[78] To the extent that this is true, the phenomenon of hybridity tended to undermine the very dichotomy upon which the whole enterprise was premised. Ireland bred 'dreadfull doubts' of a more intimate nature than the mere threat of violence in a hostile landscape (I. I. 12). The phenomenon of assimilation betrayed the insecurity of English culture. 'One would not beleeve', remarked Camden, 'in how short a time some English . . . degenerate and grow out of kinde.'[79] In attempting to grapple with the problem of how such things 'maye be', Spenser was ultimately forced to recognize that it was not the country but the colonists who were at fault: 'as it is the nature of all men to love libertye So they become Libertines and fall to all Licentiousnes of the Irishe' (*Prose*, 211). There being no causal relationship between 'licentiousness' and race, however, the last three words are as logically redundant as they are politically essential. 'It is but even the other daye', Irenius concedes, 'since Englande grewe Civill' (*Prose*, 118). To enter Ireland was to submit this 'civility' to the severest test possible and risk regression to the uncivil self. It was correspondingly easy to allegorize the colonial project as an enterprise of soul-making. The imagery of metamorphosis which lends such dynamism to the verse encapsulates the very force that the heroes

---

[77] See Peter Berresford Ellis, *Celtic Women: Women in Celtic Society and Literature* (Grand Rapids, Mich.: William B. Eerdmans Publishing Company, 1995), 214–20; John C. Appleby, 'Women and Piracy in Ireland: from Gráinne O'Malley to Anne Bonny', in Margaret Mac-Curtain and Mary O'Dowd (eds.), *Women in Early Modern Ireland* (Edinburgh: Edinburgh University Press, 1991), 53–68.

[78] Homi K. Bhabha, *The Location of Culture* (London: Routledge, 1994), 70.

[79] Camden (1610), 148.

must resist, and their resistance generates a persistent tension between the moral and aesthetic orders. It is not just the Bowre of Blisse that Guyon must reject, but the poetics that sustain it. He must become deaf to Spenserian verse in order to become a Spenserian hero. Similarly, in order to survive the Irish experience the colonist must become an 'allegorical' reader, translating all of the temptations of Gaelic wealth, song and beauty into the prosaic, if no less energetic, diction of moral condemnation and commercial utility.

7   Noble Britons, Savage Scyths

Renowmed kings, and sacred Emperours,
Thy fruitfull Ofspring, shall from thee descend.

(3. 3. 23)

FOR the purposes of the nation state, genealogy is largely the art of self-invention. Ancestry underwrites ascendancy and the claim to an heroic past validates the quest for an imperial future. In the second book of *The Faerie Queene* Spenser provides his countrymen with a myth of origin, in the third he provides them with a myth of destiny and the two are inextricably linked. There is nothing unique in this.[1] The perceived *telos* of history frequently promotes the adoption, or fabrication, of myths of ethnic origin which exercise authority precisely (and paradoxically) because they *are* 'myths' in Roland Barthes's sense of the term, pseudo-historical fictions that facilitate contemporary policies and are stubbornly defended as historical truths for that very reason.[2] In Spenser's case, however, the creation of an 'English' myth of origin coincided uneasily with the attempt to discredit its Gaelic counterpart. The Galfridian myth of origins incorporated into *The Faerie Queene* was useful not least for the distinction that it appeared to establish between Trojan 'Britons' and Scythian 'Celts'. 'Thinke how much better tis', remarked Drayton in his defence of the matter of Britain,

for thee, and those of thine,
From Gods, and Heroës old to drawe your famous line,
Then from the *Scythian* poore.[3]

In Prince Arthur's book of 'Briton Moniments' the land 'which warlike Britons now possesse' first manifests an autonomous identity when it breaks off from 'the Celticke mayn-land' and achieves insularity (2. 10. 5).[4] The 'Celticke' world is that from which 'Brittaine' segregated itself.

---

[1] For the Paridell episode of book three see below p. 158.
[2] Roland Barthes, *Mythologies* (London: Paladin, 1973), 155–8.
[3] *Poly-Olbion*, VIII, 377–9 in Drayton (1961), iv. 148–9.
[4] See generally Carrie Anna Harper, *The Sources of the British Chronicle History in Spenser's 'Faerie Queene'* (Philadelphia: Bryn Mawr College Monographs, 1910).

This notion was well established by Spenser's day. Employing the fabulous pre-history fabricated by 'Berosus', and popularized in England by no less an authority than John Bale, Holinshed repeatedly (and inconsistently) distinguishes between 'Celts' and 'Britons'.[5] In the beginning, he records, 'Britaine' was 'a parcell of the Celtike kingdome' of which Samothes was the 'originall beginner'. The island passed 341 years 'under the Celts' before the coming of the giant Albion.[6] Thereafter came the Trojan Brutus who vanquished both the gigantic offspring of Albion and 'all such other people as he found in the Iland'. He then ordered the place '(which before hight Albion) to be called Britaine, and the inhabitants Britons after his name'.[7] Neither the 'Picts' nor the 'Scots' are to be accounted 'naturall Britans' but 'barbarous' interlopers of 'Scithian' origin—and 'the Scots and Irish are all one people'.[8] The Irish bards, for example, take their name from Bardus, 'fift king of the Celts' in descent from Samothes, and 'the word Bardus is meere Celtike'.[9]

The definition of the term 'Celt' is, of course, hotly contested by modern historians but, judging by the comments of Buchanan, Speed, and Camden, Holinshed's account is unduly muddled even by the standards of its own time. His terminological imprecision is born of the attempt to differentiate where the available evidence was increasingly seen to demand identification.[10] In exploring the genesis of the Britons he is just as concerned 'to find out the puritie of the originall' as in matters of religion.[11] The coincidence is telling since 'pure' racial origins are invariably endowed with 'spiritual' connotations. Involvement in the enterprise of Ireland threatened to reverse Britain's primal segregation from the 'Celticke mayn-land' through the dreaded process of 'degeneration', a phenomenon that acquires moral significance from implicit comparison with the biblical account of the 'fall'. According to Stanyhurst the early settlers were 'meere English' and remained careful to 'sunder themselves as well in land as in language from the Irish' in order to preserve their

---

[5] See T. D. Kendrick, *British Antiquity* (London: Methuen, 1950), 66–76.
[6] Holinshed (1808), i. 6.   [7] Ibid. 443.
[8] Ibid. 10–11. The use of Scottish mercenaries by Irish clan chiefs was regarded as a major cause of the country's instability. See Jane Ohlmeyer, 'Seventeenth-Century Ireland and the New British and Atlantic Histories', *American Historical Review*, 104 (1999), 446–62 (pp. 455–6); Willy Maley, 'Spenser and Scotland: The *View* and the Limits of Anglo-Irish Identity', *Prose Studies*, 19 (1996), 1–18.
[9] Holinshed (1808), i. 36–7.
[10] For the controversy concerning the term 'Celt' see Norman Davies, *The Isles: A History* (London: Macmillan, 1999), 51–3, 85–101.
[11] Holinshed (1808), i. 34.

ethnic purity. In other words, they preserved their sense of cultural and racial insularity even when forced into contact with the Celts. Once this segregation broke down 'the bodie that before was whole and sound, was by little and little festered, and in manner wholie putrified'.[12]

The Gaelic myth of origin that Irenius is at pains to refute received its classical recension in the eleventh-century *Lebor Gabála Érenn*, or 'Book of the Takings of Ireland', an elaborate pseudo-historiographical compilation deeply indebted in structure and methodology to such authorities as Eusebius, Osorius, and Isidore of Seville. Drawing upon centuries of oral and written tradition—known as 'seanchas' (or ancient lore)—it recounted the various waves of invaders from Noah's flood to the Milesians, the presumed forebears of the modern Irish, thereby providing a mythical history 'which sought to put Ireland on the same footing as Israel and Rome'.[13] With the passage of time, the materials to hand were fashioned and refashioned to suit the social and political realities of the age with the result that the most apparently ancient materials are often the most recent—a phenomenon not unfamiliar to Spenser. Pedigrees, in particular, were consciously altered or invented in order to legitimize the claims of powerful clans.[14] In fact, as Donnchadh Ó Corráin observes, 'the genealogists, like similar castes elsewhere, constantly re-interpreted political reality, justifying the contemporary holders of power and willingly giving retrospective validation to those who had only recently achieved it'.[15] New dynasties were ingeniously 'derived' from those they had supplanted while their real origins were deliberately obscured. 'The *métier* of the Irish genealogist', Ó Corráin concludes, 'leads on directly to the imaginative re-creation of the past.'[16] It was precisely this element of 'imaginative re-creation' that rendered the material so dangerous. The mythical past exercised a powerful hold over the political present.

The Milesians took their name from their eponymous leader Míl Espáine, the 'Soldier of Spain', and the legend could therefore be used to legitimize Spanish intervention in Ireland in much the same way that the legends of Gurgunt and Arthur were used to validate English territorial

---

[12] Holinshed (1808), vi. 4.

[13] John Carey, *The Irish National Origin-Legend: Synthetic Pseudohistory* (Cambridge: Department of Anglo-Saxon, Norse and Celtic, University of Cambridge, 1994), 1.

[14] See Kathleen Hughes, *The Early Celtic Idea of History and the Modern Historian* (Cambridge: Cambridge University Press, 1977), 4.

[15] Donnchadh Ó Corráin, 'Irish Origin Legends and Genealogy: Recurrent Aetiologies', in Tore Nyberg (ed.), *History and Heroic Tale* (Odense: Odense University Press, 1983), 69.

[16] Ibid. 71, 85.

claims. Contemporary Spanish commentators were fully aware of the potential utility of the Gaelic myth of origin, and the matter became increasingly important during the Nine Years' War when O'Neill and O'Donnell actively canvassed support from Philip II.[17] Lughaidh Ó Clérigh records how 'the Gaels of Fodhla were friendly to, and united with, the King of Spain on account of their having come from Spain long before, and a number of learned men and historians of the Irish had set down in remembrance and recollection for the King the doings and history of the sons of Míl'.[18] In order to circumvent this danger New English commentators seized upon the so-called 'Bayonne title', originally fabricated by Giraldus Cambrensis in order to bolster the claims of Henry II. According to this version of events, the Milesians hailed from the Basque country and were granted permission to settle in Ireland by one Gurguntius 'King of the Britons'. 'From this it is clear', Giraldus concluded, 'that Ireland can with some right be claimed by the kings of Britain even though the claim be from olden times.' By way of confirmation he notes that 'the city of Bayonne is on the boundary of Gascony, and belongs to it. It is also the capital of Basclonia, whence the Hibernienses came. And now Gascony and all Acquitaine rejoices in the same rule as Britain.'[19] The strategy was a clever one. By the simple expedient of reading the *Lebor Gabála Érenn* in the light of Geoffrey of Monmouth, Giraldus transforms a legendary 'King of the Britons' into an historical King of England and establishes a title that was considered sufficiently plausible to be cited in such crucial Elizabethan documents as the Act for the Attainder of Shane O'Neill [Seaán Ó Néill].[20]

Holinshed eagerly promoted a garbled version of the 'Bayonne title' in his account of Ireland's 'First Inhabitants'. He sounds a note of caution, however, by warning the reader that his sources have merely 'set downe what they have found in the Irish antiquities' and do not necessarily vouch for its veracity. It is possible that Gaelic chroniclers merely acted as 'all other nations and people that seeke to advance the glorie of their countries, in fetching their beginning . . . from some one of ancient antiquitie'.[21] The warning is salutary but soon forgotten. The story that Gurguntius graciously endowed Hiberus (a progenitor of the Gaelic Irish)

---

[17] Juan E. Tazón Salces, 'Politics, Literature and Colonization: A View of Ireland in the Sixteenth Century', in C. C. Barfoot and Theo D'haen (eds.), *The Clash of Ireland: Literary Contrasts and Connections* (Amsterdam: Rodopi Press, 1989), 23–36 (p. 25).

[18] Ó Clérigh (1948–57), i. 120, 121. [19] Giraldus Cambrensis (1982), 99–100.

[20] See Geoffrey of Monmouth (1966), 100–1; Campion (1963), introduction, 63–4.

[21] Holinshed (1808), vi. 71.

with a homeland is too valuable to discount since it proves that 'the kings of this our Britain had an elder right to the realme of Ireland, than by the conquest of Henrie the second'.[22] An Irish myth of origin is effortlessly transformed into an English myth of sovereignty. Prince Arthur's book of 'Briton Moniments' dutifully records how King Gurgunt,

> gave to fugitives of *Spayne*,
> Whom he at sea found wandring from their wayes,
> A seate in *Ireland* safely to remayne,
> Which they should hold of him, as subiect to *Britayne*.

(2. 10. 41)

This claim is not confined to Spenser's poetry. Irenius asserts that 'it appearethe by good recorde yeat extante that kinge Arthur and before him Gurgunt had all that Ilande in his Allegiance and Subieccion' (*Prose*, 95). As Seathrún Céitinn pointed out, however, the 'good recorde' in question depended wholly upon Giraldus's unfounded claim 'that Ireland owed tribute to King Arthur' in the days of 'Giolla Már', a figure unknown to Gaelic chronicle.[23] Muircheartach the Great, son of Earc, the monarch recorded as reigning in what was presumed to be the Arthurian era, had no connection with the Arthurian legend.

Spenser was fully aware of the political uses of Gaelic chronicle, but he generally preferred to treat such materials less as historical documents than as anthropological sources.[24] In fact his attitude is dichotomous. While using the story of Gurguntius to obvious political effect in both *The Faerie Queene* and *A View*, he also suggests that what purports to be an ancient myth is actually a modern fabrication: 'for beinge, as they are nowe accounted, the moste barbarous nacion in Christendome [the Irish] to avoide that reproche woulde dervive themselves from the Spaniardes whom they now see to bee a verye honorable people' (*Prose*, 90). Gaelic sources must therefore be treated in a sceptical, scholarly fashion quite distinct from that adopted by 'the Irishe themselves' who 'thoroughe theire Ignorance in matters of Learninge and deper iudgement doe moste

---

[22] Holinshed (1808), vi. 77. For Gurguntius see Andrew Hadfield, 'Briton and Scythian: Tudor Representations of Irish Origins', *IHS* 28 (1993), 390–408 (pp. 396–7).

[23] Céitinn (1902–13), i. 12, 13.

[24] For Spenser's knowledge of Gaelic sources see Roland M. Smith, 'Spenser, Holinshed, and the *Leabhar Gabhála*, *JEGP* 43 (1944), 390–401; Clare Carroll, 'Spenser and the Irish Language: The Sons of Milesio in *A View of the Present State of Ireland*, *The Faerie Queene*, Book V and the *Leabhar Gabhála*, *Irish University Review*, special issue, 'Spenser in Ireland 1596–1996', 26/2 (1996), 281–90.

Constantlye beleve and Avouch theym' (*Prose*, 84). The only reliable reader of Gaelic history, it appears, is an English reader. Approached in a proper ethnographical spirit, and with due attention to 'comparison of times, likenes of manners and Customes, Affinytie of wordes . . . and manie other like circumstances', Gaelic legend may be found to contain 'some relickes of the trewe Antiquitye thoughe disguised, which a well eyde man maye happelye discover and finde out' (*Prose*, 84–6). Encased in all of the 'Milesian lyes' Spenser detected a kernel of ethnic 'truth' which would support Barnaby Rich's allegation that Irish 'incevylyte' was 'bred in the bone, they have yt by nature' (*Prose*, 90).[25]

The *Lebor Gabála Érenn* asserts that the Milesians originated in Scythia, and Spenser seizes upon this detail as proof that the Irish are of barbarous origin and inherently 'salvage'. For him, this is the one un-doubted 'fact' beneath the fabrication. For Gaelic mythographers 'Scythia' was an appropriately exotic point of origin, a mysterious place on the vanishing point of the known world, famous not just for its mar-tial qualities of 'bravery' and 'valour' but for its civility. It was from Scythia, according to Céitinn, that 'other countries used to receive insti-tutes and laws and ordinances'.[26] For Spenser, the connotations of 'Scythia' were quite different, and he wrote in the spirit of a new breed of neo-classical historians who regarded it as their duty 'to rectify the barbarian account or to substitute a scientific hypothesis for it'.[27] The Renaissance perception of allegedly 'barbaric' contemporary cultures was largely dictated by ancient paradigms, but the phenomenon was immeas-urably strengthened by the notion that, in many cases, the modern and the ancient were one and the same. Herodotus represented Scythia as the cultural antithesis of the Athenian 'polis' and proceeded to describe it by a process of 'systematic differentiation' from the homeland, consistently employing the rhetorical figure of 'similitudo per contrarium'.[28] Scythia lay in the *eschatia*, the wild frontier beyond the pale of Greek civilization. Its lands were unenclosed and its inhabitants nomadic, despite their de-scent from the Greek hero Hercules. Seen from this viewpoint, the Scythians represent not merely the demonic alter ego of Athenian culture but the potential for anarchy within the *polis*. Their otherness was all the more threatening for representing the dark side of the Hercules myth for,

[25] Hinton (1940), 83.   [26] Céitinn (1902–13), i. 229.
[27] See Elias J. Bickerman, 'Origines Gentium', *Classical Philology*, 47 (1952), 65–81 (p. 71).
[28] François Hartog, *The Mirror of Herodotus: The Representation of the Other in the Writing of History*, trans. Janet Lloyd (Berkeley: University of California Press, 1988), 8, 227.

as François Hartog observes, 'he is not always a civilizing hero, and sometimes not even a civilized one'.[29] The remark is particularly apposite for
our purposes in view of Spenser's use of Hercules as the mythical proto-
type for Artegall.[30]

Spenser modelled his investigation of Irish origins upon Herodotus'
methodology, praising the manner in which the Greek historian discovered Homer's race by analysing his accounts of religious rituals: 'and by
the same reasone maie I as reasonablie Conclude that the Irishe are
discended from the *Scythyans* for that they use even to this daie some of
the same ceremonies which the *Scythyans* auncientlye used' (*Prose*, 107).
Yet Spenser's primary source was not Herodotus but Joannes Boemus's
Omnium Gentium Mores, Leges, et Ritus (1520), partially translated into
English as *The Fardle of Facions* (1555) and one of the earliest attempts at
comparative ethnography. What it actually compares, however, are not
peoples but descriptions of peoples, and its reliance upon secondary
sources is entirely characteristic of its age. In this respect it is little more
than an eclectic compilation from such authorities as Herodotus, Pliny,
'Berosus', Solinus, and Strabo, but its eclecticism is ideologically directed.
Boemus was at pains to represent the exotic by 'the contemporary standard of the socially good, the ultimate criterion of true civility'.[31] For him,
contemporary 'Scythians' are identical to their ancient forebears. They
continue to be bloodthirsty, cruel, nomadic, and idolatrous just as the
contemporary Irish remain 'inhospitable, uncivill and cruel', delight in
war, drink their enemies' blood, and make no account of right or
wrong.[32] Here, set in an eminently 'scientific' context, was the anthropological lore that Spenser needed in order to draw out the true 'meaning' of
the Gaelic myth of origin, and here too was ample conformation of the
dangers of 'degeneracy'. Living amongst the Scythians are the 'Budines'
who 'ware sometime Griekes whiche, put of fro their countrie, seatled
them selves there. And by processe, losing the proprietie of their owne
tongue, became in language haulfe Grekes, and haulfe Scithians.'[33] They
are the exact equivalent of the Old English, linguistically and culturally
degenerate yet of quintessentially 'civil' origin. By affording such an

[29] Hartog, *The Mirror of Herodotus*, 26.
[30] For Artegall as Hercules see Jane Aptekar, *Icons of Justice: Iconography and Thematic Imagery in Book V of 'The Faerie Queene'* (New York: Columbia University Press, 1969), 153–200.
[31] See Margaret T. Hodgen, *Early Anthropology in the Sixteenth and Seventeenth Centuries* (Philadelphia: University of Pennsylvania Press, 1964), 131–43 (p. 141).
[32] Boemus (1520), fo. 78r.   [33] Boemus (1555), sig. N5r.

exemplum Boemus supplied Spenser with a dangerously implosive template for *A View*.

Spenser prefaces his discussion of Irish customes with the observation that 'it is firste nedefull to Consider from whence they firste spronge, ffor from the sundrie manners of the nacions from whence that people which now is Called Irishe weare derived some of the Customes which now remaine amongest them have bene firste fetched' (*Prose*, 82). Cast in this form, the argument is inescapably circular. Observation of Gaelic manners provides clues to their ethnic origin and this in turn serves to explain the 'barbarity' of what has been observed. The people 'which now is Called Irishe' are actually something else. The very name that secures their identity only serves to obscure it. While he acknowledges several strands in their make-up, Spenser has no hesitation in concluding that 'the chiefest' is Scythian: their practice of transhumance is Scythian; their war cries are 'verye naturall *Scythyan*'; their penchant for 'Cryinge and howlinge' at funerals is 'uncivile and Scithianlike'; their mantle 'cometh from the *Scythyans*', and their glibs are 'mere salvage and *Scythyan*'.[34] This was only to be expected because 'it is the manner of all barbarous nacions to be verye superstitious and dilligent observers of olde Customes and Antiquities which they receave by Continuall tradicion from theire parentes by recordinge of theire bardes and Cronicles in theire songes and by dailye use and ensample of theire elders' (*Prose*, 109–10).

But how exactly did such a 'barbarous' people come to have written 'cronicles'? 'The Scythians never, that I Cane reade of olde', Irenius concedes, 'had Lettres amongest them.' The Irish had them 'ancientlye', however, 'ffor the Saxons of Englande are saide to have fetched theire Lettres and learninge and learned men from the Irishe' (*Prose*, 87). Spenser is here faced with the possibility that the very existence of the Irish chronicles confutes his interpretation of them. He is therefore driven to qualify his assertion of Scythian ancestry with a generous mingling of Gaulish blood 'wheareby it is to be gathered that the nacion which Came out of Spaine into Irelande weare ancientlye Gaules and that they broughte with them those Lettres which they had learned in Spaine' (*Prose*, 88). At this point the whole structure of the argument teeters on the verge of collapse. The people 'called Irishe' do not speak 'Scythian'. The Gaelic language, Spenser acknowledges, is rich in Gallic vocabulary and 'the Gallish speache is the verye *Brittish* the which was generallye used heare in all

---

[34] *Prose*, 82, 97–8, 99, 103, 105, 106.

Britany before the Comminge in of the Saxons and yeat is retained of the welchemen the Cornishemen and the *Britones* of ffraunce' (*Prose*, 93). This single sentence tends to conflate all of the various peoples that Spenser is elsewhere so anxious to differentiate. He is everywhere at pains to discredit the Irish myth of origin in the interests of establishing ethnic difference, but the irresistible conclusion to his own arguments is that the contemporary Irish are closely akin to the ancient Britons and, therefore, to the major protagonists of *The Faerie Queene*. And yet that conclusion *is resisted throughout*, despite the assertion that the east coast of Ireland was populated 'from the *Brittanes* themselves' and, consequently, that even the notorious Feagh mac Hugh O'Byrne is of ancient Briton stock (*Prose*, 94, 170–1).

Because both the Gaelic and the 'Briton' myths of origin employ essentially the same techniques of fabricated chronology and anachronistic reference, to explode one is tantamount to discrediting the other. In the manuscript of *A View* held at the PRO (as in the edition published by Sir James Ware in 1633), Irenius concedes that in formulating their myth of origin 'the Iryshe doe hearin no otherwise then our vayne Englyshemen doe in the tale of Brutus . . . it beeinge as impossible to prove that ther ever was anie suche Brutus of Albanye, as it is, that ther [was] anie suche Gathelus of Spaine. But hearin theye shewe their great lightnes, which beeinge a barbarous and salvage nation, woulde faine fetche them selves from Spaine, Lyke as wee and the French also woulde from the Troians' (*Prose*, 86).[35] It would be hard to decide which element of this assertion is the most damaging. The dismissal of *The Faerie Queene*'s myth of origin threatens to confound the racial distinctions insisted upon throughout *A View*. The whole fabric of difference would then prove to be raised upon a foundation of identity: 'they' would become 'lyke as wee' in every sense. But this, of course, is to suppose that *The Faerie Queene* is intended to be read as 'history'—a questionable supposition, as we shall shortly see. Nevertheless Céitinn was quick to exploit the apparent confusion. 'British authors', he asserts, 'themselves confess that the Saxons did not leave them any ancient texts, or monuments, by which they might know the condition of the time which preceded the Saxons.' It was unlikely, he concluded, that 'Britannia' took its name from Brutus, 'and since they knew not whence is the name of their own country, it was no wonder they should be in ignorance of many of the ancient concerns of Britain and,

---

[35] SP, 63, 202 , Part 4, item 58.

therefore, it is not strange that Spenser likewise should be ignorant of them'.[36]

The juxtaposing of Brutus and Gathelus is not original to Spenser but derives from George Buchanan's *Rerum Scoticarum Historia* (1582), the work to which Irenius gives 'moste Credite' in such matters (*Prose*, 86).[37] Although he defended much of Hector Boece's legendary Scottish history for political reasons, Buchanan's views on Geoffrey of Monmouth were uncompromising.[38] It was clear from classical sources, he argued, that the Britons 'descended from the Gauls' and that Britain in the age of Julius Caesar 'was exactly what Gaul had been before the invasion of the Romans'.[39] The Gauls were an offshoot of the 'Celts', and 'the British tongue . . . was the same with the Gallic, or not widely different from it'. The notion that the Trojans spoke 'British' was a piece of 'shameless effrontery' easily confuted by classical authority.[40] The early Britons were 'miserably poor', 'rarely applied themselves to agriculture', 'easily changed their places of residence', and were correctly categorized as 'barbarous' by Tacitus.[41] The 'romance of Brutus' was nothing more than a fabrication designed to confer vicarious lustre on a primitive people. The same was true of the myth of Gathelus, a figure wholly unknown to classical authorities. The fact of the matter was that the Irish sprang 'from the Celtic inhabitants of Spain' and spoke a version of the Celtic tongue.[42] Many English commentators were slowly coming to the same conclusion, and the veracity of Geoffrey of Monmouth fell under intense scrutiny.

The *Historia Regum Britanniae* had first appeared around 1138 and was intended, according to William of Newburgh, 'to please the Britons' at a time when their Welsh descendants were frequently dismissed as 'brutish creatures without a history'.[43] This mattered because, according to Henry of Huntington's *Historia Anglorum*, a people ignorant of its 'origins' was scarcely human.[44] Bede's *Gesta Anglorum* (731) had 'created the English as a single people by giving them a single historical mythology, by emphasising their common Germanic origins . . . and by consigning the Britons to

[36] Céitinn (1902–13), i. 24–5.

[37] For Buchanan's reputation see James E. Phillips, 'George Buchanan and the Sidney Circle', *HLQ* 12 (1948), 23–55.

[38] See I. D. McFarlane, *Buchanan* (London: Duckworth, 1981), 418–21, 425–8.

[39] Buchanan (1856), i. 84.   [40] Ibid. 76, 81, 83.   [41] Ibid. 69, 135.

[42] Ibid. 77–9, 101.

[43] John Gillingham, 'The Context and Purposes of Geoffrey of Monmouth's *History of the Kings of Britain*', *Anglo-Norman Studies*, 13 (1990), 99–118 (pp. 103, 110).

[44] Huntington (1996), 5.

a historical oubliette'.[45] Geoffrey rectified the disparity by supplying two thousand years of missing history and a powerful claim to illustrious provenance. His Britons are not the 'barbarians' of Saxon record, but a highly civilized race of gifted individuals who built cities, cultivated lands, embraced Christianity, and established an empire.[46] Although fallen on hard times, and subjected in turn to Saxons and Normans, they are destined to 'occupy the island again at some time in the future, once the appointed moment should come'.[47] Geoffrey's intentions in all of this remain highly debatable, but there can be little doubt as to whose interests his labours eventually served. Despite the allegation that he wrote 'to please the Britons', he dedicated his work not to a member of the Welsh nobility but to Robert, Earl of Gloucester, the illegitimate son of Henry I.[48] 'Towards the Norman kings', remarks J. S. P. Tatlock, 'he is no disaffected Celt.'[49] The Arthurian legend was warmly embraced by a royal family with strong Breton antecedents, and Arthur soon became 'rex Angliae' instead of 'rex Britonum'—and it was only a short step, from being King of England to being an English king.[50] Wace's *Roman de Brut* or *Gestes des Bretons* was dedicated to Eleanor of Aquitane and, although Geoffrey of Monmouth had never used the term 'England', Henry II's grandson, and prospective heir, was astutely christened Arthur.[51] The spirit of ancient heroism was to be reborn in a Norman monarchy thereby establishing continuity between an illustrious 'Briton' past and a glorious 'English' future.[52] As in the Gaelic *Lebor Gabála Érenn*, a break with the past would be represented as its fulfilment. The ancient 'Britons' were being made 'English' at just the time that their Welsh descendants were being subjected to a violent policy of 'Anglicization'.

Geoffrey alleged that he derived his tale of Trojan ancestry from 'a certain very ancient book written in the British language', but it was not long before Layamon's *Brut* (c. 1200) made its substance available in

[45] R. R. Davies, 'The Peoples of Britain and Ireland, 1100–1400: IV. Language and Historical Mythology', *Transactions of the Royal Historical Society*, 7 (1997), 1–24 (p. 19).

[46] See Nancy F. Parker, *Serious Entertainment: The Writing of History in Twelfth-Century England* (Chicago: University of Chicago Press, 1977), 62–6; 194–211.

[47] *Geoffrey of Monmouth* (1966), 283.

[48] Robert, Earl of Gloucester is the sole dedicatee in most manuscripts but some have an additional dedication to Waleran, Count of Mellent, son of Robert de Beaumont.

[49] J. S. P. Tatlock, *The Legendary History of Britain: Geoffrey of Monmouth's 'Historia Regum Britanniae' and its Early Vernacular Versions* (Berkeley: University of California Press, 1950), 399.

[50] Rees Davies, *The Matter of Britain and the Matter of England* (Oxford: Clarendon Press, 1996), 16–17.

[51] Ibid. 4; Kendrick, *British Antiquity*, 14–15.

[52] See Gordon Hall Gerould, 'King Arthur and Politics', *Speculum*, 2 (1927), 33–51.

the rival vernacular.[53] 'By the late twelfth century', observes Rees Davies, 'Geoffrey's early history of Britain had been fully absorbed into the current canon of English historiography; it had become the colourful extensive backcloth to the history of England.'[54] In Spenser's House of Alma, Prince Arthur reads his 'Briton Moniments' in English, the language described in the prefatory material to *The Shepheardes Calender* as the 'mother tongue' of the English nation. The contradictions proliferate but are swept aside by what Arthur B. Ferguson refers to as 'the myth of continuity', perhaps the most potent of all political myths.[55] Tudor apologists were quick to recognize its power when they emphasized the Welsh, and consequently 'Briton', antecedents of Henry VII. Moving in their wake, Spenser presents the advent of the Tudors as the miraculous restoration foretold by Geoffrey: 'so shall the Briton bloud their crowne againe reclame' (3. 3. 48). So much has long been recognized, but Spenser proceeds to make a far more important, if relatively neglected, claim: 'Thenceforth eternall union shall be made | Betweene the nations different afore' (49). The Tudor accession is nothing less than the vehicle for the birth of what modern readers might regard as the nation-state. 'Nations different afore'— Britons, Saxons, Danes, and Normans—are eternally united in civil harmony. Arthur and George are foundlings of different races but discover their true political identities in the service of the fairy queen, just as their respective Briton and Saxon descendants will be united in the service of her Tudor counterpart. 'The Legend of Holinesse' defies received chronology to allow its Briton Prince to redeem its Saxon saint, as Archbishop Parker credited the Tudors with reclaiming an independent 'Saxon' church from bondage to Rome. Similarly Britomart, the fictive progenitor of the Tudor line, rides forth in the armour of the '*Saxon* Virgin' who gave her name to the Angles (3. 3. 55–8). But Spenser makes even greater claims for coalescence than those of mere political union. Generally speaking, he employs the term 'nation' as a synonym for 'race'. When Britomart learns how the Greeks destroyed Troy, for example, she laments their cruelty,

> Against that nation, from whose race of old
> She heard, that she was lineally extract:
> For noble *Britons* sprong from *Troians* bold,
> And *Troynovant* was built of old *Troyes* ashes cold.

> (3. 9. 38)

---

[53] Geoffrey of Monmouth (1966), 51.   [54] Davies, *The Matter of Britain*, 16.
[55] Arthur B. Ferguson, *Clio Unbound: Perception of the Social and Cultural Past in Renaissance England* (Durham, NC: Duke University Press, 1979), 116.

'Nation' and 'race' are primarily a matter of 'lineage'. When Una asks Arthur to relate his 'name and nation' (1. 9. 2), he replies that 'the lignage and the certain Sire, | From which I sprong, from me are hidden yit' (3). The narrator, however, invariably identifies him as a 'Briton Prince'. His 'nation' is his 'race' and his homeland, like that of Britomart, is invariably called 'Britayne'. By contrast, St George is destined to become the patron saint 'of mery England' (1. 10. 61)—astonishingly the sole use of the term 'England' in *The Faerie Queene* despite its recurrence throughout *A View*. The reason for this disparity is not far to seek. Unlike the 'Briton' prince, George is born 'of English blood' (64). He comes 'from English race' (60) and specifically,

> from ancient race
> Of *Saxon* kings, that have with mightie hand
> And many bloudie battailes fought in place
> High reard their royall throne in *Britaine* land,
> And vanquisht them, unable to withstand.   (65)

In Arthur's book of 'Briton Moniments', as in Merlin's prophecies, the Saxons are the Britons' 'fone' (3. 3. 33). The poem's action is contextualized by the ongoing struggle between these two races. Britomart begins her quest for Artegall towards the close of the reign of Uther Pendragon as the conflict intensifies and 'all *Britanie* doth burne in armes bright' (52). When Spenser speaks of the establishment of 'eternall union . . . Betweene the nations different afore' he is not, in fact, alluding to the emergence of a modern nation state (which might continue to contain several distinct 'races'), but rather to a successful process of ethnic assimilation whereby racial difference has been eradicated. The 'nations' that were 'different afore' are no longer 'different' at all, politically or ethnically. The implications for Spenser's Irish policy are far-reaching.

Spenser's Merlin is usually associated with Geoffrey of Monmouth, but Merlin also figures prominently in Giraldus Cambrensis's *Expugnatio Hibernica* where he is employed to 'prophesy' the victory of the 'English' ['Angli'] over the Irish ['Hiberni']. In fact, for Elizabethan readers generally, he served as the 'magus' who linked the destiny of the two countries to the Tudor crown.[56] In Spenser he is careful to predict how Britomart's great-grandson, Malgo, will re-establish the claim to Ireland (3. 3. 32) which the 'Briton Moniments' identify as originating with Gurgunt

---

[56] Tatlock, *Legendary History of Britain*, 410–11.

(2. 10. 41). William of Newburgh dismissed Arthur's supposed conquest of Ireland, but Giraldus insisted upon it, just as he insisted upon the Trojan ancestry of its would-be reconquerors.[57] The materials lay ready to hand and may even have been designed for the purpose. At least one commentator has argued that Geoffrey deliberately fabricated Arthur's Irish adventures with an eye towards future Norman expansion. He therefore depicted the Irish as 'barbarians' who freely intermarried with 'Scythian' Picts when the more self-respecting 'Britons' refused to do so.[58] This was grist to Spenser's mill. So far as he is concerned, Ireland is one of the '*British* Islands' in a political as well as a geographical sense (7. 6. 38).[59] The preferred destiny for its people is one of racial assimilation: 'I thinke it best by an union of manners and Conformitye of mindes to bringe them to be one people, and to put awaie the dislikefull Conceite bothe of thone and thother' (*Prose*, 211–12). The process whereby the various 'nations' of the 'Briton Moniments' became 'one people' must be repeated in Ireland, so that the Gaelic Irish will, in the words of Sir John Davies, 'in tongue and heart, and every way else, becom *English*'.[60] For the reverse to occur would be racially and politically regressive for the simple reason that Spenser's 'Britons' are not barbarous 'Celts', like the Irish, but Trojans. So it is in 'fairyland' at least.

In the midst of his forthright condemnation of the Brutan legend, Buchanan pauses to make one very significant qualification: 'we must grant a liberty', he concedes, 'to poets when they endeavour to embellish, with fictitious ornaments, the origin either of families or of nations.'[61] Similarly, in his 'Letter to Ralegh', Spenser reminds us that 'the methode of a Poet historical is not suche, as of an historiographer'. Far more is involved in this assertion than matters of narrative chronology. The apparently contradictory attitudes adopted towards Brutus in *A View* and *The Faerie Queene* are the products of differences in genre and intent.[62] Sir Philip Sidney defended the poet against the charge of mendacity on the grounds that 'he nothing affirmes, and therefore never lyeth', but this is so only with respect to the factual veracity of the fable.[63] Sidney's poet

---

[57] Gillingham, 'Context and Purposes', 102; Giraldus Cambrensis (1978), 49.
[58] Tatlock, *Legendary History of Britain*, 78–81.
[59] See Andrew Hadfield, *Spenser's Irish Experience: Wilde Fruit and Salvage Soyl* (Cambridge: Cambridge University Press, 1997), 101.
[60] Davies (1612), 272.   [61] Buchanan (1856), i. 72.
[62] See Judith H. Anderson, 'The Antiquities of Fairyland and Ireland', *JEGP* 86 (1987), 199–214.
[63] Smith (1904), i. 184.

'affirmes' moral values just as Spenser's 'poet historicall' endows selected political policies with 'moral' validation. As employed within *The Faerie Queene* the myth of Brutus expresses a particular interpretation of history—as does the whole conceit of 'faery' which E.K. dismisses just as resolutely as Irenius dismisses that of Brutus.[64] Within the poetry the Brutan legend functions both as the fictive expression of the nation's perceived identity and as the 'divination' of its presumed destiny. What matters is not the historical reality of Brutus or Arthur, but the 'once and future' dimension of both legends. They 'exist' as fictive representatives of collective endeavour. Commenting upon the Brutan legend in his sceptical annotations to Drayton's *Poly-Olbion*, John Selden shrewdly remarked that 'no nationall storie' can 'justifie' itself 'but by tradition'.[65] 'Nationalism', Ernest Gellner reminds us, 'is not the awakening of nations to self-consciousness: it invents nations where they do not exist.'[66] For the Elizabethans, however, such 'invention' was by no means illicit. The faculty of 'inventio'—in the dual senses of 'discovery' and 'fabrication'—was central to the rhetorical art and poetical fictions were perceived to address 'real' political questions. In this respect, Sidney argued, 'the fayned *Aeneas* in *Virgil*' was 'more doctrinable' than 'the right *Aeneas* in *Dares Phrigius*'.[67] George Puttenham agreed and concluded that 'for these regards the Poesie historicall is of all other next the divine most honorable and worthy'.[68] Through the genre of epic, the 'poet historicall' provided the supreme articulation of the national spirit. His myths of origin are actually myths of outcome serving to 'justifie' current attitudes and promote future projects. It is comforting to believe that we 'are' what we were meant to be. 'Do by all dew meanes thy destiny fulfill' is the best advice that Merlin can offer Britomart and it is also Spenser's advice to the 'nation' (3. 3. 24). *The Faerie Queene* is intended to have the same effect upon its readers as the act of reading the 'Briton Moniments' has on Arthur. We are invited to become his fellow readers, uniting with him in the 'delight' of a common mythology (2. 10. 69):

---

[64] See E.K.'s gloss to *The Shepheardes Calender*, 'June', 25.

[65] Drayton (1961), iv. 22–3. See also Anthony D. Smith, *The Ethnic Origin of Nations* (Oxford: Basil Blackwell, 1986), 24–6.

[66] Ernest Gellner, *Thought and Change* (London: Weidenfeld, 1964), 168.

[67] Smith (1904), i. 168.

[68] Ibid, ii. 41. See Arthur B. Ferguson, *Utter Antiquity: Perceptions of Prehistory in Renaissance England* (Durham, NC: Duke University Press, 1993), 114–33.

> How brutish is it not to understand,
> How much to her we owe, that all us gave,
> That gave unto us all, what ever good we have.

(2. 10. 69)

The clever wordplay enforces the point. Brutus (or Brute as he was commonly known) is the patron of 'civility', but his very name conjures up the 'brutishness' he is credited with suppressing.[69] Endemic to civilization are the anarchic forces it struggles to contain. Not to 'understand' this is to risk the sort of regression that overtook the Old English in Ireland. 'Coulde they ever Conceave anye suche divillishe dislike of theire owne naturall Contries', Eudoxus asks, 'as that they woulde be ashamed of her name and bite at the dug from which they sucked liffe?' (*Prose*, 116). Spenser's myth of origin unwittingly betrays the origin of his myth, the urgent need to generate forebears in his self-image. He accordingly located his personal ancestors amongst the Spencers of Althorp, who traced their own antecedents to the great medieval family of Despenciers.[70] The new poets, and the new rich, of Elizabethan England shared their monarch's need for the validation of history. They needed to see their genealogies written, like *The Shepheardes Calender*, in antique letters.

The inscription of the Brutan legend within what Northrop Frye terms the 'secular scripture' of romance recognizes its status as political allegory rather than historical fact.[71] The story serves as the secular equivalent of the 'holy fictions' through which the Bible was held to inculcate spiritual truths.[72] But the act of inscription into romance also draws attention to the fictive nature of all historiographical and ethnographical narration. In the chamber of Eumnestes [Good Memory] the 'Briton Moniments' lie side by side with 'another booke, | that hight *Antiquite* of *Faerie* lond' although one might have expected the latter to reside in the chamber of Phantastes (2. 9. 60). Its actual location constitutes a comment on the nature of both texts. It is only in 'fairyland' that the fragmented versions of

---

[69] See Jeffrey Knapp, *An Empire Nowhere: England, America, and Literature from 'Utopia' to 'The Tempest'* (Berkeley: University of California Press, 1992), 66.

[70] See Ernest A. Strathmann, 'Lady Carey and Spenser', *ELH* 2 (1935), 33–57 (pp. 46–7).

[71] See Northrop Frye, *The Secular Scripture: A Study of the Structure of Romance* (Cambridge Mass.: Harvard University Press, 1976), 3–31. For *The Faerie Queene* as 'secular scripture' see Richard A. McCabe, *The Pillars of Eternity: Time and Providence in 'The Faerie Queene'* (Dublin: Irish Academic Press, 1989), 118–27.

[72] For the concept of 'holy fiction' see Colet (1876), 14–15.

'history' supplied by Merlin, Paridell, and the 'Briton Moniments' constitute a continuous narrative or share a thematic link—although it is
noteworthy that even here Paridell's contribution, which envisions history in terms of destructive cycles rather than linear progress, demonstrates the inherent dangers of 'Trojan' descent.[73] As the 'Letter to Ralegh'
implies, the 'poet historicall' employs all three faculties of the mind: 'the
first of them could things to come foresee: | The next could of things pre-
sent best advize; | The third things past could keep in memoree' (2. 9. 49).
The book that Prince Arthur reads as historical fact is presented to
Spenser's readers as exemplary fiction—as indeed is Prince Arthur himself.[74] The poem is intended not as an historical record but as an intervention in the historical process. Anticipating Frye's designation of
romance as sacred scripture, Drayton noted how allegory transforms
mere romance into 'legend', 'so called of the Latine Gerund, *Legendum*,
and signifying . . . things specially worthy to be read . . . Master *Edmund
Spenser* was the very first among us, who transferred the use of the word,
Legend, from Prose to Verse: nor that unfortunately; the Argument of his
Bookes being of a kind of sacred Nature, as comprehending in them
things as well Divine as Humane.'[75] Allegory transforms historical fictions into parables of political grace. Otherwise Spenser might expose
himself to the same criticisms as Geoffrey of Monmouth, namely,

> That all this famous antique history,
> Of some th'aboundance of an idle braine
> Will iudged be, and painted forgery,
> Rather then matter of iust memory.

> (2 Proem 1)

This would reduce him to the level of the Gaelic poets who 'use to forge
and falsefye everie thinge as they liste to please or displease anie man'
(*Prose*, 84). It is significant that this issue is addressed in the proem to the
very book that contains the 'Briton Moniments', and that Spenser is at
pains to reassert the allegorical nature of the enterprise in terms of 'covert
vele' and 'shadowes light' (5). According to James Clifford 'culturalist and
humanist allegories stand behind the controlled fictions of difference and

---

[73] See Heather Dubrow, 'The Arraignment of Paridell: Tudor Historiography in *The Faerie Queene*, III. ix.', *SP* 87 (1990), 312–27.
[74] See Wayne Erickson, 'Spenser's Letter to Ralegh and the Literary Politics of *The Faerie Queene*'s 1590 Publication', *SSt* 10 (1989—but pub. 1992), 139–74 (pp. 161–7).
[75] Drayton (1961), ii. 382.

similitude that we call ethnographic accounts'.[76] Integral to Spenser's 'culturalist and humanist allegory', however, is the contrary contention, born of colonial need, that the myth of Gathelus has no civilizing function because the bards who espouse it are 'so farre from instructinge yonge men in morall discipline that they themselves doe more deserve to be sharpelye discipled' (*Prose*, 125). Since the Gaelic myth of origin can only serve to legitimize barbarity, it cannot be classed amongst the 'sweete invencions' for which 'in all ages Poets have bene in speciall reputacion' (*Prose*, 124). It is the secular equivalent of an 'unholy fiction' and exercises a corrupting influence. The central dichotomy in Spenser's thinking lies not in conflicting attitudes towards the historicity of the matter of Britain but in his treatment of historical mythography which is variously configured both as the highest attainment of poetic skill and as the worst expression of primitive ignorance.

The most remarkable feature of Spenser's mythography is not that he chose to exercise poetic licence by utilizing a myth of origin that he elsewhere recognized to have no factual validity, but that he chose the Briton myth when the Teutonic alternative might have seemed more viable, particularly to someone who repeatedly emphasized the centrality of language to nationality. He chose an ancient myth of origin at a time when much of the intellectual endeavour of the 'nation' he celebrated was engaged upon the creation of a new one.[77] Camden's *Britannia* (1586) did far more than cast grave doubt upon the myth of Brutus; it threatened to render the issue redundant. The long-term effects were very considerable since the new admiration for the Saxons went hand in hand with renewed denigration of the Celts.[78] The notion of Saxon descent established the sort of clear ethnic distinction between colonists and colonized that the myth of 'Briton' ancestry threatened to overturn at every point. The 'English', so far as Camden was concerned, were primarily of Germanic origin, and their ancestors were not the ancient Britons but the Saxons who 'became one nation' with the Angles and Jutes 'and were called by one generall name, one while Saxons, another while, Englishmen, and

[76] James Clifford, 'On Ethnographic Allegory', in James Clifford (ed.), *Writing Culture: The Poetics and Politics of Ethnography* (Berkeley: University of California Press, 1986), 98–121 (p. 101).

[77] Hugh A. MacDougall, *Racial Myth in English History: Trojans, Teutons, and Anglo-Saxons* (Montreal: Harvest House, 1982), 31–50.

[78] See Rudolf B. Gottfried, 'The Early Development of the Section on Ireland in Camden's *Britannia*', *ELH* 10 (1943), 117–30; Sam Smiles, *The Image of Antiquity: Ancient Britain and the Romantic Imagination* (New Haven: Yale University Press for the Paul Mellon Centre for Studies in British Art, 1994), 113–28.

English-Saxons'.[79] Whereas the 'Briton Moniments' suggest that all of the country's various 'nations' somehow became one 'Briton' nation, Camden asserts the exact opposite: the Anglo-Saxon conquest was so complete that 'all the conquered, except some few, whom in the Westerne tract the roughnesse of the countrey defended and kept safe, became one nation, used the same lawes, tooke their name, and spake one and the selfesame language, with the conquerours . . . Which tongue we and they together for the space now of 1150. yeeres, have kept after a sort uncorrupt, and with it the possession also of the Land.'[80] Once again territorial and linguistic integrity are inextricably related. The 'uncorrupt' nature of the language in which Spenser took such pride served for Camden as the clearest indication of the nation's Saxon origins: 'if all the histories that ever were had miscarried and perished; if no writer had recorded, that we Englishmen are descended from Germanes, the true and naturall Scots from the Irish, the Britons of Armorica in France from our Britans; the society of their tongues would easily confirme the same.'[81]

Regarded from this viewpoint, the very language of *The Faerie Queene* might be seen to refute its choice of historical mythology in that Spenser's myth of linguistic purity is at odds with his myth of ethnic identity.[82] Like Buchanan, Camden concluded that 'the ancient Gauls inhabitants of the country now named *France* and Britans of this Isle spake one and the same language: and by necessary consequence the originall of the Britans is to bee reduced unto the Gauls'.[83] 'No man, I hope, will deny', he argued, 'that they which joine[d] in community of language, concurred also in one and the same originall.'[84] In the *Remains Concerning Britain* he asserts that the '*English-Saxon* tongue came in by the *English-Saxons* out of *Germany,* who valiantly and wisely performed heere all the three things which implie a full conquest, viz. the alteration of lawes, language, and attire'.[85] Richard Verstegan drove the point home by asserting that 'Englishmen are descended of German race, and were heertofore generally called Saxons . . . In lyke manner are wee stil termed by the name of Sasons, of the Scotishmen that yet retain their ancient Irish toung, as also of the Irishmen in their own language, who in their ortography wryte us Saxsonach, but pronounce us Sasonagh.'[86] The notion that the Irish had a better understanding of the ethnic nature of the English than they possessed themselves certainly afforded matter for reflection. Although the

---

[79] Camden (1610), 131.   [80] Ibid. 132–3.   [81] Ibid. 16.

[82] See below ch. 9.   [83] Camden (1610), 22.   [84] Ibid. 16.

[85] Camden (1605), 13.   [86] Verstegan (1605), 1.

assertion was made in 1605, six years after Spenser's death, Verstegan was merely stating what many Elizabethan historians and antiquarians had already come to believe, and Spenser, had he cared to look, would indeed have found Queen Elizabeth referred to as a 'Saxon queen' in contemporary Irish poems and chronicles. It is true, of course, that the legend of Brutus continued to find stalwart defenders, such as Richard Harvey, the brother of Spenser's closest friend, but their efforts seemed increasingly irrelevant.[87] Those interested in promoting the causes of the Reformation, parliamentary privilege, or common law found their well-documented Anglo-Saxon heritage far more useful.

As an avid reader of Camden, whom he termed 'the rource of antiquitie', Spenser must have been well aware of contemporary developments in Anglo-Saxon studies.[88] John Twyne's *De Rebus Albionicis Britannicis atque Anglicis* (1590), which dismisses the Brutan legend, was published the same year as his 'Briton Moniments'.[39] From the mid-sixteenth century onwards the portrayal of the ancient Britons was in a state of transition as the myth of cultural sophistication was increasingly supplanted by an equally misleading myth of barbarity. In the early 1570s Lucas de Heere portrayed the Britons of Caesar's day as naked, painted, and hirsute, with clear similarities to his depictions of the 'wilde Irish'.[90] Spenser may never have seen De Heere's illustrations, but a considerable volume of Anglo-Saxon scholarship had accumulated from the time of Archbishop Parker and was readily available in the public domain. It is significant, therefore, that the Saxons play such a comparatively negative and adversarial role in Merlin's account of the country's history. Their eventual hegemony is summarized in the allegation that they won the crown 'first ill, and after ruled wickedly' (3. 3. 46). Holinshed, by contrast, contends that the Britons were so marginalized by the Saxon conquest that 'their whole race must needs have sustained the uttermost confusion, and thereby the memorie of the Britons utterlie have perished among us' were it not for the survivors' intermarriage with their enemies.[91] When he uses the term 'us' he is speaking primarily as a descendant of the Anglo-Saxons.

[87] See Harvey (1593), 97. [88] See *The Ruines of Time*, l. 169.

[89] See Kendrick, *British Antiquity*, 105–8.

[90] Stuart Piggott, *Ancient Britons and the Antiquarian Imagination: Ideas from the Renaissance to the Regency* (London: Thames and Hudson, 1989), 75. For later illustrations by De Bry see Stephanie Moser, *Ancestral Images: the Iconography of Human Origins* (Stroud: Sutton, 1998), 71–6; Stephen Orgel, 'Shakespeare and the Cannibals', in Margorie Garber (ed.), *Cannibals, Witches, and Divorce: Estranging the Renaissance* (Baltimore: Johns Hopkins University Press, 1987), 40–66 (pp. 44–7).

[91] Holinshed (1808), i. 13–14.

The reason for the difference in emphasis, I believe, is that Spenser attempts to serve the cause of the 'nation' through that of the Tudor monarchy. As a result, their myth of dynastic origin becomes the nation's myth of genealogical origin, and their ascent to power marks the Britons' return (3. 3. 48). The primary purpose of the 'auncient booke, hight *Briton moniments*' is to record how the country's various 'regiments' were eventually 'reduced . . . to one mans gouernments' (2. 9. 59). The significance of Spenser's choice of vocabulary is clarified by contrast with Samuel Daniel who asserts that, even as late as the time of Caesar, Britain 'was no Monarchy' but lay 'divided into a multitude of petty Regiments' like Gaul. He dismisses the opposing view as nothing more than 'the invention of such, as take all their reason from the example and *Idea* of the present Customs they see in use'.[92] But such 'idealism' was the cornerstone of Spenser's 'invention'. He set out to recreate the Briton past in the image of the Tudor present, motivated as much by political philosophy (and colonial need) as by the urge to flatter. 'The Inglishe weare at firste as stoute and warlike a people as ever weare the Irishe', reports Irenius, but they gained 'civilytie' primarily 'by reasone of the Continuall presence of theire Kinge whose onelye persone is often times in steade of an Armye to Contayne the unrulye people from a thowsande evill occasions which that wretched kingedome [Ireland] is for wante thereof daylye Carryed into' (*Prose*, 54–5). The tale of Brutus, as Spenser tells it, is a civic parable directed as much towards the monarch as the nation. What the Trojan Britons effected in England, the Tudor Britons must effect in Ireland. Brutus redeems England's 'gentle soyle' from the 'salvage' race that inhabits it and transforms a mere 'land' into a 'realme' (2. 10. 9–13). The people he displaces are scarcely human and therefore have no creditable myth of origin—or, perhaps, one should say that they have no myth of origin and are therefore regarded as scarcely human: 'whence they sprong, or how they were begot, | Uneath is to assure'. Their antecedents are lost in 'monstrous' tales of 'lust unclene', unholy fictions that the narrator simultaneously refutes and perpetuates (8). The land that such people occupy may consequently be regarded as *terra nullius*: 'unpeopled, unmanurd, unprov'd, unpraysd' (5).[93] Following the conquest, Brutus

---

[92] Daniel (1685), 2.
[93] See Anthony Pagden, *Lords of All the World: Ideologies of Empire in Spain, Britain and France c.1500–c.1800* (New Haven: Yale University Press, 1995), 76, 90.

ensures the progress of civility—and the beginnings of 'empire'—by establishing the 'cities' of Troynovant [London] and Lincoln (3. 9. 46–51).[94] This aspect of the Galfridian fable was recognized by John Stow when he chose to open his *Survey of London* (1598) with the assertion that 'as the Roman writers, to glorify the city of Rome, derive the original thereof from gods and demi-gods, by the Trojan progeny, so Geoffrey of Monmouth, the Welsh historian, deduceth the foundation of this famous city of London, for the greater glory thereof, and emulation of Rome, from the very same original'.[95]

Stow's reference to Geoffrey as 'the Welsh historian' illustrates the difficulty under which Spenser laboured. As recently as the fifteenth century Owain Glyn Dwr had invoked Brutus in an attempt to unite the Welsh and Scots against the English. By rallying to Glyn Dwr's cause the Tudors had strenuously opposed the very 'nation' they would later claim to personify. Spenser celebrates their Welsh ancestry in the language of those who obscured their identity by Anglicizing the Christian name 'Tudwr' (or Theodore) as the surname 'Tudor'.[96] The Welsh 'Britons' credited by Spenser's Merlin with keeping the spirit of independence alive during the period of Saxon domination are characteristic of those who violently opposed the process of Anglicization that led to the incorporation of Wales into England in 1536 (3. 3. 45)—and many of Spenser's fellow planters espoused a 'Welsh solution' for the Irish problem.[97] Spenser's concerns are such that he frequently needs to obscure the very distinctions upon which he elsewhere insists. The Gaelic 'bards' whose mythography Irenius condemns as 'forgery' operated in a society that was far more homogenous than his own, and their work was more deeply rooted in the collective consciousness of its audience. By contrast, Spenser's choice of materials ensured that *The Faerie Queene* would never become England's *Aeneid*. By the 1650s Englishmen would increasingly celebrate their descent from the 'pure fountain' of a manly Teutonic nation and the Britons would be judged effeminate by comparison.[98] An emergent 'English' nation had

---

[94] See S. K. Heninger, 'The Tudor Myth of Troy-novant', *South Atlantic Quarterly*, 61 (1962), 378–87. See also Heather James, *Shakespeare's Troy: Drama, Politics and the Translation of Empire* (Cambridge: Cambridge University Press, 1997), 7–41.

[95] Stow (1956), 3. [96] Davies, *The Isles*, 433–4, 441–2.

[97] See Ciaran Brady, 'Comparable Histories?: Tudor Reform in Wales and Ireland', in Steven G. Ellis and Sarah Barber (eds.), *Conquest and Union: Fashioning a British State, 1485–1725* (London: Longman, 1995), 64–86; Quinn (1942), 166.

[98] MacDougall, *Racial Myth*, 43, 55, 63.

no use for what would increasingly be recognized as a Celtic myth of origin.[99]

*

Spenser characterizes the 1590 edition of *The Faerie Queene* as 'bred' in 'salvage soyl' and its quests for 'moral virtue' are conducted within the parameters of that 'savagery'. It is not so much that the poem is 'about' Ireland as that Ireland is inescapable within it, permeating language and imagery as well as theme. Holinesse must distinguish itself from the 'barbarous truth' of a 'salvage nation' (1. 6. 11–12); Temperaunce must resist 'an uncouth, salvage, and uncivile wight' (2. 7. 3); and Chastity must preserve the integrity of a pure bloodline destined to 'indew | The salvage minds with skill of iust and trew' (3. 3. 45). It is the Britons' peculiar task to subdue 'salvage nations' (2. 10. 7) and cultivate 'salvage parts' (2. 10. 25). The 'private morall virtues' are, ideally, appropriated to collective political policies. But the reality of the Irish campaign forced a reassessment of the relationship between private virtues and public ethics, and established an alienating frame of reference against which both were severely tested. The more deeply Ireland informed Spenser's notions of difference, the more profoundly it challenged his myths of identity.

---

[99] One of the earliest accounts of Brutus is to be found in the 9th-cent. Welsh *Historia Brittonum*. See David N. Dumville, 'The Historical Value of the *Historia Brittonum*' in his *Histories and Pseudo-histories of the Insular Middle Ages* (Aldershot: Variorum, 1990), 1–26.

Part IV: Dialogues of Displacement

8   *Colin Clout's Other Island*

WITHIN less than a year of the appearance of *The Faerie Queene* the reading public was confronted by Spenser's *Complaints. Containing sundrie small Poemes of the Worlds Vanitie* (1591). The epic poet now revealed himself as a satirist, or perhaps it might be more accurate to say that the satiric subtext of his heroic verse received explicit articulation.[1] *The Ruines of Time* refers to a paradisal garden more beautiful than that 'which *Merlin* by his *Magicke* flights | Made for the gentle squire, to entertaine | His fayre *Belphœbe*' (523–5). This sounds like a reminiscence of *The Faerie Queene* but no such incident had occurred in the first instalment nor was destined to occur in the second. Instead, as we have seen, the relationship between Belphœbe and Timias is increasingly fraught with frustration, jealousy, and disappointment. Merlin never arranges their rendezvous in an amorous *locus amoenus*, and within *The Ruines of Time* itself the beautiful garden (or garden state?) is 'wasted quite' (529). If there were few correlatives in the real world for the wonders of fairyland there were plenty, it seemed, for its problems.

  Asserting that he acted independently of the author, William Ponsonby, publisher of both *The Faerie Queene* and the *Complaints*, claimed that the 'favourable' reception of the epic had encouraged him 'to get into my handes such smale Poemes of the same Authors; as I heard were disperst abroad in sundrie hands, and not easie to bee come by, by himselfe; some of them having bene diverslie imbeziled and purloyned from him,

---

[1] The recent experience of the Marprelate tracts (1588–9) would have rendered the ecclesiastical satire of *Mother Hubberds Tale* particularly unwelcome.

since his departure over Sea'.[2] This assertion has sometimes been taken at face value, but given the elaborate mystification cast about the publication of *The Shepheardes Calender* and the Spenser–Harvey *Letters*, there seems little reason to doubt Spenser's active involvement in the issuing of the volume, particularly since five of the works included are furnished with separate authorial dedications.[3] The *Complaints* dealt with dangerous matter and, as the outcome was to demonstrate, there was every reason to cloud the fact of publication with fictions of authorial detachment. Gabriel Harvey's assertion that *Mother Hubberds Tale* was called in by the censors has recently been corroborated by Richard S. Peterson's discovery of contemporary allusions to the matter in the papers of Sir Thomas Tresham: 'He that writ this discourse', Tresham remarks,

is a Cantabrigian and of the blood of the Spencers. Yt is nott yett a yeare since he writt his booke in the prayse of the Quene . . . which was so well liked, that her maiestie gave him ane hundred marks pencion forthe of the Exchequer: and so clerklie was yt penned, that he beareth the name of a Poett Laurell. But nowe in medlinge with his apes tayle he is gott into Ireland; also in hazard to loose his forsayd annuall reward: and fynallie hereby proove himselfe a Poett Lorrell.[4]

Of particular interest here is the perceived relationship between *The Faerie Queene* and the *Complaints*. Ponsonby's letter presents the second volume as somehow complementary to the first, at least aesthetically, and suggests that the author's 'departure over Sea' to Ireland has disrupted a brilliant poetic career by leading to the dispersal, and even theft, of his manuscripts. Tresham, by contrast, sees the two volumes as contradictory. The would-be laureate is actually a 'lorrell', or fool, for hazarding the royal patronage he had so lately won. His association with Ireland is less a matter of literary inconvenience than of personal security. In the prevailing circumstances being distant from Gloriana is seen as a distinct advantage.

It is usually assumed that the calling in of the *Complaints* was occasioned solely by the detection of derogatory references to Lord Burghley and his family in *The Ruines of Time* and *Mother Hubberds Tale*. The offending passages in *The Ruines of Time* were thoroughly excised in the first folio of Spenser's collected poems (1611) and *Mother Hubberds Tale* was

---

[2] See Spenser (1999), 165.

[3] For the argument against Spenser's involvement see Jean R. Brink, 'Who Fashioned Edmund Spenser?: The Textual History of *Complaints*', *SP* 88 (1991), 153–68.

[4] Richard S. Peterson, 'Laurel Crown and Ape's Tail: New Light on Spenser's Career from Sir Thomas Tresham', *SSt* 12 (1991, but pub. 1998), 1–35 (p. 8).

never republished in Robert Cecil's lifetime.[5] It may well be, however, that Burghley was not the only one to take offence. There was much in the volume to annoy the queen herself. Writing of the incident in 1592 Gabriel Harvey observes how 'Mother-Hubbard in the heat of choler, forgetting the pure sanguine of her sweete Feary Queene, wilfully overshot her malcontented selfe'.[6] As in the Tresham letter, the contrast is between the tone of Spenser's epic and satiric work. This is significant in view of Spenser's assertion that *Mother Hubberds Tale* was 'long sithens composed in the raw conceipt of my youth'.[7] It is clear from internal evidence that the poem was revised as late as 1590 but if, as has long been suspected, the final episode originally tackled the queen's proposed marriage to the Duc d'Alençon (whose ambassador, Simier, is thought to be figured in the etymologically appropriate ape), some sections of the work must date from 1579 or 1580 and entail the same sort of political disenchantment that is evident in *The Shepheardes Calender*. Since references to the Alençon affair were censored even as late as 1587 in the second edition of Holinshed's *Chronicles*, the renewal of such a theme in 1591 can hardly have been welcomed.[8] As represented in Spenser's beast fable the state of the nation reflects poorly on the royal 'lion', just as the state of the Church, as represented in *The Shepheardes Calender*, reflects poorly on 'fayre Elisa'.[9] The lion is gendered male at line 953, but female—like the eagle that destroys the good shepherd Algrind in the *Julye* eclogue—at line 629 (and by implication at 901). This variation underscores the continuing relevance of *Mother Hubberds Tale* to the issue of female regiment whatever its original date of composition.

The poem's sovereign lioness rejoices in her favourite 'beast' but is offended by the 'late chayne' that has been laid about his neck (628). Depending on how one dates the passage, the allusion may refer either to the Earl of Leicester's clandestine marriage to Lettice Knollys (1578) or to the Earl of Essex's clandestine marriage to Frances Walsingham (1590). On

---

[5] See *The Ruines of Time*, ll.216–17, 447–53; *Mother Hubberds Tale*, ll. 1111–204. See Spenser (1999), 584, 609–10.

[6] Harvey (1884–5), i. 164. Harvey's account is largely corroborated by Nashe (1958), i. 281–2.

[7] Spenser (1999), 234.

[8] See Cyndia Susan Clegg, *Press Censorship in Elizabethan England* (Cambridge: Cambridge University Press, 1997), 146–7.

[9] See my discussion in ' "Little booke: thy selfe present": The Politics of Presentation in *The Shepheardes Calender*', in Howard Erskine-Hill and Richard A. McCabe (eds.), *Presenting Poetry: Composition, Publication, Reception. Essays in Honour of Ian Jack* (Cambridge: Cambridge University Press, 1995), 15–40 (pp. 28–31).

the deepest level, however, it matters little which we choose since Elizabeth was fated to recurrent disappointments of this nature, and the political dynamics of the Elizabethan court were correspondingly unstable. As I have argued elsewhere, what the poem exposes is not an isolated personal problem but an endemic political condition, a vicious circle of private jealousy and public disarray.[10] The appalling portrait of the lioness's court anticipates that of *Colin Clouts Come Home Againe*. Contrary to Spenser's fairy mythology the court of Gloriana is not, it seems, a haven for pure aesthetic inspiration. *The Teares of the Muses* depicts a land beset by 'ugly Barbarisme' and 'brutish Ignorance' (187–8), not unlike (and certainly not sufficiently unlike) the Ireland that Spenser describes as 'overspredd' with 'brutish barbarisme' in *The Faerie Queene*'s dedicatory sonnet to Ormond. *The Teares of the Muses* constitutes a series of nine descants upon the seminal complaint voiced in the 'October' eclogue: 'O pierlesse Poesye, where is then thy place? (79). The Muses' tears—provocatively attributed to 'virgin Queenes' (309)—are those that Elizabeth herself should shed. The theme is continued in *Virgil's Gnat* where the idealized relationship between Virgil and Augustus, evoked in the opening lines, stands in marked contrast to the translator's sense of betrayal.[11] It is true, of course, that the queen is officially exempted from the Muses' general condemnation: according to Polyhymnia she is a 'peereles Poëtresse, | The true *Pandora* of all heavenly graces, | Divine *Elisa*, sacred Emperesse' (577–9). Yet even here, where poetry is harmoniously linked to empire, all is not what it seems. Interpreted on a purely etymological level the comparison with Pandora (meaning 'all gifts') is undoubtedly complimentary; interpreted on a broader mythological level it is potentially far less so. Pandora, the source of all gifts, was also the source of all ills and, according to Eudoxus, the 'evills' of contemporary Ireland are 'verye manye and allmoste Countable with those which weare hidden in the baskett of *Pandora*' (*Prose*, 45). If Elizabeth is Pandora, Ireland is Pandora's box.

The 'October' eclogue had canvassed the prospect of an heroic poem based upon the achievements of courtiers such as Leicester (45–8), but

---

[10] See Spenser (1999), p. xvii.

[11] Ibid., p. 599. Attempts to interpret the poem as a lament for Spenser's 'exile' to Ireland in 1580 are purely speculative. See Edwin Greenlaw, *Studies in Spenser's Historical Allegory* (Baltimore: Johns Hopkins University Press, 1932), 128–30; Vincent P. Carey and Clare Carroll, 'Factions and Fictions: Spenser's Reflections of and on Elizabethan Politics', in Judith H. Anderson, Donald Cheney, and David A. Richardson (eds.), *Spenser's Life and the Subject of Biography* (Amherst: University of Massachusetts Press, 1996), 31–44 (pp. 33–7).

The Teares of Muses laments not just the lack of heroic poetry but of heroic material. The complaints of Calliope are closely related to those of Clio. Spenser's imperial song still lacks an imperial hero. In *The Ruines of Time* Verlame's lament for Roman Britain is ingeniously modulated into a lament for the House of Leicester and the inglorious ascendancy of Burghley: 'he now is gone, the whiles the Foxe is crept | Into the hole, the which the Badger swept' (216–17).[12] Leicester and Sidney are belatedly commemorated, but there is no disguising the fact that erstwhile candidates for heroic celebration have become the subjects of elegy. Similarly, the view of England presented in *Colin Clouts Come Home Againe* is greatly darkened by its publication with *Astrophel,* Spenser's official lament for the man who never succeeded his father as Lord Deputy of Ireland. In retrospect, his death amongst 'salvage beasts' during Leicester's ineffectual campaign in the Lowlands seems less heroic than foolhardy.[13] In *The Faerie Queene* Merlin had prophesied Elizabeth's dominance 'over the *Belgicke* shore' (3. 3. 49), but *The Ruines of Time* and *Astrophel* confront us with the dismal aftermath to these ventures.

But what if a suitable hero could be found? Polyhymnia's reference to Elizabeth as an 'emperesse' evokes the volume's preoccupation with both the matter and the vanity of empire, particularly as exemplified in *The Ruines of Rome,* newly translated from Joachim Du Bellay's *Les Antiquitez de Rome contenant une generale description de sa grandeur, et comme une deploration de sa ruine.* The original had first appeared in 1558 together with *Une Songe ou Vision sur le mesme subject* which Spenser translated as early as 1569 but substantially revised for republication in the *Complaints* as *The Visions of Bellay.* I have suggested in Chapter 1 that Spenser's reception of Virgilian imperialism was much influenced by Du Bellay's ambivalent response to Rome's architectural and cultural legacy.[14] As contextualized in Van der Noot's Protestant anthology, the Catholic poet's work acquired overtones that led Spenser into an increasingly sombre dialogue with his source.[15] It is by no means clear, for example,

---

[12] For the imagery see Spenser (1999), 587.

[13] See Theodore L. Steinberg, 'Spenser, Sidney and the Myth of Astrophel', *SSt* 11 (1990—but pub. 1994), 187–202.

[14] See above pp. 25–6. See also Andrew Fichter, ' "And nought of *Rome* in *Rome* perceiv'st at all": Spenser's *Ruines of Rome*', *SSt* 2 (1981), 183–92; Thomas M. Greene, *The Light in Troy: Imitation and Discovery in Renaissance Poetry* (New Haven: Yale University Press, 1982), 220–41; G. H. Tucker, *The Poet's Odyssey: Joachim Du Bellay and the 'Antiquitez de Rome'* (Oxford: Clarendon Press, 1990), 81–104.

[15] See Richard Danson Brown, *'The New Poet': Novelty and Tradition in Spenser's 'Complaints'* (Liverpool: Liverpool University Press, 1999), 63–95.

that the architecture of epic verse that Spenser hopes to 'builde' in imitation of Virgil will prove any more durable than the prematurely triumphal forms that provide its subject (345–50). When viewed through the lens of Reformation polemic, 'ambition' is found to be 'engendred easily' amongst would-be imperialists, 'as in a vicious bodie, grose disease | Soone growes through humours superfluitie' (*Ruines of Rome*, 318–20). The image of a sick body politic, one of the central tropes of *A View*, suggests an implicit application to the Irish enterprise. The correspondences were imagined to be close. The Roman Empire was perceived to have begun in a drive for urban 'civility' and the city itself to have arisen from 'enclosures . . . of salvage soyle', but there came a point at which imperial success bred the 'idlenes' and 'civill rage' which rendered the empire vulnerable to the barbarians (*Ruines of Rome*, 240, 315)—just as the initial victories of the Old English were held to have precipitated their 'degeneration'. 'Thorowe greatnes of theire late Conquestes and seigniories', Irenius records, they 'grewe insolente and bente . . . theire private powers one againste another to the utter subvercion of themselves and strenghtheninge of the Irishe againe' (*Prose*, 114). A similar fate might await the New English.

Read in the context of Spenser's *Complaints, Colin Clouts Come Home Againe* (1595) may be seen to occupy a pivotal position in Spenser's poetry of displacement, indicative of changed moods and shifting attitudes.[16] It is as though, or is made to seem as though, geographical distance from court has bred a new political consciousness. The reappearance of the solitary, disconsolate Colin Clout of *The Shepheardes Calender* is symptomatic of such developments. Considered in the light of Spenser's later career, such early work seems rich in proleptic irony. By skilfully blending Skelton's satiric persona of Collyn Clout with that of Clément Marot's elegiac Colin, Spenser had 'shadowed' a highly discontented 'selfe'.[17] Though native to Arcadia, Colin is made to endure a sort of internal exile in a pastoral setting that might have been the site of wish-fulfilment but figures instead as an ironic backdrop to wish-frustration.[18] In eclogue after eclogue shepherds travel 'homeward' but few, if any, seem to arrive,

[16] The dedicatory epistle is dated 27 December 1591, but internal evidence suggests that the work was revised as late as 1594.

[17] See Annabel Patterson, 'Re-opening the Green Cabinet: Clément Marot and Edmund Spenser', *ELR* 16 (1986), 44–70.

[18] For pastoral as the poetry of experience see Paul Alpers, 'The Eclogue Tradition and the Nature of Pastoral', *College English*, 34 (1972), 352–71; S. K. Heninger, Jr., 'The Renaissance Perversion of Pastoral', *JHI* 22 (1961), 254–61.

and Colin is not of their number. The title of *Colin Clouts Come Home Againe* is all the more arresting, therefore, in its apparent assertion of achieved security, in the implication that not merely epic heroes but epic poets are made in exile. In the intervening years the persona of Colin Clout had become a great deal more complex. For a start, all elements of anonymity had vanished. *The Shepheardes Calender* had run through four editions and the question 'who knows not Colin Clout?' had, on one level, become entirely rhetorical. To a degree hitherto unique in English literature a fictional persona had been cultivated into a personal trademark. But knowing that Spenser in some sense 'was' Colin Clout implied knowledge of the opposite, and Spenser deftly exploits this dual outlook in order to develop the persona both as a medium of self-expression and as a mechanism of self-occlusion. Now native to Ireland, not Arcadia, Colin views Elisa's kingdom through the penetrating eyes of a stranger and returns 'home againe' in disgust. To him, England is 'another world of land . . . floting amid the sea in ieopardie' (272–3), the distant goal of a rough and hazardous sea voyage. But Colin's voyage out is Spenser's voyage home and subtle reminiscences of Ovid's *Tristia* evoke something of the ambivalent emotion the act of composition must inevitably have aroused.[19] The returning exile adopts the persona of an alien to gain clarity of vision.[20] The suspicion that he has become alienated in the process is neither endorsed nor refuted.

When first we encounter him, Colin Clout seems relatively contented where he is, 'desart' though the place be, and unrequited though his 'love' remains (90–1). The situation is completely altered, however, by the intrusion of 'the shepheard of the Ocean' (66)—his fellow undertaker Sir Walter Ralegh—who has been driven from the court through unrequited 'love' of Cynthia.[21] The obvious coincidence of circumstances allows the stranger to articulate 'Colin's' suppressed anxieties:

> He gan to cast great lyking to my lore,
> And great dislyking to my lucklesse lot:
> That banisht had my selfe, like wight forlore,
> Into that waste, where I was quite forgot.
> The which to leave, thenceforth he counseld mee.   (180–4)

[19] See Sam Meyer, *An Interpretation of Edmund Spenser's 'Colin Clout'* (Cork: Cork University Press, 1969), 65–6.

[20] For Spenser's decentralized perspective see John Breen, ' "Imaginative Groundplot": *A Vewe of the Present State of Ireland*', *SSt* 12 (1991, but pub. 1998), 151–68.

[21] See Stephen Greenblatt, *Sir Walter Ralegh: The Renaissance Man and his Roles* (New Haven: Yale University Press, 1973), 60–3.

The political connotations of 'banisht' slyly fuse the fates of these two ambitious expatriates, raising a spectre of public oblivion equally anathema to both. The passage is all the more potent in relation to Spenser's fear of cultural assimilation to the 'waste' world where even noble families lose their names and confound their genealogies, a fear implicit in Colin's fable of the River Bregog who 'did lose his name' through sexual assimilation into the waters of the River Mulla (155).[22] Spenser was particularly proud of the national heritage encoded in his surname—so much so that he violates generic convention to remind us, as he was later to do in *Prothalamion* (130–1), of the 'noble familie' of the Spencers of Althorp, 'of which I meanest boast my selfe to be' (537–8). The personal pronoun 'I' is hereby rendered intriguingly unstable, sometimes signifying Colin, sometimes Spenser, sometimes both, and the whole exercise is seen to centre upon elaborately reflexive strategies of 'selfe-regard' (682).[23] In the present instance the oxymoronic conjunction of 'boast' and 'meanest' reflect the intensely personal dilemma at the heart of the issue. The 'Shepheard of the Ocean' ['he'] chooses his ground carefully in urging 'Colin' ['I'] to accompany him to England and place his 'oaten quill' at the service of Cynthia (184–94). Ralegh had doubtless lent similar encouragement, but far more important than such factual correspondence is the tangled web of complex, conflicting emotions teased out through the apparently impersonal conventions of pastoral. The poem, I would suggest, is more powerfully autobiographical in its 'fiction' than in its 'fact'.

Colin's first impression of England prompts bitter reassessment of the 'pastoral' landscape he has left behind. In England he discovers that,

> all happie peace and plenteous store
> Conspire in one to make contented blisse:
> No wayling there nor wretchednesse is heard
>
> .   .   .   .   .
>
> No griesly famine, nor no raging sweard
>
> .   .   .   .   .
>
> The shepheards there abroad may safely lie,
> On hills and downes, withouten dread or daunger.   (310–17)

---

[22] For the Mulla fable see below pp. 202–3. See also John D. Bernard, *Ceremonies of Innocence: Pastoralism in the Poetry of Edmund Spenser* (Cambridge: Cambridge University Press, 1989), 128–9.

[23] See Nancy Jo Hoffman, *Spenser's Pastorals: 'The Shepheardes Calender' and 'Colin Clout'* (Baltimore: Johns Hopkins University Press, 1977), 120–42; Terry Comito, 'The Lady in a Landscape and the Poetics of Elizabethan Pastoral', *UTQ* 41 (1972), 200–18 (p. 204).

As the prolonged technique of negative appraisal continues, the poem seems poised to defy one of the oldest conventions of pastoral whereby shepherds journey abroad (as in the *September* eclogue) only to discover that true contentment resides at home. By succeeding in reaching Cynthia's court Colin and his guide appear to have achieved the sublime goal of *The Faerie Queene*, an impression enhanced by Spenser's use of increasingly abstract vocabulary and mystical symbolism that 'transcend' political reality by the simple process of ignoring it:

> There she beholds with high aspiring thought,
> The cradle of her owne creation:
> Emongst the seats of Angels heavenly wrought,
> Much like an Angell in all forme and fashion.   (608–15)

The closer one examines Colin's eulogy of the queen, the more remarkable becomes its lack of specificity, yet it is precisely at the point of furthest abstraction that Spenser exploits the rhetorical mechanisms of pastoral dialogue to break the Neo-Platonic spell and return us to more mundane issues of salary and survival. Thestylis (alias Lodowick Bryskett, Spenser's closest colleague in the Irish service) abruptly enquires:

> Why *Colin*, since thou foundst such grace
> With *Cynthia* and all her noble crew:
> Why didst thou ever leave that happie place,
> In which such wealth might unto thee accrew?   (652–5)[24]

The deliciously ironic possibilities of 'Cynthia and all her noble crew' are admirably glossed in the appropriately mercenary, flat rhyme on 'accrew'—easily, and I suspect deliberately, one of the weakest in the poem. Described as breaking the prolonged silence arising from the mystical description of Cynthia, this forthright query derives additional force from its equal application to Colin and his creator.[25] It is the inevitable question suggested both by Spenser's career and the fictional manner in which he chose to represent it. Like throwing a stone through a stained-glass window, it shatters the fragile tracery of courtly fable, exposing majestic icons as painted ornament. As the perspective alters, all of the apparently trivial qualifications covertly insinuated into Colin's

---

[24] For Bryskett's own hopes of pastoral retreat in Ireland see Raymond Jenkins, 'Spenser and the Clerkship in Munster', *PMLA* 47 (1932), 109–21 (p. 113).

[25] For an equivalent effect see 'with that *Alexis* broke his tale asunder' (352). Alexis links praise of the queen to the possible elevation of the poet's station, asking 'what grace' Cynthia afforded Colin (356), a central crux of the poem's professional concerns.

expressions of wonder emerge into sudden prominence. It now appears that the reality falls far short of the ideal, and Colin retreats from stylized panegyric to colloquial retraction: 'for sooth to say' (as though he had not said 'sooth' till now),

> it is no sort of life,
> For shepheard fit to lead in that same place,
> Where each one seeks with malice and with strife,
> To thrust downe other into foule disgrace.   (688–91)

What is particularly remarkable in the ensuing passage is that many of the adjectives applied to Cynthia's courtiers are identical to those applied to the 'wild' Irish: 'guilefull' (699), 'ydle' (704), 'wastefull' (762), 'laesie' (766), and even 'lewd' and 'licentious' (787). There exists, it would appear, a sophisticated form of barbarity all the worse for its pretence to civility. The only possible consolation is the apparent dissociation of Cynthia from her court but that is like dissociating the spider from its web, an operation that *Muiopotmos* shows to be impossible.[26] When the praise and the blame of the same institution are both absolute, the impression created is one of wilful dichotomy. Up to this point Spenser seemed personally engaged in the creation of the very myth that entices lowly 'shepheards' to seek out Cynthia's court where, in theory, 'learned arts do florish in great honor, | And Poets wits are had in peerlesse price' (320–1). Since such poets 'do their *Cynthia* immortall make', they may now be regarded as victims of their own propaganda (453). The poem seems to be intentionally ambivalent as to whether greatness is innate or ascribed, whether monarchs are more beholden to poets or poets to monarchs (333–5). The condition of many is far from reassuring: Harpalus, 'woxen aged, | In faithfull service' (380–1); Corydon, 'meanly waged' though 'ablest' of all (382–3); Alcyon, 'bent to mourne' (384); Palemon, 'that sung so long untill quite hoarse he grew' (399), and the Shepherd of the Ocean himself, 'that spends his wit in loves consuming smart' (429). Most interesting of all is the case of William Alabaster, neglected author of an unfinished epic in praise of Elizabeth. Colin's heartfelt appeal on his behalf surely owes much of its intensity to a deep empathy in disappointment:

---

[26] See Robert A. Brinkley, Spenser's *Muiopotmos* and the Poetics of Metamorphosis', *ELH* 48 (1981), 668–76.

Who lives that can match that heroick song,
Which he hath of that mightie Princesse made?
O dreaded Dread, do not thy selfe that wrong,
To let thy fame lie so in hidden shade:
But call it forth, O call him forth to thee,
To end thy glorie which he hath begun.   (404–9)

Ominously the catalogue concludes with Sir Philip Sidney now 'dead and gone' (449). His passing is further lamented in the accompanying *Astrophel*, which is complemented by contributions from a variety of other poets including Lodowick Bryskett, Spenser's 'Thestylis'. The whole volume is unified in its morbid preoccupation with themes of lost potential and wasted opportunity. The lament for Sidney is essentially a continuation of *Colin Clout*, a lament for the England of courtly patronage he had come to symbolize, for his own inimitable version of pastoral. Elegy, as 'Clorinda' shrewdly notes, invariably finds us 'mourning in others, our owne miseries'.[27]

At the end of his list of court poets, Colin admits that Cynthia received him not for his 'skill' but for his patron's sake, thereby revealing the little esteem afforded to 'oaten quills' however worthy. It is not in the least surprising, therefore, that he 'chooses' to come home again since what Spenser actually 'shadows' under this persona is not himself but his poetic ambitions. The principal reason Colin comes home is that his creator cannot. Spenser signs the poem's dedication not from his 'home' (as its title seems to demand) but merely from his 'house' at Kilcolman. Whatever the literary opportunities afforded by displacement, the personal cost was immense. Tomis was never Ovid's home, nor Ireland Spenser's. Despite the ostensible celebration of Colin's 'homecoming', little contentment is evident at the sombre close when the company disperses under 'glooming skies'. The conclusion echoes that of Virgil's tenth eclogue but significantly omits the one phrase that, in other circumstances, might have been the most important of all: 'ite domum' ['go home']. We have heard far too much of Ireland's 'barrein soyle' (656) with its 'nightly bodrags' (315) and 'ravenous wolves' (318) to allow of any happier outcome.[28] Colin's 'love' remains as unrequited as ever: 'So hie

---

[27] *Doleful Lay of Clorinda*, 96.
[28] For the significance of 'bodrags' see below p. 177. For the contrary view that Spenser regarded Ireland as home after 1591 see John T. Shawcross, 'Assumptions and Reading Spenser', *Explorations in Renaissance Culture*, 26 (1996), 1–20.

her thoughts as she her selfe have place, | And loath each lowly thing with loftie eie' (937–8).[29] As in *The Shepheardes Calender* one detects a carefully constructed correspondence between Colin's relationship with Rosalind, and the nation's relationship with Cynthia. The despairing summary elicits another unwelcome 'sooth' that appears to apply to both ladies:

> And sooth to say, it is foolhardie thing,
> Rashly to wyten creatures so divine,
> For demigods they be and first did spring
> From heaven, though graft in frailnesse feminine.   (915–18)

Here again is the discordant clash between the monarch's and the lover's 'two bodies'—not to say the *monarch as lover*'s 'two bodies' since Cynthia is Ralegh's 'lifes Regent' in both the amorous and the political sense (235).[30] The ideal lady is 'graft in frailnesse feminine', the particular variety of frailty that female regiment throws into high relief. In making this assertion 'Colin' is responding yet again to an objection raised by one of his interlocutors and the device serves to remind us that the poem is no less engaged in the continuing dialectic of contemporary Irish politics than the formal discussion conducted 'by waye of a diologue' between Irenius and Eudoxus (*Prose*, 43). Indeed it is not unfair to say that the discussion begun in *Colin Clouts Come Home Againe* is continued, if not concluded, in *A View*.

---

[29] See David R. Shore, *Spenser and the Poetics of Pastoral: A Study of the World of Colin Clout* (Kingston: McGill–Queen's University Press, 1985), 129.

[30] See Jane Tylus, *Writing and Vulnerability in the Late Renaissance* (Stanford, Calif.: Stanford University Press, 1993), 113–43.

9   Irenius's Mother Tongue

Of me no lines are lov'd, nor letters are of price,
Of all which speak our English tongue, but those of thy device.

(Sir Walter Ralegh on *The Faerie Queene*)[1]

FOR Sir Walter Ralegh, Spenser is the pre-eminent poet of 'our English tongue' and *The Faerie Queene* marks both his and the language's coming of age. Yet the phrase 'our English tongue' begs a number of crucial questions. On whose behalf is Ralegh speaking? Their mutual involvement in the Irish colonial enterprise had familiarized Spenser and Ralegh with varieties of English unknown to most of their countrymen. Colin Clout complains to the Shepheard of the Ocean of the 'nightly bodrags' that characterize life in Ireland (314–15), but the allusion would be opaque to most English readers. The word 'bodrag', which recurs as a verbal noun in *The Faerie Queene* (2. 10. 63), appears to be a corruption of the Gaelic term, 'buaidhreach' or 'buadre' (meaning disturbance or uproar). Though uncommon elsewhere, it recurs, as do many other Gaelic words, throughout the Irish State Papers and would have been familiar to all of Spenser's fellow planters. In his contribution to the 1587 edition of Holinshed, for example, John Hooker records Ralegh's own complaint about Irish 'bodrages'.[2] Colin is using a term already associated, in print, with the Shepherd of the Ocean's turbulent Irish campaign. Its recurrence in *The Faerie Queene* as though it were an indigenous English word, and without any perceived need for gloss or explanation, is indicative of the growing influence of Spenser's Irish experience upon his vocabulary and the political outlook it articulates. A similar effect is evident in Spenser's orthography. Roland Smith notes that 'the only significant changes in Spenser's spelling are not so much individual or personal as social, and reflect the poet's increasing familiarity with his Irish background. They concern not English but Irish words, such as *kerne* and *Aherloa*.'[3] Given

---

[1] Spenser (1978), 19.   [2] Holinshed (1808), vi. 440.
[3] Roland M. Smith, 'Spenser's Scholarly Script and "Right Writing"', in Don Cameron Allen (ed.), *Studies in Honor of T. W. Baldwin* (Urbana: University of Illinois Press, 1958), 66–111 (p. 89).

Spenser's relentless insistence upon the association between language and nationalism, such developments are highly ironic. Spenser's outlook is everywhere informed by a morbid fear of infiltration—both territorial and sexual—but the very language in which he expresses such anxieties increasingly illustrates the process it deplores.

As I have argued in Chapter 2, Spenser's hostility towards the Gaelic language represents a considerable hardening in colonial attitude.[4] The appearance in 1571 of Seaán Ó Cearnaigh's *Aibidil Gaoidheilge & Caiticiosma* [*Irish Alphabet and Catechism*]—which includes translations from the Book of Common Prayer and Sir Henry Sidney's 'Principall Articles of Religion' (originally promulgated in 1566)—is indicative of earlier attempts to 'Anglicize' the Gaelic Irish through the medium of their own tongue.[5] Even as late as 1591 Sir William Herbert suggested that 'there should be set before the people songs in the Irish language which will encourage them to virtue and entice them to moderation and tranquillity of spirit'.[6] This, however, was on the assumption that the message could subvert the medium, that linguistic translation *from English to Irish* could promote cultural 'translation' from Irish to English. When Herbert quotes Gaelic verse he does so for the sole purpose of establishing the exact extent of Irish townlands with a view to imposing suitable taxation.[7] The aesthetic values of the native serve the political needs of the colonist.

Spenser's sense of the formative power of language rendered him far less sanguine than Herbert. For him, it is not so much a matter of different vocabularies as of different mentalities: 'wordes are the Image of the minde So as they procedinge from the minde the minde must be nedes affected with the wordes So that the speache beinge Irishe the harte muste nedes be Irishe for out of the abundance of the harte the tongue speakethe' (*Prose*, 119). Irenius's remarks reflect the contemporary debate as to whether 'meaning' was in some sense imminent in language or solely a matter of arbitrary attribution, but he was well ahead of his time in recognizing how language functions to shape, rather than merely express, familial and political bonds.[8] Modern linguistic analysis has demonstrated how 'bilinguals can build up very different emotive and affective meanings associated with each of their languages', and the language of 'family experience' has been shown to exercise a particularly emotive influence—

---

[4] See above pp. 31–2.   [5] Ó Cuív (1994), 11–16.   [6] Herbert (1992), 115.
[7] Ibid. 102, 103.
[8] See Richard Waswo, *Language and Meaning in the Renaissance* (Princeton: Princeton University Press, 1987), 150–6.

more than validating Spenser's fears concerning the role of Irish mothers and wet-nurses.[9] Fynes Moryson similarly regarded the adoption of the Gaelic tongue as a 'tuchstone' of 'inward affection' indicating the unwillingness of the 'English Irish' to 'apply themselves any way to the English, or not to followe the Irish in all things'.[10]

Such remarks activate habits of linguistic discrimination stretching back to the ancient Greeks for whom 'barbarism' was primarily a semantic concept. Originally 'barbarians' were those who could not speak Greek but made incomprehensible 'babbling' noises, incomprehensible, that is, to the Greeks.[11] By extension 'barbarians' were those who did not share in what were held to be the superior cultural attainments of the Greek-speaking world. Latin speakers were initially regarded as 'barbarians' but, after the conquest of Greece and the consequent Hellenizing of Roman civilization, the Romans redefined the notion of barbarity in such a way as to exclude themselves but to embrace all those living beyond the boundaries—and against the perceived values—of the Graeco-Roman world. The category of the 'barbaric' was therefore fluid and changeable, constructed and deconstructed as the need arose.[12] Commenting upon the first printed edition of *A View* (1633), Richard Bellings observed that 'if the English fell in a dislike of our habit and language, as deeming them both, and ourselves, barbarous, and hold us in scorn, because they understand not our language, might we, è converso, as justly repute them barbarous, that they learn not our language, whereby they receive more than ordinary benefits'.[13]

Adopting an attitude very similar to that of the ancient Greeks and Romans, Stanyhurst observed that 'the inhabitants of the English pale have beene in old time so much addicted to their civilitie, and so farre sequestered from barbarous sauagenesse, as their onelie mother toong was English. And trulie, so long as these impaled dwellers did sunder themselves as well in land as in language from the Irish: rudenesse was daie by daie in the countrie supplanted, civilitie ingraffed.'[14] Underlying all such arguments, however, lay a singularly ironic semantic fallacy. According to Spenser's neighbour Hugh Cuffe, the degenerate Old English had adopted the Gaelic language 'scorning our old English speech, which our

[9] See Suzanne Romaine, *Bilingualism* (Oxford: Basil Blackwell, 1989), 81.

[10] Moryson (1903), 214.

[11] Eric Cheyfitz, *The Poetics of Imperialism: Translation and Colonization from 'The Tempest' to 'Tarzan'* (Oxford: Oxford University Press, 1991), 89–90.

[12] See the comments of St Paul at 1 Corinthians 14: 11.   [13] Gilbert (1882–91), i, p. xiv.

[14] Holinshed (1808), vi. 4.

ancestors brought with them at the first conquest'.[15] But what exactly was this 'old English speech'? The form of 'English' by which Cuffe, Stany-hurst, and Spenser place such store—'the old ancient Chaucer English'—scarcely existed 'at the first conquest' but evolved slowly over the next two centuries through a complex process of linguistic change.[16] Its status as 'undefyled' (in the sense of aboriginally 'pure') is the most untenable of all Spenserian 'myths' and was challenged, as we shall see, even in his own time. In any case, the settlers whom Giraldus Cambrensis refers to as 'Angli' ('English') were predominantly of Norman ancestry. Many, like Giraldus himself, were of mixed race and spoke either Norman French or Welsh, and possibly a mingling of both.[17] The learned amongst them also spoke Latin but few, if any, spoke the 'English' of the day. It therefore follows that linguistic 'degeneration', in the form that Irenius and Eudoxus imagine it, could never have occurred. Even Stanyhurst is driven to admit, in an unguarded moment, that the 'progenitors' of the Pale were 'English and Welsh men'.[18] The latter would have spoken a language closely akin to that of the Gaelic Irish. Over the coming centuries they exchanged one variety of Celtic for another.

Rees Davies has convincingly traced the origins of Spenser's linguistic nationalism to the late middle ages, and Spenser's identification of Chaucer as his 'well of English undefyled' tends to corroborate the point (4. 2. 32).[19] Yet it is essential to recognize that Spenser's Chaucer, like Milton's Spenser or Blake's Milton, is a highly polemical construct, fashioned to serve the needs of the moment. Spenser's appreciation of Chaucer's linguistic purity was by no means universal. In *A Restitution of Decayed Intelligence* (1605), for example, Richard Verstegan challenges Chaucer's claims to be regarded as 'the first illuminator of the English toung' on the grounds that 'he was in deed a great mingler of English with French, unto which language by lyke for that hee was descended of French or rather wallon race, hee caryed a great affection'.[20] For Verstegan, Chaucer's linguistic impurity was symptomatic of his racial hybridity. The figure upon whom Spenser fathered his linguistic nationalism was himself of alien descent. Most commentators agreed with Holinshed

---

[15] *CSPI* (1598–99), 507.   [16] Holinshed (1808), i. 4.

[17] See Robert Bartlett, *Gerald of Wales 1146–1223* (Oxford: Clarendon Press, 1982), 9–26, 158–77.

[18] Holinshed (1808), vi. 67.

[19] R. R. Davies, 'The Peoples of Britain and Ireland, 1100–1400: IV. Language and Historical Mythology', *Transactions of the Royal Historical Society*, 7 (1997), 1–24 (pp. 8–15).

[20] Verstegan (1605), 203–4.

that the English language 'never came unto the type of perfection, until the time of Queene Elizabeth'. 'Although', he adds, 'not a few . . . doo greatlie seeke to staine the same, by fond affectation of forren and strange words.'[21] The intrusion of a Gaelic word such as 'bodrag' would certainly fall within the strictures of such criticism. In any case, according to George Puttenham, Chaucer's language 'is now out of use with us' and should not be imitated.[22] To employ Chaucerian language is to promote linguistic regression. Yet once again we must ask for whom Puttenham is speaking when he asserts that Chaucerian English is 'out of use *with us*'. Readers of Holinshed would encounter Stanyhurst's assertion that the speech of the Old English preserved 'the dregs' of Chaucerian diction, including the sort of archaism that Spenser had laboured to introduce into *The Shepheardes Calender* and *The Faerie Queene*—thereby leading Ben Jonson to complain that he 'writ no Language'.[23] The same phenomenon was noted by Gaelic commentators. According to Ó Súilleabháin Béarra, for example, most Palesmen of English descent preserved 'the English language, albeit in a crude and archaic form'.[24] Spenser's New English epic had ironically adopted the antiquated diction of the Old English faction he opposed, a diction which was commonly taken to denote their failure to keep abreast of linguistic and political developments in the home country.

Puttenham's association of linguistic 'perfection' with the advent of Queen Elizabeth implies a relationship between political and linguistic identity that is quite typical of its era. Throughout Europe emergent nationalism promoted, and was promoted by, the rise of vernacular tongues and the issue of linguistic difference was accordingly cast into high prominence. In his *Défense et Illustration de la Langue Française* (1549), for example, Joachim Du Bellay fulminates against the arrogance of ancient Greece which 'admiring only its own inventions, had neither law nor privilege to legitimize its own nation and bastardize all the others . . . the Scythians were barbarians among the Greeks, but the Athenians were also barbarians among the Scythians'.[25] The passage is of particular interest in the present context because of Spenser's reliance upon the alleged Scythian ancestry of the Irish to bolster his claim that contemporary Gaelic society was inherently 'salvage'. Here, as elsewhere, the thrust of

[21] Holinshed (1808), i. 24–5.   [22] Smith (1904), ii. 150.
[23] Holinshed (1808), vi. 4; Jonson (1925–52), viii. 618. See Alan Bliss, *Spoken English in Ireland 1600–1740* (Dublin: Cadenus Press, 1979), 11–30.
[24] O'Sullivan Beare (1903), 51.   [25] Du Bellay (1939), 23.

his cultural analysis is pervasively semantic and he relies very heavily upon highly politicized exercises in 'etymology' to support his arguments.[26] Thus the practice of 'tanistry' or elective leadership is denigrated by association with the 'Barbarous nacions' that destroyed Rome 'and so it maye well be That from thence the firste originall of this worde *Tanist and Tanistry* came And the Custome theareof hathe sithence As manye others else bene Contynewed' (*Prose*, 51). One of the principal institutions of Gaelic society is hereby 'revealed' as little more than an unwelcome survival from a primitive age. Because speech was regarded, in Ben Jonson's potent phrase, as 'the Instrument of *Society*', the users of a 'savage' language were deemed incapable of producing anything other than a barbarous culture.[27]

As Umberto Eco has demonstrated, Renaissance commentators were unanimous in positing the existence of a primeval or 'natural' language spoken in Eden and common to all men until the confounding of tongues at the Tower of Babel.[28] This language was regarded as superior to its successors because it was believed to have afforded an absolute correspondence between signifier and signified. The names Adam ascribed to the various creatures somehow encapsulated their true natures thereby establishing a unique coherence between language and reality (Genesis 2: 19–20).[29] The fragmentation of this primal language was held to have ushered in the phenomenon of linguistic degeneracy and to have facilitated racial conflict. Verstegan suggests that the origin of racial diversity was itself linguistic for following the disaster at Babel,

many new distinct and different nations were begun, even of such as a litle before, were all one nation, and used all one language, and each troop . . . having a naturall desyre to remain by it self, seperated from the others whose language it understood not . . . whereby such as but a litle before used all one language and were all one nation, were now become meer strangers the one unto the other, and thenceforward dayly grew unto more and more alienation.[30]

---

[26] For comparison see Herbert (1992), 5.   [27] Jonson (1925–52), viii. 621.

[28] Umberto Eco, *The Search for the Perfect Language*, trans. James Fentress (London: Fontana Press, 1997—first pub. 1993), 73–116.

[29] Platonic theory lent support to the biblical notion. See Norman Kretzmann, 'Plato on the Correctness of Names', *American Philosophical Quarterly*, 8 (1971), 126–38; Gail Fine, 'Plato on Naming', *The Philosophical Quarterly*, 27 (1977), 289–301; Bernard Williams, 'Cratylus' Theory of Names and its Refutation', in Malcolm Schofield and Martha Craven Nussbaum (eds.), *Language and Logos: Studies in Ancient Greek Philosophy presented to G. E. L. Owen* (Cambridge: Cambridge University Press, 1982), 83–93.

[30] Verstegan (1605), 6.

The concept of 'otherness' is here seen to originate in linguistic difference. The frontispiece to Verstegan's work shows the various peoples of the world dispersing in different directions towards the margins of the picture in order to establish new nations linguistically distinct, and geographically separate, from one another (Fig. 11, p. 184). The central space, occupied by the incomplete and abandoned tower, represents the insuperable problem of cultural diversity, the point at which unity of purpose breaks down through the collapse of mutual comprehension. Hence Du Bellay's contention that linguistic diversity articulates diversity of political perception, 'for languages are not born of themselves after the fashion of herbs, roots, or trees . . . but all their virtue is born in the world of the desire and will of mortals'.[31]

Du Bellay concludes that no vernacular language should be deemed superior or inferior to any other, but such tolerant relativism had little place in colonial thinking. Rather, it was assumed that some languages preserved more of the primeval purity than others. Thus Verstegan makes high claims for 'Teutonic', of which English was held to be a variant, on the grounds that the etymology of so many of its words revealed them to be singularly appropriate to the things they signified.[32] Although the Gaelic language was itself commonly regarded as one of the seventy-two mother tongues deriving from Babel, the common association between cultural degeneracy and geographical marginality could be used to diminish its prestige.[33] Stanyhurst comments upon the inherent 'obscuritie' of classical Gaelic: the 'strangenesse of the phrase, and the curious featnes of the pronuntiation' was such that 'scarse one in five hundred can either read, write, or understand it'.[34] As the language spoken beyond the borders of civility, by a race Spenser accuses of being congenitally prone to lying, Gaelic was by definition a 'barbarous tongue' (*Prose*, 67–8). Stanyhurst cites the alleged absence of a word for 'knave' as indicative of the moral values it encodes.[35] In point of fact there was a plethora of words for knave, all liberally used in descriptions of the English, but none of that

---

[31] Du Bellay (1939), 21. [32] Verstegan (1605), 191–4.

[33] Holinshed (1808), vi. 6. For the perceived virtues of English see Camden (1605), 20–1.

[34] Holinshed (1808), vi. 7. See also Campion (1963), 17–18. Both admit that demotic Gaelic 'is sharpe and sententious, and offerethe great occasion to quicke apothegms and proper allusions'. In *De Rebus in Hibernia Gestis* (1584) Stanyhurst later denied that he had intended to denigrate the Irish langage per se but continued to assert that it was 'not in the interests of our community for Irish (which our ancestors shunned as they would rocky crags) to be spoken widely and freely'. See Colm Lennon, *Richard Stanyhurst: The Dubliner 1547–1618* (Dublin: Irish Academic Press, 1981), 144.

[35] Holinshed (1808), vi. 7–8.

A RESTITVTION
of
DECAYED INTELLIGENCE:
In antiquities.
Concerning the most noble and renovv-
med English nation.

By the studie and trauaile of R. V.

Dedicated vnto the Kings most excellent Maiestie.

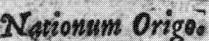

Nationum Origo.

Printed at Antvverp by Robert Bruney.
1605.

*And to be sold at London in Paules-Churchyeard,
by Iohn Norton and Iohn Bill.*

11. Richard Verstegan, *A Restitution of Decayed Intelligence* (1605). Title page.

mattered. The ethnographic argument lent comfort not only to the politics of the colonial enterprise but, perhaps even more vitally, to its psychology. Within living memory English itself, as an emergent vernacular, had struggled to throw off imputations of 'barbarity', of being, in Thomas Heywood's description, 'the most harsh, uneven, and broken language of the world, part *Dutch*, part *Irish*, *Saxon*, *Scotch*, *Welsh*, and indeed a gallimaffrey of many, but perfect in none'.[36] To denigrate the Gaelic language in such circumstances was tantamount to appropriating 'classical' status for English, and civilized status for English speakers.

The ultimate expression of the tendency towards linguistic denigration was the denial that the sounds uttered by unfamiliar peoples properly qualified as human language.[37] This too had its origins in the ancient world for, as Anthony Pagden argues, 'a close association in the Greek mind between intelligible speech and reason made it possible to take the view that those who were devoid of *logos* in one sense might also be devoid of it in another . . . Non-Greek speakers, furthermore, lived, by definition, outside the Greek family of man, the *oikumene*.'[38] The matter is relevant here in view of the common Elizabethan comparison between the Irish and American frontiers and the 'savagery' allegedly endemic to both.[39] The savage man of the sixth book of *The Faerie Queene* has no 'other language . . . nor speech',

> But a soft murmure, and confused sound
> Of senselesse words, which nature did him teach,
> T'expresse his passions, which his reason did empeach.
>
> (6. 4. 11)

It is noteworthy that 'natural' expression is here seen to impede rational discourse rather than facilitate a return to Edenic eloquence, and the connotations of 'naturall' vary throughout *A View* from the pejorative to the favourable depending upon whether English or Irish customs are in question.[40] The savage man's appearance in *The Legende of Courtesie* is

---

[36] Heywood (1612), sig. F3r. See also Michael Neill, 'Broken English and Broken Irish: Nation, Language, and the Optic of Power in Shakespeare's Histories', *SQ* 45 (1994), 1–33 (p. 19).

[37] See Margaret T. Hodgen, *Early Anthropology in the Sixteenth and Seventeenth Centuries* (Philadelphia: University of Pennsylvania Press, 1964), 411–12.

[38] See Anthony Pagden, *The Fall of Natural Man: The American Indian and the Origins of Comparative Ethnology* (Cambridge: Cambridge University Press, 1982), 16.

[39] See D. B. Quinn, *The Elizabethans and the Irish* (Ithaca, NY: Cornell University Press, 1966), 21–7, 106–22; Nicholas Canny, *Kingdom and Colony: Ireland in the Atlantic World, 1560–1800* (Baltimore: Johns Hopkins University Press, 1988), 7–13, 35.

[40] For further discussion of this episode see below p. 240.

particularly significant in view of Stanyhurst's assertion that 'the courtesie of the English language is cleane contrarie' to the self-centred values encoded in such Irish constructions as 'I and you' (rather than 'you and I').[41] The Gaelic language, he suggests, impedes the cultivation of social courtesy and consequently of civility itself. Owing to their incorporation into Holinshed's *Chronicles*, Stanyhurst's views were generally regarded as authoritative, and the association between geographical segregation, linguistic difference, and cultural inferiority was commonly taken for granted—hence the passage into common parlance of the term 'beyond the pale'. It was only 'thoroughe nearenesse of the State', Irenius argues, that the Pale had been preserved 'in reasonable Civillitye' (*Prose*, 115). For those 'planted' further off, the result was increasing alienation from the mother tongue and the political and cultural values of those who spoke it. Yet, as both Stanyhurst and Spenser were well aware, the boundaries of the Pale (a concept, like that of 'degeneracy', effectively reinvented by the New English) were so fluid and shifting as to render entirely relative all notions of 'beyond' and 'within'. Irenius notes that areas once considered central now constituted 'the moste outboundes and abandoned places in the Englishe pale, And inded [are] not Counted of the Englishe pale at all' (*Prose*, 61). His terminology serves to remind us that the sense of a boundary, and particularly an unstable boundary, implies not merely a spatial division but also a point of contact, an area of ambiguity which is neither beyond nor within but between. The inevitable process of semantic and sexual infiltration proved fatal to the colonial project for, according to Fynes Moryson (echoing the words of King James I), 'communion or difference of language, hath allwayes beene observed, a speciall motive to unite or allienate the myndes of all nations, so as the wise Romans as they inlarged theire Conquests, so they did spreade theire language . . . and in generall all nations have thought nothing more powerfull to unite myndes then the Community of language'.[42] Following the same line of thinking, Edmund Campion suggested that 'babes from their cradells should be enured under learned schoolemasters with a pure Englishe tonge, habite, fasshion, discipline' so that they might 'in time utterlie

---

[41] Holinshed (1808), vi. 67. For the Gaelic response to Stanyhurst see Brendan Bradshaw, 'Geoffrey Keating: Apologist of Irish Ireland', in Brendan Bradshaw, Andrew Hadfield and Willy Maley (eds.), *Representing Ireland: Literature and the Origins of Conflict, 1534–1660* (Cambridge: Cambridge University Press, 1993), 166–90.

[42] Moryson (1903), 213. In 1604 James I asserted that 'communitie of Language' was 'the principall meanes of Civil societie'. See Larkin and Hughes (1973), i. 95.

forgett the affinitie of their unbroken borderers'.[43] It was precisely this 'affinitie' with 'borderers', however, that threatened to unravel the entire ideology of New English colonialism.

In the 'epistle' to *The Shepheardes Calender*, E.K. warns against the contamination of the 'good and naturall English' of 'our Mother tonge' by the importation of foreign words, owing to the danger that Englishmen may eventually become 'straungers' and 'alienes' in their own language. The variety of dialectical forms employed within *The Shepheardes Calender* better illustrates the inherent diversity of Elizabethan English than its emergent standardization, but E.K. is firmly of the opinion that it is indiscriminate borrowing from foreign languages that has, as Heywood noted, 'made our English tongue, a gallimaufray or hodgepodge of al other speches'.[44] This closely corresponds to Stanyhurst's complaint (published just two years previously) that the Old English 'have so acquainted themselves with the Irish, as they have made a mingle mangle or gallimaufreie of both the languages . . . as commonlie the inhabitants of the meaner sort speake neither good English nor good Irish'.[45] As perceived by Spenser, the Old English families represent extreme examples of linguistic estrangement and alienation to the point at which they 'quite forgett theire Countrie and theire owne names' (*Prose*, 115). In so doing they derogate not only from civility but from the avowed colonial ideal of civilizing others, 'for it hathe bene ever the use of the Conquerour to despise the Language of the Conquered and to force him by all meanes to learne his. So did the Romaines allwaies use in soe muche that there is allmoste no nacion in the worlde but is sprinckled with theire language' (*Prose*, 118–19).[46] Contemporary Spanish imperialists were of much the same opinion.[47] In Ireland, however, the 'conquered' had linguistically colonized the 'conqueror'.

As the origin of nations was commonly held to be linguistic, the Old English families were generally perceived to have adopted the Irish political outlook along with the Irish tongue. Stanyhurst illustrates the imagined stages of such declension into political apostasy quite graphically:

---

[43] Campion (1963), 144.   [44] Spenser (1999), 27.
[45] Holinshed (1808), vi. 4. See Paula Blank, *Broken English: Dialects and the Politics of Language in Renaissance Writings* (London: Routledge, 1996), 144–53.
[46] For the politics of linguistic colonialism see Stephen Greenblatt, *Learning to Curse: Essays in Early Modern Culture* (London: Routledge, 1990), 16–39.
[47] See Anthony Pagden, *Lords of All the World: Ideologies of Empire in Spain, Britain and France c.1500–c.1800* (New Haven: Yale University Press, 1995), 148; Bruce Mannheim, *The Language of the Inka since the European Invasion* (Austin: University of Texas Press, 1991), 68–71.

'neighbourhood bred acquaintance, acquaintance waffed in the Irish toong, the Irish hooked with it attire, attire haled rudenesse, rudenesse ingendered ignorance, ignorance brought contempt of lawes, the contempt of lawes bred rebellion.'[48] According to Spenser's version of events, geographical proximity encouraged practices of fosterage and intermarriage which in turn precipitated the process of cultural degeneration by promoting the dangerously emotive influence of 'salvage' women as wetnurses and mothers,

> for firste the Childe that suckethe the milke of the nurse muste of necessitye learne his firste speache of her, the which beinge the firste that is enured to his tongue is ever after moste pleasinge unto him In so muche as thoughe he afterwardes be taughte Englishe yeat the smacke of the firste will allwaies abide with him and not onelye of the speche but allsoe of the manners and Condicions . . . they moreover drawe into themselves togeather with theire sucke even the nature and disposicion of theire nurses ffor the minde followethe muche the Temperature of the bodye. (*Prose*, 119)

The term 'mother tongue' is here interpreted in a very literal sense to create the impression that the child somehow 'sucks' his allegiance with his milk, that political and cultural inclinations are largely determined by familial affection. If wet-nursing and fosterage could occasion such profound shifts in political sympathy, the practice of intermarriage rendered the process irreversible.[49] As one of Spenser's fellow planters asserted, 'the blood of theire Irishe mothers, hathe wasted away the naturall love they bare to theire mother England'.[50] The linguistically hybrid were feared to be racially impure and politically unsound. Sexual intercourse and what Stanyhurst refers to as the 'intercourse of languages' were seen to facilitate one another.[51]

For Spenser, the ultimate linguistic sign of cultural degeneracy is the adoption of an Irish patronym by Old English families. As his evident pride in his own surname suggests, to name oneself is to invoke a lineage and assert a loyalty.[52] During the events that led to the Battle of Kinsale (1601), Sir John Harington recalled the official anxiety that Hugh O'Neill should style himself 'Hugh Tyrone' after the fashion of the English peerage rather than simply Ó Néill in the traditional Gaelic manner.[53] This mattered because 'Hugh Tyrone' was an English invention designed

[48] Holinshed (1808), vi. 5.   [49] Davies (1612), 178–80.   [50] Maley (1995), 33
[51] Holinshed (1808), vi. 6.   [52] See below p. 172.
[53] Hadfield and McVeagh (1994), 93.

to frustrate the 'barbarous' and 'Scythian' custom of 'tanistry', whereas
Ó Néill, despite his upbringing in the household of Sir Henry Sidney, remained very much a part of the Gaelic world. The official view was that
'the name of the O'Neill, in the judgements of the uncivil people of this
Realm, doth carry in itself so great a sovereignty, as they [the Irish] suppose that all of the lords and people of Ulster should rather live in servi-
tude to that name, than in subjection to the crown of England'.[54] With
the abolition of Irish surnames, however, Spenser predicts that the clansmen 'shall not onelye not depende uppon the heade of theire septe as now
they doe but allso shall in shorte time learne quite to forgett his Irishe nacion' (*Prose*, 215). Those who derived their new names from their 'trades'
or 'facultyes' would simultaneously redefine both their nationality and
their social class. In most cases racial difference would be translated into
social inferiority.

Among the Old English families that Spenser regards as 'degenerate'
were the Fitz Ursulas, now allegedly calling themselves the 'MacMahons',
who 'did quite caste of theire Englishe name and Allegeance . . . and have
still sithens bene Counted mere Irishe'. Spenser associates the two surnames by means of a questionable etymology whereby MacMahon is rendered as 'the bear's son' the better to correspond with its supposed
equivalent (*Prose*, 116).[55] Through acquaintance with the Gaelic Irish,
John Derricke alleged, 'civil' persons degenerated into 'bores' and
'beares'.[56] A similar conceit supplies the cultural subtext for the episode
in which Sir Calepine rescues an infant from the clutches of a marauding
bear, carries him out of the forest unto the 'plaine champion', and con-
signs him to the care of Sir Bruin and Matilda to 'traine in chevalry, | Or
noursle up in lore of learn'd Philosophy' (6. 4. 17–35). Sir Bruin and the
'bear' represent twin aspects of the one persona, the latter indicative of the
savagery latent within the civil knight, just as Fitz Ursula and MacMahon
are taken to *mean* the same thing but to *signify* contrary things.[57] The
reclamation of the child from trackless woodlands may, therefore, be seen
to reflect the hope that a number of Old English families may also be

[54] Maxwell (1923), 174.
[55] See Roland M. Smith, 'The Irish Background of Spenser's *View*', *JEGP* 42 (1943), 499–515
(pp. 507–8).
[56] Derricke (1985), 29.
[57] Michael D. Bristol notes that while 'bears are connected with violence, rape, and destruction' they 'are equally important as symbols of nurture and creativity'. *Big-Time Shakespeare*
(London: Routledge, 1996), 165.

reclaimed, perhaps through the intervention of the Court of Wards.[58] By contrast, those who spoke Irish were thought likely to follow the dictates of the brehon law which was erroneously held to be a matter of verbal tradition rather than written code.[59] Oral Irish could thus be represented as the exclusive medium of a legal system which was, according to Irenius, 'in manye thinges repugninge quite to godes lawe and mans' (*Prose*, 47). The Irish 'community of language' is that of a criminal confraternity because Gaelic is, quite literally, the language of the 'outlaw'. To translate a bardic poem or a daily conversation from Gaelic to English is to decode a criminal cypher, to expose the treason that lies hidden in the sinister jargon of the enemy. And such 'translation' must occur on every level.

Perceiving the association between the Gaelic clans and their ancestral homelands, the symbiotic relationship between culture and place, Spenser would destroy this sustaining link by uprooting the entire population or, as he terms it, by 'translating' the clans from place to place: 'I will translate all that remaine of them [of Leinster] into the places of the other in ulster' (*Prose*, 179). The entire Gaelic population is to be 'translated' out of its geographical context so that it may be translated in cultural terms as well. Similarly, in the anonymous tract *A Discourse of Ireland* (1599), we encounter an even more radical plan for 'all the race of them [the Irish] to be translated out of Ireland, and English with some Flemmings to be onely planted in their Roomes because the Flemming is a People of more propinquity to our Nature'. As a result of such 'translation' Ireland would become 'mearely a West England'.[60] The act of translation is, in a very real sense, an act of *translatio imperii*. While Spenser realized the obvious impracticability of the plan outlined in *A Discourse of Ireland* his ultimate intention remained very similar: 'to bringe them to be one people . . . which wilbe by no meanes better then by there enterminglinge of them, that neither all the Irishe maye dwell togeather, nor all the Englishe, but by translatinge of them and scatteringe them in smalle nombers amonge the Englishe' (*Prose*, 211–12). This directly contradicts Irenius's previous assertion that the Irish outnumber the New English so overwhelmingly that cultural integrity can be preserved only through strict racial segregation because in all such cases 'the fewer will followe the more' (*Prose*, 211). The ensuing dichotomy reveals the profound ambivalence of the colonial enterprise since it is agreed to be 'unnaturall that anye people shoulde love

---

[58] For the Court of Wards see below p. 240.
[59] See Spenser, *Prose*, 47; Moryson (1903), 224.   [60] Quinn (1942), 164, 166.

anothers language more then theire owne' (*Prose*, 118). By implication, therefore, a conquered people, even when in the majority, must be forced to adopt an 'unnatural' state in order to preserve the 'natural' condition of the conqueror.

In his *Enquiries Touching the Diversity of Languages, and Religions* (1614) Edward Brerewood analysed the difficulties involved in realizing a cultural programme such as Spenser's. 'How hard a matter it is', he observed,

utterly to abolish a vulgar language, in a populous country, where the Conquerers are in number farre inferiour to the native inhabitants . . . may well appeare by the vaine attempt of our *Norman* Conquerour: who although he compelled the *English*, to teach their young children in the Schooles nothing but *French* . . . and inforced all pleadings at the Law to be performed in that language . . . yet, the number of *English* farre exceeding the *Normans*, all was but labour lost.

Complete linguistic transformation had occurred, Brerewood asserts, only in those countries 'where either the ancient inhabitants have beene destroyed or driven forth, as wee see in our Country to have followed of the *Saxons* victories, against the *Brittains*'.[61] The force of the Saxon precedent was evident to Gaelic observers. Seathrún Céitinn argues that Hengist effected a 'pagan' rather than a Christian conquest and that 'Stanihurst would desire to act the same way by the Irish; for it is not possible to banish the language without banishing the folk whose language it is'.[62] In the Gaelic mind 'translation' of the sort that Spenser promoted was tantamount to cultural annihilation, and the bards viciously satirized all those who 'corrupted' their speech with English vocabulary.[63]

Although conscious of the problems outlined by Brerewood, Spenser relied upon the panacea of total military conquest to bring about a situation comparable to that which obtained amongst the Britons and the Saxons. Under existing conditions, however, he realized that only reverse examples of 'translation', in all senses of the term, were likely to occur. Thus he deplored the manner in which 'Irishe Captaines of Countries have encroched upon the Quenes freholders and Tennantes, how they have translated the Tenures of them from Englishe houldinge unto Irishe *Tanistrye*' (*Prose*, 208). For Spenser, as for Sir John Davies, the proper business of translation would be accomplished only when a complete

---

[61] Brerewood (1614), 22–3.   [62] Céitinn (1902–13), i. 37.

[63] See Joseph Th. Leerssen, *Mere Irish & Fíor-Ghael: Studies in the Idea of Irish Nationality, its Development and Literary Expression Prior to the Nineteenth Century* (Amsterdam: John Benjamins Publishing Company, 1986), 232–5, 300–2.

absence of Gaelic speakers rendered the practice redundant.[64] In other words, to return to Irenius's point of departure, if the tongue be English the heart must needs be English. At that stage, it was assumed, political opposition would cease not merely for lack of expression but, more profoundly, for lack of motivation because 'wordes are the Image of the minde' (*Prose*, 119)—an idea that optimistically ignores the sense of political alienation evident in the writings of even such staunchly 'English' writers as Spenser himself. Holinshed records the opinion that Hugh O'Neill 'would not frame himselfe to speake English' on the grounds that it was dishonourable to a high-born Gael to 'writh his mouth' in so 'clattering' a tongue, but in John Derricke's *Image of Ireland*, his close kinsman Turlough Luineach O'Neill, whose assimilation was then regarded as imminent, is endowed with a 'civil' English voice.[65] By contrast, the 'outlaw' Rory Oge O'More is made to confesse his crimes 'in plaine Irishe', which is actually plain English, the received medium of moral awareness.[66] In *The Famous Historye of the Life and Death of Captaine Thomas Stukeley* (1605), Shane O'Neill, Turlough's notorious predecessor, is made to deliver a similarly humiliating confession.[67] The ideal Irishman is Barnaby Rich's 'Patrick Plain'—English-speaking, Protestant, and grateful for both such gifts—a perfect product of the 'new Colledge' in Dublin of which Irenius had such great expectations (*Prose*, 142).[68]

The dialogue conducted between Irenius and Eudoxus constitutes a rhetorical paradigm of the English-speaking state envisaged by Spenser, for whereas the form of the work suggests an exchange of views, a dialectical argument logically 'rehearsed' as 'the verie matter it selfe offereth' (*Prose*, 45), the medium necessarily excludes the Gaelic voice from any possibility of participation. It is heard only in garbled translation or parodic paraphrase, or when quoted as etymological evidence of racial barbarity. It is translated not to be understood but to ensure that the reasons for its suppression are understood. Genuine dialogue arises only from comparison of *A View* with the Gaelic response in works such as Céitinn's *Foras Feasa ar Éirinn*. Spenser's 'dialogue' functions to exclude those voices that are deemed to be too primitive to participate in civil debate, much as, in *The Faerie Queene*, the savage man's 'natural' tongue excludes him so effectively from rational discourse that more civilized protagonists must speak for him (6. 5. 30). The destiny of Ireland must be decided by

---

[64] Davies (1612), 272.
[65] Holinshed (1808), vi. 6; Derricke (1985), 83, 88–9.
[66] Ibid. 92.
[67] Levinson (1975), sigs. E4^{r-v} (lines 1280–291).
[68] See Rich (1612).

those who speak English because English is defined a priori as the medium of civility. In so far as metaphor may be regarded as 'a translation of wordes frome their propre sygnifycation', Spenser employs the metaphor of barbarity to translate the culturally different into the morally reprehensible, into 'the evill that is of it selfe evill' and must be destroyed because it 'will never become good' (*Prose*, 148), which is to say that it can never be assimilated.[69]

Despite Spenser's best efforts, however, the Gaelic voice manages to be heard even in the language that condemns it, but the nature of the problem has often been misunderstood. It has recently been suggested, for example, that Spenser's use of Chaucerian archaisms was initially inspired by contact with 'the Irish colonial milieu', if only at second hand through the Sidneys.[70] It might then appear that aesthetic sophistication and linguistic degeneracy display a disconcerting similarity. It is important to recognize, however, that Spenser objected not to the retention of Chaucerian words in the diction of the Old English, but to the intrusion of Anglicized Gaelic words. E.K.'s epistle to *The Shepheardes Calender* defends the new poet's practice of attempting 'to restore, as to theyr rightfull heritage such good and naturall English words, as have ben long time out of use and almost cleare disherited'.[71] The prevalence of Chaucerian vocabulary in the Pale would in no sense taint it with an imputation of Irishness. There is, therefore, no reason to believe that Spenser would regard a word such as 'churl' as 'peculiarly Irish', as has been claimed, since it originates in Anglo-Saxon and remained current in sixteenth-century England.[72] As Edmund Campion explains, 'churl' was merely the current English translation of the opprobrious Gaelic term 'bodagh': 'the symple Irish are utterly another people then our Englishe of Ireland, whome they call dispitefully *boddai Sassonis* and *boddai Ghalt*, that is Englishe and Saxon chorles.'[73]

Spenser's use of the word 'kernes' at *Julye*, 199 is more significant. 'Kerne' is an Anglicization of the Gaelic 'ceithearnach' or 'ceithearn', meaning foot-soldier or band of foot-soldiers, and its occurrence demonstrates the chimerical nature of the search for absolute linguistic purity.

---

[69] Elyot (1538), sig. N5r.

[70] Willy Maley, *Salvaging Spenser: Colonialism, Culture and Identity* (London: Macmillan, 1997), 34–47.

[71] Spenser (1999), 27.

[72] Ibid. 42. See also my review essay 'Embarrassing Spenser' in *Bullán: An Irish Studies Journal*, 4 (1999–2000), 164–73 (pp. 168–9).

[73] Campion (1963), 20.

Yet the matter is a good deal more complex than may at first appear for, as E.K.'s gloss recognizes, the primary Gaelic sense is quite inappropriate in the context. Rather, the word is being used, as the *OED* indicates it sometimes was, in a derivative sense. One might even argue that it was only Spenser's subsequent contact with genuine 'kernes' that transformed a loose derivative usage into a more semantically accurate, if polemically aggressive, one. Irenius's kerns are not pastoral 'churles' or 'farmers' but 'Cruell and bloddye [men] full of revenge and delightinge in deadlye execucion licentious swearers and blasphemours Comon ravishers of weomen and murderers of Children' (*Prose*, 123). The use of loan words in English was countenanced by Spenser's schoolmaster, Richard Mulcaster, provided that they obeyed the rules of 'enfranchisment' or naturalization by which they 'becom bond to the rules of our writing . . . as the stranger denisons be to the lawes of our cuntrie'.[74] The simile is particularly apt in that it reveals the perceived relationship between language and sovereignty. As naturalized aliens become subject to English law, naturalized words must become subject to the laws of English grammar and pronunciation. A 'kerne' who became a 'farmer' was quite acceptable; a kern who remained a foot-soldier, adhered to the brehon law and corrupted his Old English neighbours, was not. The kerns of *The Shepheardes Calender* have been assimilated, those of *A View* remain 'salvage'. What Spenser and Stanyhurst condemn is not the 'enfranchisment' of foreign words envisaged by Mulcaster, but the insidious alienation of English itself. It was only when 'the Irish language was free dennized in the English pale' that the process of degeneration began.[75] 'Why a Gods name', Spenser asked in the *Familiar Letters* of 1580, 'may not we, as else the Greekes, haue the kingdome of oure owne Language?' (*Prose*, 16). His allusion to the Greeks, who invented the concept of 'barbarity', is very telling in that it indicates both the hopes and the fears of linguistic nationalism. In the coming years, however, Ireland would supply an unsettling answer to Spenser's question.

In the *Tristia,* Ovid identified linguistic contamination as the inevitable fate of an exiled poet. 'I fear', he wrote, 'that you may find Sintic and Pontic words mixed with Latin in my writings' (III. xiv. 49–50). The process, as he saw it, was insidious. The sheer prevalence of alien tongues made it impossible not to acquire them. In the *Epistulae ex Ponto* he confesses to the shameful act of having written a eulogy of Augustus 'in the

---

[74] Mulcaster (1582), 154–5.   [75] Holinshed (1808), vi. 4.

Getic tongue, setting barbarian words to our measures' (IV. xiii. 19–20). In attempting to eulogise Elizabeth from abroad, Spenser faced a comparable problem. When describing the process of linguistic 'degeneracy' in Ireland, Stanyhurst complains of 'meere Irish word[s] that crept unwares into the English, through the dailie intercourse of the English and Irish inhabitants'.[76] Although Spenser agreed, similar usages were already creeping 'unawares' into his own diction. One of the most surprising features of *A View*, when considered as a 'dialogue', is the repeated necessity for Irenius to explain elements of his vocabulary to Eudoxus, an Englishman who has never been to Ireland. At the outset, for example, Eudoxus enquires, 'what is that which youe call the *Brehon* lawe it is a worde to us alltogeather unknowen' (*Prose*, 47). For a brief moment, the distinction between 'you' and 'us' locates Irenius with the Irish rather than the English, identifying him as the habitual user of an alien vocabulary. 'Brehon' is an everyday component of the colonists' language, but is 'alltogeather unknowen' to Eudoxus. Already the English 'community of language', so highly extolled by Fynes Moryson, is showing signs of strain under the pressure of the colonial enterprise. Similarly, a little further on, we find Eudoxus asking 'what is this youe call *Tanist* and *Tanistrye*? They be names and tenures never harde of or knowen to us' (*Prose*, 50). Here the distinction between 'you' and 'us' appears to have grown more acute. Eudoxus has not understood the tenor of Irenius's remarks and the burden of comment grows exponentially. The following paragraphs are necessarily devoted to lengthy explanation and semantic analysis of the terms Eudoxus has failed to understand. Gradually but surely the language, and also, by implication, the political interests, of the colonist, are beginning to diverge from those of his fellow countrymen.

Despite E.K.'s insistence upon preserving the purity of the 'mother tongue' by excluding foreign words, the 'well' of Spenser's English is considerably 'defyled' within *A View* and the effect extends beyond the use of Gaelic vocabulary to the creation of an imaginative frame of reference that is remarkably un-English.[77] We are told, for example, that those who 'have degendred from theire antiente dignities' have grown to be 'as Irishe as Ohanlans breeche, (as the proverbe theare is)' (*Prose*, 117). Although the phrase in parenthesis is clearly intended to distance the expression from Irenius, both linguistically and geographically, the proverb has effectively

---

[76] Ibid. 4.
[77] See Roland M. Smith, 'The Irish Background of Spenser's *View*', 501–6; 'More Irish Words in Spenser', *MLN* 59 (1944), 472–7.

become his own. Indeed the very presence of the parenthesis signals an element of unease on Spenser's part. At the outset we are given to understand that Irenius has 'latelye come' from Ireland to England, and thereafter that the dialogue is conducted 'heare' in England rather than 'theare'.[78] The language, however, tells a different story. It is not only the Gaelic Irish, and the 'degenerate' Old English, who speak a different political language to the English but the new colonists as well. Dialogue is the perfect form for simultaneously expressing and containing doubt, and at times it appears that Spenser is conducting a debate with himself. In recommending the resumption of Grey's notorious policy of famine, for example, 'Irenius' tells 'Eudoxus' that 'the ende will I assure me be verye shorte' (*Prose*, 158). One might have expected 'I assure you', given the work's dialogical format, but self-reassurance is paramount in a world in which it is impossible to tell whether the majority of 'uncivil' customs 'weare Englishe or Irishe' in origin, and where language affords little assistance (*Prose*, 118).[79] The term 'kincongish', for example, is regarded as 'a worde mingled of Englishe and Irishe togeather so as I ame partelye led to thinke that the Custome thearof was firste Englishe and after warde made Irishe' (*Prose*, 81). But 'Irenius' is wrong. 'Kincongishe' was actually a corruption of the Gaelic 'cin cómfhocais' or 'liability of kindred'.[80]

Whatever its theoretical insistence upon segregation and difference, English colonial experience tends to find that everything has become 'mingled' and, more often than not, to resent or fear the discovery. Implicit in New English attacks upon the Gaelic language is the dreadful suspicion that it articulates 'English' nature better than the 'mother tonge'. The subtle alterations in Spenser's own language, the infiltration of his 'mother tongue' by words derived from the language of the Irish, bears witness to an unconscious process of assimilation of which his conscious polemic fights shy. It remains quite unclear where, if anywhere, Colin Clout and Irenius may identify as 'home' when even the rhetorical structures they inhabit are infused with 'alien' elements.

---

[78] *Prose*, 43, 44, 68, 229.

[79] When similar phrasing is used elsewhere Spenser is publicly reassuring himself. See e.g. the dedicatory epistle to *Daphnaïda*: 'I doo assure my selfe, that no due honour done to the white Lyon, but will be most gratefull to your Ladiship.' Spenser (1999), 324. For the shifting relationship between the personae of Irenius and Eudoxus see John Breen, 'Imagining Voices in *A View of the Present State of Ireland*: A Discussion of Recent Studies Concerning Edmund Spenser's Dialogue', *Connotations*, 4 (1994/95), 119–32.

[80] For the practice of 'kincongish' see *Prose*, 80–1, 307–8.

Part V: *The Faerie Queene* (1596)

10   'Friendships Faultie Guile'

AT the crisis of 'The Legend of Cambel and Telamond, or of Friendship'
Spenser inserts an epic simile that perfectly evokes the repetitive violence
of an interminable conflict between equally matched opponents.[1] The
story purports to be a continuation of Chaucer's *Squire's Tale* and may
therefore claim to be, in Spenserian terms, quintessentially 'English', but
the choice of imagery has a dislocating effect:

> Like as the tide that comes from th'Ocean mayne,
>   Flowes up the Shenan with contrarie forse,
>   And overruling him in his owne rayne,
>   Drives backe the current of his kindly course,
>   And makes it seeme to have some other sourse:
>   But when the floud is spent, then backe againe
>   His borrowed waters forst to redisbourse,
>   He sends the sea his owne with double gaine,
> And tribute eke withall, as to his Soveraine.
>
> (4 . 3. 27.)[2]

---

[1] Spenser distinguishes three different forms of friendship at 4. 9. 1. See generally Charles G.
Smith, *Spenser's Theory of Friendship* (Baltimore: Johns Hopkins University Press, 1935). For the
wider cultural implications see Lorna Hutson, *The Usurer's Daughter: Male Friendship and
Fictions of Women in Sixteenth-Century England* (London: Routledge, 1994), 52–64; Steven Mullaney, 'Brothers and Others, or the Art of Alienation', in Marjorie Garber (ed.), *Cannibals,
Witches, and Divorce: Estranging the Renaissance* (Baltimore: Johns Hopkins University Press,
1987), 67–89.

[2] See Patrick Cheney, 'Spenser's Completion of *The Squire's Tale*: Love, Magic and Heroic
Action in "The Legend of Cambell and Triamond"', *JMRS* 15 (1985), 135–55; Anthony M. Esolen,
'The Disingenuous Poet Laureate: Spenser's Adoption of Chaucer', *SP* 87 (1990), 285–311.

Of particular note is the ambiguity as to the river's true 'source', an ambiguity with obvious political import. Spenser was intrigued by the Augustinian notion that all of the world's rivers shared a common oceanic, subterranean 'source'.[3] Its theological overtones only lent strength to its political applications: 'So from the Ocean all rivers spring, | And tribute backe repay as to their King' (6 Proem 7). The 'tide' that first appears to usurp the Shannon's 'owne rayne' actually serves its true 'Soveraine', and the violent influx of foreign waters—'borrowed' by the river they seemed to oppress—eventually occasions the payment of double 'tribute', amply rewarding the expenditure of the invading 'floud'. Spenser's fellow planters would appreciate the point particularly well. The Irish State Papers attest with equal frequency to the Shannon's inexhaustible 'commodity' and to the 'idle' kerns who infest its banks.[4] The apparently unnatural effort to 'drive backe the current' of the river's 'kindly course' effects a paradoxical restoration of natural order analogous to the imposition of 'civility' through violence. A very comforting image, this, of the colonial enterprise. Yet latent within the imagery is the nightmare of perpetual recurrence. The peculiar nature of the conflicts described in book four is that they are potentially unending, and therefore inherently futile:

> As when two billowes in the Irish sowndes,
> Forcibly driven with contrarie tydes
> Do meete together, each abacke rebowndes
> With roaring rage; and dashing on all sides,
> That filleth all the sea with fome, divydes
> The doubtfull current into divers wayes.

> (4. 1. 42)

Irish topography affords ready similes for all that is 'contrarie', 'doubtfull', raging, and 'divers'. More Irish place names are mentioned in book four than in any other book of *The Faerie Queene* but the web of allusion spreads wider still: lust is a 'wilde and salvage man' who preys on civil ladies (4. 7. 5), Timias is disfigured by an Irish 'glib' (4. 8. 12), Sir Ferraugh takes his name from an Irish war cry (4. 2. 4), and the chaotic tournament presided over by the half-savage, half-civil Sir Satyrane is described as a 'folke-mote' (4. 4. 6), presumably of the sort at which 'manye mischiefs

---

[3] See David Quint, *Origin and Originality in Renaissance Literature: Versions of the Source* (New Haven: Yale University Press, 1983), 151–7.

[4] See e.g. SP 63/72/33; 63/75/71.

have bene bothe practised and wroughte' in Ireland (*Prose*, 129).[5] It is during this tournament that Artegall is introduced as the 'salvage knight' (4. 4. 39–42). So far as book four is concerned, landscape is mindscape.

River symbolism is particularly important.[6] Book four concludes with the marriage of Thames and Medway, an episode often interpreted as an exercise in 'epideictic topography' intended to symbolize the queen's 'marriage' to her country—although its emphasis upon 'the seas abundant progeny' introduces a very problematic note (4. 12. 1).[7] Regarded from this viewpoint, the final cantos constitute a sort of royal epithalamion, a public counterpart to the private *Epithalamion* that Spenser published the previous year in celebration of his own marriage. In the *Familiar Letters* of 1580 he speaks of having written an *Epithalamion Thamesis* in which 'in setting forth the marriage of the Thames: I shewe his first beginning, and offspring, and all the Countrey, that he passeth thorough, and also describe all the Rivers throughout Englande, whyche came to this Wedding' (*Prose*, 17). The source is given as 'Master *Holinshed*' and the reference is clearly to Harrison's prefatory 'Description of England' which devotes six lengthy chapters to the historical topography of the country's rivers.[8] It has often been suggested that the marriage of Thames and Medway represents a revised version of the poem described in the *Familiar Letters* but, if so, one crucial change has been introduced. The *Epithalamion Thamesis* confined itself to 'all the Rivers throughout Englande' but the marriage festivities in *The Faerie Queene* are attended by the rivers of the world. As Jonathan Goldberg has noted, the pageant is so replete with the vocabulary of empire that it may be seen to constitute an 'imperialistic fantasy', yet it is precisely these imperial elements that strike the most discordant notes and return 'fantasy' to the realm of political reality.[9]

In the preceding book Britomart tells Paridell of Troynovant's perilous foothold upon 'the waves | Of wealthy *Thamis*' (3. 9. 45), but now we read

[5] Irenius asserts that 'theare be yeat at this daie in Irelande manye Irishe men Chieflye in the Northern partes called by the name of *Ferragh*' (*Prose*, 103–4).

[6] See W. H. Herendeen, 'The Rhetoric of Rivers: The River and the Pursuit of Knowledge', *SP* 78 (1981), 107–27.

[7] See Robin Headlam Wells, *Spenser's 'Faerie Queene' and the Cult of Elizabeth* (London: Croom Helm, 1983), 105–6. See also Alastair Fowler, *Spenser and the Numbers of Time* (London: Routledge and Kegan Paul, 1964), 174–5.

[8] Holinshed (1808), i. 78–181. See Jack B. Oruch, 'Spenser, Camden, and the Poetic Marriages of Rivers', *SP* 64 (1967), 606–24 (pp. 614–15).

[9] Jonathan Goldberg, *Endlesse Worke: Spenser and the Structures of Discourse* (Baltimore: Johns Hopkins University Press, 1981), 139.

how 'divine Scamander', which flowed past the original city of Troy, is 'purpled yet with blood | Of Greekes and Troians', reflecting the human cost of epic endeavour (4. 11. 20). Even the English rivers, summoned up to symbolize the nation's unity, attest its violent and divided history, their waters being 'often stainde with bloud of many a band | Of Scots and English both' (36). The approach of the Amazon and 'rich Oranochy, though but knowen late' (21) prompts the narrator to complain of England's lack of commitment to the imperial enterprise in the New World. As the description of the Orinoco suggests, the matter was highly topical; Ralegh's *Discovery of Guiana* had appeared the previous year. The 'warlike women' of the Amazon are praised for holding their own against 'all men', but only because the 'men' are lacking in resolve:

> But this to you, ô Britons, most pertaines,
> To whom the right hereof it selfe hath sold;
> The which for sparing litle cost or paines,
> Loose so immortall glory, and so endlesse gaines.   (22)

The manner of address that is employed here is crucial. The narrator evokes his readers' imperial destiny in terms of their heroic past. They deserve to possess the New World because their ancestors previously possessed the Old.[10] The nature of the impediment is equally significant. All is lost 'for sparing litle cost or paines'—an accusation that recurs throughout Spenser's secretarial letters. His own 'Amazonian' queen was too parsimonious to promote the great global enterprise.

Inevitably, as one might expect from the proleptic introduction of the Shannon into canto three, attention turns to England's closest colony:

> Ne thence the Irishe Rivers absent were,
> Sith no lesse famous then the rest they bee,
> And ioyne in neighbourhood of kingdome nere,
> Why should they not likewise in love agree,
> And ioy likewise this solemne day to see?   (40)

Why not indeed? Ending as it does with the 'balefull Oure, late staind with English blood' the pageant itself supplies a series of possible answers (44). The allusion, as we have previously noted, is to Lord Grey's disastrous defeat at Glenmalure in 1580, but the epithet 'late' lends political urgency to personal reminiscence. The Oure was the Avonbeg or 'little river'

[10] See Benedict Anderson, *Imagined Communities: Reflections on the Origin and Spread of Nationalism* (London: Verso, 1991), 5–12.

which flowed through Glenmalure, the Wicklow stronghold of Feagh mac Hugh O'Byrne. The process whereby it becomes 'baleful' well illustrates the politics of Spenserian wordplay. Ignoring both the river's actual name and the proper etymology of Glenmalure, he concentrates upon the sinister-sounding central syllable, 'mal'. The river is pejoratively renamed after Grey's defeat. Henceforth it is the mal-Oure, or 'balefull Oure', the topographical equivalent of Malegar. The strategy was common. As New English place names were inscribed over Gaelic strongholds on the map, New English 'history' supplanted Gaelic 'legend' in contemporary chronicles. Richard Helgerson has reminded us that in chorographical terms 'the land speaks', but in reading Spenser it is essential to remember that most Irish land 'spoke' Gaelic and unsettled the New English sense of self-identity.[11] Ireland's rivers symbolized the evil population that needed to be 'broken into manie smalle partes like little streames that they Cannot easelye come togeather into one heade' (*Prose*, 205). Irenius reports that the 'base sort' of Irish people are commonly 'drawn by the graund Rebells into theire accion and Carryed awaie with the violence of the streame' (*Prose*, 156), yet his main concern is that the queen may 'stopp the streame of suche violence' as the Lord Deputy deems necessary to contain them (*Prose*, 159). Control of the country's innumerable rivers was generally regarded as the key to its political and commercial subjection and Irenius's shifting metaphors reflect his anxiety on this score.[12] As Spenser describes them, Irish rivers invariably divide, submerge, overflow, or run blood red. The 'spreading Lee' that 'encloseth Corke with his devided flood' (4. 11. 44) is the river that was 'stayned' with the 'filthy bloud' of John of Desmond.[13] At the time of composition the city of Cork was, in fact, largely confined to an island in the Lee, but 'divided' suggests the wider 'flood' of Irish history. It was on that island that Spenser and his family took refuge in 1598.

Among the other Irish rivers marshalled for the wedding ceremony is 'Swift Awniduff, which of the English man | Is cal'de Blacke water' (4. 11. 41).[14] Here was yet another reason for dissent. Colonial cartography erases the Irish rivers' proper names even when, as here, it purports to 'translate' them. The river which 'the English man' calls 'Blacke water'

---

[11] See Richard Helgerson, *Forms of Nationhood: The Elizabethan Writing of England* (Chicago: University of Chicago Press, 1992), 105–47.

[12] For the securing of rivers and fords see *Prose*, 224.   [13] See above p. 70.

[14] See the seminal article by P. W. Joyce 'Spenser's Irish Rivers', *Fraser's Magazine*, NS 17 (1878), 315–33, republished in *The Wonders of Ireland* (Dublin, 1911), 72–114.

marked the heavily contested boundary between Armagh and Tyrone, between the forces of the crown and those of O'Neill. Ó Súilleabháin Béarra comments that the river is called the 'Abhainn-mhór' [Great River] by the Irish but Blackwater by the English 'either because it is more turbid than other Irish rivers . . . or because the English often met with defeat and disaster on its banks'.[15] In *A View* Irenius recommends that 'two thowsande footemen' be placed 'uppon the Blacke water in some Conveniente place as highe up to the River as might be' (*Prose*, 152). He had good reason to do so. Just a year previously O'Neill had razed the so-called 'Blackfort' which garrisoned the river a few miles to the north of Armagh.[16] A well-fortified English 'Blackwater' might be compelled to attend the triumphal marriage of Thames and Medway, but a Gaelic 'Awniduff', or 'Abhainn-mhor', was unlikely to respond to the summons. The 'Irish' rivers can join in the celebrations only when they, like the people living along their banks, become 'English' and bear English names. The 'Liffar deep' that follows the Blackwater is the Gaelic Leithbhearr, and another potential flashpoint. Irenius therefore proposes to place a garrison at 'Castlecliffer or Castlefin' in order to secure 'all the passages upon the River to Loghfoile' (*Prose*, 152).[17] Castleliffer (the modern Lifford) and Castle Finn were the chief residences of O'Neill's major ally Red Hugh O'Donnell. Underlying the courtly conventions of the pageant lurk the colonial anxieties of the planter.

In the Liffar's wake come 'Strong *Allo* tombling from Slewlogher steep, | And *Mulla* mine, whose waves I whilom taught to weep' (4. 11. 41). The Allo had previously featured in *Colin Clouts Come Home Againe* as the 'neighbour flood . . . Broad water called farre' (122–3) to which 'old father Mole' wishes to wed his daughter. It rises, as the pageant correctly records, from Slieve Lougher (Spenser's 'Slewlogher'), an area identified by Irenius as one of the principal havens of the enemy (*Prose*, 115). The Allo, that is to say, finds the source of its 'strength' deep within the heartland of the 'uncivil' and bends its course towards the Galtymore Mountains ('old father Mole'), a notorious bastion of resistance just twenty miles to the northeast of Kilcolman. The perilous proximity of such places was 'one of the occasions by which all those Countries which . . . had bynne planted with Englishe weare shortelye displanted and loste' (*Prose*, 57). The topography

---

[15] O'Sullivan Beare (1903), 84.
[16] Cyril Falls, *Elizabeth's Irish Wars* (London: Constable, 1996—first pub. 1950), 213–20.
[17] See Rudolf Gottfried, 'Irish Geography in Spenser's View', *ELH* 6 (1939), 114–37 (pp. 116–17).

of the Allo and the Mulla charts the psychology of Spenser's deepest fears. As John O'Donovan pointed out in his commentary to *Annála Ríoghachta Éireann*, the name 'Allo' (or Ealla) was anciently applied to that section of the Munster Blackwater (the Gaelic 'Avonmore' or Great River, hence Spenser's 'Broad water') which flows from Kenturk to Mallow (i.e. Magh Ealla, the plain of the Ealla).[18] Spenser was probably aware of this, yet his choice of name eradicates rather than recuperates the river's ancient identity. *The Faerie Queene* is recalling Spenserian pastoral, not Gaelic legend, and the possessive pronouns ('Mulla mine') accurately reflect the narrator's proprietorial stake in what he describes. The Mulla is actually the Awbeg (or 'little river') which rose to the north of Kilcolman and skirted Spenser's property before flowing on to Castletownroche, the principal seat of Lord Roche, his greatest personal enemy amongst the Old English.[19] It is the subject of the etiological fable with which Colin entertains the Shepherd of the Ocean in *Colin Clouts Come Home Againe* (88–155). Not only has the planter poet renamed his territory, he has created his own territorial 'myth'. Yet Colin claims that his tale is 'no leasing new . . . But auncient truth confirm'd with credence old' (102–3), thereby prompting the suggestion that Spenser must have been drawing on Gaelic legend.[20] If so, he has appropriated local folklore as thoroughly as local land.[21] Despite Lord Roche, he claims not merely the Mulla but all literary rights to its tale (41). Once again, as in *The Shepheardes Calender*, the 'new poet' has invented his own 'antiquity', supplying the Mulla with a legend that the Awbeg lacks. It serves as the focus of a story told by one planter poet to another planter poet before both set out for London and the banks of the river to whose wedding all of the Irish rivers are summoned. The Irish section of the river pageant ends by gesturing towards 'many more, whose names no tongue can tell' (44). The topos is, of course, time-honoured, but in the present instance it might be more accurate to record the 'many more' whose names no Englishman can tell. Among them are all of the 'names' and associated etiological myths

---

[18] Ó Clérigh (1856), vi. 2080. Mallow was originally a Desmond manor but was granted to Sir John Norris after the earl's attainder.

[19] As the account in *Colin Clouts Come Home Againe* suggests, Spenser derived the name from Kilnemullah (Cill na mullach) the ancient name for the nearby town of Buttevant (108–13). For Spenser's disputes with Lord Roche see Raymond Jenkins, 'Spenser: The Uncertain Years 1584–1589', *PMLA* 53 (1938), 350–62 (pp. 358–9).

[20] Roland M. Smith, 'Spenser's Irish River Stories', *PMLA* 50 (1935), 1047–56 (pp. 1048–9).

[21] Colin's tale *is* ancient in that it adapts Ovid's story of Alpheus and Arethusa (*Metamorphoses*, 5. 585–641).

commemorated in prose and verse in the great collections of *Dindshenchas Érenn* ['Ireland's Toponymic Lore'] formally compiled in the eleventh or twelfth centuries and still liberally employed by Gaelic poets in the sixteenth.[22] Giolla-na-Naomh Ó Huidhrín spoke for all of them when he asserted that 'the story teller is not good who is not old' ['Ní maith seanchaidh nach seanóir'].[23] He had no use for 'new' antiquities.

The treatment of 'the three renowned brethren' (the Rivers Barrow, Nore, and Suir) enforces the relevance of the pageant to the 'Legend of Friendship' as politically conceived. According to Spenser's (topographically incorrect) account, the three rivers rise in the Slieve Bloom Mountains, run their separate courses through wide stretches of civil and uncivil territory, and finally converge in the great valley north of Waterford to flow together into the sea:

> All which long sundred, doe at last accord
> To ioyne in one, ere to the sea they come,
> So flowing all from one, all one at last become.   (43)[24]

In this they closely resemble the three sons of Agape whose coalescence is central to the allegory of friendship. Further similarities emerge in the account of their origins. Agape is a 'fay' who gives birth to 'three lovely babes' when raped in a 'salvage wood' by 'a noble youthly knight' (4. 2. 45). Rheusa is a 'nimph' who gives birth to 'three faire sons' when forcibly 'deflowr'd' by the Gyant Blomius under 'Slewbloome in shady grove' (4. 11. 42). In both cases civil 'accord' is born of violent miscegenation. The correspondences are clearly deliberate. The three rivers were traditionally know as 'sisters', but the change in gender immensely strengthens the comparison. Spenser has slyly rewritten the legend of Agape and Triamond into the topography of the Irish landscape, and comparison with the very different stories recorded in the metrical *Dindshenchas* reveals the degree to which he has ignored, or written in ignorance of, Gaelic tradition. Except for the sound of his name, the Giant Blomius has little in common with the Gaelic hero Bladh who was generally credited with giving his name to Slieve Bladhma (Bladhma being commonly pronounced as Bloma, hence 'Blomius'):

[22] See Tomás Ó Concheanainn, 'The Three Forms of Dinnshenchas Érenn', *Journal of Celtic Sudies*, 3 (1981–2), 88–131.
[23] John O'Donovan (ed.), *The Topographical Poems of John O'Dubhagain and Giolla Na Naomh O'Huidhrin* (Dublin: The Irish Archaeological and Celtic Society, 1862), 80, 81.
[24] For Seathrún Céitinn's response to this see below pp. 278–9.

Atbath fer find, figed gail,
i Sléib Bladma, blad adbail,
Blad mac Bregoin, buidnib tor,
do thám i Sléib bledaig Blod.

[A valiant man who used to wage battle died
at Sliab Bladma—[a man of] vast renown!
even Blad, son of Bregon, with troops of warriors,
died of disease in the monster-haunted Sliab Blod.][25]

In Spenser's version the celebrated Gaelic hero has become just another of the mountain's many 'monsters'. Occasionally, as in the case of 'sad Trowis, that once his people overran' (41), Spenser does appear to possess knowledge of local topographical myth but the needs of his political allegory invariably determine the manner in which it is handled.[26] In his tale of 'the three renowmed brethren', for example, the emphasis falls on the creation of unity out of multiplicity and looks forward to the eventual coalescence of Gaelic Irish, Old English, and New English into what Irenius describes as 'one people' (*Prose*, 211). Yet, from Spenser's point of view, there was already too much 'friendship' in Ireland—indeed the whole nature of 'friendship' was problematized there. The Old English had become 'one people' with the 'meare Irishe', and it was generally agreed that the strongest alliances to be found in the country were those between Gaelic-speaking foster brothers.[27] Even Love and Hate, though 'strongly arm'd, as fearing one another', are described as

brethren both of halfe the blood,
Begotten by two fathers of one mother,
Though of contrarie natures each to other.

(4. 10. 32)

As in Elizabethan Ireland, even the most diametrically opposed factions prove to be blood-related, at least on one side of their lineage. The most 'contrarie natures' are traceable to a common origin. Irenius's aspirations

---

[25] See Gwynn (1991), ii. 54, 55. For the Barrow see pp. 62–3.

[26] The Four Masters record how an inundation of the River Drowes (properly Drobhais), Spenser's Trowis, overran the countryside and created Lough Melvin (originally Melghe) during the burial ceremonies of Melghe Molbhthach. See Ó Clérigh (1856), i. 79. P. W. Joyce points out that Spenser appears to have derived the epithet 'sad' from the supposed etymology of Trowis, which he mistakenly regarded as cognate with 'truaghas' or sorrow. 'Spenser's Irish Rivers', 317–18.

[27] See David Beers Quinn, *The Elizabethans and the Irish* (Ithaca, NY: Cornell University Press, 1966), 84.

towards unity are wholly at odds with his obsessive opposition to 'mar-ryinge and fosteringe' with the enemy (*Prose*, 117). Yet the resolution of the conflict between Cambell and Triamond is sealed through the union of their families. They wed each other's sisters and became 'allide with bands of mutuall couplement' (4. 3. 52), just as Aeneas, the paradigm of all imperial heroes, secures his position in Latium through intermarriage, an event considered important enough to become the subject of a 'thir-teenth' book by Maffeo Vegio. The perfection of friendship appears to re-quire precisely the sort of 'intermingling' that Irenius opposes. Book four ends in the celebration of marriage, but Spenser's Irish policy resists the *telos* of his poetics.

The centrality of Irish topography to the legend of Cambell and Tria-mond reflects Irenius's persistent concern with the issue of 'friendship' throughout *A View*. According to Giraldus Cambrensis civic friendship was a virtue in which the Irish were conspicuously lacking.[28] Irenius agrees: 'I reasonablie Conclude', he informs Eudoxus, 'that the Irishe are discended from the *Scythyans* for that they use even to this daie some of the same ceremonies which the *Scythyans* auncientlye used As for exam-ple ye maye read in Lucian in that swete *Dialouge* which is intituled *Toxaris* or of frendshippe' (*Prose*, 107). Lucian's treatment of the matter, however, is a good deal more complex than this statement allows. The burden of his work is that the Scythians are just as capable of friendship as the Greeks and may therefore claim to be equally 'civilized'. It pits the Greek Mnesippus against the Scythian Toxaris in a duel of anecdotes de-signed to overturn the reader's expectations. Lucian's 'Scythian' is articu-late and educated; he admires Greek culture but defends his own. The contestants eventually conclude by pledging mutual friendship in recog-nition of the 'similarity of their ideals'. In other words, the dialogue from which Irenius fabricates racial difference is designed to illustrate common humanity. Only when filtered through the voices of Irenius and Eudoxus do those of Mnesippus and Toxaris begin to say what Spenser's argument requires. The basic premise of Irenius's stance is that the Irish, like the an-cient Scythians, form bonds of friendship solely for the purposes of milit-ary expediency. He cites Lucian's 'tale of *Arsacomas*' as evidence of this (*Prose*, 108).[29] This 'tale' is particularly relevant to our present pur-poses since it recounts the manner in which three friends unite 'into a sin-gle person'—and those three friends are Scythian not Greek.[30] It also

---

[28] See above p. 61.   [29] See Lucian (1936), v. 173–95 (pp. 163, 179–80).
[30] Ibid. 189.

illustrates Toxaris' contention that friendship is more severely tested amongst a warlike people than a peaceful one.[31] If Lucian's *Toxaris* is to be accounted amongst the sources for the legend of Cambell and Triamond, Spenser's supreme exemplum of 'civil' friendship is fashioned from a 'salvage' tale of 'Scythian' heroism. But Irenius's reading of *Toxaris* necessitates the rejection of its conclusions. He interprets Lucian's dialogue 'of frendshippe' as a dialogue of difference. 'If people are friends', Aristotle asserts, 'there is no need of justice between them; but people may be just, and yet need friendship. Indeed it seems that justice, in its supreme form, assumes the character of friendship'.[32] But the 'Legend of Justice', towards which book four inexorably moves, does not assume the character of friendship. Quite the contrary. The mythical figure of Geryon, presented in *Toxaris* as the ultimate symbol of friendship, should be displaced from book four to book five and transformed into an emblem of monstrosity (5. 10. 8–13).[33]

When read in the context of Spenser's Irish experience the epic simile of the Shannon seems a good deal better suited to its 'Chaucerian' context than might at first appear. As we have seen in the previous chapter, Chaucer figured prominently in contemporary discussions of the ethnicity of the Old English. Reacting to Irenius's call for the 'reformacion of Apparrell' in Ireland, Eudoxus is astonished to learn that,

all these which I have rehearsed to youe be not Irishe garmentes but Englishe, for the quilted leather Iacke is olde Englishe for it was the proper wede of the horsemen as ye maye reade in *Chaucer* wheare he describeth: *Sr Thopas* apparrell and armour when he wente to fighte againste the Geaunte, which Checklaton is that kinde of gilden leather with which they use to imbrother theire Irishe Iackes and theare likewise by all that discripcion ye maye see the verye fashion and manner of the Irishe horsmen moste livelye set forthe in his longe hose, his Rydinge shoes of Costelye Cordwaine his hacqueton and his habericion with all the rest thereunto belonginge. (*Prose*, 121)

It is intensely ironic that the 'moste livelye' description of wild 'Irishe horsmen' should be found in Chaucer and reproduced in *The Faerie Queene* where Arthur wears the hacqueton (2. 8. 38) and Britomart the habergeon (3. 3. 57). Irish horsemen reminded Stanyhurst of 'arrant knights of the round table', but Irenius informs us that even their odd

---

[31] Ibid. 161–3.   [32] Aristotle (1892), 246.
[33] For Geryon see Lucian (1936), v. 205. For Spenser's Geryoneo see Jane Aptekar, *Icons of Justice: Iconography and Thematic Imagery in Book V of 'The Faerie Queene'* (New York: Columbia University Press, 1969), 140–52.

'fashion of ridinge' is in fact 'native Englishe' (*Prose*, 122).[34] 'Whye then', asks Eudoxus with good reason, 'woulde youe have the quilted Iacke layed awaye?' 'Under a shirte of male it is allowable', Irenius explains, 'but to be worne daylie at home and in Townes and Civill places it is a rude habitt and moste uncomelye seminge like a players painted Coate' (*Prose*, 122). Yet it was worn 'at home'. The Elizabethan fascination with all things medieval had produced a second 'Indian summer' for English chivalry of which Spenser's own work was but one manifestation.[35] Elaborately costumed 'Chaucerian' tournaments marked the queen's Accession Day and pervaded contemporary fiction.[36] Most of the garments displayed on such occasions did indeed resemble 'a players painted Coate', but in Ireland the 'play' was for real. It was one of the few places, for example, where trial by combat was still practised.[37] The squire's tale that Spenser attempted to continue in verse was being lived around him.

'Friendship' is to the second instalment of *The Faerie Queene* what 'Holinesse' is to the first. As Richard McCoy observes, friendship was 'the virtue the Order of the Garter was supposed to inculcate in its members' and the connection between books one and four is enforced by Artegall's recollection of the Order's motto: 'Shame be his meede . . . that meaneth shame' (4. 6. 6).[38] St George is aptly described as England's 'frend | And Patrone' (1. 10. 61), and book four reintroduces Duessa, his foremost antagonist. Yet the proem to book four complains of the poem's rejection by one of the most senior members of the Order of the Garter, 'the rugged forhead that with grave foresight | Welds kingdomes causes, and affaires of state' (1). The dedicatory sonnet originally addressed to Burghley, 'on whose mightie shoulders most doth rest | The burdein of this kingdomes governement', had asked him to consider the 'deeper sence' hidden from 'comune vew' behind the poem's 'dim vele' of allegory. Precisely the opposite is now alleged to have occurred. Burghley has condemned the poem's 'looser rimes' for misleading young readers 'that better were in

[34] Holinshed (1808), vi. 68.
[35] For the analogous chivalric revival of the 15th cent. see Arthur B. Ferguson, *The Indian Summer of English Chivalry, Studies in the Decline and Transformation of Chivalric Idealism* (Durham, NC: Duke University Press, 1960).
[36] Roy Strong, *The Cult of Elizabeth: Elizabethan Portraiture and Pageantry* (London: Thames and Hudson, 1987—first pub. 1977), 129–63.
[37] See Holinshed (1808), vi. 455; Raymond Jenkins, 'Spenser in Ireland', *ELH* 19 (1952), 131–42 (p. 133).
[38] Richard C. McCoy, *The Rites of Knighthood: The Literature and Politics of Elizabethan Chivalry* (Berkeley: University of California Press, 1989), 134. For the motto of the Order of the Garter, 'Honi soit qui mal y pense', see Holinshed (1808), i. 272.

vertues discipled, | Then with vaine poemes weeds to have their fancies fed' (1). In view of Spenser's avowed intention of inculcating 'vertuous and gentle discipline', this is the most serious criticism that might be levelled against him. It equates him with the Gaelic bards who are allegedly 'so farre from instructinge yonge men in morrall disciplne that they themselves doe more deserve to be sharpelye discipled' (*Prose*, 125). Burghley has read the poem not as a national epic but as a lurid romance. The dedicatory sonnets to the first edition are notable for their inclusiveness.[39] It is as though Spenser were trying to unite a divided nation, and a divided court, through epic verse: here is something, he suggests, that every Englishman can support.[40] Its rejection at the very heart of English government was potentially devastating, and for the first time the poem sounds an exclusionist note: 'to such therefore I do not sing at all' (4). The remark recalls Colin Clout's assertion 'I play to please my selfe, all be it ill' (*June*, 72) and adumbrates his reappearance in book six. The reminiscence is ominous. Spenser was well aware that a national poet could not afford to retreat into pastoral solitude.

Spenser's alteration to the ending of book three gives notice that the second instalment of *The Faerie Queene* serves as a revision, as much as a continuation, of the first. His habits of self-quotation, first commented upon by Thomas Warton, now function as procedures of self-examination.[41] The tone of the narrator alters, as does the nature of the dialogue between narrator and narrative. By the time of publication the Nine Years' War had already begun and *A View* was already in preparation. Sir Henry Wallop had told Walsingham in August 1581 that there was no way to 'daunt' the Irish 'but by the edge off the sworde, and to plant better in there places'.[42] Spenser was the precarious beneficiary of precisely such a policy, a circumstance which now comes to inform every aspect of his work. The planter has dispossessed the native, and the poetry replicates both the act and the anxiety of dislocation. The authorial stance is no longer that of Aristotle's detached narrator but of an interested party. To a greater degree than ever before, the poem labours to convey a sense of all that is fragmentary and unfinished, an impression greatly heightened by the deletion of the 'Letter

---

[39] The first edition survives in two issues in one of which the Burghley sonnet and six others are missing. See Francis R. Johnson, *A Critical Bibliography of the Works of Edmund Spenser* (Baltimore: Johns Hopkins University Press, 1933), 11–18.

[40] See Carol A. Stillman, 'Politics, Precedence, and the Order of the Dedicatory Sonnets in *The Faerie Queene*', *SSt* 5 (1984—but pub. 1985), 143–8.

[41] Warton (1807), ii. 1–46.   [42] SP 63/85/27.

to Ralegh'.[43] The title page to book four calls Triamond 'Telamond'—or perfect world—but throughout the second instalment it is this sense of 'telos' that is increasingly obscured. Such limited closure as the earlier books afforded is conspicuously undone, and the hermaphroditic image of united lovers that concludes the first instalment—a figure for the perfect complementarity of male and female—is displaced from the human protagonists unto the 'idol' of Venus (4. 10. 41). The gap between aesthetic ideals and lived experience widens exponentially.[44]

In response to Burghley's criticism, Spenser turns to 'that sacred Saint my soveraigne Queene' as the poem's ideal reader, yet his depiction of Belphœbe is hardly flattering (4 Proem 4). Her Platonic ideals are tainted by sexual jealousy and she stands in unseemly delay 'long gazing' over the fallen members of 'Lust' (4. 7. 32).[45] A 'Legend of Friendship' should, in theory, provide the perfect context for praise of a virgin queen and book four makes due provision for Platonic lovers—they are accorded a separate space outside the Temple of Venus (4. 10. 26–8)—but its major concern is with betrothal and marriage. It is here that Britomart accepts the love of Artegall, that the virginal Marinell learns to love Florimell, that Cambel marries Cambina, that Triamond marries Canacee, that Amyas is reunited with Æmylia, that Placidas marries Pœana, and that Thames marries Medway.[46] By contrast, Spenser's 'Queene of love, & Prince of peace' can neither show love nor secure peace (4 Proem 4). The river marriage often taken to represent her union with England is beset with ironies. The comparison of Thames to 'old *Cybele*, arayd with pompous pride' recalls Du Bellay's description of ancient Rome but seems particularly incongruous for a bridegroom, and raises yet again the effeminizing spectre of female regiment (4. 11. 28).[47] In Camden's *De Connubio Tamae et Isis*, one of Spenser's undoubted sources, the Thames is female, and readers of *The Shepheardes Calender* might well remember that the 'bride' was originally male (*Julye*, 81–4).[48] Once again a great heroic simile functions to problematize what it ostensibly illustrates. On a wider scale, the protracted

---

[43] See Balachandra Rajan, *The Form of the Unfinished: English Poetics from Spenser to Pound* (Princeton: Princeton University Press, 1985), 44–84.

[44] See Mark Heberle, 'The Limitations of Friendship', *SSt* 8 (1987—but pub. 1990), 101–18.

[45] See William A. Oram, 'Elizabethan Fact and Spenserian Fiction', *SSt* 4 (1983), 33–47 (pp. 42–4).

[46] It is retrospectively implied in book four that Amoret's sufferings are related to her determination to remain a 'virgine wife'—to avoid consummation (4. 1. 6).

[47] See Alan MacColl, 'The Temple of Venus, The Wedding of the Thames and the Medway, and the end of *The Faerie Queene*, Book IV', *RES* 40 (1989), 26–47 (42–3).

[48] Oruch, 'Spenser, Camden, and the Poetic Marriages of Rivers', 611, 616.

episode of the two Florimells recalls Plato's insinuation that the war at Troy was fought for a mere phantom, that the heroic ideal may well be vain.[49]

By 1596 all of Spenser's former patrons—Sidney, Leicester, Grey, and Ralegh—were either dead or out of favour. Book five makes the most of their achievements, and a good deal more than they actually merited. The role of 'magnificence' was vacant, but there remained one leading candidate. It is hardly coincidental that Spenser's dedicatory sonnet to the Earl of Essex addresses him as 'Magnificke Lord', thereby expressly associating him with the virtue which is 'sette forth' in Prince Arthur.[50] The year that saw the publication of the marriage of Thames and Medway also offered a contrary view of the poet's relationship to the Thames. Readers of *Prothalamion* found the narrator walking in despondent mood 'along the shoare of silver streaming *Themmes*' (11). A direct link with book four is established by his characterization as 'freendles' (140). His plight arises,

> Through discontent of my long fruitlesse stay
> In Princes Court, and expectation vayne
> Of idle hopes, which still doe fly away,
> Like empty shaddowes . . .   (6–9)

The banks, by contrast, are in vivid bloom 'against the Brydale day, which is not long' (17). The title page advises the reader, however, that the subject is not the marriage of Thames and Medway but the double espousals of Katherine and Elizabeth Somerset, daughters of the Earl of Worcester, whose weddings were due to be celebrated on 8 November at Essex House. It was the former residence of the Earl of Leicester and the place from which 'Immerito' addressed one of the letters outlining his poetic ambitions in 1579. The poem is likely to have been composed sometime after mid-August when Essex returned in triumph from the Cadiz expedition. Essex House was then the centre of great heroic expectations and, as the husband of Sidney's widow and Leicester's heir, Robert Devereux may well have appeared to offer everything that Spenser might desire in a literary patron and a prospective governor of Ireland.[51] Since the swan

---

[49] For the phantom Helen see Plato, *Republic*, 9. 586c; Thomas P. Roche, *The Kindly Flame: A Study of the Third and Fourth Books of Spenser's 'Faerie Queene'* (Princeton: Princeton University Press, 1964), 153–5; James Nohrnberg, *The Analogy of 'The Faerie Queene'* (Princeton: Princeton University Press, 1976), 572–5.

[50] For the hostility between Ralegh and Essex see Charles E. Mounts, 'The Ralegh–Essex Rivalry and *Mother Hubberds Tale*', *MLN* 65 (1950), 509–13.

[51] See Alastair Fox, 'The Complaint of Poetry for the Death of Liberality: the Decline of Literary Patronage in the 1590s', in John Guy (ed.), *The Reign of Elizabeth I: Court and Culture in the Last Decade* (Cambridge: Cambridge University Press, 1995), 229–57 (pp. 235–8).

traditionally serves as an emblem of the poet, a direct relationship is established between the fate of the poem's 'brides' and that of the narrator. Their journey towards espousal is also the narrator's journey towards promise. At Essex House, where the Somerset sisters find loving partners, the 'freendles' poet finds a potential patron in 'Great *Englands* glory and the Worlds wide wonder, | Whose dreadfull name, late through all *Spaine* did thunder'. The emphasis is on masculine, martial endeavour. It is principally through Essex's 'prowesse and victorious armes' that '*Elisaes* glorious name may ring | Through al the world' (155–8)—and that, of necessity, includes Ireland, 'in regarde of the troblelous times and dailye daunger which is threatned to this realme by the kinge of Spaine' (*Prose*, 198). English epic needs a new hero whose deeds 'some brave muse may sing | To ages following' (159–60), just as Ireland needs a new Lord Grey. 'Suche an one', remarks Irenius, 'I Coulde name upon whom the ey of all Englande is fixed and our laste hopes now rest' (*Prose*, 228).[52] One of the surviving manuscripts of *A View* was prepared for Essex, and the work itself may well have been intended to strengthen the resolve of the bellicose faction he headed at court. [53] With Essex as personal 'friend' and 'Lord Liuetennante' the sweet Thames might well run softly till Spenser ended his song. How could 'Irenius' have known that Essex's experiences in Ireland would help to impel him towards the last, futile challenge to female regiment during Elizabeth's reign?

[52] See Rudolf B. Gottfried, 'Spenser's *View* and Essex', *PMLA* 52 (1937), 645–51.
[53] The copy prepared for Essex is Folger Shakespeare Library MS 6158. See Ray Heffner, 'Spenser's *View of Ireland*: Some Observations', *MLQ* 3 (1942), 507–15 (p. 509).

11   Poetic Justice

> The Legend of Justice is a charming romance, and its moral allegory
> . . . answers to the fondness of the Renaissance for the ep_c of the
> perfect man . . . Of course, it seems a trifle hard that a poet should
> advise the extermination of brother poets, however richly t1ey may
> merit destruction; it depends on the point of view however . . .
> Dreamer of dreams, Galahad of the quest for Beauty, [Spenser] was
> also of good right a member of that little group of men who saw
> beyond the welter of court intrigue and petty politics the glorious
> vision of an imperial England.
>
> (Edwin Greenlaw)[1]

ATTITUDES change. Since 1912 Greenlaw's 'charming romance' has occasioned more controversy than any of Spenser's other works. As confidence in the empire declined it came to seem more than a 'trifle hard' that 'a poet should advise the extermination of brother poets' and, in the wake of the Second World War, the term 'extermination' appeared particularly unfortunate. Yet modern disquiet on this account is less anachronistic than is sometimes claimed. It is well to remember that the age of Pizarro was also the age of Las Casas. The issue of 'extirpation' was raised by Queen Elizabeth in the letter that confirmed Lord Grey's appointment to Ireland:

wheras our subjects of that contrie birthe have (as we are informed) conceaved that we have a determination as it were to roote them out, with an intention to place there our subjects borne in this realme, we would have you seeke, by all the meanes you can, to remove that false impression wrought in them, by certayne sedetious and ill-disposed persons.[2]

Lord Grey's subsequent activities were ill calculated to dispel such 'false impressions'. After his departure, as famine gave way to plantation, the fears of the indigenous population seemed more than justified, and Sir William Herbert warned that worse might well be in store:

---

[1] Edwin Greenlaw, 'Spenser and British Imperialism', *MP* 9 (1912), 347–70 (pp. 355, 361, 370).
[2] Grey (1847), 75.

If the Irish are not disposed by any laws, persuasion or examples to embrace from the heart a way of life distinguished by the best principles and ordinances . . . then I avow and predict with quite as much truth as force that some king of England and Ireland, of great prudence and power, prompted by political considerations and designs, will disperse that entire race and will extirpate all the inhabitants there [omnesque ibi incolas . . . exstirpaturum] who have lapsed into the habits and customs of the Irish.[3]

The point was well taken. At least one poem in the *Leabhar Branach* warns that the official English policy is one of extermination or total banishment ('ionnarbadh'), that the 'hatchet' is hanging over the Gaels' heads ['ós cionn do chinn tarla an tuagh'].[4] Transportation was sometimes presented as a humane alternative to extermination but, more often than not, the one was seen to entail the other. 'I like a plantation in a pure soil,' asserts Lord Bacon, 'that is, where people are not displanted to the end to plant in others. For else it is rather an extirpation than a plantation.'[5] Other commentators had no such compunction. Nicholas Dawtrey recommended the total extermination of whole clans, including the O'Neills, O'Donnells, O'Rourkes, O'Briens, and MacMurraghs, 'nether pardon, nor protection, to be given or graunted to any of them, so longe as any of these surnames were found alive'. Underlings might be spared partly 'to avoid . . . great effusion of bloode' but principally because 'these inferiour people, will . . . yeild a good revennue unto the Crowne of England'.[6]

Spenser was particularly sensitive on this issue. In recommending the use of the 'sword', Irenius explains, 'I doe not meane The Cuttinge of all that nacion with the sworde, which farr be it from me that ever I shoulde thinke soe desperatlye or wishe so uncharatablie' *(Prose,* 148). Such a policy would be quite impracticable in any case 'since Irelande is full of her owne nacion that maye not be roted out' *(Prose,* 211). The quality of 'maye' is admittedly uncertain. Does it connote a moral imperative or a military impossibility? The point was important. When *A View* was first published by Sir James Ware in the very different political circumstances of 1633, 'maye not' was carefully altered to 'ought not'.[7] By the 'sword' Irenius intends 'the Royall power of the Prince which oughte to stretche it selfe forthe in her Chiefe strengthe to the redressinge and Cuttinge of all those evills which I before blamed, and not of the people which are evill'

---

[3] Herbert (1992), 85–7.   [4] Mac Airt (1944), 147–8.
[5] See Bacon (1857–74), vi. 457. See also Quinn (1942), 151–66.
[6] Dawtrey (1995), 112. See also pp. 87, 100, 123.
[7] For Ware's changes to Spenser's text see below pp. 275–6.

(*Prose*, 148). Abstracted from the daily carnage, violence becomes 'powre', an integral component of justice (5. 4. 1) and the concept which (in its various synonyms) most often attracts the epithet 'imperial' in Spenserian verse. The problem for book five, however, is that while Mercilla's sword is 'rusted' through prolonged disuse (5. 9. 30), Artegall's positively glistens (5. 1. 10).[8] The contrast is particularly incongruous given the expansionist context in which Mercilla is introduced. She is credited with extending her power 'from th'utmost brinke of the *Armericke* shore, | Unto the margent of the Molucas' (5. 10. 3). Judging from the effect upon his writing, there can be little doubt that Spenser found violence aesthetically stimulating. He displays considerable imaginative sympathy with what, he knew, should more properly be deplored. He has the contemplative hermit of book one tell St George that 'bloud can nought but sin, & wars but sorrowes yield' (1. 10. 60). Despite the articulation of such pious truths, however, Ireland's 'fierce warres' must somehow 'moralize' his song, the solution must be found in the problem (1 Proem 1).

It is all the more significant in this regard that the 'Legend of Justice' should begin with the departure of Astraea (5. 1. 11), an ominous episode that unwittingly recalls John Knox's allegation that female regiment 'repugneth to Justice'.[9] For the purposes of formal Elizabethan panegyric 'Eliza' was 'Astraea'. Spenser's own *Aprill* eclogue is modelled upon Virgil's prediction that Astraea is destined to return to earth and renew the Golden Age ('iam redit et Virgo, redeunt Saturnia regna').[10] In *Mother Hubberds Tale*, by contrast, the keynote for Spenser's vitriolic attack upon the state of the nation is struck by Astraea's absence (1–4).[11] Her departure at the outset of the 'Legend of Justice' signals an unprecedented convergence of epideictic and satiric modes, and the result not infrequently reads like mock-heroic, or even self-parody.[12] Artegall operates in the vacuum created by Astraea's absence, as Grey operated in the absence of royal favour, and the nature of his activities is inevitably compromised. As if to prepare the reader for what lies ahead, the proem warns us to expect little by way of

---

[8] See William Nelson, 'Queen Elizabeth, Spenser's Mercilla and a Rusty Sword', *Renaissance News*, 18 (1965), 113–17.

[9] Knox (1846–64), iv. 400.   [10] Virgil, *Eclogues*, iv. 6.

[11] Richard Danson Brown, *'The New Poet': Novelty and Tradition in Spenser's 'Complaints'* (Liverpool: Liverpool University Press, 1999), 160.

[12] See Donald Cheney, *Spenser's Image of Nature: Wild Man and Shepherd in 'The Faerie Queene'* (New Haven: Yale University Press, 1966), 146–75. For the element of parody see Michael West, 'Spenser's Art of War: Chivalric Allegory, Military Technology, and the Elizabethan Mock-Heroic Sensibility', *RQ* 41 (1988), 654–704.

idealization: 'for from the golden age, that first was named, | It's now at earst become a stonie one' (2). Appeal is made to common experience: 'who so list into the heavens looke' will discover chaotic violence rather than Ptolemaic order (5–7). The world 'is runne quite out of square' (1) and in such circumstances there could be but one solution: 'a severe Magistrate is herein required', maintained Spenser's fellow planter Richard Beacon, 'for that a common-weale mightily corrupted in manners, is *squared and reformed* onely by the rule and line of Justice which wee call distributive, the which for the inequality thereof, may not without great motions and sharpe remedies reforme the enormities and mischiefes of the common-weale'.[13] Like Grey, Beacon is vocal in his support for Sir Richard Bingham whose ruthless tactics—including a notorious massacre at Ardnaree which claimed the lives of as many women and children as combatants—made his name a byword for 'excessive cruelty' amongst the Irish.[14]

There can be little doubt that Spenser shared Beacon's outlook. He was fully aware of the compromise with 'civility' that Grey's 'thorough' policy entailed, but was quite prepared to see the strategy repeated 'seinge that by no other meanes it is possible to recure them [the Irish], and that these are not of will but of verye urgente necessitye' (*Prose*, 163). Political necessity would thus appear to dispense with justice and 'moral' allegory to rationalize the dispensation. Irenius warmly endorses Machiavelli's opinion that 'absolute power' should be ceded to colonial 'governours' in order to enable them to 'followe the necessitye of present occacions' (*Prose*, 229).[15] At issue here is a crucial distinction between '*jurisdictio* (the saying of the law) and *gubernaculum* (the holding of the tiller)'. The latter was very much 'a craft rather than a science, concerned with the unique rather than the recurrent, with the management of policy rather than the establishment of laws'.[16] 'Gubernator' is, of course, cognate with governor. When

---

[13] Beacon (1996), 82. For Beacon see Brendan Bradshaw, 'Robe and Sword in the Conquest of Ireland', in Claire Cross, David Loades, and J. J. Scarisbrick (eds.), *Law and Government under the Tudors: Essays Presented to Sir Geoffrey Elton* (Cambridge: Cambridge University Press, 1988), 139–62 (pp. 152–4); Alexander C. Judson, 'Spenser and the Munster Officials', *SP* 44 (1947), 157–73 (pp. 165–8).

[14] Beacon (1996), 22, 23, 65. For the massacre at Ardnaree see Cyril Falls, *Elizabeth's Irish Wars* (London: Constable, 1996—first pub. 1950), 158–60. Lord Grey regarded Bingham as 'a great jewel', the Irish saw him as a butcher. See SP 63/78/29; Lombard (1930), 65. For his disregard for common law see Christopher Highley, *Shakespeare, Spenser, and the Crisis in Ireland* (Cambridge: Cambridge University Press, 1997), 117–20.

[15] See Edwin A. Greenlaw, 'The Influence of Machiavelli on Spenser', *MP* 7 (1909–10), 187–202.

[16] See J. G. A. Pocock, *The Machiavellian Moment: Florentine Political Thought and the Atlantic Republican Tradition* (Princeton: Princeton University Press, 1975), 25, 29.

the realm of Ireland was left 'like a shippe in a storme amiddest all the raginge surges unruled and undirected of anye', Lord Grey behaved 'like a moste wise Pilott' and 'kepte her Course Carefullye and helde her moste strongelye even againste those roringe billowes' (*Prose*, 63). He did only what was necessary to save the ship of state from foundering. In a fallen world, Irenius assures us, 'no lawes of man, according to the straighte rule of righte, are iuste'. Rather, they are justifiable solely 'in regarde of the evills which they prevente and the safetye of the Comon weale' (*Prose*, 65). If Lord Burghley had dismissed the first instalment of *The Faerie Queene* as frivolous, here at last was a theme he might favour. In *The Execution of Justice in England for Maintenance of Public and Christian Peace* (1584), he too relies heavily upon arguments from necessity in order to justify the massacre at Smerwick and the appalling fate of the House of Desmond. Like Spenser, he fully endorses the use of the 'sword' in promoting the security of the queen's 'two realms'.[17]

Commentators such as Herbert and Beacon were content to concede that the realm of ethics was distinct from that of realpolitik, but Spenser was not.[18] He would, if possible, 'moralize' Machiavelli. Despite all disclaimers and qualifications to the contrary, justice remains the 'most sacred virtue . . . of all the rest, | Resembling God in his imperiall might' (5 Proem 10). It is, in fact, the supreme 'imperiall' virtue, and the defence of Lord Grey is reserved to book five for that very reason. The 'Legend of Justice' is hereby committed to the paradoxical endeavour of making a 'virtue' of 'necessity'—quite literally. All too often when 'necessity' dictates a choice between evils, the lesser (as Spenser conceives it) is presented as an absolute good, a process which subjects the poem's moral logic to severe strain.[19] During his encounter with the demagogic Giant of canto two, Artegall reasserts the cosmic order denied in the proem, insisting, one might say, upon an obsolete metaphor to justify the perceived inequalities of lived experience.[20] Yet the Giant is ultimately defeated not by argument but by violence. Artegall's ideals seem to be at constant

---

[17] Cecil (1965), 29–30, 34–5.

[18] See Vincent Carey, 'The Irish Face of Machiavelli: Richard Beacon's *Solon His Follie* (1594) and Republican Ideology in the Conquest of Ireland', in Hiram Morgan (ed.), *Political Ideology in Ireland 1541–1641* (Dublin: Four Courts Press, 1999), 83–109.

[19] See the excellent account by Elizabeth Fowler, 'The Failure of Moral Philosophy in the Work of Edmund Spenser', in *Representations*, 51 (1995), 47–76.

[20] See Annabel Patterson, *Reading Between the Lines* (London: Routledge, 1993), 96, 111; Walter S. H. Lim, 'Figuring Justice: Imperial Ideology and the Discourse of Colonialism in Book V of *The Faerie Queene* and *A View of the Present State of Ireland*', *Renaissance & Reformation*, 19/1 (1995), 45–67.

variance with his actions. When the concept of political 'necessitie' is explicitly invoked by the wily Burbon, he deplores it without hesitation (5. 11. 56). The reaction is understandable in view of Burbon's cynical apostasy, yet the episode as a whole endorses Elizabeth's highly expedient recognition of Henry of Navarre as King of France.[21] Here as elsewhere the 'Legend of Justice' mounts a moral defence of moral compromise and, as we have seen in Chapter 4, the resulting tensions are writ large in the character of its hero.

In the eighteenth chapter of *The Prince* Machiavelli asserts that 'there are two ways of fighting, by law or by force':

> The first way is natural to men, and the second to beasts. But as the first way often proves inadequate one must needs have recourse to the second. So a prince must understand how to make a nice use of the beast and the man. The ancient writers taught princes about this by an allegory, when they described how Achilles and many other princes of the ancient world were sent to be brought up by Chiron, the centaur, so that he might train them his way. All the allegory means, in making the teacher half beast and half man, is that a prince must know how to act according to the nature of both, and that he cannot survive otherwise.[22]

It is precisely this lesson that Spenser's allegory of the 'salvage knight' aims to teach Elizabeth while at the same time paying homage to the doctrine of the 'just war'.[23] Artegall's savagery is at once regrettable and necessary. He begins to practise 'justice' in the 'woods' upon 'wyld beasts' for 'want there of mankind' and the phrase has an ominous ring (5. 1. 7). Animal imagery is associated with the Irish throughout *A View*, but how 'humane' is their governor? Does he bring humanity to the 'beasts' or does he also lack 'mans kind'? His activity attests to the measure of Spenser's personal assimilation into the Irish problem. The notorious 'yron flayle' is merely one case in point (5. 11. 59). Much effort has been expended on Talus's iconography, and the flail is usually related to that brandished by Mars.[24] But as such Gaelic texts as *Pairlement Chloinne Tomáis* illustrate, the 'flail' ['súiste'] was

[21] See Anne Lake Prescott, 'Foreign Policy in Fairyland: Henri IV and Spenser's Burbon', *SSt* 14 (2000), 189–214.

[22] Machiavelli (1961), 99.

[23] For the doctrine of the just war and the association with chivalry see Richard A. McCabe, 'The Fate of Irena: Spenser and Political Violence', in Patricia Coughlan (ed.), *Spenser and Ireland: An Interdisciplinary Perspective* (Cork: Cork University Press, 1989), 109–25 (pp. 111–12). For sceptical responses to the doctrine see Alastair Fowler, 'Spenser and War', in J. R. Mulryne and Margaret Shewring (eds.), *War, Literature and the Arts in Sixteenth-Century Europe* (London: Macmillan, 1989), 147–64 (pp. 152–5).

[24] See Jane Aptekar, *Icons of Justice: Iconography and Thematic Imagery in Book V of 'The Faerie Queene'* (New York: Columbia University Press, 1969), 41–52.

in common, and most unchivalric, use in Irish faction-fighting.[25] The grand attribute of Mars is also the weapon of choice for the 'bodach' or low-born churl, and the conflation of classical and 'salvage' imagery well evokes the contradictions underlying the heroic aspirations of book five.[26]

Talus is excluded from the Temple of Isis but so too, and more disturbingly, is Artegall. The vision of Isis is central to the 'legend' of justice but peripheral to the development of its patron who must depart *from* Britomart (and all that she has come to represent in Isis Church) in order to settle the affairs of Ireland. The dichotomy suggests a disturbing disjunction between the poem's poetic and political values: between the civility of the heroic ideal and the incivility of the policies it celebrates. For Artegall, the 'allegorical' centre of the book is not Isis Church but Mercilla's court.[27] According to the narrator, Isis represents 'that part of Iustice, which is Equity' (5. 7. 3), but this is precisely the virtue that Artegall appears to lack despite his childhood training (5. 1. 7).[28] Three times he places his hand upon his sword with the intention of killing Braggadocchio but is restrained by Sir Guyon on the grounds that 'it would dishonour bee | To you, that are our iudge of equity, | To wreake your wrath on such a carle as hee' (5. 3. 36). Lord Grey had few such scruples: 'I take no Delight', he told Burghley, 'to advertise of every common Person's Head that is taken of. Otherwise I could have certified of an Hundreth or two of their Lives ended since my coming from those Parts.'[29] So far as Irenius was concerned, the Irish had received far too much 'equity' through the issuing of royal pardons. *A Brief Note of Ireland*, written at the crisis of the Nine Years' War, demands a change of policy: only through 'the terror of your wrath', Elizabeth is told, is it possible to 'spreade the honorable fame of your Iustice and redeeme both your owne honour and allso the reputacion of your people' (*Prose*, 241). Two decades previously Grey had similarly attempted to 'reclaim' the country 'by terrour' on the

---

[25] Williams (1981), 35, 93.

[26] Angus Fletcher notes that Hercules carries a flail rather than a club in the Gaelic life of the hero, *Stair Ercueil Ocus a Bás*. See *The Prophetic Moment: An Essay on Spenser* (Chicago: University of Chicago Press, 1971), 142.

[27] See Donald V. Stump, 'Isis Versus Mercilla: The Allegorical Shrines in Spenser's Legend of Justice', *SSt* 3 (1982), 87–98.

[28] For equity and the Temple of Isis see Fletcher, *The Prophetic Moment*, 276–87; Michael O'Connell, *Mirror and Veil: The Historical Dimension of Spenser's 'Faerie Queene'* (Chapel Hill: University of North Carolina Press, 1977), 139–47. For Bodin's influence on Spenser's notion of equity see Andrew Hadfield, *Spenser's Irish Experience: Wilde Fruit and Salvage Soyl* (Oxford: Clarendon Press, 1997), 73–6.

[29] Murdin (1759), 347.

pretext that law per se is useless in Ireland (*Prose*, 160). 'It is then a verye unseasonable time to pleade lawe when swordes are in the handes of the vulgare', agrees Eudoxus (*Prose*, 55). 'Lawe' is what 'necessitye' obliges the patron of Justice to put aside. Yet contradictions inevitably creep into the argument. The tract that promotes violence also deplores it. What it values, as it repeatedly insists, is 'civilitye'. The intention of such insistence is to justify means by ends, but the effect is to compromise ends by means.

The dichotomy is most evident in the area of religious reform. Here Irenius's tone changes quite noticeably. He has no doubt that the 'powerfull grace' of the 'mightye Saviour' will 'worke Sallvacion' in 'manye' of the Irish (*Prose*, 137). The sense of otherness so carefully cultivated up to this point now appears to be greatly diminished. Yet throughout both *A View* and *The Faerie Queene* Roman Catholicism is construed as the arch-enemy. It is cited as one of the principal reasons for the savagery of the Irish and is alleged to have 'bred greate Contagion in theire Soules' (*Prose*, 137). In works of this kind, as Johannes Fabian wryly observes, the 'pagan' is customarily regarded as '*already* marked for salvation' although the 'savage' is '*not yet* ready for civilization'.[30] Yet the 'pagan' is the 'savage'. Irenius's fleeting recognition of spiritual kinship cannot dispel the enduring sense of cultural difference nor mitigate the rigour of colonial policy. Rather the opposite. The religious impulse justifies military endeavour, 'for it is an ill time to preache amongest swordes and moste harde or rather impossible it is to settle a good opinion in the mindes of men for matters of Religion doubtfull which have a doubtlesse evill opinion of ourselves' (*Prose*, 138). Rapprochement is 'doubtfull' but difference is 'doubtlesse'. Not surprisingly, Gaelic commentators such as Ó Súilleabháin Béarra concluded that 'the Catholic religion could not be stamped out in any other way than by annihilating those in whose breasts it was deeply rooted'.[31] The pious rhetoric of conversion was seen to promote 'extirpation'.

If, as has often been argued, the tale of the two sons of Milesio is modelled upon that of the two sons of Míl Espáinne, the legendary progenitor of the Gaelic Irish, the episode illustrates the desired relationship between governor and governed (5. 4. 4–20).[32] Every undertaker in the Plantation

---

[30] Johannes Fabian, *Time and the Other: How Anthropology Makes its Object* (New York: Columbia University Press, 1983), 26.

[31] O'Sullivan Beare (1903), 48–9.

[32] See Roland M. Smith, 'Spenser's Tale of the Two Sons of Milesio', *MLQ* 3 (1942), 547–57; Clare Carroll, 'Spenser and the Irish Language: The Sons of Milesio in *A View of the Present State of Ireland*, *The Faerie Queene*, Book V and the *Leabhar Gabhála*', *Irish University Review*, special issue, 'Spenser in Ireland 1596–1996', 26/2 (1996), 281–90.

of Munster was obliged to set up courts leet and courts baron in order to facilitate the introduction of English common law.[33] This was held to be particularly beneficial to the native community by providing impartial arbitration in their disputes. John Hooker claims that the Irish 'did fall in love' with Sir Henry Sidney for 'his uprightnesse, indifferencie, and iustice, in determining of everie mans cause'.[34] In Spenser's version of the legend, Milesio's sons willingly assent to Artegall's judgement, recognizing that without his influence there can be nothing but unending, internecine conflict. In this idealized version of events, violence is what Artegall eliminates. He takes neither land nor 'threasure' for himself. Functioning in the 'Land of Ire' (as Ireland was often termed) he restrains the 'ires' of the contending brethren (4) while at the same time justifying the apparently inequitable relationship between the 'two Ilands' (7) at the heart of the dispute by upholding the 'imperiall might' of the 'mighty Sea' (19).[35] It is noteworthy, however, that even here, though 'each one had his right', one party to the dispute remains 'displeased' (20).

The theme of 'necessity' is articulated most strongly through the structure of book five.[36] The business of Ireland is presented as the climax of a much wider conflict between the forces of corruption and reform. Hence the prevalence of intrusive Apocalyptic imagery.[37] If, as I have argued, Ireland figures not merely in book five but throughout *The Faerie Queene*, it is equally true that European issues are present throughout book five, including the final canto. It is no coincidence that Grantorto has been identified both as the Earl of Desmond and Philip II.[38] The former was commonly regarded as a client of the latter and foreign policy was duly informed by paranoia. 'As warre is denounced, and threatned from forraine parts', warned Francis Hastings, 'so conspiracies lye and lurk closely at home in our owne bosomes. *Foris* they prepare;

---

[33] Michael MacCarthy-Morrogh, *The Munster Plantation: English Migration to Southern Ireland 1583–1641* (Oxford: Clarendon Press, 1986), 31.

[34] Holinshed (1808), vi. 403.

[35] For Ireland as the Land of Ire see Davies (1612), 284.

[36] For other accounts of the structure see T. K. Dunseath, *Spenser's Allegory of Justice in Book Five of 'The Faerie Queene'* (Princeton: Princeton University Press, 1968); James E. Phillips, 'Renaissance Concepts of Justice and the Structure of *The Faerie Queene*, Book V', *HLQ* 33 (1970), 103–20.

[37] See Richard Mallette, 'Book Five of *The Faerie Queene*: An Elizabethan Apocalypse', *SSt* 11 (1990—but pub. 1994), 129–59; Kenneth Borris, *Spenser's Poetics of Prophecy in 'The Faerie Queene' V* (Victoria, BC: University of Victoria, English Literary Studies, 1991), 19–35.

[38] See Anon., 'Ms Notes to Spenser's *Faerie Queene*', *N&Q* 202 (1957), 509–15 (p. 513); Mallette, 'Book Five of *The Faerie Queene*', 144–5.

intus they conspire.'³⁹ It was suggested in 1580 that the landing of Spanish forces at Smerwick was intended to distract Elizabeth's attention
from the growing crisis in the Netherlands and even to 'turn Ireland into
an English Flanders'.⁴⁰ Book five accordingly heaps undue praise on
Leicester's ineffectual campaign in the Low Countries as an instance of
'Arthurian' heroism in the face of idolatry and oppression (5. 10. 3–39).⁴¹
This was no mere act of posthumous flattery. The English reception of
the so-called 'black legend' was heavily informed by the Spaniards' reaction to the revolt of the Netherlands.⁴² In having Prince Arthur aid
'Belgæ' at Mercilla's behest, Spenser recalls Leicester's rapturous reception at the Hague as another 'Arthur of Britaine'. In Utrecht he 'kept
most honourablie the feast of S. George . . . invested in his robes of the
order' thereby affording a perfect example of proper national commitment to the cause betrayed by Lord Grey's recall.⁴³ Although chronology demands otherwise, the episode of Belgæ precedes that of Irena as
does the episode of Duessa's trial. As we have seen in Chapter 4,
Spenser's account of the latter affair takes due note of Grey's involvement but ignores the queen's attempt to dissociate herself from the out-
come.⁴⁴ The details of the trial have been altered to reflect the
widespread hope that a turning point had finally been reached.⁴⁵

The effect upon the poetry is immediate and stark. Mercilla, in defi-
ance of allegorical precedent, acts against the expectations of her name.

³⁹ Francis Hastings, *A Watchword to all Religious, and True Hearted English-men* (London,
1598), 110.
⁴⁰ See O'Rahilly (1938), 28–9. See also Juan E. Tazón Salces, 'Politics, Literature and Colonization: A View of Ireland in the Sixteenth Century', in C. C. Barfoot and Theo D'haen (eds.),
The Clash of Ireland: Literary Contrasts and Connections (Amsterdam: Rodopi Press, 1989), 23–36
(p. 26).
⁴¹ See Douglas A. Northrop, 'Spenser's Defence of Elizabeth', *UTQ* 38 (1969), 277–94
(p. 282); Wallace T. MacCaffrey, *Queen Elizabeth and the Making of Policy, 1572–1588* (Princeton: Princeton University Press, 1992), 340–2. See also Charles Wilson, *Queen Elizabeth and the
Revolt of the Netherlands* (London: Macmillan, 1970).
⁴² William S. Maltby, *The Black Legend in England: The Development of Anti-Spanish Sentiment, 1558–1660* (Durham, NC: Duke University Press, 1971), 44–60.
⁴³ Holinshed (1808), iv. 645, 658. Contemporary annotators attempted to identify the various parties. See Alastair Fowler, 'Oxford and London Marginalia to *The Faerie Queene*', *N&Q*
206 (1961), 416–19 (pp. 416–17); John Manning, 'Notes and Marginalia in Bishop Percy's Copy
of Spenser's *Works* (1611)', *N&Q* 229 (1984), 225–7 (p. 226).
⁴⁴ See Camden (1675), 391–2; Kerby Neill, '*The Faerie Queene* and the Mary Stuart Controversy', *ELH* 2 (1935), 192–214.
⁴⁵ See René Graziani, 'Elizabeth at Isis Church', *PMLA* 79 (1964), 376–89 (pp. 379–80);
Peter E. McCullough, 'Out of Egypt: Richard Fletcher's Sermon before Elizabeth I after the
Execution of Mary Queen of Scots', in Julia M. Walker, *Dissing Elizabeth: Negative Representations of Gloriana* (Durham, NC: Duke University Press, 1998), 118–49.

She grants no mercy. Rather, like Grey at Smerwick, she is represented as grieving for the need to act against her better nature in the interests of the state (5. 10. 4).[46] Having opposed her Lord Deputy, she is now recast in his image. Spenser has taken to heart Ralegh's advice to 'behold her Princely mind aright, and write thy Queene anew'.[47] In canto nine she is 'just' rather than merciful; in cantos ten and eleven she is militaristic and interventionist rather than isolationist and cautious. There then follows the episode of Irena, chronologically prior to all that precedes it, but strategically posterior. As Spenser wrote, the fate of Irena still hovered in the balance. Grantorto had 'died' in the person of Desmond only to be re-born in the person of O'Neill. If the queen takes the message of cantos nine to eleven, and remembers the representation of the Armada in canto eight, the next 'Artegall' may be allowed to do what 'necessity' demands. *A View* presents itself to the reader not as history or chronicle but as a 'verye nedefull' pre-emptive discourse designed to 'searche into the refor-macion of abuses' with an eye to the 'prevencion' of 'the evills to Come' (*Prose*, 65). Recalling Grey from Ireland 'ere he could reforme it thor-oughly' is shown, in the course of this 'searche', to have been a grave error of moral and political judgement (5. 12. 27). Elizabeth and her Privy Council are therefore invited to respond not emotionally, but logically, to her second, and perhaps final, chance to bring the country to heel. Cele-bration of the late Lord Grey encodes an appeal for the man upon whom 'the ey of all Englande is fixed and our laste hopes now rest' (*Prose*, 228).[48] In fact, the substitution has already occurred: Essex, not Grey, was the 'Artegall' dispatched by Elizabeth to assist Henry of Navarre at the siege of Rouen in 1591. The Irish career of the first Earl of Essex may well have assured Spenser of his son's commitment to a 'thorough' policy. Gaelic commentators held him responsible for the massacre of the entire popu-lation of Rathlin Island in 1574, an event generally regarded as one of the worst atrocities in Ulster's history.[49]

If the 'Legend of Justice' represents an aberration in *The Faerie Queene*'s moral temper, it is largely because it also represents a perfect articulation of its political outlook. Aristotle held that justice sought 'the good of

---

[46] See above p. 87.   [47] Spenser (1978), 19.

[48] It is likely that Beacon's Pisistratus who leads 'a strong army by the commaundement of the councell of *Athens* unto *Salamina* [Ireland]' also represents Essex. See Beacon (1996), 13–14.

[49] The queen condoned the massacre on the grounds of 'necessity'. See Bart Westerweel, 'Astrophel and Ulster: Sidney's Ireland', in Barfoot and D'haen (eds.), *The Clash of Ireland*, 5–22 (p. 9).

others', but in colonial terms the Other's good was held to depend upon the imposition of 'civil' laws.[50] 'Where the countrie is subdued', Stanyhurst asserted, 'there the inhabitants ought to be ruled by the same law that the conqueror is governed.'[51] Adherence to an agreed code of law was now commonly regarded as one of the defining characteristics of the centralized state.[52] In Ireland, from the passing of the Statutes of Kilkenny (1366), adherence to the brehon law by families of Old English descent was officially regarded as treasonable.[53] The issue was both political and cultural. The brehon law, like other native legal codes, was regarded as inherently inferior to English common law. It was at once the best a primitive people could manage and the principal barrier to their development. 'It is a certaine rule of righte', declares Irenius, 'unwritten but delivered by tradicion from one to another in which often tymes theare appeareth great shewe of equitye in determyninge the righte betwene partie and partie but in manye thinges repugninge quite to godes lawe and mans' *(Prose*, 47).[54] Such, as the choice of name suggests, is the essence of 'Grantorto's' nature: Gaelic society is nothing more than institutionalized 'tort'. Sir John Davies asserts that the first Earl of Desmond, the direct ancestor of Grey's principal opponent, 'was the first English Lord that imposed *Coign* and *Livery* upon the Kings subiectes; and the first that raised his estate to immoderate greatnesse, by that wicked Extortion and Oppression . . . the first that reiected the English Lawes and Governement'.[55] Unfortunately for all such arguments the brehon law was a written code, whereas English common law had its roots in oral tradition.[56] For Irenius's purposes, however, the allegation of orality better suited the characterization of Gaelic society as 'salvage', just as the unfounded suggestion that English common law originated with William the Conqueror better suited the characterization of English society as civil.[57] In law as in religion the Irish

---

[50] Aristotle (1892), 138.   [51] Holinshed (1808), vi. 5.

[52] D. R. Woolf, *The Idea of History in Early Stuart England: Erudition, Ideology, and 'The Light of Truth' from the Accession of James I to the Civil War* (Toronto: University of Toronto Press, 1990), 83–9.

[53] For the Statutes of Kilkenny see A. J. Otway-Ruthven, *A History of Medieval Ireland* (London: Barnes and Noble, 1993—first pub. 1968), 291–4.

[54] For English attitudes to the brehon law see Davies, (1612), 165–75. For a strong Gaelic defence see O'Sullivan Beare (1960), 82–9.

[55] Davies (1612), 206.

[56] For the alleged orality of brehon law see Moryson (1903), 224.

[57] Other commentators acknowledged that English common law was in place 'long before the Conquest'. See Davies (1612), 127; David J. Baker, *Between Nations: Shakespeare, Spenser, Marvell, and the Question of Britain* (Stanford, Calif.: Stanford University Press, 1997), 91–3, 100–14.

were seen to depend upon 'tradicion' and every good Protestant would draw the appropriate conclusion. Yet Irenius proceeds to admit that throughout much of Ireland the brehon law is the only law: 'for theare are manye wide Countries in Irelande in which the lawes of Englande weare never established nor anye acknowledgement of subieccion made, and all-soe even in those which are subdued and seme to acknowledge subieccion yeat the same *Brehon* lawe is privilye practized amongesᵗe themselves' (*Prose*, 48). Worse still, even the 'common law' originally introduced by the Old English has grown 'corrupt', although the nature of its corruption is quite unusual.

In theory, the common law was the colonists' greatest asset. Far from ignoring it, however, the Irish and Old English employed it to great advantage in opposing New English interests. 'They are for the moste parte so cautelous and wily headed', Irenius reports, 'speciallye beinge men of so small experience and practize in lawe matters that youe woulde wonder whence they borrowe such subtilties and slye shiftes' (*Prose*, 67). This is a familiar manoeuvre in colonial discourse. Native intelligence is always 'wily', crafty, or criminal (like that of Spenser's Malengin) even when it expresses itself through the colonists' own legal code.[58] And Spenser knew whereof he spoke. The single greatest threat to the Plantation of Munster came from the law courts. As Michael MacCarthy-Morrogh points out, 'from the 1590s well into the seventeenth century an increasing number of lawsuits evicted the settlers from various portions of their lands. Ultimately, instead of expanding, the official plantation decreased in size.'[59] The legal 'quirkes' that Irenius spurns were frequently upheld in court (*Prose*, 67).[60] Similar problems arose with the common law practice of trial by a jury 'chosen out of the honestest and moste substantiall fre-houlders' (*Prose*, 66). As it was allegedly impossible to impanel a fair jury in Ireland, ministers of the crown frequently had recourse to summary justice—which is to say that their activities contravened English common law.[61] Hence Irenius's assertion that '*Ius Politicum* thoughe it be not of it selfe iuste yeat by applicacion or rather necessitye is made iuste' (*Prose*,

[58] See Elizabeth Heale, 'Spenser's Malengine, Missionary Priests, and the Means of Justice', *RES* NS, 41 (1990), 171–84. For the Irish dimension of the setting see Thomas Herron, 'Irish Den of Thieves: Souterrains (and a Crannog?) in Books V and VI of Edmund Spenser's *Faerie Queene*', *SSt* 14 (2000), 303–17.

[59] MacCarthy-Morrogh, *The Munster Plantation*, 19 (see also pp. 70–106).

[60] See David J. Baker, ' "Some Quirk, Some Subtle Evasion": Legal Subversion in Spenser's *A View of the Present State of Ireland*', *SSt* 6 (1985, but pub. 1986), 147–63.

[61] For Grey's attitude to Irish juries see Murdin (1759), 348.

66). This is tantamount to admitting that law is something with which policy may dispense. Elsewhere, however, Irenius blames the 'degeneration' of the colonists on the progressive relaxation of legal restraints: 'so sone as they Come thither wheare they see lawes more slacklye tended . . . they growe more lose and Careles of theire duetie . . . more boldlie daringe to disobaie the lawe thoroughe presumpcion of favour and friendeshippe then anye Irishe dareth' (*Prose*, 211). What Irenius does not admit at this point is that the same might hold true for the governors. Acting outside the constraints of common law, crown agents became increasingly erratic and conducted themselves in a manner virtually indistinguishable from the most oppressive of the Gaelic and Old English overlords.[62] They became what they professed to oppose, and Catholic commentators such as Richard Verstegan were quick to point to the birth of a new 'black legend'.[63]

In dedicating his translation of Giraldus Cambrensis's *Expugnatio Hibernica* to Sir Walter Ralegh, Hooker seeks to draw a sharp distinction between English colonial methods and those of Spain.[64] Writing in the immediate aftermath of the Desmond rebellion and amid preparations for the plantation of Munster, he negotiates the by now familiar correspondence between Ireland and the New World. Ralegh was 'a partie and a dooer in some part of the Desmonds wars' and has since created in Virginia 'the first English colonie that ever was there planted'.[65] He was soon to receive the single largest 'seignory' in the Plantation of Munster and to replicate his American efforts in Ireland. He was held to act solely in the interests of 'civility' in both spheres, however, unlike the Spaniards who 'subdued a naked and a yeelding people, whom they sought for gaine and not for anie religion or plantation of a commonwelth'. An implicit contrast with the Spaniards is everywhere operative in the defence of the English imperial enterprise both in Ireland and the New World. In *A Report of the Truth of the Fight about the Isles of Azores* (1591), for example, Ralegh—who served as one of Grey's two principal henchmen in the massacre at Smerwick—bitterly complains of Spanish cruelty in Hispaniola, 'the Story whereof is at large written by a Bishop of their own nation called *Bartholome de las Casas*, and translated into English and many

---

[62]   See Ciaran Brady, *The Chief Governors: The Rise and Fall of Reform Government in Tudor Ireland 1536–1588* (Cambridge: Cambridge University Press, 1994), 139–40.

[63]   For Richard Verstegan's *Theatrum Crudelitatum Haereticorum Nostri Temporis* (1588) see Highley, *Shakespeare, Spenser, and the Crisis in Ireland*, 153–4.

[64]   See Maltby, *The Black Legend in England*, 12–28.   [65]   Holinshed (1808), vi. 107.

other languages, entitled *The Spanish cruelties*'. He proceeds to attribute the fall of the Earl of Desmond to 'his adhering to the Spaniards' in their attempt to establish a powerbase in Ireland.[66] Similarly, in *A Briefe Description of Ireland* (1589) Robert Payne suggests that Las Casas's account of the 'monsterous cruelties' of the Spanish in the West Indies should be more than sufficient to deter the Irish from placng their hopes in Spain.[67] Survivors of the Munster famine were unlikely to agree but the adoption of 'Spanish' methods could always be justified by alleging a difference in motivation: what the Spaniards did for gold the English did for God. It was no more, according to one seventeenth-century commentator, than the imposition of a 'loving terrour' intended 'not only [to] subdue those people, but convert them'.[68]

One of the foremost practitioners of this 'loving terrour' was Sir Humphrey Gilbert, Ralegh's half-brother. Gilbert served his colonial apprenticeship in Ireland and his methods are graphically described in Thomas Churchyard's *A Generall Rehearsall of Warres* (1579). Just as the Spaniards were careful to observe the letter of the infamous 'Requerimiento', Gilbert was equally scrupulous. 'Wheresoever he came to doe her Maiestie service', Churchyard records, 'before he attempted any thyng, he proferred her highnesse mercie to the Rebelles . . . whiche if thei once refused . . . he would never after by any meanes receive theim to grace, but would subdue theim by the sworde or [*sic*] he departed, how dearly so ever he bought it.'[69] This procedure served as both moral and legal justification for the slaughter of 'manne, woman, and child'. Noncombatants were judged to be legitimate targets on the grounds that they afforded succour to 'rebels'.[70] The argument was not without precedent but even Churchyard begins to exhibit signs of unease at the ritualized terror in which Gilbert indulged. 'His maner', he tells us,

was that the heddes of all those (of what sort soever thei were) whiche were killed in the daie, should bee cutte of from their bodies, and . . . laied on the ground, by eche side of the waie leadyng into his owne Tente: so that none could come into his Tente for any cause, but commonly he muste passe through a lane of heddes, whiche he used *ad terrorem*, the hedde feelyng nothyng the more paines thereby: and yet did it bryng great terrour to the people, when thei sawe the heddes of their dedde fathers, brothers, children, kinsfolke, and freendes, lye on the grounde before their faces . . . Whiche course of governemente maie by some bee

---

[66] See Ralegh (1986), 74, 75.   [67] Payne (1589), 7.

[68] Hadfield and McVeagh (1994), 71.

[69] See Las Casas (1992), pp. xxiv–xxv; Churchyard (1579), sig. Q1v.   [70] Ibid., sig. Q2r.

thought to cruell, in excuse whereof it is to bee aunswered, That he did but then beginne that order with theim, whiche thei had in effecte ever tofore used toward the Englishe.[71]

But doubts linger and Churchyard labours to assure the reader that 'certainly by this course of governemente (although to some it maie seeme otherwise) there was muche blood saved, and greate peace ensued in haste'.[72] Since Gilbert was knighted by Sir Henry Sidney for his efforts, it is principally in such sources as Churchyard that we must seek for the literary and political genesis of the 'salvage' knighthood exhibited in Artegall. Gilbert defended his methods by alleging that he had merely adopted those of his opponents. This, if true, would be ironic enough, but what he had actually adopted were the habits indiscriminately attributed to Gaels and 'Scythians' by contemporary ethnographers. According to Boemus, for example, whenever the Scyths were victorious in battle 'every manne cutteth of his prisoners head, and carieth it home: and fasteneth it upon the ende of a long pole, and setteth it up: some upon their house toppe some upon their chimneis as high as thei can'.[73] The paragon of civility had assimilated himself to a stereotype of barbarity. Because he invariably refused to negotiate with his enemies Gilbert had little real knowledge of Gaelic society but, in any case, as Eric Cheyfitz has argued, 'stereotypes function to repress such knowledge, so that the other can become a screen for the repressed and projected crimes of the self'.[74] In Ireland's 'permissive frontier' the greatest anxiety was to determine what might be done 'by coloure of Justice' rather than by its stricter course.[75]

Gilbert's interest in Ireland was primarily economic rather than religious or cultural. From the late 1560s he was engaged in drafting schemes for the plantation of 'rebel' lands with New English servitors such as himself. In all such proposals 'commodity' functions as the subtext to 'civiletie'.[76] In the New World, as we have seen, land inhabited by 'savages' was regarded as 'terra nullius' and the image of the 'salvage' Irishman would have served much the same purpose were it not for the legal acumen displayed by the 'salvages' in question. In practical terms the image of the 'salvage' was less serviceable than that of the 'rebel' since escheated

---

[71] See Las Casas (1992), pp. xxiv–xxv; Churchyard (1579), sig. Q3v.
[72] Ibid., sig. Q4r.   [73] Boemus (1555), sig. N4r.
[74] Eric Cheyfitz, *The Poetics of Imperialism: Translation and Colonization from 'The Tempest' to 'Tarzan'* (Oxford: Oxford University Press, 1991), 161.
[75] Churchyard (1579), sig. Q3r.   [76] See Quinn (1940), i. 12, 122–8; ii. 490–7.

lands came with unassailable 'title'. In the wake of the Desmond wars, and the ensuing famine, depopulation reached such levels that it became possible to combine both claims. All of Desmond's demesne lands escheated to the crown but Lord Grey had effectively created a 'terra nullius' in the literal sense. In area after area the commissioners for the plantation reported that 'the people be dead, the inhabitants gone'.[77] The twelfth canto of the 'Legend of Justice' creates a very different impression. In a reprise of the apocalyptic overtones of book one, crowds of people rush forth to rejoice at the death of Grantorto, 'glad to be quit from that proud Tyrants awe'. Yet these people are not, as Elizabethan readers might be led to imagine, the native Irish. Rather, they are those who acknowledge Irena as 'their true Liege and Princesse naturall' (5. 12. 24). But who exactly is Irena? In dispatching Artegall to 'worke *Irenaes* franchisement' (5. 11. 36) Gloriana is represented as the compassionate 'Patronesse' of 'weake Princes' (5. 1. 4), but in this instance the cause she supports is quite evidently her own. Ireland can have but one 'true Liege and Princesse naturall', and Irena, by a highly solipsistic rhetorical stratagem, proves to be yet another surrogate for Gloriana herself. In supporting Irena she ensures the elimination of all 'lewde disposed Traitours that shall care to lifte up theire heele Againste theire Soveraigne Ladie' (*Prose*, 149). At the outset of Artegall's quest, Irena blossoms 'like as a tender Rose in open plaine' (5. 12. 13). The imagery is borrowed from Ariosto, but the flower in question is clearly the Tudor rose.[78]

The creation of Irena was a masterstroke of polemic invention since it functions to dissociate 'Ireland' from its native population in a fictive reenactment of the act of plantation. Irena is near kin to Irenius. As presented in canto twelve, however, the object of justified violence is not evil people but evil itself, 'for evill people by good ordinaunces and government maye be made good, but the evill that is of it selfe evill will never become good' (*Prose*, 148). 'O, that we then could come by Cæsar's spirit', remarks Shakespeare's Brutus, 'and not dismember Cæsar' (2. 1. 169–70). Political allegory is uniquely equipped to gratify such conflicting aspirations. In practice, of course, it is wholly impossible to maintain Irenius's distinction and only a few sentences later we hear of the need to destroy 'all that Rebellious route of loose people' who oppose the crown (*Prose*, 149). The reader of *The Faerie Queene* is inured to the slaughter of such

[77] MacCarthy-Morrogh, *The Munster Plantation*, 12, 28.
[78] See Ariosto, *Orlando Furioso*, xxxii. 108. Compare E.K.'s gloss to *The Shepheardes Calender*, *Aprill*, 68.

'evil' people by a number of subtle rhetorical devices. The victims, for example, are invariably presented as indistinguishable members of a 'rebellious route' with the result that military victories are allegorically translated into conceptual triumphs. The 'real' casualties are discreetly buried in the gap between tenor and vehicle. And just as the common people are presented as a 'route', their leaders are metamorphosed into dragons and giants. Transposed to 'fairyland' the colonial enterprise becomes a fairytale, a 'charming romance' of knights and giants of the sort conventionally resolved 'by the sworde' (*Prose*, 148). Artegall performs a modern version of the labours of Hercules by ridding the world of 'monsters' not men.[79] One hardly notices how, after the giant's fall, Talus is sent abroad to deal with 'all such persons, as did late maintayne | That Tyrants part'. He is so effective in promoting Irena's cause 'that in short space, whiles there with her he stayd, | Not one was left, that durst her once have disobayd' (5. 12. 25). The sense is ambiguous. It may mean that everyone has become obedient or that everyone is dead. There is a disturbing echo of Irenius's account of the Munster famine: 'in shorte space theare weare non allmoste lefte and a moste populous and plentifull Countrye sodenlye lefte voide of man or beaste' (*Prose*, 158).

Only through the careful interaction of politicized image and poeticized policy may the mechanized brutality of book five be presented as a serious instance of moral or chivalric 'achievement', yet the tenor repeatedly resists the vehicle. Unspoken accusations shape the rhetoric of innocence and the inherent volatility of the medium entails an inevitable slippage between assertion and implication. New English ideology was wholly premised upon the legal fiction that Henry II's incursions into Ireland constituted a total conquest, and that his claim to sovereignty was endorsed, like that of Irena, by 'the consentes and shoutes' of the whole people.[80] The 'Legend of Justice' may therefore be regarded as a legal fiction written in support of a legal fiction. But Spenser's attitudes were self-contradictory. Irenius never quite decides whether Ireland was conquered or not, nor whether 'lawes' should be 'fashioned' to the nature of the people or the people to the nature of the laws. Although the latter procedure 'maie worke ill, and perverte iustice to extreame inustice' (*Prose*, 54), it is a risk he is finally prepared to take: 'sithens we Cannot now applie Lawes fitt to the people . . . we will applie the people and fitt them to the Lawes' (*Prose*, 199). The poetry takes even greater risks and wrestles

---

[79] For Hercules as tyrant-slayer see Holinshed (1808), i. 433.   [80] Campion (1963), 80.

with the consequences. Such discordance is all the more remarkable in that historical romance generally tends to 'resolve the real contradictions of history in imaginative form'.[81] More particularly, as Fredric Jameson argues, it serves to supply 'a symbolic answer to the perplexing question of how my enemy can be thought of as being *evil* (that is, as other than myself and marked by some absolute difference), when what is responsible for his being so characterized is quite simply the *identity* of his own conduct with mine, the which—points of honour, challenges, tests of strength—he reflects as in a mirror image'.[82] Spenserian romance frustrates such resolution even on a fictional level.

It is with a fine sense of polemic irony that Seathrún Céitinn chose to conclude *Foras Feasa ar Éirinn* by turning his attention to the New English legend of Gaelic injustice which provides the subtext for book five:

I do not think there is a race in Europe who would be more obedient to law than the Irish if the law were justly administered to them. And this is the testimony which John Davies gives of them in the last page of the first book which he has written on Ireland . . . 'There is no nation under the sun that love equal and indifferent justice better than the Irish.'[83]

The answer to Spenser is found not just in the common law, but in the writings of one of its most distinguished New English practitioners. It is, in Irenius's terms, the ultimate legal 'quirk'.

---

[81] See Laurence Coupe, *Myth* (London: Routledge, 1997), 175.

[82] Fredric Jameson, *The Political Unconscious: Narrative as a Socially Symbolic Act* (London: Methuen, 1983—first pub. 1981), 118.

[83] Céitinn (1902–13), iii. 369. For the argument that the Gaelic Irish were never accorded proper access to English common law see Davies (1612), 102–32.

12 Savage Courtesy

> There is nothing in that nation, that is either barbarous or savage,
> unless men call that barbarisme which is not common to them. As
> indeed, we have no other ayme of truth and reason, than the exam-
> ple and *Idea* of the opinions and customes of the countrie we live in.
>
> (Montaigne, 'Of the Caniballes')[1]

AT the very outset of book six courtesy is identified as the virtue proper to
the 'court' (6. 1. 1), yet it is Artegall's untimely 'recall' to 'faerie court' that
frustrates the 'reforme' of Irena's kingdom (5. 12. 27). It is hardly surprising, therefore, that the pattern of violence begun in book five continues
into book six. 'Courtesy', as commonly conceived, was generally regarded
as inappropriate to the colonial enterprise. According to Thomas
Churchyard, for example, 'severe and straight handely [*sic*] of rebellious
people, reformes them sooner to obedience, then any courteous
dealyng'.[2] Although Calidore compliments Artegall on the success of his
quest, he is fated to struggle, like Grey's successors, with the implications
of its failure:

> But where ye ended have, now I begin
>   To tread an endlesse trace, withouten guyde,
>   Or good direction . . .
>
> (6. 1. 6)[3]

The words 'wild' and 'salvage' occur more often in the sixth book of *The
Faerie Queene* than any other, and its visions, or illusions, of pastoral tranquillity invariably degenerate into scenes of carnage. The 'salvage' landscape of book six reflects the failed politics of book five. None of
Calidore's predecessors ever succeed in reaching the court of Gloriana but
only the patron of 'courtesy' actively shuns it, preferring to live 'amongst
the rusticke sort',

---

[1] Montaigne (1910), i. 219.   [2] Churchyard (1579), sig. Q1r.
[3] See Donald Cheney, *Spenser's Image of Nature: Wild Man and Shepherd in 'The Faerie
Queene'* (New Haven: Yale University Press, 1966), 186.

> Rather then hunt still after shadowes vaine
> Of courtly favour, fed with light report,
> Of every blaste, and sayling alwaies in the port.
>
> (6. 10. 2)

The narrator displays considerable sympathy with this attitude, and the image of a ship that never makes it out of port aptly fuses Spenser's colonial and poetic frustrations. Things fall apart on every level because the centre does not hold. It is particularly incongruous, but also entirely fitting, that it should be Calidore himself, rather than any of the book's 'salvages', who dispels the vision of the Graces.

On Mount Acidale we encounter not Gloriana but Colin Clout and the shock is, or should be, as great as if Virgil's Tityrus were to reappear in the sixth book of the *Aeneid*. The first instalment of *The Faerie Queene* had signalled its Virgilian credentials by emulating the most famous movement from pastoral to epic in literary history: 'Lo I the man, whose Muse whilome did maske, | As time her taught in lowly Shepheards weeds' (1 Proem 1). Viewed in this light, the unprecedented reversion to pastoral in book six signals no less than a radical reappraisal of the epic enterprise. 'Who knowes not *Colin Clout?*' (6. 10. 16), asks the narrator, and the question is apt to evoke memories of both *The Shepheardes Calender* and *Colin Clouts Come Home Againe*. The political discontent of Spenserian pastoral is hereby infused into the heart of Spenserian epic: the poem has reached its most critically self-reflexive stage. Precisely because the 'seat' of virtue is 'deepe within the mynd', the sense of alienation is most acutely intimate in book six (6 Proem 5). The Blatant Beast is irrepressible partly, at least, because it denotes a tendency towards satire within the epic itself: it is as though the poem has been infected by the culture of 'sclaunder' that poisons the court.[4] The proem identifies the queen as the source and end of courtesy but the marked absence of an effective surrogate within the ensuing narrative stands in stark contrast to the virtual omnipresence of the beast, a monster that first emerges at the close of book five to further the ruin of Artegall's reputation (5. 12. 37). Sir John Perrot, Lord Grey's successor, fared no better in this regard than Spenser's patron: 'Why are prablers heard against me?', he asked, 'And why are all my best actions misconstrued or misreported? Do I ill? Have I benn trulie backbited?'[5] By

---

[4] See Elizabeth J. Bellamy, 'The Vocative and the Vocational: the Unreadability of Elizabeth in *The Faerie Queene*', *ELH* 54 (1987), 1–30.

[5] Perrot (1943), 47.

the close of the narrative, as the 'gentle poet' himself falls prey to the Blatant Beast, it is impossible to resist the suggestion that detraction, and not courtesy, is the lot of all who serve the court. Yet the court remains essential. Spenser cannot 'displace' Elizabeth without displacing himself. If there was to be no second Augustus, there could be no second Virgil. It is significant that he resumes the role of Colin Clout at precisely the point at which he substitutes a private for a public love and generically violates the most basic expectations of the Virgilian 'rota' to which he had appeared to commit himself in the proem to book one.

The displacement of Gloriana on Mount Acidale, combined with Calidore's apparent preference for pastoral leisure over heroic achievement, has given rise to the suggestion that the 'Legend of Courtesie' expresses Spenser's desire to retreat from the pressures of 'history', and the role of 'poet historicall', and supplant epic verse with lyric. But exactly the opposite is the case.[6] Like the episode on Mount Acidale, book six as a whole is carefully structured to interrogate the folly of escapism by illustrating the urgency of 'history'. Pastoral is a courtly genre that merely feigns rusticity, and Pastorella is a courtly foundling mistaken for a shepherdess. Without realizing it Calidore loves the court *in her* and, in order to protect what he loves, he is forced to resume his discarded armour beneath his shepherd's clothes in a scene that anticipates the pastoral imperialism of Claude Lorrain's *The Landing of Aeneas in Latium*.[7] It is Calidore's ignorance of the true nature of civic 'grace' that leads him to dispel Colin's vision. The argument to canto ten enforces the point: 'Calidore sees the Graces daunce, | To Colins melody: | The whiles his Pastorell is led, | Into captivity'. In the ensuing narrative these events occur sequentially, not simultaneously, and there is no causal relationship between them. Yet the association implicit in the argument is thematically consistent with the presentation of the Graces as the source of 'civility'.[8] Their mother is identified as Eurynome or 'wide rule' because, as Natalis Comes explains, the blessings of civic felicity are the exclusive products of the rule of law: 'when law and equity reign, violence, theft and brigandage cease, then fields rejoice, homes are happy, the temples of the gods are joyous, and everything is resplendent.'[9] Only when active *as a knight* can

---

[6] See David Norbrook, *Poetry and Politics in the English Renaissance* (London: Routledge, 1984), 145.

[7] See Marcel Röthlisberger, *Claude Lorraine: The Paintings*, 2 vols. (London: Zwemmer, 1961), i. 436–8; ii. fig. 301.

[8] For the Graces and (urban) civility see Bryskett (1606), 78.

[9] Comes (1581), 274. The translation is mine.

Calidore possess 'Pastorella'. The nature of her abductors would be familiar to all readers of John Derricke's *Image of Irelande*:

> A lawlesse people, *Brigants* hight of yore,
> That never usde to live by plough nor spade,
> But fed on spoile and booty, which they made
> Upon their neighbours, which did nigh them border.

(6. 10. 39)

Their incursion into Calidore's rural idyll is merciless. The aged Meliboeus, who derives his name from the dispossessed victim of Virgil's first
eclogue, is not only dispossessed but murdered. His abandonment of the
'roiall court' with all of its attendant ills has availed him little (6. 9. 24).
'Pastorals' need protectors. Sir John Davies aptly quotes from the famous
lament of Virgil's Meliboeus to illustrate what he sees as the alternative to
colonial rule in Ireland:

> Impius hæc tam culta novalia miles habebit?
> Barbarus has segetes? En quo discordia Cives
> Perduxit miseros? En queis consevimus agros?   (70–2)

[Shall a godless soldier have these well-tilled fallows? A barbarian these crops? See
to what misery strife has reduced our hapless citizens. Have we sown our fields for
these?][10]

By a deft sleight of hand the dispossessors have been recast as the dispossessed. For Davies, as for Spenser, the settlers are the new 'natives'.[11]

If Colin's lady is to be identified with the lady celebrated in the
Amoretti and Epithalamion—and she is described as the fairy queen's
'handmayd' in both works—she was a New English colonist, a close
kinswoman of Richard Boyle whose life and fortune depended on the
preservation of 'civility' in Ireland. Like Calidore, Spenser found his mate
in the wilderness but she was a 'civil' lady nonetheless. The marriage
celebrated in the *Epithalamion* is as vulnerable to history's 'hasty accid-
ents' as the poem itself (429). The vision in which his lady dances before
Colin is parodically anticipated in that of the naked Serena exposed to the
'lustfull fantasyes' of marauding 'cannibals' (6. 8. 41). The disturbing col-
location of such discordant, yet strangely complimentary, visions recalls
one of the illustrations to Thomas Harriot's *A Briefe and True Report of the*

---

[10] Davies (1612), 175.
[11] See Julia Reinhard Lupton, 'Home-Making in Ireland: Virgil's *Eclogue* 1 and Book VI of
The Faerie Queene', *SSt* 8 (1987—but pub. 1990), 119–45 (pp. 132–3).

236 The Faerie Queene (1596)

New Found Land of Virginia, which displays three native 'graces' dancing at the centre of a savage ritual (Fig. 12). As Stephen Orgel points out, however, the earliest depiction of the scene is wholly devoid of De Bry's classicism and more closely resembles a witches' coven.[12] The argument to canto ten may therefore be seen to highlight the most disconcerting, and characteristic, feature of book six: its incongruous conflation of the civil and the savage.

A good analogy to the paradoxical effects produced in the 'Legend of Courtesie' is supplied in Lodowick Bryskett's *A Discourse of Civill Life: Containing the Ethike part of Moral Philosophie. Fit for the instructing of a Gentleman in the Course of a Vertuous Life.*[13] The close correspondence with Spenser's project is evident even from the title. The work is largely a translation from Giambattista Giraldi Cinthio's *Tre Dialoghi della Vita Civile* (1565), but the setting is transferred from Italy to the Pale, and the act of translation is very much in the nature of an exercise in *translatio civilitatis*. Despite his insistence on the importance of restricting Irish civic office to Englishmen, Bryskett was of Italian blood and labours to appropriate the humanist educational agenda to the circumstances of the colonist.[14] His chosen speakers are not Italian luminaries but New English officials engaged in the process of 'civilizing' an uncivil nation, of importing courtesy into the wilderness. Although publication was delayed until 1606 when the work appeared with a dedication to the Earl of Salisbury, it was composed around 1584 for Lord Grey while the escheated lands of the Desmonds were being surveyed for plantation. Grey is described as having 'plowed and harrowed the rough ground to his hand', but the business of sowing 'the seede' and harvesting the rewards remains to be undertaken. 'God of his goodnesse graunt', remarks Sir Robert Dillon, 'that this poore countrey may by a wel ordered and setled forme of governement, and by due and equall administration of iustice beginne to flourish as other Common-weales do.'[15] The setting is a 'little cottage ... neare unto Dublin' on the borders of the Pale and within its Anglicized

---

[12] Stephen Orgel, 'Shakespeare and the Cannibals', in Marjorie Garber (ed.), *Cannibals, Witches, and Divorce: Estranging the Renaissance* (Baltimore: Johns Hopkins University Press, 1987), 40–66 (pp. 44, 49, 50).

[13] For a detailed account of Bryskett's career see Deborah Jones, 'Lodowick Bryskett and his Family', in Charles J. Sisson (ed.), *Thomas Lodge and Other Elizabethans* (Cambridge, Mass.: Harvard University Press, 1933), 243–363.

[14] The irony of Bryskett's ethnic attitudes was duly noted by his Old English opponents. See Bryskett (1927), 54.

[15] Bryskett (1606), 158.

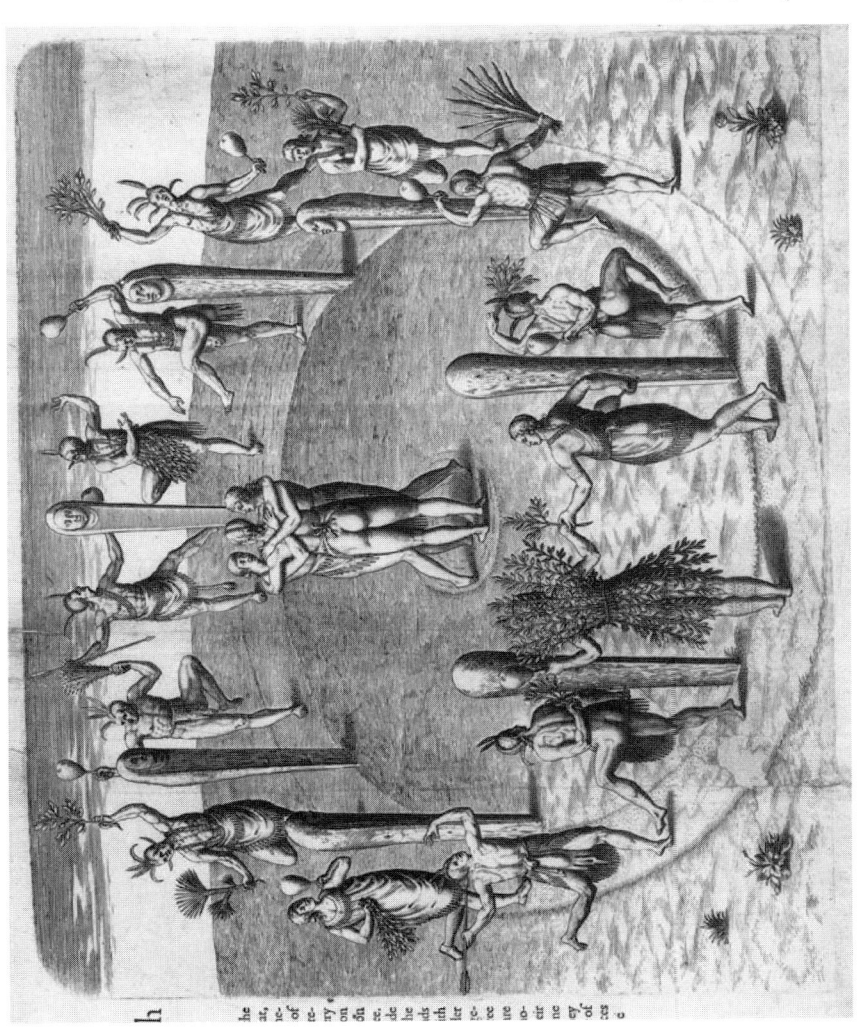

12. Thomas Harriott, *A Briefe and True Report of the New Found Land of Virginia* (1590). Native American Dances.

precincts the Gaelic evils of coyne and livery are said to have been abolished. Its well-cultivated garden, 'planted on both sides with yong ashes', serves as a model for plantation in general since the Irish were unaccustomed to 'plant any Gardens or Orchards, Inclose or improve their Lands, [or] live together in setled Villages or Townes'.[16] The participants constitute a microcosm of New English society: Bryskett was secretary to the Council of Munster and employed Spenser as his deputy; the Church of Ireland is represented by Archbishop John Long; the legal establishment by Sir Robert Dillon and Walter Dormer, 'the Queenes sollicitor'; the 'civil' professions are represented by the respected apothecary Thomas Smyth; and finally the military profession—significantly, and in marked contrast to Giraldi, the single largest group—is represented by Captains Christopher Carlyle, Warham St Leger, Nicholas Dawtrey, and Thomas Norris.[17] At the conclusion of their deliberations they all depart 'towards the Citie' and the urban civility it represents.[18]

It is to such a gathering that Bryskett has 'Spenser' recount his plans for *The Faerie Queene* thereby contextualizing the work as a product of the New English community.[19] Because the poem is not yet finished, however, 'Spenser' suggests that Bryskett's dialogue be read in its place thus confirming the cultural and political affinity of the two projects. The act of translating Giraldi proves that Bryskett 'hath not withdrawne himself from service of the State, to live idle or wholy private to himselfe, but hath spent some time in doing that which may greatly benefit others'.[20] The remark is quite apposite. Bryskett's letters frequently express a Meliboeus-like intention to retire from public life. 'I have taken a farme here', he tells Sir Francis Walsingham, 'to see if a just and honest simple lyfe, may not even emong the most Barbarous people of the world breede securitie to him that shall live nere them or emong them.' The fate of Spenser's Meliboeus would suggest otherwise and, as subsequent letters demonstrate, Bryskett is endeavouring to present himself as an embattled frontiersman valiantly attempting 'to sitt downe upon a border and to oppose my self to the hazard of their wicked and rebellious attempts, who will never cease to disturbe the quyett of the State'.[21] Such attitudes inform every aspect of his translation and Irenius's opinions are anticipated throughout.

---

[16] Bryskett (1606), 5, 92, 157; Davies (1612), 170.

[17] Bryskett, Norris, and St Leger had accompanied Lord Grey at the execution of Nicholas Nugent on 8 April 1582. Bryskett (1927), 35.

[18] Bryskett (1606), 279.   [19] Ibid. 25–7.   [20] Ibid. 28, 31. See also pp. 11–12.

[21] Bryskett (1927), 33, 37.

Fathers, we learn, must exercise 'great care' in 'framing the manners and disposition of their children' in order to ensure that they be 'fashioned to such customes and conditions as may best beseeme them'. In particular, 'because the milk of the mother, or of the nurse, is the first fit food for the infant; it were to be wished, that it should receive the same rather from the mother, then from any strange woman'. At the very least it must be ensured 'that the nurse to be chosen for a child . . . be not of strange nation, lest she should give it strange or unseemely manners'.[22] Care must also be given to the moral, and by implication the ethnic, propriety of the language spoken in civil households because 'yong children marke such things' and respond accordingly.[23]

Civic education was seen to form the strongest bastion of England's 'precarium imperium'—the precarious tenure of the planter.[24] According to Chancellor Gerrard, the only way to reclaim the Old English was to awaken within them the residual 'instincte of Englishe nature'. Force was unequal to such a task: 'for can the swoord teache theim to speake Englishe, to use Englishe apparrell, to restrayne theim from Irishe exactions and extorcions, and to shonne all the manners and orders of the Irishe?'[25] Ideally considered, the movement of *The Faerie Queene* from justice to courtesy describes the progress from military conquest to civil reclamation desired by Gerrard and prescribed in *A View* (*Prose*, 201), yet the very form of book six militates against the notion of linear progress. Courtesy is the 'roote of all civill conversation' (6. 1. 1) and, according to Irenius, the essential virtue 'whearby they [the Irish] will in shorte space growe up to that Civill Conversacion that bothe the Children will loathe the former rudenes in which they weare bredd and allsoe theire parentes will even by thensample of theire younge Children perceave the fowlenes of theire owne brutishe behaviour Compared to theires' (*Prose*, 218).[26] If fosterage and intermarriage had formerly promoted the process of 'degeneration', an official policy of counter-fosterage in English-speaking schools would now undo it. Education would achieve what warfare could not, and eventually result in cultural 'extirpation': the 'salvage' would 'in shorte time learne quite to forgett

---

[22] Bryskett (1606), 50–1, 52, 53.   [23] Ibid. 56.   [24] Bryskett (1927), 34.
[25] Gerrard (1931), 96.
[26] For the argument that Spenser is referring specifically to Stefano Guazzo's *La Civil Conversatione* (1574), trans. as *The Civile Conversation* in 1586, see John Leon Lievsay, *Stefano Guazzo and the English Renaissance 1575–1675* (Chapel Hill: University of North Carolina Press, 1961), 96–9.

his Irishe nacion' (*Prose*, 215).[27] The reclamation of book six's various foundlings, including the 'bear's son', serves to encode such aspirations.

Yet this, at best, is only half of the story. Working contrary to, and persistently undermining, the imagery of reclamation is that of regression. In practice, as Irenius notes, Sir Bruin's son was more likely to be delivered to a 'bear' since 'gentlemens children' commonly fell 'in the warde' of Gaelic overlords and were 'not onelye theareby broughte up lewdlye and Irishe like but allsoe for ever after soe bounden to theire services as that they will run with them unto anye disloyall accion' (*Prose*, 73).[28] Preferred servitors were men such as Barnaby Fitzpatrick, Baron of Upper Ossory, who had been educated at court and were to some extent estranged from their Gaelicized families. Sir Henry Sidney warmly refers to Fitzpatrick (whom he knighted in 1560) as 'my particular sworn brother, and the faithfullest man for the Queen's service for martiall action that ever I found of that country'. Refusing excessive rewards for his services, Fitzpatrick informed Sidney that 'he had received by nurture under the good and religious King Edward Vith. more good, and by pension greater gayne, confirmed by the Queen's most excellent majesty, than his service deserved'.[29] Here, it seemed, was the ultimate colonial success story, a tale of 'nurture' as generously given as gratefully received. Yet, as Ciaran Brady points out, Fitzpatrick's personal demeanour 'did little to further the Anglicisation of his lordship'.[30] It was nature's apparent imperviousness to nurture that preoccupied most contemporary commentators. For Spenser, a powerful counter example to Barnaby Fitzpatrick was Hugh O'Neill whom Sidney claims to have 'bred in my house from a little boy'.[31] John Hooker similarly calls attention to the example of Patrick Fitzmaurice, son of the Baron of Lixnaw, who

notwithstanding he was trained up in the court of England . . . and apparelled according to his degree, and dailie nurtured and brought up in all civilitie: he was no sooner come home, but awaie with his English attires, and on with his brogs, his shirt, and other Irish rags, being become as verie a traitor as the veriest knave of them all.

---

[27] For education as an instrument of control see Campion (1963), 144. See also Patricia Fumerton, 'Exchanging Gifts: The Elizabethan Currency of Children and Poetry', *ELH* 53 (1986), 241–78.

[28] For the bear's son see above pp. 189–90.   [29] See Sidney (1860), 188–9.

[30] Ciaran Brady, *The Chief Governors: The Rise and Fall of Reform Government in Tudor Ireland, 1536–1588* (Cambridge: Cambridge University Press, 1994), 288.

[31] Sidney (1856), 92.

'An ape is but an ape', Hooker concludes, 'albeit he be clothed in purple and velvet'.[32] Attitudes such as these go a long way towards explaining the paradoxical profusion of 'salvages' in the 'Legend of Courtesie'.

Central to the fractured structure of book six is the unresolved, and apparently irresolvable, dichotomy between the presentation of the 'salvage man' and that of the 'salvage nation' with whom, contrary to all logical expectations, he appears to share no kinship. Contemporary commentators were agreed that the most dangerous aspect of Ireland's 'salvage nation' was its sense of kindred. 'All the surnames their [*sic*] dwell together', complains Nicholas Dawtrey, 'for as they rebell together so they dwell together.'[33] By contrast, Spenser's 'salvage man' is represented as solitary, and it was essential to the colonial agenda that he should be. It was imperative that Ireland's 'salvage nation' should not be reformed *as a nation*. Their sense of 'nationhood' was precisely what had to be destroyed so that individuals might be 'reclaimed' from it. Hence Irenius's insistence upon the abolition of the 'surnames' of which Dawtrey complains (*Prose*, 215). The encounter between Serena and the 'salvage man', who rushes to her aid with such incongruous gallantry, represents the ideal relationship between the civil and the savage, the colonist and the native. It recreates the 'real' savage in the image of a literary type—a type that was easy to co-opt into a vision of beneficent conquest. To figure the native as a child, or childlike, is to transform the colonist into a parent and sentimentalize the relationship between ruler and ruled:

> But the wyld man, contrarie to her feare,
>   Came to her creeping like a fawning hound,
>   And by rude tokens made to her appeare
>   His deepe compassion of her dolefull stound,
>   Kissing his hands, and crouching to the ground.
>
> (6. 4. 11)[34]

In this, the best of all possible scenarios, the native's 'love' for the colonist endorses the colonist's self-image and vindicates his policy. Gazing in the 'mirror' of his opponents' savagery, the colonial narcissist sees the image of his own superiority. Except that it never quite works out that way. As

---

[32] Holinshed (1808), vi. 417.   [33] Dawtrey (1995), 131.

[34] For the literary ancestry of the 'salvage man' see Humphrey Tonkin, *Spenser's Courteous Pastoral: Book Six of the 'Faerie Queene'* (Oxford: Clarendon Press, 1972), 58–65. See also Richard Bernheimer, *Wild Men in the Middle Ages* (Cambridge, Mass.: Harvard University Press, 1952); Bernard W. Sheehan, *Savagism and Civility: Indians and Englishmen in Coloniat Virginia* (Cambridge: Cambridge University Press, 1980).

Homi Bhabha has wryly observed, the 'mirror phase' of colonial self-identity is 'always threatened by *lack*', and *The Faerie Queene*'s proliferation of mirrors was calculated to promote an increasingly self-critical awareness.[35] The Irish 'loved' neither Colin nor Eliza and, unlike the speechless 'salvage man', were all too vocal in their response (6. 5. 30).

The contrast between the 'salvage' man's reaction to Serena and that of the 'salvage' nation is remarkable. They 'spoile' her of her 'rich array' and drool with 'sordid eyes' over the blazon of 'those daintie parts . . . Which mote not be prophan'd of common eyes',

> Her goodly thighes, whose glorie did appeare
> Like a triumphall Arch, and thereupon,
> The spoiles of Princes hang'd, which were in battel won.
>
> (6. 8. 42)

The reminiscence of Belphœbe's blazon is striking (2. 3. 28).[36] The 'salvage man' instinctively adopts an attitude of subservience towards Serena and treats her as his sovereign, just as he later takes Arthur for 'his Lord' (6. 6. 39) and loves him for 'his royall usage and array' (6. 5. 41). The 'salvage nation' defiles a standard icon of Elizabethan sovereignty by exposing the vulnerable woman beneath the courtly costume. The 'salvage man' is not merely a noble savage but an ideal savage fashioned in the image of colonial wish-fulfilment. He has neither language nor identity and will say and be whatever he is trained to say and be.[37] He is therefore carefully detached from the 'salvage nation' of which he should properly form a part in order to be recreated as a feral child—a foundling in whom Chancellor Gerrard's 'instincte of Englishe nature' lies dormant: 'for certes he was borne of noble blood, | How ever by hard hap he hether came; | As ye may know, when time shall be to tell the same' (6. 5. 2).[38] We have heard this before. Serena's encounter with the 'salvage man' is antic-

[35] Homi K. Bhabha, *The Location of Culture* (London: Routledge, 1994), 77. See also Lucien Dällenbach, *The Mirror in the Text*, trans. Jeremy Whiteley and Emma Hughes (Cambridge: Polity Press, 1989), 44.

[36] See Andrew Hadfield, 'Another Look at Serena and Irena', *Irish University Review*, special issue, 'Spenser in Ireland 1596–1996', 26/2 (1996), 291–302 (pp. 299–300).

[37] See Anne Fogarty, 'The Colonization of Language: Narrative Strategy in *A View of the Present State of Ireland* and *The Faerie Queene*, Book VI', in Patricia Coughlan (ed.), *Spenser and Ireland: An Interdisciplinary Perspective* (Cork: Cork University Press, 1989), 75–108; William M. Hamlin, *The Image of America in Montaigne, Spenser, and Shakespeare: Renaissance Ethnography and Literary Reflection* (Macmillan: London, 1995), 85–7.

[38] See A. Bartlett Giamatti, 'Primitivism and the Process of Civility in Spenser's *Faerie Queene*', in Fredi Chiapelli (ed.), *First Images of America* (Berkeley: University of California Press, 1976), 71–82 (pp. 72–3, 76).

ipated by Calidore's encounter with Tristram, a Barnaby Fitzpatrick figure exiled to the woods by political circumstance but retaining a clear sense of his 'Briton' antecedents (6. 2. 27). His sole ambition is knighthood and, just like the savage man, he dons another man's armour in order to protect a lady in distress (32–3). He is what the salvage man may become when the eventual discovery of his antecedents 'dilates' into a myth of origin that appropriates difference to identity. The 'salvage man' is destined to be 'one of us' but primarily because, like the Old English, he formerly was 'one of us'. The case of the 'salvage nation' is quite different. Its reclamation depends on the recognition that its culture is mere barbarity. Thus Richard Beacon argues that the notion of autonomous Gaelic 'nationality' is merely an illusion. In order to prove the point, however, it was imperative to do away with all 'difference of lawes, religion, habite, and language, which by the eie deceiveth the multitude, and persuadeth them that they bee of sundry sortes, nations, and countries, when they be wholy together but one body'.[39] By suppressing all of the outward manifestations of native culture, one might demonstrate to the 'multitude' that they were—as the relevant 'statutes and records' asserted—really 'English' in so far as Englishness and civility were coincident. The contrasting depictions of the 'salvage man' and the 'salvage nation' may therefore be seen to reflect the dichotomous nature of Spenser's project both literary and political. Difference must be represented as simultaneously absolute and illusory. The 'salvage man' and the 'salvage nation' are fated to exist side by side but never to meet. They are, in fact, mutually exclusive. In a work designed to 'fashion a gentleman' Spenser has gone to great pains to fashion two very different forms of savage, thereby recreating native culture in the dual image necessary to justify its suppression—that of social barbarity and natural potential.

The latent civility of the 'salvage man' is demonstrated by his response to Arthur and Serena, just as the latent civility of the 'salvage' Irish was gauged by their attitude towards English government. In fact, it is little exaggeration to say that contemporary documents use the notion of 'savagery' as a metaphor for political disaffection. The more politically hostile the clan, the more 'salvage' their nature. The argument was flexible enough to run in both directions: if political subservience was a touchstone of 'civility', civility necessitated the surrender of political independence. As Rees Davies valuably reminds us, the policy of 'surrender and regrant' ultimately

---

[39] Beacon (1996), 121.

entailed the abandonment of native culture.[40] The suppliant 'surrendered' not merely his lands but his ethnic identity and received a new identity through the 'grant' of an English title. Regarded from this viewpoint, Irenius's various proposals for civil reform reveal themselves as so many strategies of political control. Sir John Davies points to Agricola's success with the Britons: 'the *Roman* Attire grew to be in account, and the *Gowne* to be in use among them; and so by little and little . . . beeing come to the heighth of Civility, they were thereby brought to an absolute subiection.'[41] The keyword is 'thereby' and its force was well appreciated on the opposing side. Red Hugh O'Donnell complained that soldiers were being sent into his territory 'under a colour of teaching his people civility' while in a poem addressed to Brian na Múrtha Ó Ruairc, Tadhg Dall Ó hUiginn wryly observed that whereas 'warlike men are left in peace . . . Gaels of civil behaviour can expect no peace from the foreigners' ['D'fhior chogaidh comhailtear síothcháin . . . Ní fhuighid siad síodh ó Ghallaibh | Gaoidhil na ngníomh gcathardha'].[42] But the onslaught was relentless. 'If wee consider the Nature of the Irish Customes', asserts Davies, 'wee shall finde that the people which doth use them, must of necessitie bee Rebelles to all good Government . . . and bring Barbarisme and desolation upon the richest and most fruitfull Land of the world.'[43] Such are Serena's enemies:

> In these wylde deserts, where she now abode,
>   There dwelt a salvage nation, which did live
>   Of stealth and spoile, and making nightly rode
>   Into their neighbours borders: ne did give
>   Them selves to any trade, as for to drive
>   The painefull plough, or cattell for to breed,
>   Or by adventrous marchandize to thrive;
>   But on the labours of poore men to feed,
> And serve their owne necessities with others need.

>   (6. 8. 35)

Figured in this way, the 'salvages' are equally related to the 'brigants' who abduct Pastorella and to the 'salvage nation' that Eudoxus wishes to see reduced 'to better goverment and Cyvilitye' (*Prose*, 43). But the

[40] R. R. Davies, 'The Peoples of Britain and Ireland, 1100–1400: IV. Language and Historical Mythology', *Transactions of the Royal Historical Society*, 7 (1997), 1–24 (p. 15).

[41] Davies (1612), 126.

[42] Camden (1610), 125 (mispaginated as p. 113); Ó hUiginn (1922–6) i. 108; ii. 72 (my translation).

[43] Davies (1612), 165.

'Legend of Courtesie' is less interested in brigandage per se than in the ethos that allegedly promotes it, in the ethnographic roots of incivility. 'Manners' reveal not only one's 'degree' but also one's 'race' (6. 3. 1) and *The Faerie Queene* is accordingly supplied with its first race of 'cannibals':

> Thereto they used one most accursed order,
> To eate the flesh of men, whom they mote fynde,
> And straungers to devoure, which on their border
> Were brought by errour, or by wreckfull wynde.
> A monstrous cruelty gainst course of kynde.
>
> (6. 8. 36)

As we have previously seen, accusations of cannibalism were familiar in accounts of the New World but they served an equally vital purpose in anti-Gaelic polemic.[44] In the present instance the sounding of 'bagpypes' as well as 'hornes' about the captive Serena attests to the potent conflation of New and Old World imagery. As Spenser was well aware, what began as mere comparison might develop through metaphor and 'continued allegory' into identification, 'for what els is your *Metaphor*', asked George Puttenham, 'but an inversion of sence by transport; your *allegorie* by a duplicitie of meaning or dissimulation under covert and darke intendments?'[45] According to Sir John Davies, those living in accordance with Gaelic law 'were little better then *canniballes*, who doe hunt one another; and hee that hath most strength and swiftnes, doth eate and devoure all his fellowes'.[46] Although they might not literally eat flesh—and the only instances of actual cannibalism recorded by Spenser and Fynes Moryson were occasioned by the use of famine as a military weapon—their way of life constituted a form of institutionalized 'cannibalism' and was therefore indefensible.[47]

   The activities of the 'salvage nation' of book six constitute a belated justification for the violence of book five. As Bryskett observed, 'the valour of those men that defend their countrey from barbarous people, is full of iustice'.[48] In such circumstances, Calidore agreed, 'bloud is no blemish'—although it is notable that even he is 'much . . . abashed' at the contrary assertion for in ideal terms there is 'no greater shame to man then inhumanitie' (6. 1. 26). Embarrassment plays a surprisingly large role in

---

[44] See Roy Harvey Pearce, 'Primitivistic Ideas in *The Faerie Queene*', *JEGP* 44 (1945), 139–51 (p. 150).

[45] Puttenham (1936), 154.

[46] Davies (1612), 166–7.

[47] See *Prose*, 158; Moryson (1907–8), iii. 282.

[48] Bryskett (1612¹, 72–3.

the lives of most of Spenser's questing knights. It is quite unclear how Calidore's principles may be made to accord with an incident such as the Smerwick massacre: 'Perdie great blame, (then said Sir *Calidore*) | For armed knight a wight unarm'd to wrong' (6. 2. 8). Although the 'salvage man' is distinguished in so many ways from the savage nation, the narrator concedes that the trait that renders him indispensable to both Serena and Arthur is his innate savagery. He has no fear of harm because 'the salvage nation doth all dread despize' (6. 4. 6).[49] In this crucial respect he is one of the 'salvage nation' after all. As he clambers awkwardly into Calepine's abandoned armour the figure of book five's 'salvage knight' is parodically reconstituted in a manner that reflects very disquietingly on Artegall's own hybrid nature (6. 5. 8). Like Irenius, Lord Grey was scathing in his assessment of the savagery of Irish kerns and Spenser duly recorded his opinions in the secretarial letters.[50] What neither openly acknowledged, however, was the government's reliance upon selected bands of 'Queen's kerns'—Serena's savages, one might say—to sustain their efforts against the native Irish.[51] 'Knight and Salvage' stand side by side in the conflict with Sir Turpine (6. 6. 23), a figure who himself personifies the problem of 'degeneracy'.

Given the role assigned to the fictional 'Spenser' in Bryskett's *Discourse of Civill Life*, it is doubly appropriate that Spenser should address to Bryskett, the 'Thestylis' of *Colin Clouts Come Home Againe*, his anxieties concerning the completion of *The Faerie Queene*:

> Great wrong I doe, I can it not deny,
>   to that most sacred Empresse my dear dred,
>   not finishing her Queene of faëry,
>   that mote enlarge her living prayses dead.
>
> (*Amoretti*, 33)

Love traditionally impedes heroic endeavour in both the martial and the literary spheres, but the problem here is more complex. Time is running out. The 'Empresse' is fated to die before either her real or fictive empire is perfected and 'living' praise will soon be posthumous praise. It is as though the poem has lost its race with history. To continue with *The*

---

[49] Like Shakespeare's Caliban, the 'salvage man' provides Serena and Calepine with food, shelter and healing herbs (6. 4. 12–16).

[50] For Lord Grey's views see SP 63/78/29.

[51] See Richard Bagwell, *Ireland Under the Tudors*, 3 vols. (London: Longman, 1885–90), iii. 61. See also Hogan and O'Farrell (1959), 60, 172.

Faerie Queene in such circumstances is to engage in 'tædious toyle' and, in
any case, Spenser's 'wit' is preoccupied by other concerns. Both the nature
and the location of those concerns are highly significant. From the very
outset the *Amoretti* is associated with Spenser's Irish experience.[52] Acting
in the author's 'absence' (and allegedly in independence of him),
Ponsonby states that he has chosen to dedicate the work to Sir Robert
Needham in order to 'gratulate' his 'safe return from Ireland'. Needham
had been knighted by the Lord Deputy and was returning in some triumph. The 'weldeserving' Spenser, by contrast, had returned only in
manuscript although his 'gentle Muse for her former perfection' has been
'long wished for in Englande'.[53] This information may well be biograph-
ically correct, but the topos is ancient: Ovid begins his *Tristia* by sending
the book to the city to which he cannot go (I. 1. 1–4). The note of absence
is intensified in the first commendatory sonnet by Geoffrey Witney Sr.:
'So while this Muse in forrraine landes doth stay', the reader is told, 'in-
vention weepes': 'Then, hie thee home, that art our perfect guide, | and
with thy wit illustrate Englands fame'. In effect, Spenser is asked to 'come
home again' to finish *The Faerie Queene* as if it were impossible to do so
from abroad. Ireland is a 'forraine' land and quite unsuited for the herald
of 'Englands fame'. Both Ponsonby and Witney emphasize the 'perfection' of Spenser's art (a term that at least implies completion), yet within
the *Amoretti* Spenser suggests that *The Faerie Queene* may be destined to
remain imperfect. Sonnet 80 insinuates that, like Calidore, Spenser needs
to abandon the 'quest' at least temporarily:

> After so long a race as I have run
> Through Faery land, which those six books compile,
> give leave to rest me being halfe fordonne,
> and gather to my selfe new breath awhile . . .

The effect created here is consciously unsettling. To a degree quite unusual in Spenser, there can be no doubt as to the speaker's identity. The author of the *Amoretti* speaks as the author of *The Faerie Queene*. Since the
second instalment had yet to appear, however, the reader is informed both
that the narrative has been continued beyond the first three books and that
the process of composition has stalled. The sonnet serves notice that the
promise of 'twelve books', which the title page to the second instalment

[52] For the association of the love imagery with Spenser's Irish concerns see James Fleming, 'A
View from the Bridge: Ireland and Violence in Spenser's *Amoretti*', *SSt* 15 (2001), 135–64.
[53] Spenser (1999), 386.

repeats, may never be fulfilled. Coupled with the opening allusions to the poet's 'absence' in 'forraine landes', the *Amoretti*'s reference to six completed books is apt to recall one of the most famous instances of incompletion in literary history: 'do not suppose that all of my work is trivial', the exiled Ovid tells Augustus in the *Tristia*, 'I have often set grand sails upon my bark. Six books of *Fasti* and as many more have I written ... This work, Caesar, I recently composed under your name, and dedicated to you, but my fate has broken it off' (2. 547–52). Only six books of the *Fasti* are extant, but Ovid suggests that all twelve have at least been drafted. Spenser, by contrast, indefinitely defers the great project in honour of his 'dear dread', an oxymoron that perfectly conveys the ambivalence of his attitude towards one of his primary sources of inspiration—if she is still to be accounted as such. As in *The Shepheardes Calender* one suspects that amorous discontent encodes its political equivalent, and to some extent it does. Of both Elizabeths, lover and queen, Spenser might reasonably say, 'So I her absens will my penaunce make, | that of her presens I my meed may take' (sonnet 52), but a wholly new element has entered the equation. Elizabeth Boyle is not Rosalind. Unlike most contemporary sonnet sequences, the *Amoretti* leads to consummated desire and fulfilment can hardly symbolize dissatisfaction. It can, however, displace the object of dissatisfaction. In the *Epithalamion* it is Elizabeth Boyle who resembles 'some mayden Queene' (158) and it is in her face that 'vertue raynes as Queene in royal throne' (194). The wedding night is compared to that on which Jove 'begot Maiesty' (331), but 'Cinthia' is consigned to the role of potentially envious (and certainly barren) voyeur peeping through the bedroom windows (372–7). As on Mount Acidale, the sense is conveyed that Spenser's poetic vision no longer centres on Elizabeth Tudor.[54] Unlike Ovid, who laments the loss of his wife's company in the *Epistulae ex Ponto*, he has found something on the margins that has displaced the centre, and he has found it within Ireland's New English community. The literary expectations aroused by the volume's initial echoes of Ovid are dramatically overturned. The 'Nymphes of Mulla' (the River Awbeg) are called upon to bind up the lady's locks (56), and the reference would be familiar to all readers of *Colin Clouts Come Home Againe*. Not only is the *Epithalamion* set in Ireland, it is set on the new plantation—hence the subtext of peril that 'echoes' through the poetry of celebration in the hauntingly uncertain

---

[54] See Tonkin's suggestion that Mount Acidale's fourth Grace represents the poem's '*Idea* or fore conceit'. *Spenser's Courteous Pastoral*, 140–1.

refrain. The poet is marrying in a 'forraine' land within the Planter community, and 'Cinthia' is asked to favour a work of 'generation' (384) that will counteract the country's 'degeneration' by restocking it with Englishmen.

Publication of the *Amoretti and Epithalamion* preceded that of the second instalment of *The Faerie Queene* by about a year. Readers of book six might therefore perceive in Calidore's apparent dereliction of duty—'unmyndfull of his vow and high beheast, | Which by the Faery Queene was on him layd' (6. 10. 1)—a reflection of Spenser's attitude towards *The Faerie Queene*. Sonnet 80 promises a return to heroic endeavour following a period of 'sport' in 'pleasant mew', but the concluding stanzas of book six call that possibility in doubt. Disillusioned with the court, Calidore enters his pastoral retreat suffering something approaching the collective weariness of all of the poem's questing knight's, but it is in that retreat that he eventually discovers something worth fighting for—and it is not the fairy queen. Something similar appears to have happened to his creator during his stay in Munster. Calidore's defeat of the Blatant Beast is effectively negated by its subsequent escape, but this 'deferral of closure' is like none other in the poem. All previous instances can be attributed to the demands of narrative continuity, but this is occasioned by the narrator's highly dramatic intrusion into his tale. Virgil's authorial presence is often felt in the *Aeneid*, but never like this—and that, perhaps, is the poetic point. The tone is now unmistakably Ovidian, and the reader experiences a remarkable *frisson*. The narrator is now 'in' his narrative, and making aesthetic capital out of personal disappointment. The second instalment of *The Faerie Queene* opens on a note of complaint but ends on a note of provocative cynicism. The notion that the court has rendered epic impossible is, perhaps, the single greatest stroke of satire in the entire Spenserian canon:

> Ne may this homely verse, of many meanest,
>   Hope to escape his venemous despite,
>   More then my former writs, all were they clearest
>   From blamefull blot, and free from all that wite,
>   With which some wicked tongues did it backebite,
>   And bring into a mighty Peres displeasure,
>   That never so deserved to endite.
>   Therfore do you my rimes keep better measure,
> And seeke to please, that now is counted wisemens threasure.

(6. 12. 41)

If the 'mighty Pere' alluded to in this passage, and in the Proem to book four, is indeed Lord Burghley, Elizabeth's Lord Treasurer, Spenser has packed considerable insult into his final line.[55] Not heroic endeavour, in either the political or the literary sense, but money motivates the court. Only those 'rimes' fashioned to 'please' or flatter may be 'counted wisemens threasure'. As the proem to book six alleges, it is at court that courtesy is degraded from a moral vertue to a social manner 'fashion'd to please the eies of them, that pas, | Which see not perfect things but in a glas' (6 Proem 5). In order to be the 'Courtly figure' that Puttenham described, allegoria must now become 'the figure of false semblant' in every sense of the term.[56] The image of Colin on Mount Acidale is, perhaps, Spenser's single greatest act of 'self-fashioning', but it is located, significantly, in a wilderness beset by 'brigants' and 'savages'. This is hardly a recipe for continuity. Rather, it suggests that the poem has taken on what Balachandra Rajan terms 'the form of the unfinished', in the sense that the project has become inherently inconclusive.[57] Allegorical fiction usually functions to resolve thematic contradictions through narrative 'dilation', but Spenser has reached the point at which narrative continuity can only serve to generate further thematic inconsistency. To continue the story is to compromise the ideal and, in so doing, to demonstrate the political impotence of poetry. After six books of epic endeavour Spenser returns once more to the question first posed by Piers in *The Shepheardes Calender* and bitterly recapitulated by Colin himself in *Colin Clouts Come Home Againe*: 'O pierlesse Poesye, where is then thy place?' Not, it would finally seem, in 'Princes pallace'. 'And yet', as Piers maintains, 'is Princes pallace the most fitt' (*October*, 79–81). The banning of the *The Faerie Queene* in Scotland in 1596 by one of Gloriana's most likely successors was perhaps the final, and most discouraging, intimation of Spenser's permanent exclusion from the court, from the centre of his political world.

---

[55] See David Lee Miller,'The Earl of Cork's Lute', in Judith H. Anderson, Donald Cheney, David A. Richardson (eds.), *Spenser's Life and the Subject of Biography* (Amherst: University of Massachusetts Press, 1996), 146–71 (p. 170).

[56] Puttenham (1936), 186.

[57] Balachandra Rajan, *The Form of the Unfinished: English Poetics from Spenser to Pound* (Princeton: Princeton University Press, 1985), 71. See also Susanne Woods, 'Closure in *The Faerie Queene*', *JEGP* 76 (1977), 195–216; Stanley Stewart, 'Sir Calidore and "Closure"', *SEL* 24 (1984), 69–86.

*

The second instalment of *The Faerie Queene* is infused with a greater sense of political urgency than the first. We are presented here with no more ancient chronicles. Rather, the allegory enforces the immediacy of current events. The narrator's voice is more insistent, defensive and plaintive. The 'Queen of England' is more harshly assessed against her perceived failure as 'Queen of Ireland', and the status of female regiment suffers accordingly. The effect is all the more disquieting to the extent that Spenser had constructed his sense of the nation about that of its sovereign. The failure of courtesy *in the court* threatens to reduce Arthur and his fellow knights to so many empty signifiers in desperate search of a signified. But however politically disquieting this may have been, it also afforded boundless poetic opportunities. If the great national poem could not be completed, it could instead explore the nature of its own incompletion, infusing Ovidian moods into Virgilian forms. The exile would find a 'home' in verse. The vision of Mount Acidale is born of geographical and emotional displacement. Whenever he begins to 'feele decay of might', the narrator tells us, poetry itself supplies 'secret comfort' (6 Proem 1–2). The problem was that poetic comfort was impotent in the absence of political support. It provided no defence against brigands. Far from turning from 'history' to 'myth', book six demonstrates the vulnerability of myth to history. The murder of Meliboeus speaks directly to the fears of the planter community. 'Amid such wars', Virgil's Moeris tells Lycidas, 'our songs avail as little as Chaonian doves against the approaching eagle.'[58] 'Colin Clout' was being driven to the same conclusion.

[58] *Eclogues*, IX. 11–13.

Part VI: Spenser's Ireland 1609–1650

13 *Diana's Spite*

And tell how *Arlo* through *Dianaes* spights
(Beeing of old the best and fairest Hill,
That was in all this holy-Islands hights)
Was made the most unpleasant, and most ill.

(7. 6. 37)

IN presenting the *Mutability Cantos* to the reading public in 1609,
Matthew Lownes judged his moment shrewdly. During the 1590s Spenser
was one of the most popular authors published by his rival, William Ponsonby, and his success was greatly enhanced by a reputation for topicality.
Lownes had sought to capitalize on this by attempting to publish *A View
of the Present State of Ireland* at the very height of the Nine Years' War.
That project had come to nothing but now, with Ireland at the top of the
political agenda once again, Spenser could be made to address current
issues from beyond the grave. The appearance of the *Mutability Cantos*,
set in the devastated wastelands of the Munster plantation, coincided
with the issuing of James I's 'Orders and Conditions' for the plantation of
Ulster. Applications were plentiful and the first 'undertakers' were required to take possession of their lands by September 1610.[1] As in the
mid-1580s the mood was again optimistic, and with some justification.[2]
The Nine Years' War had ended in 1603 with the Treaty of Mellifont just
a few days after Queen Elizabeth's death. It was as though Gaelic regiment
and female regiment had perished together. The new Britannia had risen

---

[1] See Cyril Falls, *The Birth of Ulster* (London: Constable, 1996—first pub. 1936), 161–89;
John McCavitt, 'The Political Background to the Ulster Plantation, 1607–1620', in Brian Mac
Cuarta SJ (ed.), *Ulster 1641: Aspects of the Rising*, rev. edn. (Belfast: Institute of Irish Studies,
Queen's University of Belfast, 1997), 7–23.
[2] See R. A. Butlin, 'Land and People, *c*.1600', *NHI* iii. 142–67.

from the deathbed of the virgin queen and Ireland had again become a '*British*' island in the political sense (7. 6. 38).

In reality, matters were somewhat less clear cut. O'Neill had secured surprisingly favourable terms, but his subsequent departure for Spain in the so-called 'Flight of the Earls' (1607), and the suppression of Sir Cahir O'Doherty's feeble uprising (1608), had created a power vacuum in Ulster. The new plantation could therefore be represented as the belated completion of Lord Mountjoy's heroic victory, a victory that had continually eluded Elizabeth. The lands of the 'Arch Rebel' had at last escheated to the crown. By 1612 the enterprise had proceeded well enough for Sir John Davies to claim that it was only 'since the crown of this kingdom, with the undoubted right and Title thereof, discended upon his Maiesty' that 'the whole Island' had been subdued 'and all the Inhabitants, in every corner thereof . . . absolutely reduced under his immediate subiection'.[3] Elizabeth is never expressly criticized, but the implication is plain: both realms have profitably returned to 'mans well ruling hand' (5. 5. 25). Not only had Ireland survived the 'curse' drawn upon it by Diana's 'spight', it had been restored to something like the golden age recalled in Spenser's fable of Faunus and Molanna and predicted in numerous promotional pamphlets for the new plantation.[4] But for readers considering a future in Ireland, the *Mutability Cantos* also sounded a sombre note of warning. Its account of the dangers confronting 'that lands in-dwellers' lent perfect articulation to the fears that the projectors were labouring to overcome (7. 6. 55). Ulster was as well supplied with wolves and woodkerns as Munster, and its dispossessed population was described in official reports as amongst the most 'discontented' in Christendom.[5]

Spenser's biography offered little encouragement to prospective settlers. Legends of the sack of Kilcolman were already in circulation—as doubtless was the story, later recorded by Sir James Ware, that the remaining six books of *The Faerie Queene* had either perished in the flames or been lost in the turmoil of flight. 'He was cast forth of doores by the Rebels,' Camden recorded, 'robbed of his goods, and sent over very poore into *England.*'[6] So far as the reading public was concerned, Colin Clout had 'come home' only to die in neglect. His remains lay in Westminster Abbey 'under unwritten

---

[3] Davies (1612), 286.

[4] For Ulster as 'Eden' and 'new Troy' see Blenerhasset (1610), sigs. D3r–v.

[5] See R. F. Foster, *Modern Ireland, 1600–1972* (Harmondsworth: Penguin Books, 1989—first pub. 1988), 65.

[6] See Alexander C. Judson, 'The Seventeenth-Century Lives of Edmund Spenser', *HLQ* 10 (1946), 35–48 (pp. 37–8); Wells (1971–2), 178.

stones, that who goes by | Cannot once read, Lo Here doth Collin ly'.⁷ The fragmentary form of the *Mutability Cantos* encoded a grim warning. The six completed books of *The Faerie Queene* present the reader with the literary equivalent of shired land and it is no coincidence that Spenser frequently describes his poetic art in terms of husbandry.⁸ Every episode, every thought, every image can be precisely located by book, canto, stanza, and line. Structural coincidences and variants are as easy to plot as distances on a map. But the relationship of the *Mutability Cantos* to the rest of the poem remains enigmatic. To the six previous books Ponsonby appends 'Two Cantos of Mutabilitie: Which, both for Forme and Matter, appeare to be parcell of some following Booke of the Faerie Queene, under the Legend of Constancie. Never before imprinted.' But there are three cantos, not two, and they are numbered six, seven, and eight. The latter consists of just two stanzas and lacks an argument, or perhaps it would be more accurate to say that the place of the argument is supplied by the word 'unperfite'. The addition of this fragment to a fragment—two stanzas for two cantos—immensely enhances the contradictory sense of incompletion *and* finality that has always informed the critical response to this text. For readers of the first edition, it must have appeared as if the pages had been snatched from the ashes of the former plantation.

In book six the narrator had asked 'who knowes not *Colin Clout*?' (6. 10. 16). Now he asks 'who knowes not *Arlo-Hill*?' and the answer was likely to be discouraging (7. 6. 36). Readers familiar with the 1587 edition of Holinshed would have encountered 'Arlo' in John Hooker's account of the Desmond wars, but the majority would 'know' it only in relation to Colin Clout.⁹ Recognizing this, Spenser explains his topography in highly self-referential terms. Arlo is said to 'over-looke' the Munster plantation and the adjacent counties, 'the richest champian that may else be rid, | And the faire *Shure*, in which are thousand Salmons bred' (7. 6. 54). It is 'located' in the landscape of Spenserian ambition and, consequently, of Spenserian myth. The River Behanna accordingly becomes the Molanna,

> daughter of old father *Mole*,
> And sister unto *Mulla*, faire and bright:
> Unto whose bed false *Bregog* whylome stole,
> That Shepheard *Colin* dearely did condole,
> And made her lucklesse loves well knowne to be.
>
> (7. 6. 40)

---

⁷ Ibid. 98.   ⁸ See particularly 6. 9. 1.   ⁹ Holinshed (1808), vi. 451–2.

The reader is referred to the literary setting of *Colin Clouts Come Home Againe* and might even recall the 'fowle *Arlo*' of the accompanying *Astrophel* (96). But the literary is also the political. At a crucial point during the discussion conducted in *A View*, Eudoxus consults a map.[10] The context of the action well illustrates the nature of colonial cartography:

> I see now all your men bestowed but in what places woulde youe sett theire Garrison that they mighte rise out moste Convenientlie to service? and thoughe perhaps I ame ignorante of the places yeat I will take the mapp of Irelande before me and make myne eyes in the meane while my Scollemasters to guide my understandinge to iudge of your plott. (*Prose*, 152)[11]

Such maps 'chart' not just landscape but land-hunger, and the military and colonial 'plotts' or strategies devised to satisfy it. Irenius admits that he is no 'marshall man' but positions his various garrisons 'by the purposes and plottes which the Lord Grey whoe was well experienced in that service . . . did laye downe' (*Prose*, 173–4).[12] In recommending Meredith Hanmer's *Chronicle of Ireland*—published together with *A View* in 1633—Matthew Manwaring asks 'to whom could a mapp of the world be more fitly presented then to an *Alexander*? And to whom more fitly the History of a kingdome then to him that sits at the helme of that kingdome? Historie is a Charte and Mappe of government.'[13] These remarks are directed to Viscount Wentworth, the newly appointed Lord Deputy and would-be architect of the plantation of Connaught. In Ireland, maps were accordingly perceived by both sides as instruments of conquest. While Lord Burghley was busy annotating maps of Ireland with strategic

---

[10] For the sort of maps available see R. Dunlop, 'Sixteenth-Century Maps of Ireland', *EHR*, 20 (1905), 309–37; J. H. Andrews, 'Geography and Government in Elizabethan Ireland', in Nicholas Stephen and Robin E. Glasscock (eds.), *Irish Geographical Studies in Honour of E. Estyn Evans* (Belfast: Queen's University of Belfast, 1970), 178–91; J. H. Andrews, *Plantation Acres: An Historical Study of the Irish Land Surveyor and his Maps* (Belfast: Ulster Historical Foundation, 1985), 28–51.

[11] For Irenius's use of the map see Bruce Avery, 'Mapping the Irish Other: Spenser's *A View of the Present State of Ireland*', *ELH* 57 (1990), 263–79; Mercedes Maroto Camino, ' "Methinks I See an Evil Lurk Unespied": Visualizing Conquest in Spenser's *A View of the Present State of Ireland*', *SSt* 12 (1991—but pub. 1998), 169–94; Bernhard Klein, 'The Lie of the Land: English Surveyors, Irish Rebels and *The Faerie Queene*', *Irish University Review*, special issue, 'Spenser in Ireland 1596–1996', 26/2 (1996), 207–25.

[12] For the connotations of the word 'plot' see Julia Reinhard Lupton, 'Mapping Mutability: or, Spenser's Irish Plot', in Brendan Bradshaw, Andrew Hadfield, and Willy Maley (eds.), *Representing Ireland: Literature and the Origins of Conflict, 1534–1660* (Cambridge: Cambridge University Press, 1993), 93–115 (pp. 96–7).

[13] See Ware (1633). For imperial cartography see John Breen, 'The Empirical Eye: Edmund Spenser's *A View of the Present State of Ireland*', *Irish Review*, 16 (1994), 44–52.

information, Gaelic clansmen were killing English surveyors in order to prevent the 'discovery' of their territories.[14] 'The greatest advantage that the Irish had of us in all their Rebellions', observed Sir John Davies, 'was, our Ignorance of their Countries, their Persons, and their Actions: Since the Law and her Ministers have had a passage among them . . . It is knowne, not only how they live, and what they doe, but it is foreseen what they purpose or intend to do.'[15] To characterize an area as 'wild' was to legitimize the process of shiring, and shired land was 'civilized land'.[16] It was part of the growing sense, informing works such as Hooker's *Historical Description of the Island of Britain* and Camden's *Britannia*, that the progress of territorial expansion was coincident with the advance of civilization.[17] Given such a climate of opinion, the 'topography' of self-cultivation, charted by the moral allegorist, could easily be 'mapped' onto the cartography of military conquest.

Although Irish topographical references are scattered throughout *The Faerie Queene* and become increasingly frequent in the second instalment, the *Mutability Cantos* are unique in specifying a particular, highly localized sphere of action. Here, setting and theme coalesce.[18] Ireland is the site of all that is unfinished, and possibly unfinishable, both politically and poetically. It functions as a metonym for the accumulated failures of the poem's idealism. Indeed, in their different ways, the fables of Faunus and Mutability reprise that of the Fall. Readers of the *Fowre Hymnes* might not be unduly surprised. In *An Hymne of Heavenly Love* the narrator describes how the evil angels, 'degendering' like the Old English, 'fell from above' (94). In response, the deity established a 'new unknowen Colony' to fill the 'waste and emptie place' they left behind (101–4). But this 'colony' admitted the very evil it was meant to supplant and man fell 'forgetfull of his makers grace, | No lesse then Angels' (120–2). The recurrence of such imagery in a poem so apparently remote from the concerns of colonialism indicates the degree to which such experience had come to inform every facet of Spenserian poetics.

[14] See David J. Baker, 'Off the Map: Charting Uncertainty in Renaissance Ireland', in Bradshaw et al. (eds.), *Representing Ireland*, 76–92. See also John Breen, 'Spenser's "Imaginative Groundplot": *A View of the Present State of Ireland*', *SSt* 12 (1991, but pub. 1998), 151–68 (p. 153).
[15] Davies (1612), 270–1.   [16] See e.g. Sir Henry Sidney (1860), 179.
[17] See W. H. Herendeen, 'The Rhetoric of Rivers: The River and the Pursuit of Knowledge', *SP* 78 (1981), 107–27 (p. 118).
[18] See Wayne Erickson, *Mapping 'The Faerie Queene': Quest Structures and the World of the Poem* (New York: Garland, 1996), 68.

The topography of the Faunus and Molanna episode is carefully chosen. Arlo Hill, 'the highest head (in all mens sights) | Of my old father *Mole*' (7. 6. 36), is Spenser's name for Galtymore, the highest peak in the Galty Mountains and clearly visible from Kilcolman. Both it and the adjacent Glen of Aherlow were thickly wooded and thronged with wood-kerns. In a letter of 12 September 1579 written from the outskirts of Aherlow (the Gaelic 'Eatharlach'), Lord Justice Drury informed Walsingham that the Earl of Desmond was likely to remain 'master of the woddes and mountaines whosoever were master of the fielde'.[19] After Desmond's fall, as Irenius notes, Arlo afforded a perfect refuge for the dispossessed, a people just as preoccupied as Mutability with the 'triall of their Titles and best Rights' (36). Like them, she bases her argument on primacy. As Titan's daughter she boasts the elder claim, and as 'Earths daughter' she is literally autochthonous (22).[20] Jove does not dispute this but, like the New English, rests his claim on the right, or myth, of conquest: 'For, we by Conquest of our soveraine might, | And by eternall doome of Fates decree, | Have wonne the Empire . . .' (33). I say 'myth' of conquest because of a little-noticed but vital concession that precedes this grand assertion of achievement. Reminding the gods of their conflict with 'th'Earths cursed seed', Jove admits that the 'conquest' of the Titans was far from complete. The heavenly forces 'them destroied quite',

> Yet not so quite, but that there did succeed
> An off-spring of their bloud, which did alite
> Upon the fruitfull earth, which doth us yet despite.   (20)

For this reason, he is prepared to come to terms with Mutability, as with her predecessors, by granting her 'great power' (3), but he cannot concede the issue of 'regiment' (2). That is the prerogative of superior beings. The argument from primacy can be allowed no more legitimacy here than on Bosworth Field. What matters is the perceived quality of the combatants: the autochthonous issue of the earth are conveniently dismissed as 'bad seed' (21).

It is indicative of Spenser's increasingly ambivalent attitude towards female rule that Mutability's political aspirations should be related so consistently to her gender. Though described by the patriarch of the gods as no more than a 'fraile woman' (25) or 'foolish gerle' (34), her quest is

---

[19] Hogan and O'Farrell (1959), 168.
[20] See Gordon Teskey, 'Mutability, Genealogy, and the Authority of Forms', *Representations*, 41 (1993), 104–22.

'empire' (1). In fact, the word 'empire' is used more frequently in the *Mutability Cantos* than in any of the poem's completed books and the emphasis is unrelenting. As the argument to canto six informs us, Mutability wishes to become an absolute 'Soveraine', her goal is 'rule and dominion' (4), the 'empire of the heavens hight' (7), the 'kingdoms' of the gods (18). Yet her government is universally baleful. Her sovereignty, as John Knox would eagerly have agreed, infringes the 'lawes of Nature' and confounds those 'of Iustice, and of Policie' (6). Her influence perpetuates the effects of the fall, 'by which, we all are subiect to that curse, I and death in stead of life have sucked from our Nurse' (6). Once again the anxieties of female regiment and Gaelic wet-nursing seem to fuse. If the fate of Arlo Hill is anything to go by, 'curses' are the most notable outcome of female rule. Mutability's conflict with 'Cynthia' merely serves to emphasize their inherent similarity. The temporary eclipse of the moon in stanza thirteen suggests the queen's approaching death, but its wider implications are even more disturbing. Elizabeth's motto was 'semper eadem', but Mutability demonstrates otherwise. Following in the footsteps of Sir Walter Ralegh, she reveals the fickle woman behind the mask of deity. 'Yet hath her mind some marks of human race', Ralegh had conceded in *The Book of the Ocean to Cynthia*, 'yet will she be a woman for a fashion, I So doth she please her virtues to deface' (202–4).[21] It is not just that the queen is mortal but that she is a mortal *woman*. Mutability takes the argument much further. Cynthia is 'mortall borne, how so ye crake':

> Besides, her face and countenance every day
> We changed see, and sundry forms partake,
> Now hornd, now round, now bright, now brown & gray:
> So that, as *changefull as the Moone* men use to say.

> (7. 7 50)

What is under attack here is no less than the integrity of an established icon. Cynthia is not just exposed by Mutability, she is exposed as Mutability. *The Faerie Queene* has begun to unravel its own political mythology and to make aesthetic capital from the act of destruction. The setting of the ensuing debate is, therefore, peculiarly appropriate. Nowhere was Cynthia's vacillation more evident to Spenser than in her Irish policy.

The extent to which the queen was held personally responsible for the unstable condition of the country is revealed, through the prudent

---

[21] Ralegh (1986), 41.

mechanism of a dream vision, in an astonishing passage of Richard Beacon's *Solon his Follie* (1594). Solon tells Epimenides how he,

> seemed to beholde faire *Diana* with a beautiful Dove glistering like golde, placed upon her shoulder, slyding and wavering everywhere, in such sorte, as it seemed to me to be in great jeopardy of falling, but forthwith mooved with compassion I stretched foorth my right hande, to better and reforme the place of her standing: wherewith I might beholde *Diana* with a sharpe and sowre countenaunce to threaten the losse of my hand.

Epimenides explains that 'the golden Dove, is the pleasaunt countrie of *Salamina* [Ireland]: the wavering of this Dove from place to place, is the frailty and mutability, whereunto this countrie of *Salamina* hath ever beene subject'. But who then is Diana? The official explanation is that 'the people of *Salamina*, is the threatening *Diana*, hating all reformation'.[22] No contemporary reader could fail to make a different identification. In any case, the work begins by figuring the queen as a sort of 'Circe' who has long repressed 'liberty of speech' on the issue of 'Salamina'.[23] What is remarkable in the dream vision itself is the implied conflation of polar opposites. Ireland's 'reformation' is blocked both by its people and its queen. A similar conflation appears to be operative in Spenser. Discussing the mutability of Irish policy, Irenius concludes that 'this is the wretchednes of that fatall kingedome which I thinke thearefore was in olde time not Called amisse *Banno* or *sacra Insula* takinge *sacra* for accursed' (*Prose*, 145).[24] But in the *Mutability Cantos* it is Diana herself who pronounces the 'curse' that transforms the 'holy island' into a wilderness (37).[25] Similarly, it is the royal court's 'inconstant mutabilitie' that lies at the heart of the problems of *Mother Hubberds Tale* (723).

The episode of Faunus and Molanna is particularly revealing in this respect. From the start, the prosperity of Ireland is linked to the favour of Cynthia in her capacity as 'soveraine Queene profest | Of woods and forrests, which therein abound' (7. 6. 38). 'Profest' allows for a potential discrepancy between claim and reality, however. In fact, no English monarch had ever governed the Irish woodlands and generations of planters had called, like Irenius, for large portions of them to be cut down. It is highly

---

[22] Beacon (1996), 16–17.   [23] Ibid. 6.
[24] For the mutability of Irish policy see *Prose*, 228.
[25] For Gaelic commentators it was English warfare that had 'reduced the sacred island to a rude and uncultivated place'. See O'Sullivan Beare (1621), fo. 55r. See also Rudolf B. Gottfried, 'The Early Development of the Section on Ireland in Camden's *Britannia*', *ELH* 10 (1943), 117–30 (121–2).

fitting that Cynthia's antagonist should be Faunus, the half-human, half-bestial progenitor of 'the Wood-gods breed' (50). In the *Aeneid*, by contrast, Faunus figures as the divine progenitor of the Latin race who encourages his people to intermarry with the Trojans and share in universal dominion (7. 81–106). He is an agent of empire. But Spenser's fable owes more to Ovid than to Virgil.[26] Behind it lies Ovid's account of Actaeon but very probably enhanced with a piece of local folklore. In what is clearly an adaptation of a much older Gaelic myth, Maurice Fitzgerald, second Earl of Desmond, was reported to have violated the goddess Áine (an equivalent of Diana) after watching her bathe naked in the River Camoge.[27] Since Áine symbolized the sovereignty of Munster, the legend was replete with political import for the Old English: the offspring of the alleged union was Gearóid Iarla, third Earl of Desmond, Gaelic poet, and proponent of Irish and Old English integration. The matter was celebrated in Gaelic verse.[28] As Spenser was living on Desmond lands, the legend may well have come to his attention. Like Maurice Fitzgerald, his Faunus is no respecter of persons. He treats the 'soveraine Queene profest | Of woods and forrests' as the savages of book six treat Serena. He wishes to see Cynthia naked and strip away the mystique of deity. The establishment was having similar problems in England. As the country grew increasingly 'weary of an old woman's government' (to use Bishop Goodman's words), the royal costumes became increasingly elaborate in an attempt to distract attention from the decaying body beneath.[29] Some months after Spenser's death, his fable was all but realized when the Earl of Essex, abandoning his disastrous Irish campaign, burst into the queen's bedchamber at Nonsuch while she was still dressing.[30] The perfect courtier, cautioned Castiglione, 'will never attempt to make his way into the chamber or private quarters of his master uninvited'.[31] Yet the hero of *Prothalamion* had behaved like a savage 'faun' and was shortly to be accused of conspiring with O'Neill to 'put aside' the queen and surrender

---

[26] W. P. Cumming, 'The Influence of Ovid's *Metamorphoses* upon Spenser's *Mutabilitie Cantos*', *SP* 28 (1931), 241–56; Michael Holahan, ' "Iamque opus exegi": Ovid's Changes and Spenser's Brief Epic of Mutability', *ELR* 6 (1976), 244–70.

[27] See Dáithí Ó hÓgáin, *The Hero in Irish Folk History* (Dublin: Gill and Macmillan, 1985), 79–82.

[28] McKenna (1938), 204–5.

[29] See Penry Williams, 'Court and Policy under Elizabeth I', in *Bulletin of the John Rylands Library*, 65 (1983), 259–86 (p. 270); Dennis Kay, ' "She was a queen and therefore beautiful": Sidney, his Mother, and Queen Elizabeth', *RES* 43 (1992), 18–39 (p. 21).

[30] Collins (1746), ii. 127.   [31] Castiglione (1976), 127.

the land to 'Irish kerns'.[32] 'Lorde', exclaims Eudoxus, 'how quicklye dothe that country alter mens natures' (*Prose*, 210).

The essence of pomp is awe but, spying the naked female body beneath the regalia, Faunus confronts sovereign iconography with the most corrosive response possible: he laughs at it. His laughter, we are told, 'loud profest | His foolish thought' (7. 6. 46), undermining Diana's 'profest' sovereignty over the woodlands. But even more interesting than the insult is the response. Faunus cannot be killed, or even gelded, because 'that same would spill | The Wood-gods breed, which must for ever live' (50). When considering how the Nine Years' War might have been averted Spenser asks, 'should the Irish have ben quite rooted out? That were to bloudie a course: and yet there continuall rebelliouse deedes deserve little better' (*Prose*, 240). How does one assess the suppressed violence of that desperate 'and yet'? Artegall's sword, one remembers, is identified as the sword that Jove used to quell the 'Gyants' (5. 1. 9), and the father of the gods faces a similar dilemma:

> But ah! if Gods should strive with flesh yfere,
> Then shortly should the progeny of Man
> Be rooted out, if *Iove* should doe still what he can.
>
> (7. 6. 31)

'That were to bloudie a course', however, and charity dictates that other methods of control be found. But Diana finds none. Instead she 'abandons' Arlo's 'faire forrests', apparently oblivious to the effect that this will have upon her loyal subjects:

> Since which, those Woods, and all that goodly Chase,
> Doth to this day with Wolves and Thieves abound:
> Which too-too true that lands indwellers since have found.   (54)[33]

As the Nine Years' War intensified and danger drew ever nearer to the Munster settlers, this sense of abandonment was acutely felt.[34] In October 1598 O'Neill's forces burst into Munster 'and going straight upon the English as they dwelt disparsed . . . spoiled them all . . . so many as they could catch they hewed and massacred miserablie, the rest leaving all behinde them fledd with their wives and Children to such porte townes as

---

[32] See Janet Clare, *Art Made Tongue-Tied by Authority: Elizabethan Censorship and Jacobean Dramatic Censorship* (Manchester: Manchester University Press, 1990), 64.

[33] For John of Desmond as a 'woolfe in the woods' see Holinshed (1808), iv. 528.

[34] For the defects of the Munster plantation see *Prose*, 180.

were next them' (*Prose*, 238).[35] They were now 'abandoned of all helpe and hope and exposed to extreme miserie' (*Prose*, 239). Where was their queen? *A Brief Note of Ireland* is addressed to the 'moste mightie Empresse our Dred soveraigne' from 'the ashes of disolacon and wastnes of this your wretched Realme of Ireland' (*Prose*, 236). It seeks to focus her 'mercifull eyes' upon the 'ruefull calamities' that have befallen the planter community (*Prose*, 238). The appeal is to pity, but pity is also the enemy.[36] The great fear is that 'Diana' may still pardon 'Faunus' despite his mockery. She must therefore consider 'howe great dishonour it shall be to protect or pardon them which . . . in theire Common meetings and their Priestes preachinges do speake so lewdlie and dishonorably of your moste sacred Maiestie'. Should she decide to 'temporiz any longer with pardons and proteccions . . . then we humbly beseeche your Maiestie to call us your poore subiectes alltogether away from hence that at least we may die in our Countrie' (*Prose*, 242). If Diana was to 'abandon' Arlo, the 'least' she might do was to take the 'indwellers' with her. Ireland was no longer 'our Countrie', if it ever had been. Spenser has chosen his words carefully. In the Coverdale Bible Abraham tells the Canaanites that he is merely 'a straunger and an indweller amonge you' (Genesis 23: 4). The King James version substitutes 'sojourner'.

By inserting the Ovidian fable of Faunus and Molanna between Mutability's appeal to Nature and the goddess's arrival at the opening of canto eight, Spenser politically contextualizes the ensuing contest. He ensures that the rhetorical topos of mutability is literalized in Irish topography, and his personal stake in the landscape is evident in the proliferation of possessive pronouns used to describe it.[37] By cursing the land, Diana effectively curses the narrator. As a result, Arlo Hill becomes the site of the final confrontation between the 'Ovidian' and 'Virgilian' Spenser, between the personae of would-be laureate and disaffected exile. In his *Epistulae ex Ponto* Ovid suggests—while simultaneously apologizing for the suggestion—that political 'gods' are 'made' in verse, that 'majesty' needs poets (4. 8. 55–6).[38] Spenser had done more than most to elevate Elizabeth to 'deity' but had often found her to be, as the Earl of Essex phrased it, 'a goddess not at leisure to hear prayers'.[39] Quite the opposite, in fact.

---

[35] For the Chief Justice of Munster's account of the slaughter see Maxwell (1923), 211–12. For a Gaelic account see O'Sullivan Beare (1903), 114–17.

[36] See above pp. 91–3.

[37] See Rudolf B. Gottfried, 'Spenser and the Italian Myth of Locality', *SP* 34 (1937), 107–25.

[38] Eudoxus cites the *Epistulae ex Ponto* (2. 9. 48) at *Prose*, 87.   [39] SP 63/205/14.

There is no equivalent to Diana's curse in Spenser's primary source, the tale of Actaeon and Diana recounted in the *Metamorphoses* (3. 155–252). In the *Tristia*, however, Ovid compared himself to Actaeon: 'why did I see anything?', he asks, 'why did I make my eyes guilty? Why was I so imprudent to harbour knowledge of a fault?' (2. 103–6). Just as there is something of Actaeon in Ovid, there is something of Faunus in Spenser. He too had 'harboured knowledge of a fault' in the sense that the experience of living in Ireland had afforded him a peculiarly critical perspective upon Elizabeth's government. On more than one occasion he too had 'profest | His foolish thought' and run into trouble with the censor. The 'rugged forhead that with grave foresight | Welds kingdomes causes' had even declared his 'carmen' to be his 'error' (4 Proem 1). The New English Virgil had the classical Ovid thrust upon him. The civil indweller, the father of sons called Peregrine and Sylvanus, had more in common with the feral Faunus than he cared to admit: Camden explains Peregrine as 'strange, or outlandish' and Sylvanus as 'woodman, or rather Wood-god'.[40] 'Nature' is summoned up on Arlo Hill to adjudicate not merely between Mutability and Jove but between the heroic poet and the satirist. The challenge, overtly directed towards the gods of classical epic, is ultimately directed towards heroic idealism. Nature's resolution envisages an eventual escape from contingency, but she too is a goddess 'made' by a poet and primarily drawn, as Spenser points out, from literary sources (7. 7. 9). She is summoned up on Arlo Hill in much the same way as the Graces are summoned up on Mount Acidale, and she is destined to vanish just as suddenly 'whither no man wist' (7. 7. 59). The cantos open, like the proem to book five, with an appeal from idealism to experience, but Nature represents an ideal. She is the last of Spenser's great hermaphrodites (5) and—in marked contrast to Diana whose 'doom uniust' destroys the hero Orion (39)—represents the perfect complementarity of male and female attributes. Arlo Hill withers under Diana's curse but rejuvenates at Nature's approach (11). She is the ultimate *dea ex machina* deployed when 'Cynthia' has fallen into eclipse.

The gathering of gods and goddesses on Arlo Hill resembles classical accounts of Mount Olympus, but it also recalls something closer to

---

[40] Camden (1605), 67, 70. Peregryne and Sylvyn figure as speakers in 'A Book of the State of Ireland' (1599), written (in all probability) by Spenser's neighbour Hugh Cuffe. See Rudolf B. Gottfried, 'Spenser's View and Essex', *PMLA* 52 (1937), 645–51 (pp. 647–51); Willy Maley, 'Dialogue-Wise: Some Notes on the Irish Context of Spenser's View', *Connotations*, 6 (1996), 67–77.

home. Irenius complains that the Irish were accustomed 'to make greate assemblies togeather uppon a Rathe or hill, theare to parlye (as they saie) aboute matters and wronges betwene Towneshipp and Towneshippe or one private persone and another' (*Prose*, 128).[41] The scene is reflected in book five when the demagogic Giant gathers a 'great assembly' of the 'vulgar' around a 'rocke' in expectation of 'uncontrolled freedome' (5. 2. 29–33). Such meetings originally resembled English 'folkmotes' but 'thinges beinge since alltered, and now Irelande muche differinge from that state of Englande, the good use that then was of them is now turned to abuse' (*Prose*, 129). In fact, 'manye Englishemen and other good Irishe subiectes have bene villanouslye murdered' as a result of such gatherings (*Prose*, 129). Any such assembly on Galtymore spelt imminent danger to Kilcolman, and Irenius is vocal in demanding protection (*Prose*, 48). The appearance of '*Natures* Sergeant' upon Arlo Hill is less surprising when viewed in this context. This is the sole use of the word 'sergeant' in Spenser's poetic canon and the introduction of a term so closely associated with the machinery of civic control comes as something of a shock amid the vocabulary of classical mythology, but the conflict of registers is quite deliberate. The assembly on Arlo Hill has all the makings of a riot and threatens to descend into 'much confusion and disorder' (7. 7. 4). As Sheriff of Cork, Spenser had a particular concern for such matters.[42] The identification of the 'sergeant' *as* 'Order' puts the outcome beyond dispute, despite the dramatic 'suspense' that is instilled into the episode. If it is true, as Eric Cheyfitz claims, that 'imperialism always justifies, or mystifies, the political in the name of the absolute or the natural', the decision handed down on Arlo Hill may rate as one of the foremost examples of this phenomenon.[43] Having listened to all of the contrary 'evidence', Nature 'confirms' Jove 'in his imperiall see' on the familiar grounds that the complainant needs to be governed:

> Cease therefore daughter further to aspire,
> And thee content thus to be rul'd by me:
> For thy decay thou seekst by thy desire.   (59)

---

[41] For examples of such Gaelic assemblies see Williams (1981), p. xxv.

[42] For Spenser's appointment as sheriff see Willy Maley, *A Spenser Chronology* (London: Barnes and Noble, 1994), 72, 75.

[43] Eric Cheyfitz, *The Poetics of Imperialism: Translation and Colonization from 'The Tempest' to 'Tarzan'* (Oxford: Oxford University Press, 1991), 160. See also Robert E. Stillman, 'Spenserian Autonomy and the Trial of New Historicism: Book Six of *The Faerie Queene*', *ELR* 22 (1992), 299–314.

I have hitherto referred to the 'debate' on Arlo Hill but, in view of Spenser's choice of vocabulary, it would be more appropriate to speak of the pleading of a case at law. One of the duties of an Elizabethan 'sergeant' was to summon witnesses before the courts. The *Mutability Cantos* are most usually associated in critical discussion with book three's 'Gardens of Adonis' episode, but Spenser's terminology links them just as closely, if more subtly, with the judicial concerns of book five. Astraea's departure from the earth 'after Wrong was lov'd and Iustice solde' is recalled in canto seven (37) and the argument sets the tone for all that follows by explaining how 'Pealing, from *Ioue* to *Natur's* Bar, | bold *Alteration* pleades | Large Evidence'. In the way that one might appeal from common law to Chancery, Mutability has taken her case to a higher court. Her submission identifies Jove as another Grantorto. He does her 'tortious Iniurie' (14) by denying her rights 'by heritage in Fee' (15) and 'dew descent' (16). She therefore seeks to 'dispossesse' him of the 'heavens Empire' (1). Spenser had personal experience of such suits and Patricia Coughlan has valuably called attention to a fascinating verbal reminiscence between Lord Roche's deposition against Spenser and Jove's rebuttal of Mutability's case.[44] According to Lord Roche, Spenser 'entered into three plough-lands, parcell of Ballingerath, and disseised your suppliant thereof'. Coughlan remarks that the word 'disseise' (in the sense of wrongfully dispossess or put out of 'seisin') belongs 'to the register of legal language coming from the Norman French'.[45] In the *Mutability Cantos* the position is reversed. The sort of accusation that Roche levels at Spenser is deflected unto Mutability despite the apparent legality of her claims. Jove concedes, that 'all things else that under heaven dwell | Are chaung'd of Time', but only because time 'doth them all disseise | Of being' (48). Faced with mounting 'evidence' of Mutability's de facto rights of possession, Jove has recourse to the mystique of sovereignty, a strategy much favoured by both Elizabeth and James I in their capacity as earthly 'gods'. It is not an attitude that would impress Faunus, nor does it fare any better with Mutability:

> The things,
> Which we see not how they are mov'd and swayd,
> Ye may attribute to your selves as Kings,

[44] The document is reproduced in Maley, *A Spenser Chronology*, 61. For Roche's complaint against the alleged injustice of the undertakers generally see Maxwell (1923), 246–7.

[45] Patricia Coughlan, 'The Local Context of Mutabilitie's Plea', *Irish University Review*, special issue, 'Spenser in Ireland 1596–1996', 26/2 (1996), 320–41 (p. 336).

> And say they by your secret powre are made:
> But what we see not, who shall us persuade?   (49)[46]

She proceeds to demonstrate the mortality not only of Cynthia (50), but even of Jove himself (54). Since seeing is believing, monarchy's pretensions to 'deity' are now clearly in peril. Mutability's argument articulates a suspicion that Spenser, or at least 'Colin', had long harboured. The *December* eclogue of *The Shepheardes Calender* is based on Clément Marot's *Eglogue au Roy soubz les noms de Pan et Robin*, a work which records Marot's hope that Francis I is sure to respond to his appeal for assistance. Colin, by contrast, is far less assured of the 'shepheards God' and goes so far as to insinuate the greatest of all political heresies, 'perdie God was he none' (50).

Viewed in purely philosophical terms the 'doome' delivered by Nature is exactly what one might expect from a figure so intent on the maintenance of 'order'. In Neoplatonic philosophy becoming is merely an instrument of being, and from the moment that Mutability traces her lineage back to 'Chaos' the dice are loaded against her (7. 6. 26). She is damned in her ancestry as surely as the Gaelic families that Irenius traces back to 'Scythian' origins. Her claims to primacy signal a return to primal chaos and 'Nature', as Spenser conceives of it, cannot rule in favour of chaos. The strength of Mutability's case is also its weakness. It is precisely because she is born of the soil, because she is 'native' to it, that she cannot be allowed to govern it. The very prevalence of 'chaunge' enforces the perceived need for the imposition of order. The difficulty is that the issues confronting a 'poet historicall' can never be purely 'philosophical'. Even the loftiest ideals must find their application in the world of social and political experience:

> I well consider all that ye have sayd,
>> And find that all things stedfastnes doe hate
>> And changed be: yet being rightly wayd
>> They are not changed from their first estate;
>> But by their change their being doe dilate:
>> And turning to themselves at length againe,
>> Doe worke their owne perfection so by fate:
>> Then over them Change doth not rule and raigne;
> But they raigne over change, and doe theire states maintain.

$$(7.\ 7.\ 53)$$

---

[46] Note the contrast with 2 Proem 3. For the philosophical implications see Richard A. McCabe, *The Pillars of Eternity: Time and Providence in 'The Faerie Queene'* (Dublin: Irish Academic Press, 1989), 207.

Given the way in which the legal vocabulary and the Irish setting politicize the problem of mutability, Nature's use of words such as 'estate', 'rule', 'raigne', and 'states' is particularly noteworthy. Irenius is much concerned with the problem of 'change' in Ireland. He wishes 'to beginne all as it weare anewe and to alter the whole forme of the governement', but in political matters, Eudoxus warns, 'all inovacion is perillous in so muche as thoughe it be meante for the better yeat soe manye accidentes and fearefulle eventes maye Come betwene as that it maye hazzarde the losse of the wholle' (*Prose*, 147). His words recall Artegall's warning to the demagogic Giant that 'all change is perillous, and all chaunce unsound' (5. 2. 36). Irenius concedes the general principle but, characteristically, finds it to be inapplicable to Ireland. For him, political change is essential if Ireland is to 'dilate' into its true identity and regain its 'first estate'. The problem with this, as Patricia Parker notes, is that Nature employs the term 'dilate' in a teleological sense while the poem, and its author, remain trapped 'within the period of *dilatio* as exile, or process'.[47] The 'eternall peace' that Irenius wishes to confer upon Ireland can be attained only 'by the sworde' (*Prose*, 197). Bryskett agreed: 'warre is allowed by the lawes of all those who have bin the founders of famous Common-weales, to take away seditions . . . and to maintaine temperance and order among all subiects. And God himselfe is called the God of hoasts.'[48] This 'God of hoasts' is, of course, the 'God of Sabbaoth' to whom Spenser appeals in the final lines of canto eight, and Bryskett's remarks serve to illustrate the political context of that appeal. As applied to the here and now, God's status as the Lord of Hosts justifies the use of 'warre' in order 'to maintaine temperance and order'—the sort of 'order' that Nature's sergeant promotes. The virtuosity of Spenser's wordplay at this point is quite astonishing: the God of Hoasts (Sabbaoth) is the God of Rest (Sabbath), but he is also the God of Elizabeth (Eli-Sabbath).[49] At the opening of book four Spenser had appealed from Burghley to Elizabeth. At the close of the Mutability cantos he appeals from Elizabeth to Elizabeth's God, and this God is a militant God. And, formally speaking, the poem is not concluding but continuing. The two stanzas that might well have functioned as the concluding

---

[47]   Patricia A. Parker, *Inescapable Romance: Studies in the Poetics of a Mode* (Princeton: Princeton University Press, 1979), 64. See also John Erskine Hankins, *Source and Meaning in Spenser's Allegory: A Study of 'The Faerie Queene'*, rev. edn. (Oxford: Clarendon Press, 1971), 291.

[48]   Bryskett (1606), 72.

[49]   The *OED* notes that during this period 'sabbath' was often spelt 'sabaoth' or 'sabbaoth' by confusion with the Lord of Sabbaoth. Spenser creates thematic complexity out of orthographical uncertainty.

stanzas to canto seven, serve instead to open canto eight, to gesture towards continuity and 'perfection' even as they create the contrary impression of all that is 'unperfite' and 'cut off through hasty accidents'. Readers preparing to undertake the enterprise of Ulster were left in a position similar to that confronting Prince Arthur as he contemplates the abrupt termination of the 'Briton Moniments': it is indeed 'as if the rest some wicked hand did rend, | Or th'Authour selfe could not at least attend | To finish it . . .' (2. 10. 68). They would write the next canto themselves.

14   The Response to A View

WHEN first published in 1633 in Sir James Ware's *Historie of Ireland* the work that we now know as *A View of the Present State of Ireland* seemed wholly outdated.[1] It afforded a vision of Irish affairs that most sections of the community wished to forget. 'The sense of that happy peace', observes Ware,

> which by the divine providence this Kingdome hath enjoyed, since the beginning of the raigne of his late Majestie of ever sacred memory, doth then take the deeper impression, when these our halcyon dayes are compared with the former turbulent and tempestuous times, and with the miseries . . . incident unto them. Those calamities are fully set out, and to the life by Mr. Spenser, with a discovery of their causes, and remedies, being for the most part excellent grounds of reformation.[2]

'For the most part' is the operative phrase. There was much in Spenser's text with which Ware was deeply uncomfortable. He wished it had been 'tempered with more moderation' and tempered it himself by deleting a number of contemptuous references to the Old English who now seemed on the point of securing an unprecedented measure of religious toleration and political influence.[3] The advent of another Lord Grey was desired by no-one. By the time Milton made use of Ware's text, however, the situation had altered completely. Many of the leading Old English families had made common cause with their fellow Catholics and were widely alleged to be complicit in the massacre of countless Protestants. They had apparently heeded the call to arms issued by Pádraigín Haicéad:

---

[1] Spenser's authorship of *A View* has recently been questioned but the arguments are wholly unconvincing. See Jean R. Brink, 'Constructing the *View of the Present State of Ireland*', *SSt* 11 (1990, but pub. 1994), 203–28; 'Appropriating the Author of *The Faerie Queene*: The Attribution of the *View of the Present State of Ireland* and *A Brief Note of Ireland* to Edmund Spenser', in Peter E. Medine and Joseph Wittreich (eds.), *Soundings of Things Done: Essays in Early Modern Literature in Honor of S. K. Heninger Jr.* (Newark: University of Delaware Press, 1997), 93–115. For the contrary arguments see my review of the latter in *RES* 50 (1999), 236–7; Willy Maley, *Salvaging Spenser: Colonialism, Culture and Identity* (London: Macmillan, 1997), 163–94; Andrew Hadfield, 'Certainties and Uncertainties: By Way of Response to Jean Brink', *SSt* 12 (1991, but pub. 1998), 197–202.

[2] Ware (1997), 3.   [3] Ibid. 6.

Caithfid fir Éireann uile
ó aicme go haonduine,
i dtír mbreic na mbinncheann slim,
gleic 'na timcheall nó tuitim.[4]

[All Irishmen, from whole clans to single individuals, all living in this land of graceful, dappled summits, must fight for her or fall.]

There was now a pressing need for a new Lord Grey and the person 'uppon whom the ey of all Englande [was] fixed' was the future Lord Protector (*Prose*, 228). Spenser had gone from antiquated commentator to political seer.

The complex story of the work's reception began on 14 April 1598 when 'a booke intituled A viewe of the present state of Ireland, Discoursed by way of a Dialogue betweene Eudoxus and Irenius' was entered to Matthew Lownes in the Stationers' Register 'uppon Condicion that hee gett further aucthoritie before yt be prynted'.[5] The work was entered 'under the hand' of the warden Thomas Man whose daughter was married to Humphrey Lownes, Matthew's brother.[6] The manuscript is extant and on the final page Man notes that it may be printed for Lownes whenever 'he do bringe other attoryte'.[7] To have secured such a work at a time when the Nine Years' War was moving towards its climax was to have gained a very marketable commodity. Hugh O'Neill was the centre of political attention and here was a treatise by one of the most eminent authors of the day which professed to reveal his true motives and to offer a plausible strategy for his defeat. It was a guaranteed best-seller. Yet nothing happened. *A View* remained unprinted until 1633, and Lownes's text until the 1930s.[8] Such circulation as the dialogue enjoyed was restricted to manuscript. It is necessary, therefore, to consider the nature of the 'further aucthoritie' that Lownes was enjoined to seek. The issue is complicated by the imprecision of the terminology customarily used in the

---

[4] Haicéad (1962), 35.   [5] Arber (1875–94), iii (1876), 111.

[6] See R. B. McKerrow (ed.), *A Dictionary of Printers and Booksellers in England, Scotland and Ireland, and of Foreign Printers of English Books 1557–1640* (London: Bibliographical Society, 1910), 179, 184.

[7] See Bodleian Library, MS Rawlinson B 478. This manuscript gives the date of composition as 1596. The Bodleian also holds a second manuscript of *A View*, Gough MS, Ireland 2. This also appears to have been prepared for publication. See Ray Heffner, 'Spenser's *View of Ireland*: Some Observations', *MLQ*, 3 (1942), 507–15 (pp. 509–11).

[8] Bodleian MS Rawlinson B 478 provided one of the copytexts for *A View of the Present State of Ireland*, ed. W. L. Renwick (London: Partridge at the Scholartis Press, 1934). For a convenient summary of the censorship issue see Andrew Hadfield, 'Was Spenser's *View of the Present State of Ireland* Censored? A Review of the Evidence', *N&Q* 240 (1994), 459–64.

Stationers' Registers. A work needed to be 'authorized', or 'licensed', in two quite distinct senses. The first was purely a commercial matter; the Stationers' Company would license a work for publication only if the officers were sure that the prospective publisher was not infringing another member's commercial rights. The second was a matter of public censorship; in accordance with the 'Decrees for Printing' issued by the Star Chamber in 1586 nothing could be published that was not 'first seen and perused by the Archbishop of Canterbury and Bishop of London'.[9] In the present context the term 'aucthoritie' might refer to either of these procedures. Spenser's regular publisher was not Lownes but Ponsonby and the two were already in dispute about a number of works.[10] It is possible, therefore, that the officers of the Stationers' Company sought assurance that Ponsonby would not contest Lownes's right to print a new Spenserian work. In the event of a dispute, the matter could have been referred to the Court of the Stationers' Company for adjudication, and the problem was more likely to delay printing than to prevent it. Ponsonby was in a strong position to promote his case, being elected warden of the Company in June 1598. He prosecuted a number of printers in the Star Chamber the following year in order to protect his rights in the Sidney canon.[11] In the case of *A View*, however, there is no evidence of either a legal challenge or of submission to commercial arbitration. Although Lownes eventually secured the rights to all of Spenser's works, he never produced the one he had entered in the Stationers' Register in 1598 despite the possession of an adequate manuscript. This could well suggest that the problem of 'aucthoritie' lay elsewhere.

The government had every reason for vigilance.[12] Contrary to the terms of a recent truce, O'Neill was again besieging the strategically positioned 'Blackfort' on the River Blackwater. On 14 August 1598, five months to the day after Lownes entered his copy of *A View*, the government's forces were routed at the Battle of the Yellow Ford and O'Neill

---

    [9] Arber (1875–94), ii. 807–12 (p. 810). See Peter W. M. Blayney, 'The Publication of Playbooks', in John D. Cox and David Scott Kastan (eds.), *A New History of Early English Drama* (New York: Columbia University Press, 1997), 383–422 (pp. 396–405).
    [10] See Michael Brennan, 'William Ponsonby: Elizabethan Stationer', *Analytical and Enumerative Bibliography*, 7 (1983), 91–110.
    [11] McKerrow, *Dictionary of Printers*, 218.
    [12] See the discussion by David J. Baker in ' "Some Quirk, Some Subtle Evasion": Legal Subversion in Spenser's *A View of the Present State of Ireland*', *SSt* 6 (1985, but pub. 1986), 147–63 and *Between Nations: Shakespeare, Spenser, Marvell, and the Question of Britain* (Stanford, Calif.: Stanford University Press, 1997), 116–23.

looked set to sweep the country.[13] His campaign was now being presented as a religious crusade, largely in the hope of securing the support of the Catholic Old English many of whom were already deeply hostile to the New English administration. The last thing that the government needed was the publication of a work calculated to alienate them even further, and *A View* was just such a work. Here they might learn that they needed 'a sharper reformacion then the Irishe for they are muche more stubborne and disobedient to lawe and governement then the Irishe be' (*Prose*, 210). Here too they would find their political loyalties called in question on account of their religion. In fact, the very alliance that O'Neill was labouring to create is the alliance that Irenius alleges to exist. In this respect Ware's deletions serve as a convenient index to Spenser's attitudes. Irenius asserts that 'the moste parte' of the Old English are 'degenerated' but Ware supplies the more reassuring formulation 'some of them are degenerated' and those 'some' are seldom identified (*Prose*, 96).[14] When particular Old English families (such as the Roches and the Butlers) are mentioned by Irenius, Ware not infrequently deletes the details. His readers never learn of how 'the great mortimer . . . forgettinge how greate he was once in Englande or Englishe at all is nowe become the moste barbarous of them all' (*Prose*, 117).[15] References to Old English 'barbarity' are generally excised. Customs that were alleged to be 'verye bad and barbarous' become simply 'very bad'. Those that were 'verye brute and uncivill' become simply 'very uncivill' (*Prose*, 117).[16] Enough of the original survives to testify to the phenomenon of 'degeneration' but the impression of its extent is greatly diminished. 'In that last conspiracye of the Englishe pale', Irenius asks, 'thinke youe not that theare weare manye more guiltye then [they] that felte the punishment? or was theare anie allmoste Cleare from the same?' (*Prose*, 160–1). The concluding phrase, which very accurately reflects Spenser's general suspicion of the Old English, is wholly deleted by Ware.[17]

What was still potentially embarrassing even as late as 1633 was political dynamite in 1598. So far as Irenius is concerned the needs of the New English are the needs of Ireland, but that was a perspective that the Privy Council could ill afford to adopt. To suggest that the government could not rely upon the oldest established families of the 'Englishe pale' was to articulate the very suspicions that the authorities were anxious to disclaim. If such families had already lost the trust of the crown, they had

---

[13] For a Gaelic account of the Battle of the Yellow Ford see Lombard (1930), 63.
[14] Ware (1997), 54.   [15] Ibid. 70.   [16] Ibid. 70.   [17] Ibid. 104.

little to lose by supporting O'Neill. It is sobering to think that no-one might have profited more from the publication of *A View* than its arch-villain. Commenting upon the appearance of Ware's edition, Richard Bellings, future secretary to the Supreme Council of the Confederation of Kilkenny, claimed that the work had been 'kept dormant' until 1633 in order to facilitate the implementation of its 'destructive platform . . . for the utter subversion of this kingdom'. It has been allowed to appear, he asserts, only when the Spenserian programme is 'almost finished'. This allegation, delivered in the course of a remarkable diatribe against Spenser, is impossible to prove or disprove, but constitutes an important, and neglected, element in the history of the work's reception. Even in the seventeenth century there were those who believed that censorship of *A View* was clearly in the interest of the English government.[18]

'The prospect before the Old English in 1633', writes Aidan Clarke, 'was an exciting one, and their confidence was nourished on the alarm of Irish Protestants'.[19] Ware's alterations need to be considered in this context.[20] Sir Thomas Wentworth, the newly appointed and duplicitous Lord Deputy, had hinted at the king's willingness to grant the much contested 'Graces' which were intended to secure Old English titles to various disputed lands (particularly in Connaught) and to guarantee a large measure of religious toleration.[21] Exaction of the recusancy fine had been suspended temporarily, and it was hoped that an oath of allegiance would eventually supplant the oath of supremacy so that religious and political loyalties might be distinguished.[22] Whereas Spenser was obsessed by ancient myths of racial difference, Ware sought to promote a new myth of racial unity. He assures his readers that had Spenser 'lived to see these times',

he would have omitted those passages which may seeme to lay either any particular aspersion upon some families, or generall upon the Nation. For now we may truly say, *iam cuncti gens una sumus* [we are all one people], and that upon just cause those ancient statutes [the Statutes of Kilkenny], wherein . . . those of *English* bloud were forbidden to marry and commerce with them, were repealed

[18] Gilbert (1882–91), i, p. xiv.
[19] Aidan Clarke, *The Old English in Ireland, 1625–42* (Dublin: Four Courts Press, 2000—first pub. 1966), 75.
[20] See Eiléan Ní Chuilleanáin, 'Forged and Fabulous Chronicles: Reading Spenser as an Irish Writer', in *Irish University Review*, special issue, 'Spenser in Ireland, 1596–1996', 26/2 (1996), 237–51 (243–51).
[21] For an account of Wentworth's Irish career see Hugh F. Kearney, *Strafford in Ireland 1633–41: A Study in Absolutism* (Manchester: Manchester University Press, 1959).
[22] Clarke, *The Old English in Ireland*, 37, 48, 73–4.

by act of Parlament, in the raigne of our late Soveraigne King James of ever
blessed memory.[23]

Miscegenation was now an outmoded concept. Irenius had asked 'how
cane suche matchinge but bringe forthe an evill race?' (*Prose*, 120). 'How
can such matching succeede well?' is Ware's reading, recast in the assurance that his prefatory remarks have already supplied the answer.[24]
Where Spenser refers to the 'olde Englishe' (*Prose*, 117), or more problem-
atically to the 'englishe Irishe' (*Prose*, 210), Ware frequently substitutes
'English'.[25] Similarly, Spenser's 'wilde Irishe' have become 'the Irish'
(*Prose*, 210), and are no longer to be regarded as inherently 'evill minded'
(*Prose*, 131).[26] Even Irenius's opening reference to 'that salvage nacion' is
altered to 'that nation' (*Prose*, 43).[27]

The most extensive of Ware's changes relate to matters of religion. At
the point at which Irenius launches into an uncompromising anti-
Catholic diatribe, Ware simply deletes the entire passage (*Prose*, 136–8).[28]
Most of the imagery that serves to link *A View* with the first book of *The
Faerie Queene* is hereby excised. Ware's readers are never confronted with
the suggestion that Irish Catholics are more properly to be regarded as
'*Atheists* or infidles' than Christians (*Prose*, 136). It would have been highly
impolitic to include such material at a time when Irish Catholicism
seemed certain to secure some form of official approval, but it would be
wrong to regard Ware as merely a political opportunist. His 'view' of the
state of Ireland was genuinely different from that of Spenser. He was of
New English stock but he was born in Ireland. He belonged, that is to say,
to the first generation of 'native' New Englishmen. He was educated not
at Cambridge or Oxford but at Trinity College Dublin and his interest in
Irish history led him to form an unprecedented association with Dubhaltach Mac Fhirbhisigh, the foremost Irish genealogist of his day, through
whom he gained access to a wide range of Gaelic texts, albeit in translation.[29] His scholarly account of the antiquities of Ireland is consequently
far different in scope and outlook from that projected by 'Irenius' (*Prose*,
231).[30] Ireland was Ware's homeland in a sense that it could never have
been Spenser's and his sensitivity to the text of *A View* is born of this fun-
damental difference in perspective.

[23] Ware (1997), 6.   [24] Ibid. 71.   [25] Ibid. 70, 143.   [26] Ibid. 81, 143
[27] Ibid. 1.   [28] Ibid. 85.
[29] See Nollaig Ó Muráile, *The Celebrated Antiquary Dubhaltach Mac Fhirbhisigh (c.1600–1671):
His Lineage, Life, and Learning*, Maynooth Monographs, 6 (Maynooth: An Sagart, 1996), 248–62.
[30] See Ware (1654).

Despite his best efforts, Ware's alterations to Spenser's text proved insufficient to deflect the criticisms of the Gaelic community. The thrust of the argument survived the attempted amelioration of the language and drew the immediate fire of Seathrún Céitinn who was then engaged in the composition of *Foras Feasa ar Éirinn*. This work, as its preface makes clear, is no simple narrative or 'annal' but a discursive defence of both the Gaelic Irish and the Gaelicized Old English against the unjust imputations of the 'new foreigners' ('Nua-Ghaill') of whom Spenser is one of the foremost.[31] In the case of the Gaelicized Old English, amongst whom Céitinn proudly numbers himself, he applauds the very process of acculturation that Spenser condemns as 'degeneracy'. The Keatings are dismissed as 'outlawes' by Irenius (*Prose*, 154–5), and local legend maintains that Céitinn himself took refuge in the dreaded forests of Aherlow, Spenser's 'Arlo'.[32] Had he lived to have *Foras Feasa ar Éirinn* 'translated unto him', however, Spenser would have been astonished by its political outlook. Céitinn is at pains to emphasize the traditional, and future, loyalty of the Catholic Old English to 'the crown of England' ('coróin na Sacsan').[33] Far from being merely 'a monument to a doomed civilisation', his work speaks to the needs of the 1630s and expounds a highly contemporary agenda—as Brendán Ó Buachalla has expertly demonstrated.[34] In his response to Sir John Davies, for example, he defends the institution of 'tanistry' on the grounds that, like so many related customs and institutions, it served the needs of the age in which it arose. He concedes, however, that it is 'not suitable for Ireland now'.[35] He was by no means oblivious to the sense of cultural and political loss felt by so many of his contemporaries—his poetry provides abundant evidence to the contrary—but, like Peter Lombard and Hugh McCaghwell, he saw the need to reach a practical accommodation between potentially divergent religious and political loyalties.[36]

---

[31] Céitinn (1902–13), i. 1–9.

[32] See Bernadette Cunningham, *The World of Geoffrey Keating: History, Myth and Religion in Seventeenth-Century Ireland* (Dublin: Four Courts Press, 2000), 83.

[33] Céitinn (1902–13), i. 33.

[34] See Brendán Ó Buachalla's discussion of 'coróin na hÉireann' ('the Irish crown') in *Aisling Ghéar: Na Stíobhartaigh agus an tAos Léinn 1603–1788* (Dublin: An Clóchomhar, 1996), 3–66.

[35] Céitinn (1902–13), i. 67–71.

[36] For the poetry see Céitinn (1900). For Lombard and McCaghwell see Mícheál Mac Craith, 'The Gaelic Reaction to the Reformation', in Stephen G. Ellis and Sarah Barber (eds.), *Conquest and Union: Fashioning a British State, 1485–1725* (London: Longman, 1995), 139–61 (pp. 150–7).

This process of polemical revisionism is even more evident in *Annála Ríoghachta Éireann* (or *Annals of the Kingdom of Ireland*) composed around the same time by the 'Four Masters'. The very title of the work is indicative of its outlook. Mícheál Ó Cléirigh and his fellow annalists regarded the Stuarts as the direct successors to the ancient high kings, genealogically as well as politically, and exaggerated the dignity of the ancient office with this in mind.[37] The very 'idea' of Gaelic sovereignty which had posed such a threat to the Tudors, now offered solace to the Stuarts. Spenser would again have been astonished to find the Earl of Desmond, Lord Grey's principal antagonist, presented as a traitor for betraying the 'Prince' ['Prionsa'] whose ancestors had provided his family with their 'patrimonial lands'.[38] Such passages greatly embarrassed nationalist commentators of the nineteenth century but they serve to remind us that, as well as marking the passing of the old order, works such as *Foras Feasa ar Éirinn* and *Annála Ríoghachta Éireann* looked forward with high expectations to the eventual establishment of an Irish Catholic kingdom under the Stuart crown.[39] Contemporary Gaelic poetry written for such families as the O'Briens of Thomond reconciled service to the monarchy with the retention of Gaelic ways.[40] This is not to say that older attitudes had been totally erased. The Four Masters' lament for the death of Rury O'Donnell [Ruairí Ó Dónaill], who fought for his 'religion and fatherland' ['a irri, agus a athardha'] alongside the heroic Red Hugh, bears comparison with the elegiac verse of any bard.[41] But nostalgia can be functional as well as escapist, and the shared cultural and religious heritage of the Gaelic Irish and Gaelicized Old English was seen to afford a sound basis for contemporary political cooperation.[42]

This common tradition was something in which the 'new foreigners' were frequently judged to have little share. At the heart of the matter lay the issue of 'record'. To write of Irish history or culture without access to the primary documentation, so far as Céitinn was concerned, was to offend the canons of humanist scholarship. How, he asked, could Stanyhurst find fault with Irish doctors or lawyers when 'he was not capable of reading either the law of the land or the medicine in their own language?' It was as though a blind man should seek to distinguish colours by

---

[37] See Cunningham, *The World of Geoffrey Keating*, 126.
[38] Ó Cléirigh (1856), v. 1794–7.   [39] See ibid. 1776–7.
[40] See Marc Caball, *Poets and Politics: Reaction and Continuity in Irish Poetry, 1558–1625* (Cork: Cork University Press in association with Field Day, 1998), 124–6.
[41] Ó Cléirigh (1856), vi. 2364–7.
[42] See Cunningham, *The World of Geoffrey Keating*, 110.

touch.[43] Similarly, Spenser's erroneous identification of the Mortimers with the Macnamaras is shown to display a profound ignorance of Gaelic genealogy.[44] But this, as we have already seen, is one of the passages that Ware is careful to delete and Céitinn must therefore have had access to an uncensored manuscript of *A View*. As he elsewhere refers to Ware's edition by page number, his allusion to expurgated materials may possibly have been intended to alert Old English readers to the true temper of New English thinking.[45] Similarly, Spenser's fabrication of false etymologies for family names, such as O'Byrne [properly Ó Broin], is used to demonstrate how a little knowledge of the Gaelic language, acquired in isolation from Gaelic history or mythology, can prove to be a very dangerous thing:

He says that 'brin' and 'woody' ['coillteach'] are alike in meaning; I allow that 'brin' and 'woody' are the same, yet it is not from this word 'brin' the Byrnes are called, but from the name of a young warrior called Brannút . . . wherefor the opinion of Spenser is false.[46]

Spenser used etymology to demonstrate the inherent barbarity of the O'Byrnes. In correcting his mistake, Céitinn restores their heroic ancestry by rescuing them from the realm of hostile etiological fabrication and relocating them in that of Gaelic legend. So far as Céitinn was concerned, it was Spenser's ignorance of the authentic Gaelic *Dindshenchas* [or place-lore] that necessitated his invention of spurious fables. In Ware's edition he would have found *A View* accompanied by the Irish river pageant from book four, the Faunus and Molanna episode from the *Mutability Cantos*, the sonnets to Ormond, Grey and Norris, and some extempore verses on the Earl of Cork's lute. Spenser's self-made etiology merely added insult to injury, since the verse could be seen to embody the attitudes articulated in the prose. To misunderstand the land was to misunderstand the people. Céitinn is therefore at pains to point out, for example, that Spenser's 'three renowmed brethren' (the Rivers Barrow, Nore, and Suir) do not, in fact, share a common point of origin. This is merely a popular English misconception deriving from Giraldus Cambrensis, the father of all such errors.[47] The matter was important because of the link it established between poetics and polemics. Commenting upon the classification of his countrymen as 'savages' and the elaborate pseudo-scholarship deployed in its support, Céitinn affects great surprise that 'Spenser ventured to

[43] Céitinn (1902–13), i. 39.   [44] Ibid. 27–9.   [45] Ibid. 25.   [46] Ibid. 29.
[47] Ibid. 21.

meddle in these matters, of which he was ignorant, unless that, on the score of being a poet, he allowed himself license of invention, as it was usual with him and others like him, to frame and arrange many poetic romances with sweet-sounding words to deceive the reader' ['iomad finnsgeul filidheachta do chumadh agus do chórughadh le briathraibh blasda, do bhreugadh an léaghthóra'].[48] We are here presented with a view of Spenserian romance that engages with its politics on the deepest level. Céitinn's language is parodic and mocking, its subtle rhythms and sound effects mimicking Spenser's celebrated 'rime'. That the comment should arise from an analysis of *A View* rather than *The Faerie Queene* lends it even greater weight. Céitinn was one of the first to recognize the poet in the prose writer, the fabricator of polemic 'romances' in the would-be anthropologist—and Ware's juxtaposing of the poetry and prose is likely to have played no small part in that recognition.

By the time Milton turned his attention to Ireland in the early 1640s, the political situation had altered radically. Hostilities broke out in Ulster on 23 October 1641 and spread rapidly throughout the country. The reasons were many and complex. Wentworth's denial of the Graces was certainly a key factor as were his plans for the plantation of Connaught, but the claim that the 'rebels' were acting with the king's approval proved decisive in a great many cases. The 'Royal Commission' that was used to validate this claim was certainly fraudulent but, like many of his contemporaries, Milton accepted its authenticity.[49] Given the king's ambivalent attitude towards the insurgents, his reaction is understandable. Plans were indeed afoot in 1640 to use an Irish army to crush the Scots, and the possibility of Irish intervention in England remained a perceived threat for some time to come.[50] It was quite clear to all parties that the promise of the Graces—which tended to appear and disappear as abruptly as those summoned up on Mount Acidale—could well prove sufficient to secure support for the royalist cause from both of Ireland's Catholic communities. It was the Earl of Ormond's apparent concession of the Graces on 17 January 1649 that prompted Milton's officially commissioned response, *Observations Upon the Articles of Peace with the Irish Rebels* (May 1649).[51] In point of fact, Ormond had conceded a good deal less than Milton

[48] Ibid. 31.   [49] See Clarke, *The Old English in Ireland*, 165–8, 179, 227–9.
[50] See Conrad Russell, 'The British Problem and the English Civil War', *History*, 72 (1987), 395–415 (p. 406).
[51] For the circumstances of the work's publication see William Riley Parker, *Milton: A Biography* (Oxford: Clarendon Press, 1968), 356–9; Milton (1953–82), iii. 168–83.

alleged, and the settlement was soon repudiated by Archbishop Rinuccini, the Papal Nuntio, and the majority of the Ultramontanist faction whose views find expression in the poetry of Pádraigín Haicéad.[52] To Milton's way of thinking, however, Ormond's activities confirmed the suspicion that the king had personally fomented the Irish rebellion through 'his own inclination to Popery, and the prevalence of his Queen over him'.[53] Such actions had allegedly resulted in the 'massacher' of his Protestant subjects, and Milton aggravates the matter by setting the number of casualties at six hundred thousand, greatly exceeding even the most inflated estimates proffered by Sir John Temple.[54] Given the anti-monarchical thrust of Milton's arguments, his frequent citation of a 'royalist' poet such as Spenser might well seem paradoxical were it not that the Spenserian canon could be seen to harbour its own brand of iconoclasm—and nowhere more so than in relation to crown policy in Ireland.[55]

This was not a point that Royalists were disposed to concede and Spenser was appropriated with equal enthusiasm by both parties. Ideally considered, *The Faerie Queene* could be presented as a precursor to *Eikon Basilike*, a celebration of the very 'image' that Milton was struggling to smash. For the anonymous author of *The Faerie Leveller* (1648), Spenser was Elizabeth's 'Poet Laureat' whose verses 'then propheticall are now become historicall in our dayes'. The fifth book of *The Faerie Queene* is a case in point for 'applying all to these times' the author finds that '*Arthegall Prince of justice*' is 'King Charles'; '*Talus his Executioner with his yron*

[52] See Patrick J. Corish, 'Ormond, Rinuccini, and the Confederates, 1645–9', *NHI* iii. 317–35. For Haicéad's support of Rinuccini see Haicéad (1962), 38–43.

[53] Milton (1953–82), iii. 474.

[54] Ibid. 470. The number of casualties is more likely to have been in the region of 4,000. Contemporary estimates were based on depositions taken from refugees by the Dublin administration. See Aidan Clarke, 'The 1641 Depositions', in Peter Fox (ed.), *Treasures of the Library, Trinity College Dublin* (Dublin: The Royal Irish Academy for the Library of Trinity College Dublin, 1986), 111–22. Sir John Temple drew upon this material for *The Irish Rebellion* (1646), one of the most highly influential, and highly biased, accounts of the war. A selection of the original depositions was made available for propaganda purposes in Thomas Waring, *A Brief Narration of the Plotting, Beginning and Carrying On of that Execrable Rebellion and Butcherie in Ireland* (1650). See T. C. Barnard, 'The Protestant Interest, 1641–1660', in Jane H. Ohlmeyer (ed.), *Ireland from Independence to Occupation, 1641–1660* (Cambridge: Cambridge University Press, 1995), 218–40.

[55] See Richard F. Hardin, *Civil Idolatry: Desacralizing and Monarchy in Spenser, Shakespeare and Milton* (Newark: University of Delaware Press, 1995), 91–123; Willy Maley, 'How Milton and Some Contemporaries Read Spenser's *View*', in Brendan Bradshaw, Andrew Hadfield, and Willy Maley (eds.), *Representing Ireland: Literature and the Origins of Conflict, 1534–1660* (Cambridge: Cambridge University Press, 1993), 191–208 (p. 201).

flayle' is 'the Kings forces'; '*Pollente an oppressing Saracen*' is 'the prevalent over awing Faction in the two Houses' and '*the Gyant Leveller*' is 'Col. Oliver Cromwell, L.G. of the Sts. Army'.[56] Milton may well have had this passage in mind when he came to advance his own very different inter-pretation of book five in *Eikonoklastes*. Responding to the allegation made in *Eikon Basilike* that the king's actions were dictated by the fear of popu-lar 'tumults' and the threat of anarchy, Milton quotes the king's own words against himself (although he strongly suspected that the king was not, in fact, the real author). What 'mischeifs', he asks, had these terrible 'tumults' been alleged to cause?: 'they remov'd obstructions, they purg'd the Houses, cast out rott'n members.' His response is highly 'Spenserian': 'If there were a man of iron, such as *Talus*, by our Poet *Spencer*, is fain'd to be the page of Justice, who with his iron flaile could doe all this, and ex-peditiously, without those deceitfull formes and circumstances of Law, worse then ceremonies in Religion; I say God send it don, whether by one *Talus*, or by a thousand.'[57] The deputies and governors most admired by Spenser frequently acted outside the common law for reasons of 'necessi-tye', and Milton's dismissal of all of the inconvenient 'formes and circum-stances' of the legal process accurately captures the character of the 'thorough' policy adopted by Lord Grey and symbolized by Talus. 'It was not the Kings grace or princely goodness', Milton comments, 'but this iron flaile the People, that drove the Bishops out of thir Baronies, out of thir Cathedrals, out of the Lords House.'[58] The very power that *The Faerie Leveller* interpreted as the 'Kings forces' is now reinterpreted as 'the People'. The mob that Talus habitually scatters has become Talus. Mil-ton's Spenser, it is fair to say, was very much of the revolutionary party whether he knew it or not.[59] Commenting upon the state of the Anglican Church as early as 1641, Milton observed that candidates for the ministry must not resemble 'that false Shepheard *Palinode* in the Eclogue of *May*, under whom the Poet lively personates our Prelates . . . Those our ad-mired *Spencer* inveighs against, not without some presage of these re-forming times.' He proceeds to quote the relevant lines from the *May* eclogue (103–31).[60] In 1645, in an attempt to emulate Spenser's vatic per-sona, he made similar, retrospective claims for the prescience of *Lycidas*.[61]

[56] Anon., *Faerie Leveller* (1648), sigs. A2r–v.   [57] Milton (1953–82), iii. 390.
[58] Ibid. 391.
[59] For Spenser's influence on Milton generally see Maureen Quilligan, *Milton's Spenser: The Politics of Reading* (Ithaca, NY: Cornell University Press, 1983).
[60] Milton (1953–82), i. 722–3.   [61] Milton (1968), 239.

But while Spenser took great care to tax the Anglican Church obliquely through overt criticism of Roman Catholicism, Milton collapses the distinction completely.[62] Similarly, in *The Reason of Church-governement Urg'd against Prelaty* (1641), the Anglican episcopacy is identified as the new 'dragon' that the modern St George must slay.[63]

Milton read Spenser, as he read the current political situation, very much in a 'British' context.[64] His constant concern throughout *Eikonoklastes* is with the interaction of 'the Three Kingdoms', and his *Observations* are directed as much against the Ulster Scots, who had belatedly espoused the Royalist cause, as against Gaelic Catholics.[65] To some extent *A View* had pioneered the 'British' perspective through its preoccupation with the involvement of Scots mercenaries in Ireland, and Milton's choice of language seems designed to identify the new Presbyterian planters with the wild 'Scottes and Redshankes' condemned by Irenius (*Prose*, 168). 'By thir actions', he sneers, 'we might . . . judge them to be a generation of High-land theevs and Red-shankes.' In their protests against regicide they have forgotten that '*John Knox*, who was the first founder of Presbytery in *Scotland*, taught professedly the doctrine of deposing, and of killing Kings'.[66] If the crown, by Spenser's account, had impeded the reformation of Ireland in the 1590s, it had, by Milton's account, conspired with the rebels in the 1640s. The Irish dimension to the problem of the 'three kingdomes' necessitated, and justified, regicide:

As for these Articles of Peace made with those inhumane Rebels and Papists of *Ireland* by the late King, as one of his last Masterpieces, We may be confidently perswaded, that no true borne *English-man*, can so much as barely reade them without indignation and disdaine, that those bloudy Rebels . . . should be now grac'd and rewarded with such freedomes and enlargements, as none of their Ancestors could ever merit by their best obedience, which at best was alwaies treacherous.[67]

The time for temporizing with the Irish problem was past. In his 'Commonplace Book', under the heading of 'Astutia Politica' ['Political Adroitness'], Milton notes 'the wicked policies of divers deputies & gov-

[62] Spenser (1999), 536, 544.   [63] Milton (1953–82), i. 857.

[64] See Conrad Russell, 'The British Background to the Irish Rebellion of 1641', *Historical Research*, 61 (1988), 166–82; M. Perceval-Maxwell, 'Ulster 1641 in the Context of Political Developments in the Three Kingdoms', in Brian Mac Cuarta (ed.), *Ulster 1641: Aspects of the Rising*, rev. edn. (Belfast: Institute of Irish Studies, Queen's University of Belfast, 1997), 93–106.

[65] Milton (1953–82), iii., 179–83, 472. See also David Stevenson, *Scottish Covenanters and Irish Confederates* (Belfast: Ulster Historical Foundation, 1981), 267–8.

[66] Milton (1953–82), iii. 329, 333.   [67] Ibid. 301.

ernours in Ireland see Spenser dialogue of Ireland'.[68] The passage in question alleges that various 'martiall men' amongst Grey's successors have 'cunninglye' schemed to leave the Irish unconquered in order to foster their own vested interests in the country's turmoil (*Prose*, 143–4). It was evident to Milton that Ormond fell within this category and he assures the readers of his *Observations* that Cromwell 'hath done in few yeares more eminent and remarkable Deeds whereon to *found* Nobility in his house, though it were wanting . . . then *Ormond* and all his Auncestors put together can shew from any record of thir *Irish* exploits'.[69] The path was being prepared for the imminent arrival of a new Lord Grey and an even more 'thorough' policy. Cromwell arrived in Ireland in August 1649 and the notorious massacres at Drogheda and Waterford occurred soon after. By the time he departed in May of the following year the country was effectively subdued.[70] 'And now the *Irish* are asham'd', reported Andrew Marvell, 'to see themselves in one Year tam'd.' It was the single bloodiest campaign in Cromwell's career and 'An Horatian Ode upon Cromwell's Return from Ireland' perfectly captured the morbid fascination of the moment and the man.[71]

Cromwell achieved the sort of victory for which Spenser had longed, yet it solved nothing. Mercenary considerations soon eroded heroic ideals. From the early 1640s 'adventurers' had been encouraged to speculate in the Irish market, supplying money for the campaign in the hope of gaining possession of the vast amount of land that was expected to escheat to the state.[72] There were also large numbers of potentially mutinous soldiers to be paid. But Spenser's experience was once again appropriated to present needs. In his 'Commonplace Book', under the heading 'De Disciplina Militari' ['Of Military Discipline'], Milton makes the following entry: 'Provision for souldiers after the warrs to be consider'd. Spenser dialogue of Ireland from p 84. &c.'[73] The reference is to Ware's edition and specifically to the passage in which Irenius recommends that discharged soldiers should 'be placed in parte of the landes by them wonne

---

[68] Ibid. i. 465.   [69] Ibid. iii. 312.

[70] See Toby Barnard, *Cromwellian Ireland: English Government and Reform in Ireland 1649–1660* (Oxford: Oxford University Press, 1975), 1–15.

[71] Marvell (1971), i. 93. See David Norbrook, *Writing the English Republic: Poetry, Rhetoric and Politics 1627–1660* (Cambridge: Cambridge University Press, 1999), 243–71.

[72] See R. F. Foster, *Modern Ireland, 1600–1972* (Harmondsworth: Penguin Books, 1989, first pub. 1988), 110, 112. For contemporary attitudes to this policy see Christopher Hill, 'Seventeenth-Century English Radicals in Ireland', in Patrick J. Corish (ed.), *Radicals, Rebels and Establishments, Historical Studies* 15 (Belfast: Appletree Press, 1985), 33–49.

[73] Milton (1953–82), i. 496.

at suche rate or rather better then others to whom the same shalbe sett out' (*Prose*, 177). The effect of implementing this policy was devastating. Owing to the chronic shortage of manpower most of the Catholic peasantry remained in place but about two thousand of the major landholding families were transported to the relatively poor lands of Connaught, as Éamonn an Dúna explained in the powerful lament 'Mo lá leóin go deó go n-éagad' ['My endless day sorrow']:

> Gach ar fágadh d'fhás na Féine,
> do bhí i n-oighreacht, i bhfeidhm nó i bhféile,
> go Cóige Connacht do cuireadh ar séirse
> nó go tuaisgeart Tuamhan 'na dtréinrith.
> I n-áit a dtailimh do gealladh dóibh stéigeach
> i gConnachtaibh thuaig, i dTuamhain nó i mBréifne.

[All those who remained of the Irish race who had real estate, status or wealth, were hurriedly dispatched to Connaught or North Thomond, and in place of their ancestral estates were proffered barren lands in Connaught, Thomond or Breifne.][74]

This picture is essentially accurate. In 1641 Gaelic and Old English Catholics held around 60 per cent of Irish land but only about 9 per cent by 1660.[75] Amongst the casualties, ironically, was one William Spenser, son of Sylvanus Spenser of Kilcolman and grandson of the poet. His mother, Ellen Nagle of Monaning in County Cork, was a Roman Catholic. Faced with the prospect of dispossession he appealed directly to the Lord Protector. The response is extant and casts considerable light on Spenser's reputation during this period. On 27 March 1657 Cromwell wrote in the following terms to the Lord Deputy and Council:

A petition hath been exhibited unto us by William Spencer, setting forth that being but seven years old at the beginning of the Rebellion in Ireland, he repaired with his mother, his father being then dead, to the City of Cork and during the Rebellion continued in the English quarters, that he never bore arms or acted against the Commonwealth of England, that his grandfather Edmund Spencer and his father were both Protestants, from whom an estate of lands in the Barony of Fermoy and County of Cork descended on him . . . that the said estate hath been lately given out to the soldiers in satisfaction of their arrears, only upon the account of his professing the Popish religion, which since his coming to years of discretion he hath, as he professes, utterly renounced; that his grandfather was that Spencer, who by his writings, touching the reduction of the Irish to civility,

---

[74] O'Rahilly (1977), 91.   [75] Foster, *Modern Ireland*, 115.

brought on him the odium of that nation, and for those works and his other good services Queen Elizabeth conferred upon him that estate, which the said Wm. Spencer now claims.[76]

The first half of this letter is particularly valuable in that it summarizes the substance of William Spenser's petition. It is clear that he, at least, entertained no doubts as to his grandfather's authorship of *A View*, since his reference to the poet's 'writings, touching the reduction of the Irish to civility' echoes Eudoxus's opening concern for 'reducing that salvage nacion to better gouerment and Cyvilitye' (*Prose*, 43). The implication that *A View* helped to secure Spenser his estate is, of course, misleading—although it is certainly true that the attitudes it expresses would have recommended him very strongly to the commissioners for the Plantation. William is desperate to distance his family from the insurgents and, to a large extent, defends his own reputation through that of his grandfather. His flight to Cork, for example, is obviously intended to recall the events of 1598, and the ancestral Protestantism of the Spensers is made to offset his own youthful apostasy: 'since his coming to years of discretion' William has 'utterly renounced' the 'Popish religion'. He casts himself not as a former Catholic but as a former victim of Catholicism, as someone who, like Guyon, has escaped from the degenerative power of the Bowre of Blisse through the exercise of adult 'discretion'. He has rejected the baleful influence of an Irish Catholic mother, the sort of mother repeatedly attacked in *A View*.

The second half of the letter is equally valuable in elucidating Cromwell's personal attitude to Spenser and to the current Irish situation. As he presents the matter, Spenser's estate was granted to him for his 'eminent deserts and services to the Commonwealth'. He admits, of course, that the land was granted by the crown, but the shift in emphasis makes it appear that Queen Elizabeth acted as an agent of the reformed state. Spenser is a good, Protestant 'commonwealth' poet whose 'issue' deserves well of the new regime. Unfortunately, the Lord Deputy and Council appear to have disagreed and the Spensers were never reinstated. Cromwell's letter left the authorities free to conduct further 'enquiry' into the matter and they may have found reason to doubt William Spenser's Protestant credentials. Alternatively they may have been unwilling, or unable, to dispossess the veterans who had already settled on his land. Either way, the

---

[76] Dunlop (1913), ii. 659. See also John P. Prendergast, *The Cromwellian Settlement of Ireland* (London: Constable, 1996—first pub. 1865), 43–4.

poet's descendants were fated to share in the great diaspora lamented in contemporary Gaelic poetry.[77] Its effect is particularly well articulated by the cacophonous intrusion of English words into Gaelic verse, a device intended to mimic the discordant intrusion of the settlers themselves.[78] Éamonn an Dúna duly records the most memorable of the new English sounds ['mo mheabhair ar Bhéarla'] that were now commonly to be heard:

> *Transport, transplant,* mo mheabhair ar Bhéarla,
> *Shoot him, kill him, strip him, tear him.*
> *A Tory, hack him, hang him, rebel,*
> *a rogue, a thief, a priest, a papist.*[79]

Since those responsible were 'Cromwell's frenzied, rapacious mob' ['sluaite Chromuil chuthuig chraosuig'], the poem concludes by reposing its hopes in the restoration of the monarchy and ultimately in the Catholic Duke of York.[80] Upon his accession to the throne in 1685 Dáibhí Ó Bruadair wrote some of the most powerful royalist poetry ever composed in the Stuart cause but the euphoria was necessarily short lived.[81]

Following the Williamite wars the remnants of the great Irish forests were felled, and amongst them the dreaded woods of 'Arlo'. An anonymous Gaelic poet captured the significance of this moment in a poem that asserts the centrality of Spenser's 'salvage' woodlands to Gaelic civility. The opening lines are in the nature of a reverie, a recollection of past times expressed with such verbal energy that the speaker almost forgets that they are over:

> Ar m'éirí dom ar maidin, grian an tSamhraidh ag taitneamh,
> [On rising in the morning, the summer sun ashining]
> chuala an uaill dá casadh is ceol binn na n-éan;
> [I heard the horn awinding, and the sweet birdsong]
> broic is míolta gearra, creabhair na ngoba fada,
> [the badgers and the small hares, the long-beaked woodcocks]

---

[77] See Marc Caball, 'Providence and Exile in Early Seventeenth-Century Ireland', *Irish Historical Studies*, 29 (1994), 174–88.

[78] See Seán Ó Tuama, 'Gaelic Culture in Crisis: The Literary Response 1600–1850', in Thomas Bartlett, Chris Curtin, Riana O'Dwyer, and Gearóid Ó Tuathaigh (eds.), *Irish Studies: A General Introduction* (Dublin, Gill and Macmillan, 1988), 28–41 (p. 30).

[79] O'Rahilly (1977), 90.   [80] Ibid. 96, 100.

[81] Joseph Th. Leerssen, *Mere Irish & Fíor-Ghael: Studies in the Idea of Irish Nationality, its Development and Literary Expression prior to the Nineteenth Century* (Amsterdam: John Benjamins Publishing Company, 1986), 251–60.

fuaim ag an macalla, is lámhach gunnaí tréan;
[and the loud, resounding echoes of the guns]
an sionnach rua ar an gcarraig, míle liú ag marcaigh,
[the red fox on the hillside, the shouts of the hunters]
is bean go dubhach sa mbealach ag áireamh a cuid géann.
[and an anxious woman by the roadside counting all her geese]

Then quite suddenly, with the intrusion of the word 'anois' ['now'], reality impinges upon reminiscence and the galloping rhythms progressively slow:

Ach anois tá an choill dá gearradh, triallfaimid thar caladh,
[But now the woods are being felled, we must go across the bay]
is, a Sheáin Uí Dhuibhir an Ghleanna, tá tú gan géim.
[and, Sean O'Dwyer of the Valley, your game is no more.][82]

'Géim' has much the same connotations as its English equivalent. It denotes both the game that is hunted and the pleasure derived from the hunt. The four final words, 'tá tú gan géim', hereby acquire something of the stark desolation of Keats's haunting phrase 'and no birds sing'. Arlo Hill was finally 'civilized' but the cost to the Gaelic lifestyle was immense, 'which too-too true that lands in-dwellers since have found'.

[82] See O'Connor (1970), 98–9.

Primary Sources

Anon. (1584), *A Breefe Discourse, declaring and approving the Necessarie and Inviolable Maintenance of the Laudable Customes of London* (London).

Anon. (1648), *The Faerie Leveller: or, King Charles his Leveller descried and deciphered in Queene Elizabeths dayes. By her Poet Laureat Edmond Spenser, in his Unparaleld Poeme, entituled The Faerie Queene. A Lively Representation of Our Times* (London).

ARBER, EDWARD (ed.) (1875–94), *A Transcript of the Registers of the Company of Stationers of London: 1554–1640 A.D.*, 5 vols. (London: privately printed).

ARISTOTLE (1892), *The Nicomachean Ethics*, trans. J. E. C. Welldon (London: Macmillan).

AYLMER, JOHN (1559), *An Harborowe for Faithfull and Trewe Subiectes, agaynst the late blowne Blaste, concerninge the Government of Wemen* (London).

BACON, SIR FRANCIS (1857–74), *Works*, ed. J. Spedding, R. L. Ellis and D. D. Heath, 14 vols. (London: Longman).

BALE, JOHN (1849), *Select Works of John Bale*, ed. Henry Christmas (Cambridge: Cambridge University Press).

—— (1990), *The Vocacyon of Johan Bale*, ed. Peter Happé and John N. King, Medieval and Renaissance Texts and Studies, 14 (Binghampton, NY: Renaissance English Text Society).

BASTARD, THOMAS (1598), *Chrestoleros: Seven Bookes of Epigrames* (London).

BEACON, RICHARD (1996), *Solon His Follie, or A Politique Discourse touching the Reformation of Common-weales Conquered, Declined or Corrupted*, ed. and trans. Clare Carroll and Vincent Carey, Medieval and Renaissance Texts and Studies, 154 (Binghampton NY: Renaissance English Text Society).

BEDE (1990), *Ecclesiastical History of The English People with Bede's Letter to Egbert and Cuthbert's Letter on the Death of Bede*, trans. by Leo Sherley-Price, R. E. Latham, and D. H. Farmer, rev. edn. (Harmondsworth: Penguin Books).

BERGIN, OSBORN (1970), *Irish Bardic Poetry: Texts and Translations together with an Introductory Lecture* (Dublin: Institute for Advanced Studies).

BLENERHASSET, THOMAS (1610), *A Direction for the Plantation in Ulster* (London).

BODIN, JEAN (1606), *The Six Bookes of a Commonweale*, trans. Richard Knolles (London).

BOEMUS, JOANNES (1520), *Omnium Gentium Mores Leges et Ritus* (Augsburg).

—— (1555), *The Fardle of Facions: Conteyning the Aunciente Maners, Customes, and Lawes, of the Peoples enhabiting the Two Partes of the Earth, called Affrike and Asie* (London).

BRAY, GERALD (ed.) (1994), *Documents of the English Reformation* (Cambridge: James Clark).

BREATNACH, PÁDRAIG A. (1973), 'Marbhna Aodha Ruaidh Uí Dhomhnaill', *Éigse*, 15: 31–50.

—— (1977), 'Metamorphosis 1603: Dán le hEochaidh Ó hEódhasa', *Éigse*, 17: 169–80.

BREREWOOD, EDWARD (1614), *Enquiries Touching the Diversity of Languages, and Religions through the Cheife Parts of the World* (London).

BRYSKETT, LODOWICK (1606), *A Discourse of Civill Life: Containing the Ethike Part of Moral Philosophie* (London).

—— (1927), *The Life and Correspondence of Lodowick Bryskett*, ed. Henry R. Plomer and Tom Peete Cross (Chicago: University of Chicago Press).

BUCHANAN, GEORGE (1856), *The History of Scotland*, 6 vols. (Glasgow: Blackie & Son).

CAMDEN, WILLIAM (1602), *Anglica, Normannica, Hibernica, Cambrica a Veteribus Scripta* (London).

—— (1605), *Remains of a Greater Worke, concerning Britaine* (London).

—— (1610), *Britain, or a Chorographical Description of the Most Flourishing Kingdomes, England, Scotland, and Ireland*, trans. Philemon Holland (London).

—— (1675), *The History of the Most Renowned and Victorious Princess Elizabeth*, 3rd edn. (London).

CAMÕES, LUIS VAZ DE (1952), *The Lusiads*, trans. William C. Atkinson (Harmondsworth: Penguin Books).

—— (1924), *Minor Works of Camões*, ed. Edgar Prestage (London: privately printed).

CAMPION, EDMUND (1963), *Two Bokes of the Histories of Ireland*, ed. A. F. Vossen (Assen: Van Gorcum & Co.).

CARNEY, JAMES (ed.) (1945), *Poems on the Butlers of Ormond, Cahir, and Dunboyne* (Dublin: Institute for Advanced Studies).

CASTIGLIONE, BALDESAR (1976), *The Courtier*, trans. George Bull, rev. edn. (Harmondsworth: Penguin Books).

CECIL, WILLIAM, LORD BURGHLEY, and WILLIAM ALLEN (1965), *The Execution of Justice in England; A True, Sincere, and Modest Defense of English Catholics*, ed. Robert M. Kingdon (Ithaca, NY; Cornell University Press for the Folger Shakespeare Library).

CÉITINN, SEATHRÚN [Geoffrey Keating] (1900), *Dánta, Amhráin is Caointe Sheathrúin Chéitinn*, ed. Eoin Cathmhaolach Mac Giolla Eáin (Dublin: Conradh na Gaedhilge).

CÉITINN, SEATHRÚN [Geoffrey Keating] (1902–13), *Foras Feasa ar Éirinn: The History of Ireland,* trans. David Comyn, 4 vols. (London: Irish Texts Society).

CHURCHYARD, THOMAS (1579), *A Generall Rehearsall of Warres* (London).

CLANRICARD, ULICK BURKE, Marquis of (1722), *Memoirs of the Right Honourable the Marquis of Clanricarde, Lord Deputy of Ireland* (London).

CLARK, ANDREW (ed.) (1907), *The Shirburn Ballads 1585–1616* (Oxford: Clarendon Press).

COLERIDGE, SAMUEL T. (1936), *Coleridge's Miscellaneous Criticism,* ed. T. M. Raysor (London: Constable).

COLET, JOHN (1876), *Ioannis Coleti Opuscula Quaedam Theologica: Letters to Radulphus on the Mosaic Account of the Creation,* ed. and trans. J. H. Lupton (London: George Bell & Sons).

COLLINS, ARTHUR (ed.) (1746), *Letters and Memorials of State, in the Reigns of Queen Mary, Queen Elizabeth, King James, King Charles the First, Part of the Reign of King Charles the Second, and Oliver's Usurpation,* 2 vols. (London).

COMES, NATALIS (1581), *Mythologiae* (Venice).

COX, RICHARD (1689–90), *Hibernia Anglicana: or, The History of Ireland from the Conquest thereof by the English, to this Present Time,* 2 pts. (London).

DANIEL, SAMUEL (1685), *The Collection of the History of England,* 5th edn. (London).

DAVIES, SIR JOHN (1612), *A Discoverie of the True Causes why Ireland was never entirely Subdued* (London).

DAWTREY, NICHOLAS (1995), *A Booke of Questions and Answars concerning the Warrs or Rebellions of the Kingdome of Irelande,* ed. Hiram Morgan, *Analecta Hibernica,* 36: 79–132.

DERRICKE, JOHN (1985), *The Image of Irelande, with a Discoverie of Woodkarne* (1581), ed. D. B. Quinn (Belfast: Blackstaff Press).

DRAYTON, MICHAEL (1961), *The Works of Michael Drayton,* ed. J. W. Hebel, rev. edn., 5 vols. (Oxford: Blackwell for the Shakespeare Head Press).

DU BELLAY, JOACHIM (1939), *The Defence and Illustration of the French Language,* trans. Gladys M. Turquet (London: Dent & Sons).

DUNLOP, ROBERT (1913), *Ireland under the Commonwealth: being a Selection of Documents relating to the Government of Ireland from 1651 to 1659,* 2 vols. (Manchester: Manchester University Press).

ELYOT, SIR THOMAS (1538), *The Dictionary of Syr Thomas Eliot knyght* (London).

ELIZABETH I (2000), *Collected Works,* ed. Leah S. Marcus, Janel Mueller, and Mary Beth Rose (Chicago: University of Chicago Press).

ERASMUS, DESIDERIUS (1557), *A Mery Dialogue, declaringe the Propertyes of Shrowde Shrewes, and Honest Wyves* (London).

FICINO, MARSILIO (1944), *Marsilio Ficino's Commentary on Plato's Symposium,* trans. S. R. Jayne (Columbia: University of Missouri Press).

GEOFFREY OF MONMOUTH (1966), *The History of the Kings of Britain*, trans. Lewis Thorpe (Harmondsworth: Penguin Books).

GERRARD, WILLIAM (1931), *Lord Chancellor Gerrard's Notes of his Report on Ireland (1577–8)*, ed. Charles McNeill, *Analecta Hibernica*, 2. 93–291.

GILBERT, JOHN T. (1882–91), *History of the Irish Confederation and the War in Ireland, 1641–1643*, 7 vols. (Dublin).

—— (1882), *Facsimiles of National Manuscripts of Ireland*, Part IV, Sect. 1 (London: Stationery Office).

GILLIES, W. (1970), 'A Poem on the Downfall of the Gaoidhil', *Éigse*, 13: 203–10.

GIRALDUS CAMBRENSIS (1978), *Expugnatio Hibernica: The Conquest of Ireland*, ed. and trans. A. B. Scott and F. X. Martin (Dublin: Royal Irish Academy).

—— (1982), *The History and Topography of Ireland*, trans. John J. O'Meara, rev. edn. (Harmondsworth: Penguin Books).

GOODMAN, CHRISTOPHER (1558), *How Superior Powers Oght to be Obeyd of their Subiects* (Geneva).

GREENE, DAVID (ed.) (1972), *Duanaire Mhéig Uidhir: The Poembook of Cú Chonnacht Mág Uidhir, Lord of Fermanagh 1566–1589* (Dublin: Institute for Advanced Studies).

GREY, LORD ARTHUR (1847), *A Commentary of the Services and Charges of William Lord Grey of Wilton*, ed. Sir Philip de Malpas Grey Egerton (London: Camden Society).

GRIMM, JACOB and WILHELM (1982), *Selected Tales*, trans. David Luke (Harmondsworth: Penguin Books).

GWYNN, EDWARD (ed. and trans.) (1991), *The Metrical Dindshenchas*, 4 vols. (Dublin: Institute for Advanced Studies—first pub. 1903–35).

HADFIELD, ANDREW, and JOHN McVEAGH (eds) (1994), *Strangers to that Land: British Perceptions of Ireland from the Reformation to the Famine* (Gerrards Cross, Bucks.: Colin Smythe).

HAICÉAD, PÁDRAIGÍN (1962), *Filíocht Phádraigín Haicéad*, ed. Máire Ní Cheallacháin (Dublin: An Clóchomhar).

—— (1993), *Haicéad*, trans. Michael Harnett (Loughcrew: Gallery Books).

HAKLUYT, RICHARD (1903–5), *The Principal Navigations Voyages Traffiques & Discoveries of the English Nation*, ed. Walter Raleigh, 10 vols. (Glasgow: MacLehouse & Sons).

—— (1935), *The Original Writings and Correspondence of the two Richard Hakluyts*, ed. E. G. R. Taylor, 2 vols. (London: Hakluyt Society).

HARRIOTT, THOMAS (1590), *A Briefe and True Report of the New Found Land of Virginia* (London).

HARVEY, GABRIEL (1884–5), *Works*, ed. A. B. Grosart (London).

HARVEY, RICHARD (1593), *Philadelphus, or a Defence of Brutes and the Brutan History* (London).

HERBERT, SIR WILLIAM (1992), *Croftus sive De Hibernia Liber*, ed. and trans. Arthur Keaveney and John A. Madden (Dublin: Irish Manuscripts Commission).

HEYWOOD, THOMAS (1612), *An Apology for Actors* (London).

HINTON, EDWARD M. (1940), 'Rych's *Anothomy of Ireland*, with an Account of the Author', *PMLA* 55: 73–101.

HOGAN, JAMES (ed.) (1936), *Letters and Papers relating to the Irish Rebellion between 1642–46* (Dublin: Irish Manuscripts Commission).

—— and N. McNEILL O'FARRELL (eds.) (1959), *The Walsingham Letter-Book or Register of Ireland May, 1578 to December, 1579* (Dublin: Stationery Office for the Irish Manuscripts Commission).

HOLINSHED, RAPHAEL (1808), *Chronicles of England, Scotland, and Ireland*, 6 vols. (London).

—— (1979), *Holinshed's Irish Chronicle*, ed. Liam Miller and Eileen Power (Dublin: Dolmen Press).

HOOKER, JOHN (1857), *The Life and Times of Sir Peter Carew*, ed. John Maclean (London: Bell & Dalby).

HORE, HERBERT F. (ed.) (1858), 'Irish Bardism in 1561', *UJA*, 6: 165–7, 202–12.

HUNTINGTON, HENRY (1996), *Historia Anglorum. The History of the English People*, ed. and trans. Diana Greenway (Oxford: Clarendon Press).

HURAULT, ANDRÉ (1931), *A Journal of all that was Accomplished by Monsieur de Maisse, Ambassador in England from King Henry IV to Queen Elizabeth Anno Domini 1597*, ed. and trans. G. B. Harrison and R. A. Jones (London: Nonesuch Press).

JONSON, BEN (1925–52), *Works*, ed. C. H. Herford and Percy and Evelyn Simpson, 11 vols. (Oxford: Clarendon Press).

KINNEY, ARTHUR F. (ed.) (1999), *Renaissance Drama: An Anthology of Plays and Entertainments* (Oxford: Blackwell).

KNOX, JOHN (1846–64), *The Works of John Knox*, ed. David Laing, 6 vols. (Edinburgh).

LARKIN, JAMES F., and PAUL L. HUGHES (eds.) (1973), *Stuart Royal Proclamations*, 2 vols. (Oxford: Clarendon Press).

LAS CASAS, BARTOLOMÉ DE (1583), *The Spanish Colonie, or Briefe Chronicle of the Acts and Gestes of Spaniardes* (London).

—— (1971), *Historia de las Indias: History of the Indies*, ed. and trans. Andrée Collard (New York: Harper & Row).

—— (1992), *A Short Account of the Destruction of the Indies*, trans. Nigel Griffin, intro. Anthony Pagden (Harmondsworth: Penguin Books).

LEVINSON, JUDITH C. (ed.) (1975), *The Famous History of Captain Thomas Stukeley* (Oxford: Oxford University Press for the Malone Society).

LLOYD, DAVID (1670), *State-Worthies or, The States-men and Favourites of England since the Reformation* (London).

LOMBARD, PETER (1930), *The Irish War of Defence 1598–1600: Extracts from the 'De Hibernia Insula Commentarius'*, ed. and trans. Matthew J. Byrne (Cork: Cork University Press).

LUCIAN (1936), *Works*, trans. A. M. Harmon et al., 8 vols. (Cambridge, Mass.: Harvard University Press).

LYNCH, JOHN (1848), *Cambrensis Eversus*, ed. and trans. Matthew Kelly, 3 vols. (Dublin: Celtic Society).

MAC AINGIL, AODH (1952), *Scáthán Shacramuinte na hAithridhe*, ed. Cainneach Ó Maonaigh (Dublin: Institute for Advanced Studies).

MAC AIRT, SEÁN (ed.) (1944), *Leabhar Branach: The Book of the O'Byrnes* (Dublin: Institute for Advanced Studies).

MACALISTER, R. A. S. (ed.) (1938–56), *Lebor Gabála Érenn*, 5 vols. (Dublin: Irish Texts Society).

MAC AN BHAIRD, EOGHAN RUADH (1930), *Duanta Eoghain Ruaidh Mhic an Bhaird*, ed. Tomas Ó Raghallaigh (Galway: O Gormain Teach na Clodoireachta).

MAC CUARTA, BRIAN (ed.) (1987), 'Mathew De Renzy's Letters on Irish Affairs 1613–1620', *Analecta Hibernica*, 34: 107–82.

MACHIAVELLI, NICCOLÒ (1961), *The Prince*, trans. George Bull (Harmondsworth: Penguin Books).

McKENNA, LAMBERT [Láimhbheartach Mac Cionnaith] (ed.) (1918–19), *Iomarbhágh na bhFileadh: The Contention of the Bards*, 2 vols. (London: Irish Texts Society).

—— (ed.) (1938), *Dioghluim Dána* (Dublin: Oifig an tSoláthair).

—— (1939–40), *Aithdhioghluim Dána: A Miscellany of Irish Bardic Poetry, Historical and Religious, including the Historical Poems of the Duanaire in the Yellow Book of Lecan*, 2 vols. (Dublin: Irish Texts Society).

—— (ed.) (1980), *The Book of O'Hara: Leabhar Í Eadhra* (Dublin: Institute for Advanced Studies).

MAC NIOCAILL, GEARÓID (ed.) (1963), 'Duanaire Ghearóid Iarla', *Studia Hibernica*, 3: 7–59.

MALEY, WILLY (ed.) (1995), *The Supplication of the Blood of the English most Lamentably Murdred in Ireland, Cryeng out of the Yearth for Revenge, Analecta Hibernica*, 36: 3–77.

MARVELL, ANDREW (1971), *The Poems and Letters*, ed. H. M. Margoliouth, 2 vols., 3rd edn. (Oxford: Clarendon Press).

MAXWELL, CONSTANTIA (ed.) (1923), *Irish History from Contemporary Sources (1509–1610)* (London: Allen & Unwin).

MHÁG CRAITH, CUTHBERT (ed.) (1980), *Dán na mBráthar Mionúr*, 2 vols. (Dublin: Institute for Advanced Studies).

MILTON, JOHN (1953–82), *Complete Prose Works of John Milton*, eds. Don M. Wolfe et al., 8 vols. (New Haven: Yale University Press).

MILTON, JOHN (1968), *Complete Shorter Poems*, ed. John Carey (London: Longman).

MONTAIGNE, MICHEL EYQUEM DE (1910), *Essays*, trans. John Florio, ed. L. C. Harmer, 3 vols. (London: Dent).

MORYSON, FYNES (1903), *Shakespeare's Europe: Unpublished Chapters of Fynes Moryson's Itinerary*, ed. Charles Hughes (London: Sherratt & Hughes).

—— (1907–8), *An Itinerary, Containing his Ten Yeeres Travell through the Twelve Dominions of Germany, Bohmerland, Sweitzerland, Netherland, Denmarke, Poland, Italy, Turky, France, England, Scotland & Ireland*, 4 vols. (Glasgow: James MacLehose & Sons).

MULCASTER, RICHARD (1582), *The First Part of the Elementarie which Entreateth Chefelie of the Right Writing of our English Tung* (London).

MURDIN, WILLIAM (ed.) (1759), *A Collection of State Papers Relating to Affairs in the Reign of Queen Elizabeth, from the Year 1571 to 1596* (London).

MURPHY, GERALD (1948), 'Poems of Exile by Uilliam Nuinseann Mac Barúin Dealbhna', *Éigse*, 6: 8–15.

NASHE, THOMAS (1958), *Works*, ed. R. B. McKerrow, 5 vols., rev. edn. (Oxford).

NOOT, JAN VAN DER (1569), *A Theatre wherein be represented as wel the Miseries and Calamities that follow the Voluptuous Worldlings, as also the Greate Ioyes and Plesures which the Faithfull do Enioy* (London).

Ó BRUADAIR, DÁIBHÍ (1910–17), *Duanaire Dháibhidh Uí Bhruadair: The Poems of David O Bruadair*, ed. John C. Mac Erlean, 3 vols. (London: Irish Texts Society).

Ó CLÉRIGH, LUGHAIDH (1948–57), *Beatha Aodha Ruaidh Uí Dhomhnaill: The Life of Aodh Ruadh O Domhnaill*, ed. and trans. Paul Walsh, 2 vols. (London: Irish Texts Society).

Ó CLÉRIGH, MÍCHEÁL, et al. (1856), *Annála Ríoghachta Éireann: Annals of the Kingdom of Ireland by the Four Masters*, ed. and trans. John O'Donovan, 2nd edn., 7 vols. (Dublin: Hodges & Smith).

O'CONNOR, FRANK, trans. (1970), *Kings, Lords, & Commons: An Anthology from the Irish* (Dublin: Gill and Macmillan; first pub. 1959).

Ó CRÓINÍN, DÁIBHÍ I. (ed.) (1975), 'A Poem to Toirdhealbhach Luinneach Ó Néill', *Éigse*, 16: 50–66.

Ó CUÍV, BRIAN (ed.) (1952), *Párliament na mBan* (Dublin: Institute for Advanced Studies).

—— (1973–4), 'A Sixteenth-Century Political Poem', *Éigse*, 15: 261–76.

—— (1994), *Aibidil Gaoidheilge & Caiticiosma: Seaán Ó Cearnaigh's Irish Primer of Religion published in 1571* (Dublin: Institute for Advanced Studies).

Ó DOMHNUILL, UILLIAM, trans. (1602), *Tiomna Nuadh* (Dublin).

O'FLAHERTY, RODERIC (1793), *Ogygia, or A Chronological Account of Irish Events*, trans. James Hely, 2 vols. (Dublin).

O'GRADY, STANDISH HAYES, and ROBIN FOWLER (eds.) (1953), *Catalogue of Irish Manuscripts in the British Museum*, 3 vols. (London).

Ó hUIGINN, TADGH DALL (1922–6), *The Bardic Poems of Tadgh Dall O'Huiginn*, ed. and trans. Eleanor Knott, 2 vols. (London: Irish Texts Society).

Ó LAIDHIN, TOMÁS (ed.) (1962), *Sidney State Papers, 1565–70* (Dublin: Irish Manuscripts Commission).

O'RAHILLY, ALFRED (1938), *The Massacre at Smerwick*, Historical and Archaeological Papers, 1 (Cork: Cork University Press).

O'RAHILLY, CECILE (ed.) (1977), *Five Seventeenth-Century Political Poems* (Dublin: Institute for Advanced Studies).

O'SULLIVAN, ANNE (1971), 'Tadhg O'Daly and Sir George Carew', *Éigse*, 14: 22–38.

O'SULLIVAN BEARE, PHILIP (1621), *Historiae Catholicae Iberniae Compendium* (Lisbon).

—— (1903), *Ireland Under Elizabeth: Chapters Towards a History of Ireland in the Reign of Elizabeth*, ed. Matthew J. Byrne (Dublin: Sealy, Bryers and Walker).

—— (1960), *Selections from the Zoilomastix of Philip O'Sullivan Beare*, ed. Thomas J. O'Donnell (Dublin: Stationery Office for the Irish Manuscripts Commission).

Ó TUAMA, SEÁN (1981), *An Duanaire 1600–1900: Poems of the Dispossessed*, trans. Thomas Kinsella (Portlaoise).

Ó TUATHAIL, ÉAMONN (1940), 'Nugentiana', *Éigse*, 2: 4–14.

PARKER, MATTHEW (1853), *Correspondence of Matthew Parker*, ed. John Bruce (Cambridge: Cambridge University Press).

PAUL OF ST UBALD (1654), *The Soul's Delight* (Antwerp).

PAYNE, ROBERT (1589), *A Briefe Description of Ireland* (London).

PERROT, JAMES (1933), *The Chronicle of Ireland, 1584–1608*, ed. Herbert Wood (Dublin: Irish Manuscripts Commission).

PERROT, SIR JOHN (1943), *The Letter-Book of Lord Deputy Sir John Perrot between 9 July, 1584 and 26 May, 1586*, ed. Charles McNeill, *Analecta Hibernica*, 12: 3–65.

—— (1626), *The Government of Ireland under the Honorable, Iust, and Wise Governour Sir Iohn Perrot 1584–8*, by E.C.S. (London).

PUTTENHAM, GEORGE (1936), *The Arte of English Poesie*, ed. Gladys Doidge Willcock and Alice Walker (Cambridge: Cambridge University Press).

QUINN, DAVID B. (ed.) (1940), *The Voyages and Colonising Enterprises of Sir Humphrey Gilbert*, 2 vols. (London: The Hakluyt Society).

—— (ed.) (1942), 'A Discourse of Ireland (circa 1599): A Sidelight on English Colonial Policy', *Publications of the Royal Irish Academy*, 47, Section C, no. 3: 151–66.

RALEGH, SIR WALTER (1614), *The History of the World*, 2 pts. (London).

—— (1986), *Selected Writings*, ed. Gerald Hammond (Harmondsworth: Penguin Books).

RICH, BARNABY (1604), *The Fruites of Long Experience* (London).

—— (1612), *A Catholicke Conference betweene Syr Tady Mac. Mareall a Popish Priest of Waterforde, and Patricke Plaine a young student in Trinity Colledge by Dublin in Ireland.*

ROTHE, DAVID (1616), *Analecta Sacra, Nova, et Mira. De Rebus Catholicorum in Hibernia pro Fide Gestis* (Place unknown).

SANDER, NICHOLAS (1877), *The Rise and Growth of the Anglican Schism . . . with a continuation of the History by Edward Rishton*, ed. and trans. David Lewis (London: Burns & Oates).

SHAKESPEARE, WILLIAM (1988), *The Complete Works*, ed. Stanley Wells and Gary Taylor (Oxford: Oxford University Press).

SHELL, MARC (1993), *Elizabeth's Glass with 'The Glass of the Sinfull Soul' (1544) by Elizabeth I and 'Epistle Dedicatory' and 'Conclusion' by John Bale* (Lincoln, Nebr.: University of Nebraska Press).

SIDNEY, SIR HENRY (1856; 1857; 1860), *Memoir or Narrative Addressed to Sir Francis Walsingham, 1583*, ed. Henry F. Hore, *UJA*, 1st ser., 3 (1856), 37–44, 91–9, 346–53; 5 (1857), 305–23; 8 (1860), 179–95.

SIDNEY, SIR PHILIP (1912–26), *The Works of Sir Philip Sidney*, ed. A. Feuillerat, 4 vols. (Cambridge: Cambridge University Press).

SMITH, G. GREGORY (ed.) (1904), *Elizabethan Critical Essays*, 2 vols. (Oxford: Clarendon Press).

SPENSER, EDMUND (1758), *Spenser's Faerie Queene*, ed. John Upton, 2 vols. (London).

—— (1932–58), *The Works of Edmund Spenser*, ed. Edwin Greenlaw *et al.*, Variorum Edn., 11 vols. (Baltimore: Johns Hopkins University Press).

—— (1978), *The Faerie Queene*, ed. Thomas P. Roche, Jr. (Harmondsworth).

—— (1999), *The Shorter Poems*, ed. Richard A. McCabe (Harmondsworth: Penguin Books).

STAFFORD, THOMAS (ed.) (1633), *Pacata Hibernia, Ireland Appeased and Reduced: or, an Historie of the Late Warres of Ireland, especially within the Province of Mounster, under the Government of Sir George Carew* (London).

STOW, JOHN (1956), *The Survey of London*, ed. H. B. Wheatley, rev. edn. (London: Dent).

STRYPE, JOHN (1735–7), *Annals of the Reformation and Establishment of Religion, in the Church of England*, 3 vols. (London).

—— (1821), *Historical Collections of the Life and Acts of the Right Reverend Father in God, John Aylmer* (Oxford).

STUBBS, JOHN (1968), *John Stubbs' 'Gaping Gulf' with Letters and Other Relevant Documents*, ed. Lloyd E. Berry (Charlottesville: University Press of Virginia for the Folger Shakespeare Library).

TILNEY, EDMUND (1992), *The Flower of Friendship: A Renaissance Dialogue Contesting Marriage*, ed. Valerie Wayne (Ithaca, NY: Cornell University Press).

VERSTEGAN, RICHARD (1605), *A Restitution of Decayed Intelligence: In Antiquities. Concerning the Most Noble and Renowmed English Nation* (Antwerp).

WALSH, PETER (1682), *A Prospect of the State of Ireland from the Year of the World, 1576 to the Year of Christ 1652* (London).

WARE, SIR JAMES (1633), *The Historie of Ireland, collected by Three Learned Authors viz. Meredith Hanmer Doctor in Divinitie: Edmund Campion, sometime Fellow of St Johns Colledge in Oxford: and Edmund Spenser Esq.* (Dublin).

—— (1654), *De Hibernia et Antiquitatibus eius, Disquisitiones* (London).

—— (1664), *Rerum Hibernicarum Annales* (Dublin).

—— (1997), *A View of the State of Ireland: From the First Printed Edition (1633)*, ed. Andrew Hadfield and Willy Maley (Oxford: Blackwell).

WARTON, THOMAS (1807), *Observations on 'The Fairy Queen' of Spenser* (London; first pub. 1754).

WELLS, WILLIAM (ed.) (1971–2), *Spenser Allusions in the Sixteenth and Seventeenth Centuries*, 2 pts. (Chapel Hill: University of North Carolina Press).

WHITE, STEPHEN (1849), *Apologia pro Hibernia adversus Cambri Calumnias*, ed. Matthew Kelly (Dublin: John O'Daly).

WILLIAMS, N. J. A. (ed.) (1981), *Pairlement Chloinne Tomáis* (Dublin: Dublin Institute for Advanced Studies).

Index